Development Planning in Mixed Economies

Edited by Miguel Urrutia and Setsuko Yukawa

 THE UNITED NATIONS UNIVERSITY

The views expressed in this publication are those of the authors and do not necessarily
reflect the views of the United Nations University.

The United Nations University
Toho Seimei Building, 15-1 Shibuya 2-chome, Shibuya-ku, Tokyo 150, Japan
Tel.: (03) 499-2811 Telex: J25442 Cable: UNATUNIV TOKYO

Printed in Hong Kong

DSDB-16/UNUP-637
ISBN 92-808-0637-8
United Nations Sales No. E.88.III.A.6
02500 P

CONTENTS

PREFACE

Two years after retiring from a government position, I was asked by the Universidad del Rosario in Bogotá to give a public lecture on the process of economic planning in Colombia. As I prepared the lecture, I realized how different the practice of planning in Colombia was from both the theory of planning still being taught in the universities and the types of planning that some international agencies are still trying to implant through their technical assistance programmes. That is to say, it became clear that the Colombian planning agency influenced some areas of economic policy and public expenditure in an important way, but not through the methodologies suggested by economic development textbooks.

Two years later, I had the occasion, while at the United Nations University in Tokyo, to propose a project whose purpose would be to compare the philosophies, goals, methods, procedures, and implementation of economic planning in various countries, to indicate how the planning has actually been carried out, and to measure the degree of effectiveness of different types of planning.

The measurement of the degree of effectiveness was deemed important because, even though many developing countries have had 30 years of experience with national development planning, plans have in many cases had only a marginal impact on policy-making. In spite of the limited success of this kind of government intervention, however, advocates of planning argue that even in these cases planning could have been made more effective if certain methodologies or processes had been followed. Furthermore, the governments of many developing countries continue to prepare plans and seem to consider planning indispensable as a tool which, if made more effective, could improve economic management significantly.

In view, then, of the discrepancy between the postulated advantages and high expectations of planning on the one hand and the actual results in many countries, whether encouraging or dismal, on the other, it was felt that it would be useful for the United Nations University to launch a project on development planning in mixed economies in order to identify the economic, social, and political factors that have determined its success or failure.

Further, after considering the proposal, my colleagues suggested that the project should be formulated to shed some light on the new approaches to development planning that have evolved. This seemed appropriate because, although simultaneous efforts have been made since the end of the 1960s to analyse the reasons behind poor performance and to raise questions about the effectiveness of planning, apparently no study had been made of the more recent innovations applied by developing countries as a reaction to the failure of the types of plans adopted in the 1960s.

Professor Yukawa and I initiated the project in 1983. On the basis of a detailed research proposal, we were able to interest a group of researchers from Africa, Asia, and Europe in the project. Those concerned met in Penang, Malaysia, in early 1984 to present background documents on the planning experience in their countries and to decide on the approach to the case studies of the countries under consideration. It was decided to analyse the planning history of seven countries: Sri Lanka, Malaysia, and Japan in Asia, Colombia in Latin America, Kenya and Nigeria in Africa, and Hungary in Eastern Europe. We tried to include Mexico and Brazil in the project, but the researchers who originally agreed to participate were later unable to do so.

Although the main purpose of the project was to identify the types of planning processes that seemed to work best and the areas of economic management in which planning could be instrumental in promoting efficiency and growth in less-developed countries with mixed economies, Japan and Hungary were included. Japan provides a unique example of a country that has undergone a remarkable transformation which is said to have taken place under various economic plans, and Hungary, which started as a centrally planned economy and gradually adopted the market mechanism in some productive activities, furnishes a unique example of national planning in a mixed economy.

At Penang the participants agreed that an important by-product of the project was the eye-opening occasion it provided the researchers to learn about policy-making and development processes in countries other than their own. Unfortunately, Asian and African researchers have too few occasions to study or visit Latin America, and Latin Americans and Africans can only learn about Asian development through the sometimes biased interpretations of European and North American authors. The meetings were therefore quite exciting; they revealed similar problems and attempted solutions, as well as similar interpretations of development processes — processes which, incidentally, are often quite different from what has been related in some of the development literature.

The case studies were discussed at a seminar during the International Congress of Americanists in Bogotá, Colombia, in July 1985. This conference brought together the original participants of the project and a number of experts, mainly from Latin American countries. In the discussions we tried to find common aspects in both the successful and unsuccessful planning efforts.

The fruits of our research and discussions are contained in this volume. Chapters 1 and 2 are general. Chapter 1, by way of introduction, summarizes some of the conclusions we reached about the factors that have inhibited the effectiveness of planning and concludes by identifying both the various contributions, actual and potential, attributable to the planning processes and the changes required in the planning process to accomplish certain objectives. Chapter 2 is a review of the theoretical and historical arguments for planning.

Chapters 3–9 are the case studies. Following are some brief highlights.

Sri Lanka is an interesting case of development planning in a mixed economy because the alternation of power between different administrations with different ideologies resulted in different approaches to planning. The Sri Lanka case study also shows the difficulties of planning in a small, relatively open economy, where the crucial economic variables are determined by events external to the country.

In Malaysia, while the first plans placed emphasis on economic growth, substantial efforts have been made since 1969 to incorporate social and political factors into development plans so as to achieve more equitable income distribution among the various ethnic groups that make up Malaysian society.

The Colombian experience from the 1950s to 1983 shows a change in the assumptions and practice of planning which transformed the process from the formulation of textbook macro-economic plans to plans emphasizing policy choices.

Kenya has accepted planning as an important policy instrument to attain higher rates of economic growth and a high standard of living for its people. Although it has not been very successful in putting the plans into effect at the national level, some sectoral plans have been implemented with rather satisfactory results.

In Nigeria during the last two decades national plans seem to have been ineffective in managing the effects of changing external conditions on the national economy.

Japanese economic plans in the post-war period were basically indicative, and they played an important role in forming a national consensus on the restrictions to be overcome and the efforts and sacrifices to be made by certain groups to achieve development for all.

Lastly, the Hungarian case study analyses an experience in planning which has undergone substantial change in its nature by moving from a highly centralized planning system toward a more decentralized system. The Hungarian experience is suggestive with respect to the effectiveness of centralized planning in a small economy which must trade a substantial part of its output.

Professor Yukawa has been the co-ordinator of the project, and she has carried a disproportionate part of the burden of editing this volume. We both would like to thank Mrs. Yoshie Sawada, who was not only a secretary but a friend of the project and the authors, and Ms. Kumiko Ishikawa, who, as programme officer in charge of the project at the UNU, made it possible to bring it to a happy conclusion.

Before going to print, we received the sad news of the death of Professor Ránki. His insights, personal kindness, and depth of knowledge of the history of economic transformations have been an inspiration to all of us, and his presence contributed much to making our workshops both a pleasant and a successful experience. It is only fitting, therefore, to dedicate this book to his memory.

Miguel Urrutia
Washington, D.C.

1

NEW APPROACHES TO DEVELOPMENT PLANNING

Miguel Urrutia

As Professor Yukawa points out in chapter 2 in reviewing the origins of economic planning in developing countries, in the 1960s the practice of planning and the political commitment to that concept was much influenced by its apparent success in the socialist economies and by the emergency plans implemented during the post-war recovery phase in some of the industrialized countries.

Only with time did it become obvious, as Professors Ránki and Enyedi mention in their paper (chap. 9), that central planning with detailed physical production targets was particularly well adapted to war-ravaged countries that were involved in reconstruction, or to a large continental country involved in the development of basic industries, such as the Soviet Union. However, in small economies, which necessarily must trade a large proportion of their production, many decisions are outside the control of a national planning authority. Therefore, the methodology of centralized quantitative planning cannot be indiscriminately adopted by most developing countries.

Nonetheless, in a small economy, forced to trade in order to obtain basic raw materials and to achieve economies of scale, centralized quantitave economic planning might serve as an efficient option at a time of reconstruction. The following may serve to elucidate its relative advantage. War can destroy oil pipelines and the profitability of an oil company, but not its dispersed oil wells. Market forces will in the medium run lead to the building of a new pipeline since this is profitable. But oil production can be increased more rapidly if a planning board assigns foreign exchange and investment funds to the pipeline project, thus restoring the production of the whole oil industry.

It appears that in Hungary and Japan quantitative planning and direct administrative guidance were an efficient way to bring these economies back to pre-war levels of production. Once this was achieved, however, it became increasingly clear in both countries that a more decentralized method of economic decision-making would be needed to achieve economic growth.

In the other countries we studied, reconstruction was not the problem. The challenge was the construction of modern industry and agriculture from scratch. It was, therefore, not surprising to find that new planning methodologies had to be designed. Furthermore, in all the developing countries studied, policy-makers assumed that the private sector would be responsible for a substantial part of investment and production, and therefore planning methodologies that did not rely on administrative commands and directives had to be developed.

The First Plans

In some of the countries studied, the first plans were actually programmes of public investment. In the cases of Malaysia, Kenya, Nigeria, and Sri Lanka, the pre-independence colonial administrations produced plans of this type. In Malaysia, the Draft Development Plan (1950–1955) was of this nature, as were the Post-war Development Proposals for 1946 and the post-independence Six-Year Plan in Sri Lanka, and the Ten-Year Plan of Development and Welfare for Nigeria (1946).

Even though these plans were little more than lists of public-sector projects, they led to the production of medium-term profiles of public investment, which could be matched with estimates of expected revenues. Making the investment options explicit made it necessary to choose between projects, to project expenditures into the future, and to fit public investment into a budget constraint.

The Sri Lanka study (chap. 3) evaluates the first planning efforts in the country in terms that might be applicable to some of the early planning efforts of other developing countries: "[The] claim that what it had in the collection of budgets was 'a National Plan for the economic social development of the country covering a period of six years' was certainly exaggerated. Even so, some of the explicitly stated objectives of 'planning' in this initial phase defined some of the limits within which the planning process would have to operate."[1]

The Six-Year Programme of Investment 1954/55–1956/60 advanced the planning process one step further in Sri Lanka. First, a formal Planning Secretariat attached to the Cabinet was established, and, second, the programme, for the first time, required ministries and departments to undertake a disciplined exercise of phasing their ongoing projects and future investments over a period of six years. The exercise "established a general system of financial allocations, secured the type of data pertinent to an overall public sector program, ensured the consistency of this data with the annual budgetary provision and generally integrated and aggregated individual projects and programs to a single whole."[2]

Planning was, however, rapidly transformed. Development economists in economics faculties and in the United Nations organizations were proposing a much more ambitious type of developing planning. It was felt that broad macro-economic plans could lead to fast economic growth and were therefore necessary. Further, it was felt that unless broad structural transformations were carried out in traditional societies, economic modernization would not take place.

The more ambitious plans in this second phase proposed high growth targets. They also proposed major structural changes: accelerated industrialization in largely agricultural societies, land reform, increased savings propensities, and the taxation of the most powerful and wealthiest groups in society in order to mobilize savings for ambitious investment plans. In some cases the plans even postulated a major restructuring of the economic system.

This second planning model had a very limited impact on real economic management, but it was abandoned reluctantly. There were three reasons for this reluctance:

1. This approach to planning was politically convenient since it allowed technocrats and politicians to propose radical changes in their societies without entering into conflict with interest groups that would oppose more practical and concrete proposals for reform. Interest groups never felt threatened by the largely theoretical and somewhat vague macro-economic planning models.
2. It was academically respectable for economists to work on such plans since they utilized the most modern economic tools of analysis.
3. The plans were successfully used to convince aid agencies that funding requests were well designed and would be accompanied by substantial local efforts to achieve growth rates that would make future aid unnecessary.

During the late 1950s and early 1960s, encouraged by the aid agencies, most developing countries were producing macro-economic planning documents. Many of them were nothing more than that: documents which were produced for their own sake and which had little impact on economic management.

This was certainly true in the case of the Colombian Ten-Year Plan of 1961. Produced following the framework recommended by the UN Economic Commission for Latin America, and with a heavy dose of technical assistance from that agency, "the document. . . contained a formal planning model, complete with underlying econometric projections, capital-output ratios, savings coefficients, etc. A high target rate of growth was fixed and the savings and foreign exchange gaps were calculated."[3] Griffin and Enos made a realistic evaluation of the usefulness of this plan when they wrote: "The Plan has never been used in preparing economic policy and it became evident soon after publication that its growth target was unrealistic. . . . As a diplomatic maneuver for attracting foreign capital, the plan was a success."[4]

The First National Development Plan of Nigeria (1962–1968) also contained the usual macro-economic targets and utilized the economic methodology then in vogue. None of the targets were met, and it appears that the plan had little influence on decision-making in a country that lived through a series of constitutional crises, a coup d'état, and a civil war during the plan period.

The Ceylon Ten-Year Plan (1959–1968) was in many ways representative of the best type of planning of this period. The study by the Marga Institute (chap. 3) relates how, according to the mandate given the newly created National Planning Council by the Prime Minister, it would appear that the Council was to undertake its work as a scientific professional body, examining the problems of the economy in depth and planning for the structural changes in the economy in a way that would be of lasting value to whatever government was in power. Planning was, then, defined primarily as an intellectual and technical task. As in Colombia and other developing countries, the Planning Council was not drawn into the decision-making process during the three years in which it was left to complete the preparation of the plan. When published, the Ten-Year Plan was internationally recognized as a professionally competent document and in many ways a pioneering exercise for small developing economies.[5]

Shortly after the presentation of the plan to parliament, however, the government changed and it was not accepted for implementation. Despite the sophisticated technical work that went into it, its basic forecasts also proved incorrect almost as soon as the document was published. The plan had not foreseen the possibility of deteriorating terms of trade and serious balance-of-payments problems. The balance-of-payments problems, in fact, led to a constriction of both imported consumer and investment goods, and this led to the underfulfilment of most of the macro-economic targets. More importantly, it can be argued that by not identifying the likely balance-of-payments problems, the planners biased economic policy against export promotion and diversification. The plan also overestimated fiscal revenues, and this led to deficit financing and inflationary pressures.

In summary, even though the tools and methodologies utilized in the Ten-Year Plan were those recommended by the development literature, they did not lead to the identification of the major problems that would become apparent during the plan period. This experience underlines the limitations of long-term macro-economic planning in small economies highly vulnerable to fluctuations in the international economy. In addition, the Sri Lanka experience also shows the limited impact of long-range technocratic macro-economic plans on the day-to-day economic decision-making processes. After the experience with the Ten-Year Plan, when the left-of-centre coalition came back to power, the planners abandoned long-range planning and concentrated on intervening in short-term economic decision-making.

In Malaysia, although it is hard to assess whether the early plans had a real impact on the economy or not, economic performance came closer to the targets postulated by the plan documents. In fact, to some extent the Malaysian macro-economic plans might have been fairly influential, because, instead of trying to produce major structural changes in the economy, they concentrated on setting a reasonable framework for growth which gave local and foreign investors some fairly clear rules in which to work, while the state concentrated on the provision of infrastructure and the support of agriculture.

It is significant that the highest economic growth rates among the countries studied were achieved by Malaysia, which produced national plans that, even in the 1950s, concentrated government activity in the rural sector. While the Colombian, Sri Lankan, and Nigerian governments were trying to promote large industrial projects, the Second Malaya Plan (1961–1965) and the First Malaysia Plan (1966–1970) emphasized agricultural and rural development. The First Malaysia Plan, for example, allotted only 3.3 per cent of public investment to industrial sectors. Interestingly enough, not only were high growth rates achieved during these planning periods but growth and investment turned out to be similar to the values postulated in the plans.

Lai and Tan relate (chap. 4), however, that these planning documents were produced in large part by expatriate experts. This might have given local and foreign investors some faith in the good prospects predicted for the Malaysian economy, but this type of ivory-tower planning probably had little influence on day-to-day decision-making within the government.

This brings us to the role played by expatriate technocrats and aid agencies in the planning processes in developing countries.

The Influence of Aid Agencies on National Planning

The First Malaya Plan (1956–1960)was heavily influenced by a World Bank mission, and between 1964 and 1971 expatriate technocrats working for the Harvard Development Advisory Service, in a project financed by the Ford Foundation, seem to have been responsible for preparing substantial parts of Malaysia's planning documents. In Colombia, the first planning document was prepared by a World Bank mission, and the 1961 Ten-Year Development Plan was drafted with substantial technical advice provided by the Economic Commission for Latin America (ECLA).[6] Foreigners working as technical assistants to the government also contributed substantially to the first Kenyan plan.

Aid agencies, however, influenced the economic planning process in ways other than through technical assistance.

In the 1960s foreign aid was simply not available to countries that could not justify their need for aid on the basis of economic plans which could show how foreign exchange could be absorbed in ways which would increase growth, avoid inflation, and assure an increasing welfare level for the poorest sectors of society. In Latin America, development plans were a prerequisite for qualification for loans from the Alliance for Progress programme. Even in Japan, the first attempts at integrated planning were reports produced in order to claim US aid and World Bank loans.

The macro-economic plans that calculated foreign-exchange needs and showed that a country could profitably absorb foreign aid were used by aid officers in bilateral and multilateral agencies to justify credits and grants. Since international bureaucracies had trouble convincing donors to lend to countries where such justifications, in the form of plans, did not exist, the benefits of drafting macro-economic plans increased, and this stimulated their production. The usefulness of the plans, however, was dependent not on how operational they were but rather on whether they met the criteria and the philosophy of the donors. This encouraged the production of elegant plans by agencies that had little connection with policy-makers or line ministries.

Inasmuch as these plans did generate low-cost foreign exchange, they were successful. However, that was their objective and they had very little impact on economic policy. In time, foreign-aid agencies stopped taking the plans seriously, and the technocrats within the national planning agencies became quite frustrated at their lack of influence. This led the planners to shift to short-term planning and involvement in daily economic decision-making. For example, in Colombia and Sri Lanka, two persons who had been responsible for the production of the first long-term macro-economic plans in the late 1950s came back as heads of the planning agencies in the late 1960s and radically changed the objectives of the institutions they headed.

Before analysing this shift towards involving the planning agencies in short-term policy-making, however, it is useful to discuss how foreign-aid agencies influenced the way public-investment choices were made in the developing countries.

Foreign-aid agencies have had a very substantial effect on the way public investment is carried out in many developing countries. Up to the 1950s, public-investment decisions were based on felt need, regional pressures, or engineering viability. Aid agencies started to require cost-benefit analyses and economic-feasibility studies for those investments they were going to help finance, and this led to the rationalization and prioritization of investment decisions in major sectors of the economy.

In the 1960s, the World Bank and bilateral aid agencies tended to limit their aid to so-called economically productive projects in areas such as road transport, railroads, irrigation, and electricity generation. The availability of aid for projects in these areas forced the relevant ministries and state enterprises to establish processes for evaluating the economic and technical feasibility of investment projects requested by people and organizations through the usual political channels. Although the pre-feasibility or feasibility studies were often made only to justify projects for which there was already a political commitment, the new methodologies sometimes led to the postponing or abandonment of projects where the studies identified serious technical difficulties or low economic returns. Government technocrats or officers of finance ministries could use the fact that a project did not meet the aid criteria as a reason to put such doubtful investments at the bottom of the priority lists. The planning processes forced on certain parts of the public sector increased the return on public infrastructure investments and led to improved management systems and placement of better trained people at some of the state enterprises that were recipients of foreign aid.

When in the 1960s the regional banks, such as the Inter-American Development Bank, and some bilateral donors started to make credit available for social projects in areas such as water supply and education, pressure was also created to rationalize the criteria for investment decisions in the social sectors. For example, efforts were made to make user charges more realistic, reflecting capacity to pay, and to improve the administration of health and education programmes. Evaluations of how these services reached the poorest families were also carried out, making it possible to target these programmes more effectively to benefit primarily those with low incomes.

Discussing the sectors where planning has been introduced with the greatest success, Fernando Cepeda, a prominent Colombian political scientist, stated in an interview that the rationalization of investment and management has gone farthest in those sectors that have received the greatest amount of foreign credit or aid. There has been more planning and greater efficiency of investment and government expenditure in the electricity sector than in education, in part because in Colombia much more aid has flowed to the former. Even among social programmes, public health has received more aid than primary education, and there has been much more effective planning and investment in public health. Management is very lax and investment priorities less technically determined in hospital management than in primary health care, because there has been less aid in the former sector and therefore less outside pressure to improve the way investment decisions are made. Finally, management practices and investments are particularly outdated in sectors that usually do not receive foreign aid, such as the administration of justice or local administration.

José Fernando Isaza, again in reference to the Colombian experience (chap. 5), contends that the rationalization of decision-making in only certain public-sector activities has had the effect of channelling most of the government budget to activities where it is methodologically easier to justify investments in terms of conventional measures of economic performance. It is possible that the aid agencies' insistence on projects with clearly measurable economic rates of return led to over-investment in electricity-generation projects and under-investment in rural water supply and nutrition programmes.

The experience of the late 1970s and early 1980s, when commercial banks made large untied loans to governments without requiring clear economic feasibility studies for projects, suggests, however, that the multilateral and bilateral agencies have contributed to improving the efficiency of investment. The large financial flows that led to the 1982–1983 debt crisis were often not well spent. The story of the way in which the Nigerian oil-boom money was invested might be illustrative of what happens when investment criteria are relaxed.

In summary, it would appear that in certain sectors of the economy the availability of foreign aid and the conditions for disbursement of such aid determined the growth and consolidation of certain planning practices. To be more specific, methodologies for determining the economic and technical feasibility of public investment projects were often defined in relation to the availability and the conditions for disbursement of foreign aid.

The Shift towards Short-Term Planning

As has been mentioned, in the mid-1960s, by coincidence in both Colombia and Sri Lanka former heads of the national planning agencies, who had been responsible for the production of the first long-range macro-economic plans, were reappointed to equivalent posts. In both cases it was made clear that writing a plan document was not a top priority. Rather, the planning agencies were reoriented towards participation in day-to-day economic policy-making. This transformation in Colombia and Sri Lanka reflected a more generalized frustration with the ineffectiveness of the macro-economic planning methodologies. Only a few UN agencies and academic economists continued to believe that macro-economic planning could be an effective management tool in developing countries. The attention of the planners in fact focused on short-term policy-making.

Nevertheless, the growing involvement of the planning ministries in short-term policy-making was not an unqualified success. The experience in Sri Lanka is illustrative. In 1965, when the centrist United National Party was voted back into power, the man who had been head of the planning organization in 1954–1960 was brought back as head of the newly created Ministry of Planning and Economic Affairs. The planners defined for themselves a set of tasks and responsibilities in which the formal exercise of preparing a national plan had low priority. The Ministry then concentrated on (i) evaluating public-sector projects, (ii) preparing a public-sector investment programme for the period 1966–1970, and (iii) managing a short-term 'economic recovery' strategy. To perform the latter task, the Ministry took control of a few key decision-making levers: foreign-aid approvals and negotiations, foreign-exchange budgeting, and the formulation of the government's capital budget. Although the new approach improved short-term economic policy formulation, no agency of the government continued analysing and proposing solutions for the major long-term economic disequilibria emerging in the society.

In Colombia, the re-formed planning agency concentrated on exactly the same tasks after 1966, under the leadership of Edgar Gutiérrez, who had been head of planning in the late 1950s when the Ten-Year Plan was prepared. In addition to being responsible for foreign aid and the public-investment budget, the planning agency also became involved in day-to-day public-sector decision-making when representatives of the agency were made directors of the boards of the major public-sector enterprises and members of the advisory councils of the line ministries. In addition, the head of the agency participated actively in the government committees in charge of formulating monetary, foreign-exchange, and trade policy.

The Sri Lanka study concludes that the country's experiment in 1965–1970 was unable to resolve the problem of handling the incompatibility between short-term and long-term policies. In fact, "the planning process was caught in the dilemma of applying deflationary policies to meet short-term problems on the one hand and sustaining an adequate rate of economic growth in the long-term on the other."[7]

In Colombia, the planners set the stage for inflation by becoming so involved in the preparation of projects and investment plans for specific agencies that they became partisans of ambitious public investment programmes that could not be financed with foreseeable tax revenues. Once it became obvious that it would be difficult to sustain the high investment levels made possible by the massive foreign-aid flows of the late 1960s, they took the position that the problem could be solved by a massive tax reform. The result was a period of bitter conflict between the Planning Department and the Ministry of Finance.

In addition, planning in Colombia tended to be myopic. Concentration on short-term decision-making was stressed to the exclusion of achieving a national consensus on the country's long-range economic strategy. Each public-sector agency advocated its own projects and plans, and there was no overall framework to facilitate choices between projects, investment priorities, and decisions about prices and administrative changes. However, this lack of co-ordination was not too serious a problem, because the President had his own broad and quite consistent economic strategy and was involved in most major decisions. But institutionally, the lack of a long-range plan tended to lead to uncoordinated economic decision-making dominated by the personal preferences of public-sector actors with different degrees of political strength.

In both Colombia and Sri Lanka, however, the new style of planning improved project evaluation and preparation and probably introduced investment criteria into the public sector which, in turn, permanently improved the efficiency of public investment.

At the same time, although both governments were pro–free enterprise, planning activism led to a rapid growth of the share of public investment and to some policies that discouraged private entrepreneurship by introducing the government into many important and unimportant decision-making processes.

At this point it may be useful to say something about Japan, where planning moved in a direction exactly opposite to that in the developing countries. During the post-war period economic management moved from detailed planning directives to broad indicative macro-economic plans.

In the immediate post-war period, when there were absolute shortages of materials, technologies, and capital, all aspects of economic activity were managed with tight and direct controls by the public authorities. In August 1946 the Economic Stabilization Board was set up and given authority, under close control from the General Headquarters of the Supreme Commander of the Allied Powers, to plan, implement, and inspect all aspects of economic policy, including foreign trade, finance, production, and consumption. Prime Minister Yoshida's advisory council recommended a radical programme of reconstruction to mobilize all available resources, which were in limited supply because of strict import restraints, towards basic industries (particularly coal and steel). The Reconstruction Bank was created to finance those industries, and scarce foreign exchange was rationed strictly to achieve the production targets in basic industry. The "highest priority strategy for industrial reconstruction" was successful, and pre-war production levels of steel and coal were soon reached.

The Japanese experience shows the potential benefits of adopting clear economic-policy guidelines designed by a council that is independent of the particular sectoral interests usually represented in the traditional ministries. The success of the strategy will depend on whether the many independent government agencies will follow those guidelines closely.

In the first post-war decade the government was involved in detailed quantitative planning in many sectors. Specifically, it carried out a strategic allocation of scarce foreign exchange through a foreign-exchange budget for imports. The political leadership, however, was committed to a free-enterprise mixed economy, and even during this first phase of post-war growth the government was moving towards liberalization of the economy. By 1960, an International Trade and Exchange Liberalization Plan was adopted.

The first comprehensive national plan was drafted to avoid the imminent confusion that the revival of the market economy would induce. In 1957, the second plan was also considered a mechanism for diminishing uncertainty as the economy shifted from a controlled towards a freer and more competitive economy. Because the plan was meant to create a consensus on some basic economic decisions, the process of planning was important, and an institutional structure for consultations among the various social partners was established.

In summary, the Japanese planning agency, instead of concentrating on planning in the public sector, developed a planning methodology that would diminish uncertainty in the private sector and facilitate the orderly elimination of the specific types of state intervention that were set up during the war and continued, in a changed form, during the reconstruction period. Gradually, the objective of planning became the creation of national consensus on the broad economic policies needed to achieve rapid growth and a rising level of well-being for the population. Such a consensus would need to be based on a recognition by all groups in society of the individual efforts and sacrifices that were essential for the welfare of all.

The process of planning thus became as important as the plan itself: for the consensus to occur, a broad process of participation and consultation had to take place. A special administrative structure was devised for the planning agency: instead of the agency having its own personnel, the majority of its officials were on loan from other government agencies — the Ministry of Finance, the Ministry of International Trade and Industry, and other relevant sectoral departments and agencies.

Within this scheme, econometric models and macro-economic projections played an important role, since these set the broad limits within which the sectoral ministries and private interests would negotiate. For that reason Japan shifted more and more towards broad macro-economic planning.

The Japanese experience is instructive because it points towards the useful role that long-range planning can play. By creating a consensus of what the major problems are that an economy must overcome, the planning process can organize the inevitable negotiations between the different economic agents by forcing them to accept certain basic premises. This limits the degree of conflict between them and makes economic-policy decision-making more rapid and more consistent.

The Further Shifts towards Policy Planning

By the 1970s it had become clear that limiting planning activity to the production of public-sector projects plus some short-term trouble-shooting meant that the planners were not having an influence on the economic policy decisions that affected the most important economic variables determining the way an economy develops. In that decade some of the countries studied started to experiment with plans setting out broad policy guidelines that should give clear indications on economic policy to all government decision-makers and establish a clear set of rules within which the private sector could work. The purpose of those policy plans was to make public decisions consistent with one another and to diminish the degree of uncertainty for the private sector.

This shift towards formulating a set of consistent economic policies to achieve certain objectives occurred in most countries but was reflected in the planning documents in different ways. Aid agencies, and the World Bank in particular, started also to emphasize the need for countries to adopt a broad set of consistent policies to achieve a better allocation of resources. The International Labour Organisation and many academic economists, on the other hand, emphasized the impact of different combinations of macro-economic polices on employment creation and income distribution.

A list of the principal objectives of the successive development plans in Kenya over the past two decades shows that that country's planning has closely paralleled the rapid shifts of emphasis in development theory during the period:
— 1966–1970 and 1970–1974, economic growth
— 1974–1978, employment creation and redistribution of income
— 1979–1983, alleviation of poverty
— 1984–1988, mobilizing domestic resources for equitable development
Issues of equity and environment were introduced into planning both in the academic literature and at the level of international agencies and governments. This reflected a shift from economic planning towards more comprehensive development planning.

In the 1970s there was also a growing realization that exchange-rate policies, the pricing of capital, agricultural and industrial pricing policy, tariffs, tax policy and fiscal incentives, and monetary policy all have a fundamental impact on employment creation, growth, and income distribution. Plans, therefore, began to set out guidelines for policy-making in these areas and to put less emphasis on growth targets, investment levels, and specific production targets.

In countries like Colombia and Sri Lanka, where the policy framework was clear and there was a political commitment to follow the consistent set of policies put forth in the plans, economic growth was maintained even during a period of low growth for the world economy.

In summary, plans that clearly establish a consistent set of policy guidelines seem to have effectively influenced economic policy-making and improved economic management. The shift towards policy planning seems, therefore, to have been a fairly successful innovation.

Conclusions

It would seem that thirty years of planning experience in some countries led to a planning model in which generalized project evaluation improved public sector investment, and that the development of plans which set out a broad policy framework for decision-making increased the consistency and the effectiveness of such decision-making. Unfortunately, these innovations in the methodology of planning led to the gradual abandonment of long-term planning, a development which facilitates too frequent changes in economic policies and a sense on the part of private entrepreneurs that the country lacks a permanent sense of where the economy should be going.

There is no need, however, for planners in developing countries to concentrate on either long-term or short-term planning to the exclusion of the other. It should be possible to do both. Long-term planning can provide a consensus on the basic problems that the economy must overcome and an economic framework within which all economic actors can make a contribution to the general welfare. As L. P. Mureithi mentions (chap. 6), an important objective of long-term planning is to define the image a society has of its future. The involvement of the planners in short-run policy, on the other hand, is a necessity for the maintenance of consistency in economic decision-making. Finally, since the public sector will not disappear, its efficiency is a prerequisite for economic growth in developing countries. For that reason, the planners must also continue to force governments to subject all government expenditure to strict project-evaluation criteria.

It is unforunate that planning agencies in the past have tended to shift from one role to another, emphasizing only one of these objectives at any particular time. The lesson we have derived from our survey of planning is that planners must address all three objectives simultaneously.

Other interesting lessons can also be drawn from the planning experiences in the different countries studied.

The Sri Lankan and Hungarian case studies illustrate clearly the difficulties inherent in detailed quantitative planning in small economies with large sectors that produce internationally traded goods. In those economies, the crucial economic variables are outside the control of the planners, and for that reason centralized quantitative planning is difficult. Such a planning methodology, on the other hand, may be viable in large, resource-rich nations such as China, Brazil, or the Soviet Union at certain stages of their development. The Hungarian and Japanese post-war experiences also show that quantitative planning is easier when the objective is to develop or reconstruct a small number of important basic industries.

Planning is also difficult in countries that export primary commodities, because of the great instability in the prices of these commodities. It is clear that one way to deal with this problem is for planners to plan policy reactions to external shocks. Making plans on the basis of only one set of projections for export revenues leads to the plans rapidly becoming obsolete. The new policy plans deal with external instability by specifying the actions that must be taken when certain external prices increase or decrease. It is also clear that the countries that consciously followed a policy of diversifying their exports fared best and performed better economically in those periods in which active diversification was pursued.

Another conclusion that emerged from the studies, and which was emphasized by our colleagues from Nigeria at all of our meetings, is that economic planning makes little sense in an environment of political instability.

Most countries make explicit their plans for encouraging certain sectors, but few make explicit how they will deal with declining industries. The Japanese case study shows the importance of smoothing the decline of certain economic activities when it discusses the measures taken to facilitate the absorption of labour from a declining coal industry. Unless countries plan for the absorption of the labour and capital in declining industries, these sectors will fight for survival at the cost of introducing serious rigidity in the economy, and this will be translated into low growth rates.

It was also apparent that in most countries line ministries tend to end up representing certain industries or interests. It would appear that only an agency with cabinet status but no executive functions can propose broad guidelines for development with independence from pressure groups. Planning agencies are in this position particularly if they are working closely together with the head of state, who, like them, cannot defend the interests of any specific group.

Another objective of planning is to educate the people in economics. The challenge to planners is to translate social problems into economic terminology and to explain to the public the way the economy functions. If the plans help to educate the public in economics, it will be easier to adopt rational economic policies. For that reason plans should be easy to read and widely circulated and discussed. The usual five-volume mimeographed development plan obviously cannot have this type of impact.

It is also apparent that the only way a national planning agency can affect the behaviour of the private sector is by letting representatives of the private sector and people who shape public opinion participate in the process of shaping the broad long-term development guidelines. Such participation is more difficult in short-term decisions, since these often directly affect the specific interests that would be consulted. It appears that the process of planning, and the degree of public participation in that process, must be different for short-term interventions in the economy and for the reaching of a consensus on a long-term development strategy. We were also warned that mechanisms for assuring the participation of the private sector in the planning process tend to give excessive weight to representatives of small and well-organized pressure groups. The poor are often not organized for participating in planning committees at the national level.

Finally, in most developing countries planning methodologies have not been applied to the management of certain labour-intensive sectors or significant social problems such as the administration of justice, racial policy, or crime control. One of the challenges for development economists is to develop methodologies for planning as well as for evaluating the benefits of government expenditures in such sectors. These latter methodologies should make it possible for policy-makers to choose rationally between dedicating scarce government resources to physical infrastructure projects or to these other sectors.

Little has been achieved also in the area of integrating technological change and science and technology into the planning process. This is another area where theoretical and organizational breakthroughs are needed.

The above is an imperfect summary of some of the conclusions and lessons the participants attempted to draw from the experience that the countries we studied have had with planning. Other conclusions can be drawn, and very likely the reader will disagree with some of our generalizations after reading the case studies.

Notes

1. See p. 55 of chap. 3.
2. The Planning Secretariat, *Six-Year Programme of Investment 1954/55 to 1959/60* (Govt. Press, 1955), p. 15.
3. Keith Griffin and John Enos, *Planning Development* (London, Addison-Wesley, 1970), p. 201.
4. Ibid.
5. Donald Snodgrass, *Ceylon: An Export Economy in Transition* (New Haven, Yale University Economic Growth Center, 1966).
6. During the 1960s the Ford Foundation also financed a Harvard Development Advisory Service mission to Colombia. The experts had very limited influence, and they tended to concentrate on preparing policy papers related to short-term issues of economic management. Their main success was that they helped to train the young economists who would man the planning agency in the late 1960s and 1970s.
7. See p. 63 of chap. 3.

2

THE ARGUMENTS FOR PLANNING

Setsuko Yukawa

Historical Background

Before World War II, economic planning was considered a specific characteristic of socialist countries. Although some attempts at planning were made during the 1930s in countries such as India and the Philippines, it was in the post-war period that development planning became widely accepted as a means of accelerating the rate of economic growth and raising the standard of living of people even in countries with market economies. Behind this phenomenon lay two factors: the need for reconstruction of some Western industrialized countries that had suffered serious damage from the war, and the aspirations of the less-developed countries, many of which had attained political independence after the war, for economic independence.

During the war, many industrialized market economies adopted physical planning in order to use scarce materials efficiently in certain priority areas, and this experience led them to use planning to help their economies recover from the ruins of the war. The Marshall Plan strengthened this tendency by requiring each participating country to formulate comprehensive plans before receiving aid from the United States, which considered such planning indispensable in order for these countries to attain reconstruction under their own initiative. Even after the Marshall Plan ended, some Western European

A part of this study was first published in *KSU Economic and Business Review*, no. 11 (June 1984). The author wishes to thank Dr. Miguel Urrutia and Professor Minoru Suzuki for their valuable comments and suggestions.

countries continued their planning activities to promote economic expansion consistent with their resource endowment.

On the other hand, economic development was conceived as a national goal in the less-developed countries, since it was believed that only increasing prosperity would guarantee viable independent, democratic societies. Therefore, some colonial administrations adopted planning practices to promote the modernizing process of their territories. Asian countries which either had become or were about to become independent were more active than countries in any other region in preparing development plans. The Colombo Plan, approved in 1950, took into consideration the fact that many Asian countries had shown a lot of interest in planned development and encouraged its member countries to formulate six-year development plans based on a realistic assessment of available resources. Thus it gave a new impetus to planning in South and South-East Asia.

In Latin America, some partial programmes dealing primarily with public investment in economic infrastructure were prepared and implemented in the 1940s. As the Latin American economy encountered increasing difficulties towards the end of the 1950s, the need for development planning began to be explored in order to overcome internal as well as external problems. Although a few countries drew up national development plans in this decade, at the Punta del Este Conference in 1961 all the Latin American governments accepted that planning should be the fundamental instrument for mobilizing national resources, bringing about necessary structural changes, enhancing efficiency and productivity, and securing more international co-operation. In addition, US aid under the Alliance for Progress was made conditional upon the presentation of an economic and social development plan. It was argued that sound plans that would include not only economic targets and policies but also land reform and other social programmes would be the foundation of development efforts,[1] since the United States wanted to avoid lending to governments that followed policies benefiting only the upper classes and to ensure that there would not be new social upheavals like the Cuban revolution. Although national planning was of interest only to technicians until the beginning of the 1960s, with the formation of the Alliance for Progress it became an essential factor for acquiring foreign aid and consequently a common practice in many Latin American countries.

African countries also showed enthusiasm for development planning, largely stimulated by the colonial powers. By the mid-1960s almost every African country, not only the newly independent nations but also those which had kept their independence during the colonial era, had a development plan. The basic objective of the national plans of the new nations of Africa was to fully realize their economic potentialities not only in order to accelerate the rate of economic growth and improve the level of living of the people but also to recover control over their economy.

As in the case of the Colombo Plan and the Alliance for Progress, the spread of development planning has been stimulated by the foreign-aid policies adopted by Western industrialized countries and donor agencies such as the World Bank, which has played an important role in fostering and strengthening planning efforts, in many countries, especially in the area of infrastructure. The United Nations has also strongly supported development planning in the third world. For instance, the Economic Commission for Latin America (ECLA) recommended adoption of a long-term development policy as early as the end of the 1940s, suggesting the necessity of national planning in view of deteriorating terms of trade and other structural problems inhibiting sustained growth of Latin American countries. In 1962, on the occasion of the inauguration of the Latin American Institute for Economic and Social Planning, an ECLA publication stated:

Although one of Latin America's essential problems lies in the shortage of funds to promote an intensive flow of investment, the want of concrete plans and programmes — including the study of specific projects of significant importance — had been limiting the region's capacity to absorb public and private foreign capital as a means of supplementing the scanty supply of domestic savings. The expansion of external aid opportunities . . . has underlined the importance and urgency of adopting decisive measures with regard to the planning of economic development.[2]

Roles and Patterns of Planning

In the socialist countries, national economic planning represents a form of governing and regulating the society's economic life, and the state controls the level of savings, the amount and composition of output and investment, and the structure of prices. It is believed that centralized planning is essential for a conscious establishment of priorities in distributing the society's resources among individual spheres and sectors of the national economy for the purpose of solving specific economic and social problems.[3]

In countries with mixed economies, however, the question of whether to plan or not and to what extent is decided on the basis of the effectiveness of the planning machinery in fulfilling the given development objectives compared to that of the market mechanism. In other words, the market mechanism and administrative machinery are considered alternative instruments of economic policy. Actually, there is much divergence of opinion about the extent of the role the market mechanism, formed by the free functioning of private enterprises, should play in economic development and the extent to which the government should exercise direct and indirect controls over the economy to allocate the resources in the desired direction and to the desired extent. Broadly speaking, it is admitted that the market mechanism has some advantages over direct controls by government, such as decentralization in decision-making, provision of incentives to a wide range of economic activities, and flexible adaptation to changing conditions.

To a large extent, however, three arguments favour planning over the market mechanism in developing countries. First, the market mechanism is not as effective in the developing countries as in the developed countries because the latter are provided with much greater social overhead capital and with a wider array of complementary factors of production and intermediate goods which make it possible for private enterprises to react to market signals. If the poor performance of the market mechanism in developing countries were due mainly to the lack of social capital, governments would be able to create favourable conditions by increasing investment in social capital, which would provide bases for private enterprises to invest in directly productive activities.

In addition, however, certain structural rigidities prevailing in developing countries tend to make the market imperfections even more serious and therefore represent a second reason for the need for planning. Among these rigidities is a characteristic dual structure — a division of the national economy into two sectors, modern and traditional, which are not fully integrated with each other. Under such conditions, the market mechanism can be effective in bringing about marginal changes in the economy, but it cannot generate the fundamental structural transformations that economic development requires. Where this is the case, the government should assume a leading role in certain aspects of economic and social activities.

Thirdly, when countries pursue certain national goals that would be difficult to achieve even with a well-functioning market mechanism, they must also rely on government intervention. The reduction of inequality between ethnic groups, for instance, has been one of the main objectives of planning in Malaysia. The recent tendency to favour people in low-income brackets has promoted planning practices in many developing countries. This is because resource allocation brought about through the market mechanism reflects each individual's preferences expressed in the market, but individuals can express their preferences in this way only when they have the necessary purchasing power, which in turn depends on the existing pattern of income distribution derived largely from a given distribution of human and material assets.[4] Therefore, if it is desirable to foster more equitable economic and social development, it is necessary to take some policy measures to alter the institutional conditions in which the market mechanism functions.

In spite of the widespread acceptance of development planning as a means of promoting economic growth, it has been defined in very different ways. In some countries, a plan is the product of a group of high-level economists working out a consistent set of economic targets for some single future year with an 'optimal' growth path leading to it. In other countries, it expresses the government's intention to intervene in the whole economic process to make the future very different from what it would otherwise be.

A general definition might be that planning is the establishment of a relationship between means and ends for the purpose of achieving the latter by the most efficient use of the former. It may be used for various purposes — for example, for setting up a production process in a factory, managing an enterprise, or constructing public facilities. But development planning in particular represents an attempt to select and co-ordinate the best available alternatives in order to give desirable direction to and accelerate a country's development.

A development plan may contain the following features:
— a survey and diagnoses of the present economic situation
— policy objectives, especially as related to the future development goals of the country concerned
— a set of strategies by which the objectives should be achieved
— a macro-economic projection for the whole economy[5]

In this type of orthodox planning, the review of the recent trends of the economy and its main factors such as output, investment, saving, consumption, government expenditure, balance of payments, and the population is the starting point of planning. The growth path to attain certain objectives is determined on the basis of this information.

Policy objectives naturally include not only those directly related to government activities but also the targets set for the private sector, which means that the plan strategies should be specified in the form of a list of government expenditures and other policies for the purpose of controlling or promoting the production activities of the private sector, such as the pricing policies of state enterprises and public utilities, tariffs, taxes, and subsidies, quotas, licensing, and rationing. If the government intends to induce private enterprises to employ their resources more productively and in a desirable direction, its decisions concerning these measures need to be efficient and mutually consistent.

Most textbooks recommend a macro-economic projection of the economy as useful for testing the mutual consistency of a plan's quantitative assumptions and proposals. In addition, a forecast for the whole economy helps each investor to grasp an idea of the possibilities to be created when the planned economic expansion is realized and thus, by diminishing his perceived risk, may persuade him to invest more actively than he otherwise would.

In reality, development planning takes many forms. Planning in socialist countries differs substantially from that in mixed economies; in the Soviet Union, for example, and countries of Eastern Europe resource allocation and production are determined by a highly centralized administrative system and the market mechanism is supposed to play only a minor role. The plans made by these countries are documents of authorization indicating what and how much to produce and how much to invest, while those in countries with mixed economies only express the intentions of the government and authorize nothing. But apart from this difference in social, economic, institutional, and political structure, the nature of a country's development planning is influenced by many other factors, such as the availability of natural and human resources, the effectiveness of administrative machinery, and the country's stage of development, even within a mixed economy. The stage of development has an especially decisive influence in determining the form and role of a country's planning. In very poor countries, exports are usually a stimulus to economic expansion, and development can be achieved mainly by opening up new export possibilities or by improving the productivity of existing resources. Planners therefore will concentrate their efforts on exploiting new exportable resources or allocating available resources in a more efficient way. As the economy passes on to the stage of import substitution, inter-industrial relationships begin to assume importance within the national economy and an input-output model becomes necessary to reveal the changes that occur in the whole production system. But less-developed economies usually do not have enough reliable information to manipulate input-output models.[6]

On the basis of these considerations, W. A. Lewis suggested that in a country with poor statistics the first development plan, and even the second, should concentrate on bringing order into the public sector's programmes and into economic policy. This would help administrators and technicians to acquire a certain degree of experience in planning and plan implementation and would contribute to improving the administrative machinery, which is the basis for effective planning. At the same time, the data system would be improved, and increasingly useful statistics would be made available, which would facilitate formulation of a development plan with an interdependent model for the whole economy.[7]

On the other hand, Waterston divided the planning process into three stages: a project-by-project approach, integrated public investment planning, and comprehensive planning. Many countries with mixed economies adopt the project-by-project approach to planning at the beginning of their development. It has been useful, to a certain extent, in laying a foundation for development by providing basic public utilities. But a piecemeal, project-by-project approach has serious shortcomings. Public investment projects are rarely co-ordinated with each other or with other policies within the framework of a specified development philosophy. Therefore, it is desirable to replace the project-by-project approach with integrated public investment planning, combining individual projects into sector programmes and then into an investment plan for the public sector. As a country moves into a more advanced stage of development, comprehensive planning, the most complete form of development planning, becomes feasible. It is theoretically better than partial planning because it covers the whole economy and seeks to ensure the consistency of the intended projects and policies in order to achieve a desired rate of growth in real per capita income.[8] However, Waterston advises that until a country can rely on a reasonably good statistical basis for planning and a sufficient number of administrators and experts trained and experienced in preparing an integrated public investment plan and putting it into practice, comprehensive planning covering both public and private sectors is difficult, and therefore less-developed countries lacking these conditions would do better starting with partial planning.[9]

Development plans differ as much in duration as in form, but they may be generally classified as short-, medium-, or long-term. Short-term plans are typically for one year, while medium-term plans are for periods ranging between three and seven years, with five years as the most common case, and long-term plans for periods of from ten to twenty years.

Lewis argued that countries that undertake planning should have all three kinds of plans.[10] He and other experts on planning such as Tinbergen[11] suggest that planning should start with a perspective plan incorporating the country's long-term perspectives and development objectives. Perspective plans are recommended because they can promote fundamental transformations in the social and economic structure which economic development requires by its very nature and which a shorter-term plan would not be able to bring about.

It has also been advised that after the formulation of a long-term plan, a medium-term plan must be prepared and then the annual plan. The annual plan is necessary because it is the operative document which puts into practice the intentions of the policy-makers expressed in the medium- or long-term plans by authorizing the ministers to appropriate the budget for specific purposes when it is approved by parliament. Regional and sectoral plans might be formulated with the framework of the long- and medium-term plans, with necessary budget provisions in an annual plan.

Choosing to start with a perspective plan has great advantages. First of all, it provides broad guide-lines for planners to formulate a shorter-term plan and serves as a basis for the systematic consideration of the implications of present decisions for the future. Secondly, by virtue of its comprehensive view of the economy and its long-range perspectives, this kind of planning contributes to avoiding the occurrence of bottlenecks and imbalances which may hamper growth. Lastly, it provides the people who participate in the planning process with the opportunity to consider development objectives in a wider perspective and to devise policies in order not only to tackle immediate difficulties but also to solve fundamental problems.[12] The long-term plan might also be used, as has happened in Japan, as a means of building a general consensus in wide sectors (or influential sectors) of the population concerning the broad economic and social objectives which the country should follow.

In reality, however, despite these recommendations, countries in an early stage of development tend to start planning with a short-term plan of one or two years or, more commonly, a medium-term plan of three to seven years. These countries usually face many urgent problems, and the need of fulfilling immediate development objectives is so pressing that political leaders prefer to search for solutions to immediate problems and rarely pay much attention to the long-term perspectives of the country. Therefore, little serious consideration is given to preparation of a long-term plan, in addition to short- or medium-term plans.

Moreover, the lack of political stability and economic certainty which is fairly common in the less-developed countries makes politicians reluctant to formulate perspective plans, and these conditions are also related to the "crisis in planning" which has been pointed out repeatedly since the second half of the 1960s.

Difficulties in Planning in the Less-Developed Countries

Increasing scepticism about planning has arisen mainly from the fact that many countries with a planned economy have failed to achieve satisfactory rates of economic development. Furthermore, in many countries the plans are never used as terms of reference for policy-making; and in others they are never even discussed at the political level. For example, in the mid-1960s, Waterston, after examining the experiences in more than 100 countries, reached the conclusion that "among developing nations with some kind of market economy and a sizable private sector, only one or two countries seem to have been consistently successful in carrying out plans."[13] He continues: "experience shows that countries with well-prepared projects coordinated by sound budgetary procedures and controls can dispense with comprehensive plans, at least for a time, and still maintain high rates of growth."[14]

Apart from political instability and external difficulties, the reasons which have been given for the failure in realizing theoretical advantages of planning in developing countries can be divided into two groups: one group is related to the formulation of plans and the other is concerned with their implementation. With regard to the former, it has often been pointed out that although planners in low-income countries usually follow the practices devised in and for the developed countries, theoretical models have been of limited use even in industrialized countries in the sense that they have rarely been able to provide pertinent forecasts of economic expansion and that, therefore, application of these planning techniques to developing countries with economic and social structures very different from those of developed countries may produce even more misleading results. In fact, in spite of the arguments made by many economists that all economy-wide plans have to contain quantitatively consistent planning indices, as well as some analysis of trade-offs,[15] the concepts of these indices are not necessarily the same in developing countries as in industrialized countries, which may cause inaccurate interpretation of the actual situation of the economy. Moreover, a lack of reliable data and the ability to process them adequately is one of the characteristics of less-developed countries. In some cases, even basic data for population, production, and national income are dubious or virtually non-existent. Therefore, most of the econometric techniques that have been utilized in national planning in developed countries cannot be applied in low-income countries until a good data system has been built.

Nevertheless, many professionals, including experts of international organizations such as the United Nations Economic and Social Commision for Asia and the Pacific (ESCAP), ECLA, and the Economic Commision for Africa (ECA), have advocated that less-developed countries should plan comprehensively using modern planning techniques, because, they claim, it is a way of planning that is theoretically superior to others. But attempts to adopt macro-economic models in these countries have tended to create development plans that are not necessarily relevant to the conditions of their economies, even though their figures are mutually consistent. The value of macro-economic exercises depends on the reliability of the figures. If calculations have to be made based on invented figures, which is not an exceptional practice in poor countries, the results are naturally misleading.

Secondly, in addition to the availability of data and methodological problems in planning, it has been suggested that a strictly economic approach to development is not sufficient to tackle the difficulties facing developing countries, and it is indispensable to take into consideration not only economic but also non-economic factors in preparing and implementing development plans and policies, because they are interrelated and constitute a country's social and economic structure within which the plans and policies are executed. Seers expresses this in stating that "the real point is not that the 'wrong' economic models are used, it is that any 'purely economic' model, interpreting 'economic' in the conventional way, must be of very limited use."[16]

There are several reasons why a purely economic approach is not adequate. The first is that planners with economic training are not taught to take into account social and political constraints which might impede the putting into practice of development plans. Secondly, purely economic models assume no interaction between economic, social, and political developments. But each economic decision has social and political implications, and it is even more important to realize this interrelationship if we consider that development implies structural transformation, and economic structure cannot be changed without changing social and political structures.

Moreover, the preference of planners for quantitative development models generates the tendency of choosing plans of a relatively short period, which may divert attention away from basic matters such as education, land tenure, and demographic problems by taking these factors as given. Even though preparation of a perspective plan of more than 10 years is not a necessary condition for effective development planning, it is indispensable to have a broad outlook on the long-term development objectives even in preparing short- or medium-term plans.

These considerations indicate that the planner needs to come increasingly into contact with reality. He has to learn how statistical data are collected and processed in his own country and how he can utilize them in a more adequate way. It is also necessary for him to gather a wide range of information about every sector of the country in order to broaden his view of its economy. Even more important is the establishment of a mechanism by which he can get the participation in the planning process of entrepreneurs, trade union leaders, politicians, and other agents who will be affected by the plans, because the extent to which objectives of a plan can be achieved depends largely on whether or not the opinions of all of these actors, and in particular those of the private sector, are reflected in the plan.

Thirdly, the role of planners and politicians in setting the objectives of a plan is critical. Sunkel pointed out that according to the conventional concept of the function of the planner, there exists a clear and well-defined relation between the politician and the planner; that is, the former would define objectives of the society and make choices among the alternative means available to him, and the latter would be concerned with elaborating various policy alternatives which permit the society to advance from a given situation towards those objectives. However, this conception does not correspond to reality.[17]

The first reason is that it does not seem to be feasible for the politician to make a reasonable and conscious choice among the alternatives that the planner offers to him because the politician often lacks technical knowledge and a complete understanding of the policy implications of the various alternatives the planner proposes.

An even more significant reason is that the technocrats cannot easily translate the value judgements and objectives of the politicians into the quantitative models traditionally used in planning. As observed by Hagen[18] and many other economic planners, political leaders usually state national goals and priorities in an implicit manner and express them only vaguely in quantitative terms. Given this difficulty, Roemer proposes planning by "revealed preference,"[19] in which planners begin by identifying alternative sets of national goals and priorities and then prepare alternative strategies that might result in varying satisfaction of the national goals. This provides the political authorities with full information on the goals and the means and sacrifices that each strategy would imply, enabling them to make their selection of a strategy and goal priorities.

Among the causes to which ineffective implementation of plans has been attributed, the most widely discussed are the administrative deficiencies in the less-developed countries. Waterston found that quite a few development plans failed to be executed as was originally expected due to the weakness in the administrative machinery, and "a major limitation in implementing projects and programmes, and in operating them upon completion, is not financial resources, but administrative capacity."[20]

In many less-developed countries, administrative structures do not meet the demands of accelerated development. In some of these countries, such structures may make possible decentralized development based on market signals but may not accommodate attempts at planning. A lack of co-ordination among government departments often leads to a phenomenon in which a macro plan does not have a clear link with the sectoral policies drafted by the various departments. When the planning and execution of a programme or a project within the plan involves more than one public agency, as is usually the case, the independent responsibilities and policies of each agency tend to result in confusion and paralysis. If it is necessary to involve not only the central government but also the provincial and local governments, co-ordination among their development activities becomes even more difficult. Many countries have tried to overcome administrative deficiencies by creating new organizations, but it has been made clear that "the biggest problem is how to reconcile the autonomy they need for managerial efficiency with the need for a co-ordinated development policy in the public sector."[21]

With the awareness of the need for an integrated approach to development issues, particularly those related to poverty groups, since the beginning of the 1970s greater efforts have been made to restructure the administrative system. However, a system of decentralization adopted in some countries to deal at the local level with the complex and interrelated problems of the poor in a more adequate and flexible manner has achieved only limited success, for various reasons such as local authorities' dependence on financial doles from the centre and narrow political interests favouring specific projects, as was observed in Kenya and Sri Lanka.[22] As decentralization implies power sharing from the central government to the local authorities, this kind of administrative reform would be difficult to implement without a firm political will.

On the other hand, Seers, while also admitting administrative deficiencies in developing countries, argues that the fundamental problem lies rather in the nature of the administrator and the planner. If planning means a deliberate strategy of intervention to change the shape of the country's future, it is not attractive to the traditional bureaucrats, and the planner's task can be made harder by the attitude of these government officials. Moreover, if it is necessary to introduce coherence into government policy, the planner needs a great deal of skill in handling the other departments, which is not necessarily a quality that model-builders have. On the contrary, model-builders are usually accustomed to sitting in an office and elaborating programmes or projects rather than to exercising influence on the policies of other departments.[23]

Apart from administrative deficiencies, what makes effective implementation even more difficult is the lack of the political will to execute plans. Indeed, there seems to be a growing consensus among economists that a lack of government support for the plans is one of the most important reasons why they are rarely carried out successfully. Seers also argues that "political forces encourage the production of pseudo-plans."[24] However, when there is a political consensus within the government on a series of development objectives, a national plan formulated by technocrats to achieve certain political goals in a consistent manner may well count on the support of the head of state or the governing party for the period in which the political group in question remains in power, as suggested by the Colombian experience.

Yet, this sort of relative success of a short- or medium-term plan does not necessarily mean that it will be carried out in consistency with the long-term objectives of the country. In effect, difficulties can arise even with the existence of a firm political commitment to planning when a transfer of power takes place between two administrations with substantially different ideologies, since it would lead to discontinuity in development policies which, in turn, would discourage activities of the private sector, a situation which would eventually hamper sustained growth, as occurred in Sri Lanka. This implies that the effectiveness of planning efforts, especially in developing countries, is determined to a considerable extent by the country's political arrangements, such as the country's system of party politics and political ideologies for national development.[25] Thus, when there is no broad consensus on the desired long-term nature of society due to these kinds of political problems, a long-term development plan might be of little practical use, in spite of its attractiveness as a concept.[26]

The Malaysian experience, however, indicates that programmes which have the highest priority in terms of political, economic, and social necessities are able to extract full commitment in formulation and implementation and that this commitment is made possible when the approach is politically acceptable to all major socio-economic groups and interests. If this is the case, in the absence of serious ideological conflicts concerning national development, a development plan with long-term perspectives could play an important role in forming a national consensus not only on the development objectives but also on the restrictions to be overcome and the efforts and sacrifices to be made by certain groups in order to attain those objectives for the whole nation, as is shown by the Japanese case.

Planning and Policy Implementation

The views referred to in the previous sections are still basically in favour of planning, in spite of the many shortcomings of this type of government intervention applied in developing countries. But Myint goes a little further and advocates "planning using the market mechanism."[27] Given the Asian experience, which "tends to confirm the general proposition that extensive and detailed controls by the administrative machinery are extremely inefficient and can not offer a workable method of co-ordinating the economy,"[28] he suggests making "a deliberate use of the theoretically unsophisticated but practically more dependable working of the market mechanism as an instrument of economic development policy."[29] This view apparently denies the need for planning but emphasizes the importance of policy, which recalls Lewis, an advocate of comprehensive planning, who argues that "the core of planning for higher productivity in the private sector lies in the set of policies which induce private persons to employ their time and resources more productively,"[30] thus emphasizing equally the function of the market mechanism.

The problem lies, then, not in the choice between planning and the market mechanism but in effective policy implementation. Improvements in policy-making and administrative machinery as proposed by many experts are definitely required to implement development policy in an effective way, even if a country does not adopt comprehensive planning. However, what has received relatively little attention is the importance of studying the social and institutional conditions which may influence the behavioural assumptions implicit in the planning models used. It is very important in developing economies with a substantial private sector to identify the factors that impede economic agents from following behaviour which would be economically rational. For example, if an entrepreneur does not react to a stimulus that the government offers in order to orient investment in a desirable direction, it may be due to any of various reasons, specific to a particular society, such as a lack of entrepreneurship, technical constraints, an inadequate supply of complementary inputs or facilities, a very marked aversion to risk when one is near the poverty line, and possibilities of other, more profitable, activities such as speculation or investment abroad. Needless to say, in a less-developed economy which usually consists of a small modern sector and a large traditional sector, these factors differ according to not only the nature of productive activities but also the extent to which they are modernized.

The trend in the 1970s to place emphasis on direct elimination of poverty rather than on aggregate economic growth and rather than trying to involve all socio-economic groups in the process of development has affected the planning process as well as the choice of targets. In addition to sustained economic growth, the creation of employment opportunities and the satisfaction of basic human needs of the poverty groups who had benefited little from economic growth so far achieved have become important objectives of development plans in many developing countries. This shift from growth-oriented strategies to poverty-focused strategies has stimulated the arguments in favour of people's participation in planning for the purpose of addressing the specific problems of the rural and urban poor. It was expected that the participation of the target groups would help to identify their real needs and the economic, social, and institutional factors determining their behaviour and thus would facilitate effective formulation and implementation of development plans.

The issue of participation, however, should be carefully examined in the light of the particular conditions of a given society. Although people's participation in the process of formulation of a plan can theoretically be a useful instrument to assure effectiveness in planning and plan implementation, it is not easy to find an effective way of getting the participation of the people, especially in a country where a democratic system is yet to be firmly established. Even more serious would be a case in which a plan aims at a fundamental transformation of an existing social structure. For instance, in a traditional society, local power élites do not necessarily represent the interests of the poor, and their participation in the planning process might contribute to the protection of their own interests at the expense of the real objectives of the development plans. If development planning seeks by its nature to break down structural obstacles which hamper development, it would be difficult to ensure freedom from this kind of problem, and here again the support of the central government to the plan objectives would play a decisive role.

Uncertainty is another issue which has been raised as an important factor influencing the success or failure of planning and still remains to be fully analysed. The problem of planning under uncertainty has two aspects. In the first place, countries in which exports and imports are an important proportion of the national income clearly do not have complete control of some of the strategic variables for planning, and external shocks may negate the planning schemes. Wide fluctuations in the international economy since the early 1970s in particular have brought about fundamental changes in economic policies in many countries, and economic management under uncertainty seems to have been a difficult task even for industrialized countries, calling for approaches different from the conventional ones. In such a case, it would be even more important for small- and medium-sized developing countries to devise an effective way to handle this problem. The recent shift from macro-economic to policy planning with greater flexibility might be a reaction of governments to the growing uncertainty in the world economy.

The second aspect of uncertainty is of a political nature. Many developing countries are facing political uncertainty, which constitutes a serious constraint on planning practices. Political stability is certainly a prerequisite for effective planning, and planners may have little ability to cope with this kind of uncertainty. However, if we consider that political instability is triggered by social conflicts in many cases, it should be one of the roles of planning to predict and avoid social problems so as to mitigate the causes for political turbulence. In fact, this sort of consideration is indispensable for any development plan, since economic growth almost inevitably creates structural imbalances that may increase inequalities and eventually cause serious conflicts between various social or ethnic groups in a country.

Hirschman points out that while the tolerance for economic inequalities may be large in homogeneous societies, as no language, ethnic, or other barriers keep those who are left behind from empathizing with those who are better off, this effect is not likely to come into being in segmented societies. Even in countries where great tolerance exists, however, a violent social conflict could occur in the course of development, unless the inequalities are corrected in time.[31]

Consequently, special importance should be attached to measures to increase social mobility and social integration as economic growth proceeds, particularly in countries with diverse populations in terms of race, religion, or language. In this connection, the Malaysian plans that incorporate the lessons from the social conflicts caused by racial problems in 1969 represent an interesting attempt to achieve these objectives, while the Nigerian case exemplifies the difficulty in attaining political stability in a segmented society when growing inequality accompanies high rates of economic growth.

Diverse experiences in planning in less-developed countries seem to tell us that its effectiveness very much depends on whether planners can find methodologies to incorporate economic, social, and political factors in development plans in order to cope with not only the problems rooted in underdevelopment but also the difficulties arising from the growth itself, and this will be possible only in planning based on medium- and long-term perspectives on the desirable state of the country.

Notes

1. Harvey S. Perloff, *Alliance for Progress: A Social Invention for the Making* (Baltimore and London, The Johns Hopkins University Press, 1969), pp. 20–21.
2. ECLA, "Latin American Institute for Economic and Social Planning," *Economic Bulletin for Latin America*, vol. 7, no. 2 (October 1962), p. 115.
3. United Nations Institute for Training and Research, USSR Academy of Sciences, *Planning in Developing Countries: Theory and Methodology* (USSR, 1979), p. 18.
4. Hisao Kumagai, *Kōsei Keizaigaku* (Welfare economics) (Tokyo, Sōbunsha, 1978), pp. 158–159.
5. W. A. Lewis, *Development Planning: The Essentials of Economic Policy* (London, Allen and Unwin, 1966), pp. 12–23; J. Tinbergen, *Development Planning* (London, George Weidenfeld and Nicolson, 1967 [Japanese translation, *Kaihatsu Keikaku* (Tokyo, Kajima Kenkyusho Shuppankai, 1970), pp. 29–32]); A. Foxley and E. García, "El Papel de las Proyecciones en la Planificación Nacional: Una Metodología para Proyecciones de Mediano Plazo y Su Aplicación a Chile," in E. García d'Acuña, ed., *La Planificación del Desarrollo en América Latina* (Mexico City, Fondo de Cultura Económica, 1975), p. 174; T. Killick, "The Possibilities of Development Planning," *Oxford Economic Papers*, vol. 28, no. 2 (July 1976), pp. 161–162.
6. W. A. Lewis, (note 5 above), pp. 19–20.
7. Ibid., p. 21.
8. A. Waterston, *Development Planning: Lessons of Experience* (Baltimore, The Johns Hopkins University Press, 1965), pp. 61–66.
9. Ibid., p. 68.
10. W. A. Lewis, (note 5 above), pp. 148–150.
11. J. Tinbergen, (note 5 above), pp. 36–37.
12. In addition to W. A. Lewis and Tinbergen, Waterston suggests these theoretical advantages; A. Waterston, "An Operational Approach to Development Planning,"

in M. Faber and D. Seers, eds., *The Crisis in Planning, I* (London, Chatto and Windus, 1972), p. 86.

13. A. Waterston "A Hard Look at Development Planning," *Finance and Development*, vol. 3 (June 1966), p. 85.

14. Ibid., p. 90.

15. For example, see T. Watanabe, "Quantitative Foundations and Implications of Planning Processes," in D. R. Blitzer, P. B. Clark, and L. Taylor, eds., *Economy-Wide Models and Development Planning* (London, Oxford University Press, 1975).

16. D. Seers, "The Prevalence of Pseudo-Planning," in Faber and Seers (note 12 above), p. 26.

17. O. Sunkel, "La Tarea Política y Teórica del Planificador en América Latina," in García d'Acuña (note 5 above), p. 50.

18. E. E. Hagen, *Planning Economic Development* (Homewood, R. D. Irwin, 1963), p. 335.

19. M. Roemer, "Planning by 'Revealed Preference': An Improvement upon the Traditional Method," *World Development*, vol. 4, no. 9 (1976): 775–783.

20. A. Waterston, *Development Planning* (note 8 above), p. 249.

21. Ibid., p. 290.

22. See chap. 3 this volume and also the original Sri Lankan case study available in mimeographed form at the Marga Institute, Colombo, which analyses in greater detail the issues related to decentralization of planning.

23. D. Seers (note 16 above), pp. 29–30.

24. Ibid., p. 24.

25. See chap. 7 this volume.

26. T. Killick (note 5 above), p. 179.

27. H. Myint, *Economic Theory and the Underdeveloped Countries* (London, Oxford University Press, 1971), p. 313.

28. Ibid., p. 300.

29. Ibid., p. 313.

30. W. A. Lewis (note 5 above), p. 23.

31. A. O. Hirschman, "The Changing Tolerance for Income Inequality in the Course of Economic Development," *World Development*, vol. 1, no. 12 (1973): 33.

Select Bibliography

Blitzer, C. R., P. B. Clark, and L. Taylor, eds. 1975. *Economy-wide models and development planning*. London, Oxford University Press.

Chenery, H. B., ed. 1971. *Studies in development planning*. Cambridge, Mass., Harvard University Press.

Cook, W. D., and T. E. Kuhn, eds. 1982. *Planning processes in developing countries: Techniques and achievements*. Amsterdam, North Holland.

Díaz-Alejandro, C. 1975. "Planificación del sector externo en América Latina." In E. García d'Acuña, ed., *La planificación del desarrollo en América Latina*. Mexico City. Fondo de Cultura Económica.

Faber, M., and D. Seers, eds. 1972. *The crisis in planning*. London, Chatto and Windus.

Foxley, A., and E. García. 1975. "El papel de las proyecciones en la planificación nacio-

nal: Una metodología para proyecciones de mediano plazo y su aplicación a Chileo."
In E. García d'Acuña, ed., *La planificación del desarrollo en América Latina*. Mexico City,
Fondo de Cultura Económica.

Gillis, M., D. H. Perkins, M. Roemer, and D. R. Snodgrass. 1983. *Economics of development*. New York, W. W. Norton.

Griffin, K. B., and J. L. Enos. 1970. *Planning development*. London, Addison Wesley.

Hagen, E. E. 1963. *Planning economic development*. Homewood, Illinois, R. D. Irwin.

———. 1975. *The economics of development*. rev. ed. Homewood, Illinois, R. D. Irwin.

Herrick. B., and C. P. Kindleberger. 1983. *Economic development*. 4th ed. New York,
McGraw-Hill International.

Killick, T. 1976. "The possibilities of development planning." *Oxford Economic Papers*,
vol. 28, no. 2 (July 1976).

Lewis, W. A. 1949. *The principles of economic planning*. London, Allen and Unwin.

———. 1966. *Development planning: The essentials of economic planning*. London, Allen and
Unwin.

Little, I. M. D. 1982. *Economic development: Theory, policy, and international relations*. New
York, Basic Books.

Myint, H. 1971. *Economic theory and the underdeveloped countries*. London, Oxford University
Press.

Roemer, M. 1976. "Planning by ' revealed preference': An improvement upon the traditional method." *World Development*, vol. 4, no. 9.

Seers, D. 1972. "The prevalence of pseudo-planning." In *The crisis in planning. See* Faber
and Seers 1972.

Streeten, P. 1972. *The frontiers of development studies*. London and Basingstoke, The Macmillan Press.

Todaro, M. P. 1977. *Economic development in the third world*. London and New York,
Longman.

UNITAR, USSR Academy of Sciences. 1979. *Planning in developing countries: Theory and
methodology*.

United Nations. 1963. *Planning for economic development*. New York, United Nations.

Waterston, A. *Development planning: Lessons of experience*. Baltimore, The Johns Hopkins
University Press.

———. 1966. "A hard look at development planning." *Finance and Development*, vol. 3
(June).

3

PLANNING IN UNCERTAINTY: THE CASE OF SRI LANKA

Godfrey Gunatilleke

The Economic, Social, and Political Background

Problems after Independence

At the time Sri Lanka gained independence it was part of a colonial economic system and had acquired many of the structural characteristics of a typical colonial economy. The British, who had ruled the country for about 150 years, had exploited the agricultural potential of the country and developed an export economy based on three major tropical products — tea, rubber, and coconut — which were supplied to the markets of industrialized countries. The economy was predominantly agricultural, with the three major export crops contributing over one-third of the GDP. The organized plantation sector, comprising large-scale units and operating on commercial enterprises, existed alongside a peasant economy of small holdings based on subsistence agriculture devoted mainly to rice cultivation.

This chapter is an abridged version of an original study available in mimeographed form in the Marga Institute, Colombo. The study was prepared by Mr. Godfrey Gunatilleke, director of the Marga Institute and project director for the study. He was assisted by Ms. Yvonne Schokman, senior research officer, Ms. Darshini de Alwis, research officer, and Mr. G. I. O. M. Kurukulasuriya, associate director of the Macro-Economic Studies Division, who comprised the research team of the institute assigned to this project. Ms. Schokman and Ms. de Alwis prepared working papers for section 3, on the institutionalization of the planning process. Mr. Kurukulasuriya contributed to the project by participating in the discussions and interacting with the other researchers in the course of their work. Ms. Malkanthi Nanayakkara, chief librarian/documentation officer, prepared the bibliography of plan documents.

The developments during the colonial period had created a dualistic economic structure, with one part linked to international markets and providing the resource base for the growing modern urban sector, and the other part engaged in production, barely above the subsistence level and with hardly any marketable surpluses. There were few exchanges and linkages between these two parts. One of the main tasks of the governments after independence was to attack the social and economic problems arising from this dualistic structure and to integrate the backward parts of the economy into the process of development.

The colonial period had also created a highly vulnerable and externally dependent economy. Imports and exports of goods and services accounted for approximately 61 per cent of the GDP in 1950. In that same year, food imports amounted to about 50 per cent of merchandise imports. Sri Lanka imported approximately two-thirds of its domestic requirements for the staple food rice and was wholly dependent on imports for the other major food items, sugar and wheat flour. Sri Lanka, therefore, was not merely an exporter of primary products and an importer of manufactured goods; it had to procure the bulk of its essential food supply from foreign markets. Nevertheless, at the time of independence, the Sri Lankan economy was in a relatively sound economic and financial condition. It enjoyed a favourable balance of payments, with a sizeable current account surplus and external reserves amounting to the equivalent of about one year's imports. The government expenditures were also being managed well within the revenue available without recourse to deficit financing (see table 9). But already at the time of independence, Sri Lanka was lowering its mortality and entering a phase of high population growth. At the same time, it had developed a social welfare system on which public expenditure was steadily increasing.

By the end of the 1950s, however, this favourable economic situation suffered a dramatic reversal. The balance of payments had run into heavy current account deficits, the trade gap was widening, and external reserves had declined drastically. Two decisive factors — one external and the other internal — contributed to these developments. Externally the terms of trade began to deteriorate steadily. Despite significant improvements in productivity and output in the export sector, price trends in current terms for the major export products — tea, rubber, and coconut — indicated a long-term decline, while import prices showed a rising trend. The Central Bank calculated that the increment to GDP measured in constant prices during the period 1959–1965 had to be further reduced by approximately 19 per cent in order to adjust for the adverse effects of the terms of trade.[1] Internally, government revenue was crucially dependent on the export sector and the income it generated. However, while the balance of payments deteriorated and began imposing serious constraints on the government budget and the mobilization of domestic resources, governments continued to sustain public expenditure at levels which resulted in large budget deficits. The growth of revenue and finances from non-inflationary sources lagged well behind rising government expenditures, and the government was resorting to deficit financing by borrowing from the Central Bank. The inflationary impact of these processes was being contained by depleting external reserves and maintaining supplies to match the expansion of demand created by deficit financing. By the beginning of the 1960s the country was moving into a prolonged economic crisis.

These continue to be the most serious problems and pose intractable difficulties for the management of the economy.

The Economy: Performance and Changes in Structure

Growth and Investment

Sri Lanka's GDP grew at an annual average of approximately 3.5 per cent in the decade 1950–1960, rising to an average of 4.4 per cent over the period 1960–1970 and then declining to 3.9 per cent in the next ten-year period at 1959 prices, or 4.1 per cent at 1970 prices (see table 1). These ten-year averages, however, conceal the sharp fluctuations that occurred within the three ten-year periods. The periods of high growth occurred when import capacities expanded and external resource flows increased, either through the use of reserves, as in the second half of the 1950s, or through external aid and borrowing, as in the case of the late 1960s and 1970s. The annual average rate of growth for the period 1966–1970 was 5.6 per cent,[2] and 6.1 per cent for 1976–1980.[3] It is also significant that these high rates of growth were achieved as a result of freer operation of market forces and the opening up of the economy, made possible through an expansion of import capacity.

The performance on savings and capital formation was also uneven during the 30-year period. Domestic savings, which were in the region of 12 per cent of GDP in the period 1950–1960, rose to approximately 16 per cent by the end of the 1960s, declining to 11.2 per cent in 1980 and increasing again, to 13.6 per cent, in 1983. Private transfers from abroad have, however, enhanced national savings to 14 per cent in 1980 and 16.2 per cent in 1983. Fixed capital formation increased from approximately 14.9 per cent in 1960 to 19.8 per cent in 1970 and to a record 31.3 per cent in 1980 (see table 2). The difference between national savings and capital formation was financed mainly through foreign savings, of which the preponderant share comprised foreign aid.

A significant share of the capital formation in the economy took place in the public sector. In the 1950s, the public sector share was in the region of 50 per cent. This share declined in the 1960s and early 1970s, to about 40 per cent in 1965 and roughly 30 per cent in 1970. The share rose once again to more than 50 per cent in the late 1970s with the massive investment programme of the government, which included the important Mahaweli River Diversion Project. The public sector thus played a major role in capital formation and development.

TABLE 1. Gross national product at constant factor cost prices: 1950–1980 (Rs million)

Sector	1959 factor cost prices				1970 factor cost prices		Average annual rate of growth at 1959 prices			At 1970 prices
	1950	1960	1970	1980	1970	1980	1950–60	1960–70	1970–80	1970–80
1. Agriculture, forestry, hunting, fishing	1,870.8	2,455.5	3,406.6	4,242.7	3,732	4,746	2.7	3.4	2.2	2.5
2. Mining, quarrying	27.0	32.4	65.2	412.2	95	684	2.0	7.2	20.25	22.0
3. Manufacturing	629.6	728.0	1,331.8	1,710.5	2,197	3,881	1.5	6.2	2.5	2.0
4. Construction	158.2	280.9	577.2	767.9	744	1,066	1.6	7.5	2.9	3.7
5. Electricity, gas, water, sanitation services	7.3	9.8	21.3	52.5	101	209	3.0	8.1	9.4	7.5
6. Transport, storage, communication	429.1	584.8	913.2	1,370.6	1,258	1,838	3.1	4.6	4.2	3.9
7. Wholesale and retail trade	604.9	928.8	1,393.2	2,082.5	2,533	3,849	4.4	4.2	4.1	4.3
8. Banking, insurance, real estate	38.4	51.8	118.0	311.9	152	402	3.8	8.6	10.2	10.2
9. Ownership of dwellings	154.9	211.8	301.5	415.8	399	549	3.2	3.6	3.3	3.2
10. Public administration, defence	157.0	314.4	458.8	853.9	517	959	7.2	3.8	6.4	6.4

11. Services	450.1	754.2	1,183.7	1,088.5	1,459	2,572	5.3	4.6	5.8	5.8
12. Gross domestic product	4,527.3	6,332.4	9,770.5	14,309.2	13,187	19,575	3.4	4.4	3.9	4.1
13. Net factor income from abroad	−62.4	−43.9	−84.1	−95.5	−222	−119				
14. Gross national product (12–13)	4,464.99	6,288.5	9,686.4	14,213.7	12,967	19,456				
15. Terms of trade effect	177.9	−10.6	−915.5	—	—	−1,205.8	3.5	4.4	3.9	4.1
16. Real national income (14–15)	4,642.8	6,277.9	8,778.9	—	12,967	18,250.2	3.1	3.4		3.5
17. Mid-year population (mn.)	7.7	9.9	12.5	14.7	12.5	14.7	—	—	—	—
18. Real per capita income (Rs)	603	636	774	—	1,037	1,242	—	—	—	—

Source: Annual Reports of the Central Bank.

Note: The computation of GDP for 1950–1960 at constant prices poses numerous problems of accuracy and comparability. The national accounts for the period compiled by the Department of Census and Statistics produce an average rate of GDP growth which is in the region of 4.5 per cent for the ten-year period. The revised tables provided by Snodgrass in *Ceylon: An Export Economy in Transition* yields almost the same result. The figures in this table have, however, been based on a revised series compiled by Dr. Savundranayagam (see *Estimates of Gross National Product from 1980 to 1981*, Staff Studies, Central Bank of Ceylon, vol. 13, nos. 1, 2, April/Sept 1985). The average rate of growth, it will be seen, is significantly lower than the earlier estimates. For the purpose of the overview of economic growth presented in this study, the revised estimates at 1959 data would suffice; further work would be needed for a more reliable and detailed assessment of the growth performance of the 1950–1960 period.

TABLE 2. Gross domestic capital formation at current market prices 1950–1980
(Rs mn.)

Item	1950	1960	1970	1980
1. Gross domestic fixed capital formation	401.1	991	2,350	20,845
1. Private sector and public corporations	—	605	1,780	16,139
1.1 Planting, replanting, and land development	—	52	96	462
1.2 Building and other construction	—	335	993	6,270
1.3 Plant and machinery	—	81	322	3,831
1.4 Transport equipment	—	82	245	4,549
1.5 Other capital goods	—	55	133	1,024
2. Government and other public enterprises	—	386	570	4,709
2. Changes in stock	−19.6	6	230	1,620
1. Private sector and public corporations	—	−27	192	640
2. Government and public enterprises	—	33	38	980
3. Gross domestic capital formation	381.5	997	2,589	2,465
1. Private sector	—	—	1,467 }	16,776
2. Public corporations	—	—	514 }	
3. Government and public enterprises	—	—	608	5,689
4. Gross domestic capital formation as percentage of GDP	10.17	18.6	17.9	31.3

Source: Annual Reports of the Central Bank.
Note: The figures for certain years are given as provisional by the Central Bank and revised in subsequent reports.

Government expenditure, both capital and current, amounted to about 17 per cent of GDP in 1950; it had risen to about 26 per cent by 1960, 30 per cent by 1970, and 42 per cent by 1980. It declined to 35 per cent by 1983 as heavy capital expenditures on government programmes peaked and levelled out. As government budgetary expenditures increased, government revenue was unable to keep pace. As a percentage share of GDP, government revenue registered significant increases. Total government receipts increased from about 14.6 per cent in 1950 to 21 per cent in 1960. They continued at about the same level in the beginning of the 1970s and stood at 20.9 per cent in 1980. By the end of the 1950s, government revenue was barely sufficient to finance the recurrent expenditure in revenue. A marginal surplus in some years was followed by deficits. The increasing budgetary gap was met by domestic market borrowings, aid, and expansionary financing.

Changes in the Sectoral Composition of GDP

These trends in economic growth and capital formation should be seen against the structural changes that took place during this period (see table 3). If

TABLE 3. Gross domestic product at constant (1959) factor cost prices (Rs mn.)

Sector	1950 Value	1950 Percentage of GDP	1960 Value	1960 Percentage of GDP	1970 Value	1970 Percentage of GDP	1980 Value	1980 Percentage of GDP
1. Primary sector: agriculture, forestry, hunting, fishing	1,870.8	41.3	2,435.5	38.5	3,400.0	34.9	4,242.7	29.5
2. Secondary sector:								
mining, quarrying,	27.0	0.6	32.4	0.5	65.2	0.7	412.4	2.8
manufacturing,	629.6	13.9	728.0	11.5	1,331.8	13.6	1,710.5	12.0
construction	158.2	3.5	288.9	4.4	577.2	5.9	767.9	5.4
Total	814.8	18.0	1,041.3	16.4	1,974.2	20.2	2,890.8	20.2
3. Tertiary sector:								
electricity, gas, water, sanitation services	7.3	0.2	9.8	0.2	21.3	0.2	52.5	0.4
transport, storage, communication	429.1	9.5	584.8	9.2	913.2	9.3	1,370.6	9.0
wholesale, retail trade	604.9	13.4	928.8	14.7	1,393.2	14.3	2,082.5	14.0
banking, insurance, real estate	38.4	0.8	51.8	0.8	—	1.2	311.9	2.2
ownership of dwellings	154.9	3.4	211.8	3.3	—	3.1	415.8	2.0
public administration, defence	157.0	3.5	314.4	5.0	—	4.7	853.9	6.0
services, n.i.e.	450.1	9.9	754.2	—	—	12.9	2,088.5	14.0
Total	1,841.7	40.7	2,855.6	45.1	—	44.9	7,175.7	50.0
Gross domestic product	4,525.3	100.0	6,332.4	100.0	9,770.5	100.0	14,309.2	100.0

Source: Annual Report of the Central Bank.

changes in the structure of the economy are measured as changes in the sectoral composition of GDP, it cannot be said that the economy has undergone any major structural transformation. The share of agriculture in GDP has declined from about 41 per cent of GDP in 1950 to about 30 per cent in 1980. The decline in the share of the primary sector might at first appear to reflect a dynamic process of structural change. This decline, however, is not matched by a corresponding increase in the manufacturing sector, which would normally be the major force in the transition from a primary economy to an industrial economy. The secondary sector, inclusive of construction and manufacturing, has increased from about 18 per cent in 1950 to 20 per cent in 1980. The processing of tea, rubber, and coconut contributed a major part of manufacturing in 1950. This share has declined appreciably, and the composition of industrial output has been considerably diversified. To this extent some element of structural transformation and growth of industrial capacity can be discerned. This was largely the product of the effort at import substitution undertaken by both the public and private sectors — basic industries such as cement, sugar, paper, tyre, steel rolling, and oil refining in the public sector and light consumer industries in the private sector.

The sector which increased its share of GDP was the tertiary sector, which grew from 40 per cent in 1950 to 45 per cent in 1960 and to 50 per cent in 1980.[4] This growth is partly accounted for by the expansion of public administration and welfare services. This would again point to an inherent structural weakness in the economy. The commodity producing sectors have grown slowly relative to the tertiary sector. Both agriculture and manufacturing have recorded average rates of growth for the thirty-year period below 3.5 per cent — approximately 2.8 per cent for agriculture and 3.4 per cent for manufacturing.

The sectoral aggregates, however, do not reflect certain important structural changes which occurred within the agricultural sector and which had a far-reaching impact on the Sri Lankan economy and policies. The most important of these was the steady and vigorous growth of the peasant smallholding sector engaged in rice cultivation. Mainly as a result of the contribution from this sector, the value added by small-scale production in crops other than tea, rubber, and coconut soon overtook the value added from these three major export crops. In the early 1950s, tea, rubber, and coconut contributed more than two-thirds of the agricultural product. By the beginning of the 1960s, the share had declined to about half. The value added in the paddy sector in 1983 was more than double that of tea; paddy and "other" crops together contributed two-thirds of the total value added in the agricultural sector, against one-third from the plantation crops tea, rubber, and coconut.

The successful performance of the paddy sector reduced the country's dependence on imports for its rice requirements and imparted some strength to the economy when the traditional export sector was running into grave difficulties. As the paddy sector was organized primarily on the basis of small-scale peasant production, its growth benefited the hitherto disadvantaged rural population and raised the levels of productivity and income in the backward segments of the economy. The increase of output in this sector reinforced the other efforts to improve the living conditions of the poor. To some extent, it helped to change the dualistic structure of the economy and promote its integration.

Problems of the External Sector

The country's export economy, which was relatively prosperous and strong at the time the country became independent, continued to struggle against a persistently deteriorating international market. The long-term trend in the 1950s witnessed a moderate decline. Taking 1978 as 100, the country's terms of trade fell from 200 in 1950 to 185 in 1960. But even within this period there were sharp fluctuations which created conditions of instability and uncertainty, posing grave problems for the management of the economy. External receipts rose by approximately 70 per cent between 1949 and 1951 and then fell sharply in 1952 to below the 1950 level. As a result of the failure to anticipate and manage these fluctuations, the Sri Lankan economy faced a major crisis in the ensuing years which had grave political repercussions. Between 1955 and 1960, export earnings stagnated at around Rs 1,700 million, while imports rose by approximately 40 per cent during the same period, resulting in large and persistent deficits in the current external account which amounted to 10–15 per cent of export earnings (see table 9).

In the 1960s and 1970s the situation in regard to the country's external transactions further deteriorated. The government responded with a strict regulation of external transactions and severe restriction of imports. By the mid-1960s, Sri Lanka was facing its greatest foreign exchange crisis after independence, with liquid resources down to the equivalent of less than two weeks' imports. Sri Lanka's ability to mobilize large-scale external assistance and borrowings was also curtailed by some of the policies that had been followed by the government — particularly the nationalization of the assets of the foreign oil companies. With the change of government in 1965, the efforts to deal with the crisis led to a new set of initiatives and changes in economic policy. For the first time, Sri Lanka sought external assistance and resorted to foreign borrowing on a large scale. External aid was mobilized through an aid consortium sponsored by the World Bank, which pledged a substantial flow of external resources. A dual exchange rate was introduced in an effort to relax some of the controls and partially restore the operation of market forces. The economy responded with some degree of buoyancy in the late 1960s. The first half of the 1970s, however, once again plunged the economy into recurrent crisis. Internal political upheavals and crop failures combined with global economic disruptions of the period — the world food shortage, the revaluation of the dollar, the steep increase in the prices of petroleum products — brought the economy's inherent structural imbalances to the surface and reversed the incipient trends of the late 1960s.

During this entire period the country was unable to undertake any major adjustments to cope with these basic structural problems. The problems arose primarily from the export sector, which continued to rely heavily on three primary commodities whose terms of trade were moving unfavourably. As in the case of most other developing countries, Sri Lanka's effort at diversification concentrated on import substitution. There was no serious complementary effort at export diversification in the 1950s or 1960s. Sri Lanka was unable to create a new growth sector for exports as Malaysia had with oil-palm. This was due partly to the limited base of natural resources on which Sri Lanka had to operate compared to a country like Malaysia or Thailand. But partly it derived from a failure to develop strategies which were outward-looking and consciously directed at enhancing Sri Lanka's international competitiveness. The planning efforts in the first two decades after independence paid little attention to export diversification. It is in the 1970s that export development received high priority.

Change of Direction after 1977

The new government which came into office in July 1977 initiated a number of far-reaching reforms in economic policy. The main thrust in this policy package was towards the liberalization of the economy and the removal of controls and regulations, thus enabling the market to function more efficiently in the allocation of resources. The regulatory system was dismantled and exchange control and import quotas removed for almost all import items with a few exceptions, as in the case of private cars. The rupee was devalued substantially and allowed to float against a basket of currencies. The administered prices for a range of import commodities such as petroleum and food items were corrected and the element of subsidy substantially reduced. In the new pricing policy, domestic prices were allowed to reflect the movement of international prices.

These policies of liberalization were supported by a major effort at the mobilization of external resources and a much higher level of investment in the economy. The total disbursements of aid increased substantially during this period, from US$205.9 million in 1977 to US$385.2 million in 1981 and amounted to approximately 9 per cent of GDP for the period 1978–1983. In the private sector, higher financial savings were garnered by increases in deposit interest rates. A favourable investment climate and substantial tax concessions provided incentives to bring about a higher level of foreign and domestic private investment. While the essential elements of the social welfare system, such as free health and free education, were retained and in certain instances strengthened, the government modified certain parts of the system and made it more discriminatory to ensure that the benefit of the system accrued to those who were genuinely in need. As a result, the food subsidy was replaced with a food stamp scheme, for which households below certain incomes became eligible. The net effect of these changes has been significant in reducing

the burden of subsidies on the economy and releasing resources for development. The subsidies which amounted to 9.6 per cent of GDP in 1977 were
absorbing only 3.4 per cent in 1981.[5]

In the first phase of implementation of this policy package, the economy responded with great vigour. Table 8 provides some of the key statistics relating
to the economic performance of the country during the period 1977–1982. The
liberalization of the economy combined with the substantial increases in the
flow of external resources and the unprecedented public sector investment programme resulted in high rates of economic growth in 1978 and 1979. The overall
rate of growth of GDP for the period 1978–1982 was relatively high, maintaining an annual average of 6.2 per cent. The sectors which recorded the highest
growth were paddy production, services, and construction. The rural sector did,
therefore, fully share in the economic expansion, and the real income of rural
households on the whole rose correspondingly. These were also areas which
responded quickly to the changes in relative prices and the elimination of import quotas. As against these relative successes, the outcome has been dis-
appointing in several other important sectors, particularly the plantation sector
and the manufacturing sector.

The liberalization of imports on the one hand and the massive investment
programme on the other generated a volume of domestic demand which produced both widening gaps in the balance of payments and large deficits in the
government budget. The overall budget deficit rose from 5.8 per cent of GDP in
1977 to approximately 23 per cent of GDP in 1980. Since then it has been
reduced and remained at around 14 per cent of GDP in 1982. These budget
deficits were partly financed by foreign resources, the major share of which
came in the form of concessional assistance. The government also resorted to a
fairly high level of commercial borrowing in foreign capital markets. These resources were, however, not adequate to bridge the deficits, and in the early
period the government had to have recourse to a large volume of Central Bank
borrowings. Borrowing was equivalent to 10.7 per cent of GDP in 1980 and 4.6
per cent in 1981. There has been progressive improvement in budgetary management in the recent past, and Central Bank borrowing has been reduced from
3.7 per cent of GDP in 1982 to 0.2 per cent in 1983.[6]

The removal of subsidies and the correction of administered prices, the devaluation of the rupee, the liberalization of the economy, and the transmission
of inflationary pressures from the international economy and the large budget
deficits which fuelled domestic demand — all combined to produce a rate of
inflation which was unprecedented for Sri Lanka. In the preceding period,
1970–1977, despite the major changes in the international price structure, the
rate of inflation averaged approximately 10 per cent. In the period 1978–1982,
the rate of inflation rose steeply; in certain years (e.g. 1980) it exceeded 30 per
cent. The average for the period 1979–1982 was in the region of 15 per cent.[7]

TABLE 4. Domestic and national savings 1950–1980

Category	1950	1960	1970	1980
GDP at market prices	—	6,651	13,664	66,527
Net imports of goods and non-factor services	−151	195	430	15,022
Investment	382	997	2,589	24,466
Domestic savings (3–2)	533	799	2,159	7,443
Domestic savings ratio (4 as percentage of 1)	—	12.0	15.8	11.2
Net private transfers	−73	−31	−5	2,260
National savings (4 + 6)	463	768	2,154	9,271
National savings ratio (7 as percentage of 1)	10.2	11.5	15.8	14.0

Source: Annual Reports of the Central Bank.

TABLE 5. Demographic changes

	1953	1963	1971	1980/1981
Total population (in thousands)	8,098	10,583	12,762	14,738
Rate of growth of population during each period/annum (%)		2.5	2.1	1.8
Percentage of population below 25 years of age	57.7	59.4	59.6	59.7
Percentage of population in 25–34 age group	15.1	13.3	13.27	13.26
Rate of growth of population in 25–34 age group (%)		3.0	2.4	1.8
Percentage of urban population	15.3	19.1	22.4	21.5

Sources: Ministry of Plan Implementation, *Socio-Economic Indicators of Sri Lanka*, 1983; Department of Census and Statistics, *Statistical Abstract of Sri Lanka*.

TABLE 6. Social indicators for SRI LANKA

Social Indicators	1953	1963	1971	1981
Population (in thousands)	8,098.6	10,582.0	12,689	14,850
Crude birth rate (per 1,000 population)	39.4	34.1	30.0	28.0
Crude death rate (per 1,000 population)	10.9	8.5	7.7	6.0
Infant mortality (aged 0–1 years per 1,000 live births)	71	56	45	39.0 (1980)
Life expectancy at birth (year)	58	63.5	65.25	69.0
Literacy (%)	69.0	76.9	78.5	86.5

Sources: Department of Census and Statistics, *Statistical Abstract of Ceylon*, 1955, 1965, 1977; Central Bank of Ceylon, *Sri Lanka Socio-Economic Data*, 1983; Central Bank of Ceylon, *Report on Consumer Finances and Socio-Economic Survey*, 1953, 1963, and 1978/1979; World Bank, *World Development Report*, 1983.

Social and Demographic Changes

Social Well-being

When we turn from the country's economic performance to the developments in the social sectors, some very unusual features immediately attract our attention (see table 6). The country's progress in the fields of health, education, and housing has been quite exceptional for a low-income country. Sri Lanka has been able to extend life expectancy to about 70 years, reduce infant mortality to 34 per 1,000 live births (1980) and the crude death rate to below 7. The adult literacy rate is approximately 86 per cent. These social indicators compare favourably with the average for countries at much higher levels of per capita income. These developments have been the outcome of a combination of policies pursued by successive governments in the last three decades — policies which contain many of the elements which have now become part of the conventional wisdom on poverty-oriented development strategies and the satisfaction of basic needs.

Even before Sri Lanka became independent, the base for a major set of public initiatives in the field of social development had already been laid. By the time Sri Lanka achieved independence, the government programmes which were to become the main components of the social welfare programme in the period after independence had already been put in place. In 1945, the government decided to provide universal free education up to the university level. A food distribution system with subsidized food rations was introduced during the Second World War to serve the entire population. Substantial investments were being made to increase food production to meet domestic needs, particularly rice. Government legislation during this period preserved the vast extent of arable land which was uncultivated or under forest for land settlement programmes to benefit the rural poor. These efforts continued to bring about a significant improvement in the social indicators for the population as a whole. Infant mortality, which was 175 per 1,000 live births in 1930, had dropped to 141 in 1946. Maternal mortality had declined from 21.4 to 16.1. The crude death rate for the whole population had fallen during this period from 25.4 to 19.8. The levels of literacy continued to rise during this period from approximately 45 per cent to 57 per cent.

During the period after independence the main elements of the social welfare package which had evolved in the period immediately preceding independence were elaborated and developed into a comprehensive and nation-wide programme. More than one-third of the government budget was allocated for this programme. The system of mass free education led to the establishment of educational facilities spanning the entire island. There is nearly full participation in ordinary level education and approximately 51 per cent of the relevant age group in the secondary school system. As mentioned earlier, the level of adult literacy has risen to 86 per cent. After the steep decline in mortality rates and the rise in life expectancy in the second half of the 1940s, health indicators continued to improve, but at a slower pace. The crude death rate, which had dropped from 19.8 in 1948 to 12.4 in 1950, declined further to 8.6 in 1960 and thereafter continued to decline to below 6 by the beginning of the 1980s. Similarly, infant mortality, which had dropped from 141 in 1946 to 82 in 1950, dropped, at a slower rate, to 53 in 1965. It continued to decline in the 1970s and stood at 34 in 1980.[8]

Nutrition and Income Distribution

Per capita food consumption and levels of nutrition also show fairly significant improvement during this period. Government policies assured a nation-wide distribution of essential foodstuffs at prices either subsidized or with the minimum mark-up. This was achieved through a trading system which relied on import and wholesale marketing through state agencies as well as on a scheme of retail distribution through a widely dispersed network of co-operative stores. Even during periods of acute foreign exchange scarcity, priority was assigned to supplies of the essential food items. It was a system which maintained a fairly stable structure of prices during the 1950s and 1960s. The consumer price index rose only 12 points during the entire period 1952–1965.

The distribution of income underwent major changes during the twenty-year period 1953–1973, for which relatively firm data are available (see table 7). The share of income of the highest 10 per cent of spending units in the country,

TABLE 7. Percentage of total income received by each ten per cent of ranked spending units

Decile	1953	1963	1973	1978/79
[1]	[2]	[3]	[4]	[5]
Lowest	1.90	1.50	2.79	2.12
Second	3.30	3.95	4.38	3.61
Third	4.10	4.00	5.60	4.65
Fourth	5.20	5.21	6.52	5.68
Fifth	6.40	6.27	7.45	6.59
Sixth	6.90	7.44	8.75	7.69
Seventh	8.30	9.00	9.91	8.57
Eighth	10.10	11.22	11.65	11.22
Ninth	13.20	15.54	14.92	14.03
Highest	40.60	36.77	28.03	35.84
GINI coefficient of income distribution	0.46	0.45	0.35	0.44

Source: Central Bank of Ceylon, *Report of Consumer Finances and Socio-Economic Survey*, 1978/1979.

which had been 40.6 per cent of the total in 1953, was reduced to 28.03 per cent in 1973. The share of the lowest 10 per cent had risen from 1.9 per cent to 2.79 per cent during the same period. The bottom half of society had increased its proportion of income from 20.9 per cent to 26.7 per cent. Therefore, even with a relatively low increase of per capita income, strategies which were redistributive and which also directed a larger proportion of the increment in the national income to the poorer segments of the population succeeded in eliminating some of the worst manifestations of poverty.

The post-1977 period, however, indicates a reversal of the trends observed during the 1963–1973 period.[9] Income inequalities appear to have grown during this period according to the data availabe from recent surveys. At the same time, the data show that the average income of the lowest income deciles have also increased in real terms. The key social indicators continued to improve during this period. Crude death rates fell for the first time below 7 and stood at 6.4 in 1980. Infant mortality declined from 42 in 1977 to 34 in 1980.

TABLE 8. Economic indicators for Sri Lanka, 1977–1981

Economic sectors	1977	1978	1979	1980	1981
GNP constant (1970) factor cost price (Rs mn)	15,999	17,311	18,389	19,456	20,256
Per capita GNP constant (1970) prices	1,148	1,220	1,271	1,320	1,352
GNP at constant (1970) prices	16,078	17,401	18,501	19,575	20,706
Growth rates of GNP at constant (1970) prices	4.3	8.2	6.2	5.6	4.1
Growth rate of real national income at constant (1970) prices	7.5	7.9	3.1	3.7	3.3
Growth rates of GNP per capita at constant (1970) prices	2.6	6.3	4.2	3.6	2.4
Gross domestic fixed capital formation/GDP (%) at market prices	13.83	19.97	25.28	31.3	29.11
Gross domestic savings/ GDP at market prices (%)	18.1	15.3	13.8	11.2	11.7
Colombo consumer price index (1952 = 100)	203.2	227.8	252.3	318.2	375.4

Source: Central Bank of Ceylon, *Economical and Social Statistics of Sri Lanka*; Central Bank of Ceylon, *Review of the Economy*, 1981.

TABLE 9. Government finance and the balance of payments (1950–1980) (Rs mn.)

	1950	1955	1960	1965	1970	1980
Govt. revenue and expenditure						
Revenue	623.3	1,158.6	1,403.8	1,816.4	2,736	14,068
Total expenditure	718.8	1,089.0	1,821.3	2,274.6	3,886	30,343
Overall surplus (+)/deficit (−)	−95.5	+69.6	−417.5	−458.2	−1,150	−16,275
Expenditure from current revenue	563.2	873.4	1,511.9	1,803.4	2,873	16,489
Surplus on current expenditure	60.1	285.2	−108.1	+13	−137	−2,421
Treasury bills outstanding	78.6[a]	50	550[c]	1,300[c]	1,950	9,800
	59.8[b]		62.5[d]			
Balance of payments						
1. Merchandise a/c:						
exports (fob)	1,484.7	1,962.6	1,796.0	1,909.4	2,016.6	17,603
imports (cif)	1,156.1	1,447.0	1,998.8	1,922.1	2,332.4	33,915
net	+328.6	515.6	−202.8	−12.7	−315.8	−16,312
2. Total goods and services:						
credit	1,635.3	2,194.1	2,042.4	2,107.9	2,253.3	22,207.8
debit	1,415.7	1,810.4	2,284.5	2,089.7	2,672.8	37,661.2
net	+219.6	+383.7	−242.1	+18.2	−419.5	15,453.4
3. Transfer payments, net	−72.9	−60.9	+21.6	+40.7	69.2	4,541
Current a/c balance (2 + 3)	+146.7	+322.8	−220.5	+58.9	−350.3	−10,912.4
Capital and monetary gold						
Private capital investment:						
credit	16.8	5.8	14.2	2.4	7.9	6,197.6
debit	36.2	62.2	19.5	23.9	13.3	2,216.5
net	−19.3	−56.4	−5.3	−21.5	−5.4	3,981.1

Official and banking institutions:						
credit	—	8.2	211.6	290.6	1,065.3	9,186.0
debit	139.4	282.3	15.7	322.1	758.8	3,614.9
net	−139.4	−274.1	+195.9	−31.5	306.5	5,571.1
Total capital and monetary goldf**:**						
credit	16.8	14.0	255.8	303.0	1,073.2	15,383.6
debit	175.6	341.5	35.2	346.0	772.1	5,831.4
net	−158.7	−330.5	+190.6	−53.0	301.1	9,552.2
S. D. R. allocations	—	—	—	—	78.0	258.2
Valuation adjustments	—	—	—	—	—	607.0
Errors and omissions	+12	+7.7	+29.9	−5.9	−28.8	495.0

a As at 30-9-1950.
b As at 1-1-1951.
c As at 30-9-1960.
d As at end of 1960.
e As at end of 1965.
f Monetary gold is nil in our balance-of-payments statements.

The Growth of Population and the Rural-Urban Balance

The total population of Sri Lanka as given in the census of 1946 was 6,657,000. At the 1981 census it had increased to 14.7 million. With crude birth rates continuing at levels which prevailed before the dramatic decline in mortality in the late 1940s and early 1950s, there was a rapid surge in the rate of natural increase in population, ranging from 1.6 and 1.9 per cent in the early 1940s to 3.6 per cent in the late 1950s. Population continued to grow at an average of about 2.5 per cent per annum during the period 1950–1960. By 1980, the crude birth rate had fallen to 27.6 per 1,000, the mortality rate to 6.2, and population growth net of migration to 1.7 per cent. The demographic indicators seemed to suggest that at a relatively early stage of development, with a rural population which still comprises approximately 75 per cent of the total population, Sri Lanka was entering the demographic transition, resulting in the simultaneous fall of birth rates and death rates and the slow decline in the rate of population growth.

The mounting pressure of the population on land posed another set of problems, to which succeeding governments responded with policies of planned internal migration from the congested south-west and centre to the sparsely populated dry zone in the north-central and south-western parts of the country. These policies resulted in a spatial distribution of population which relieved the pressure in the southern, western, and central regions of the island and contributed to a pattern of demographic change which prevented any major rural-to-urban shift in the population. In addition to the land policies, policies which guided the location of industry in the public sector, together with the relatively slow growth of the urban industrial sector, combined to produce a demographic and economic structure which promoted a rural-urban balance of a somewhat unusual character for a developing country.

The Growth of the Work-Force and Unemployment

The growth of Sri Lanka's population resulted in a proportionately massive expansion of the work-force in the 1960s as the new generation began entering the labour market. Between 1963 and 1971, the total work-force increased by approximately 1 million additional participants, almost all of whom were new entrants to this body. This represented an increase of approximately 29 per cent over an eight-year period, or an annual rate of growth of 3.2 per cent. The total number who succeeded in finding employment during this period was in the region of 430,000. The ensuing outcome was a massive backlog of unemployment which grew to an estimated 24 per cent in 1973 — over 1 million unemployed, most of whom were in the 15–24-year-age group.

Youth unemployment was emerging as a major problem in the second half of the 1960s, and the growing frustration and discontent was manifesting itself in extremist political activity which threatened the stability of the prevailing system. However, policy-makers were still slow to respond to this situation with strategies aimed directly at alleviating the problems of unemployment. With the change in economic policy after 1977 and the new employment opportunities that became available in Middle East countries, there has been a discernible improvement in the situation. Employment abroad accounted for approximately 100,000 jobs in the period 1977–1985, after allowing for return migration. All these factors have combined to reduce the rate of unemployment to approximately 11.7 per cent in 1981–1982 according to recent surveys.

Political Changes

The Parliamentary Framework and the Multiparty System

The somewhat unique mix of welfare and growth in Sri Lanka has to be placed in the political context if the socio-economic processes are to be fully understood. It might be said that Sri Lanka presents both the positive outcomes as well as the contradictions to be found in an experiment in social democracy at an early stage of economic development. Universal adult franchise and a limited form of responsible government was introduced in the early 1930s, about 16 years before independence. With independence, Sri Lanka took over the political institutions of British parliamentary democracy. Already in the 1940s the degree of political mobilization of the people was quite high. Several political parties representing the entire spectrum from Left to Right were established and became active. It might be noted, however, that while on the Left there were several Marxist parties which were theoretically sceptical of "bourgeois democracy," the Right was represented by a democratic conservative party, and there was no extremist Right party which was ideologically opposed to the existing system. The major Left parties themselves progressively moved away from revolutionary politics, were prepared to work within the parliamentary system and entered governments which were formed in coalition with the main centrist parties. All major political parties in the country representing the entire spectrum from Left to Right have held power and assumed governmental responsibility at one time or another during the last 30 years. This has influenced the political culture of the country and has produced a mix of institutions and a blend of the socialist and market system to which all political parties have contributed. The particular type of "mixed economy" and the proportions of state-directed and privately-owned enterprise are a product of these developments.

The Sri Lankan constitution has undergone two major changes since independence in 1948. From 1948 to 1972, Sri Lanka was a sovereign state within the British Commonwealth, with the British monarch as its own titular head of state. In 1972, Sri Lanka adopted a new constitution which, while preserving all the main features of the parliamentary system, declared itself a republic within the Commonwealth. In 1978, once again a new constitution was promulgated.

It introduced a number of far-reaching changes, incorporating some of the features of democratic constitutions of European democracies and the United States. Chief among these were the office of a popularly elected president functioning as the chief executive and the principle of proportional representation for the election of parliament, which had hitherto been elected on the basis of constituencies and the simple majority of votes.

Alternations of Power and Development Changes

Power has alternated between the right-of-centre United National Party (UNP) and the centrist Sri Lanka Freedom Party (SLFP) and its coalition with the Left. The UNP ruled from 1947 to 1956 and from 1965 to 1970 and resumed power after it was elected in 1977. The SLFP and its coalition were in power during the other periods. These changes of government have resulted in significant alternations of policy. The UNP has veered towards an economic system in which private enterprise and the market system play the major role, while the SLFP was responsible, during its tenure, for most of the institutional and structural changes, such as the nationalization of transport, banking, insurance, petroleum, ports, and the expansion of the public sector and land reform.

While the shifts in power led to discontinuity in policies which created conditions of uncertainty and instability for investment and growth, particularly in the private sector, changes of government did not result in wholesale reversal of policies. For example, the welfare system remained a constant element in government policy until 1977, and even after 1977 the modifications did not remove a large part of the system benefiting the disadvantaged and vulnerable segments of society. The land reform, nationalization, and other major social reforms were most often left intact or, if altered at all, underwent minor changes. The public sector, which accounted for approximately one-third of the economy by the mid-1970s, continued to play an important role in all governments.

It has to be mentioned, however, that the mixed economy, as it grew, posed major problems for all governments, Left or Right. No government quite succeeded in orchestrating policies for both the public and private sectors in a manner which produced an internally consistent framework of incentives for both parts of the economy. The way in which national planning itself dealt with this dilemma is examined in a later section.

Political Upheaval and Violent Conflict

The democratic political system has been able to withstand several threats which included two abortive attempts at military coups in the 1960s and a widespread youth insurrection in 1971. The resilience of the system can be attributed to the way in which it has been able to co-opt the revolutionary Left and bring them into the mainstream of the democratic political process. The revolutionary Marxist parties were gradually transformed into parliamentary Left parties and took office in coalition with the SLFP and the UNP. The pattern of socio-economic change, with its mix of welfare and growth, also played a major role in sustaining Sri Lanka's brand of social democracy. We saw how it was able to bring the benefits of development to large segments of the rural poor, ameliorating their living conditions and mitigating class conflict and socially divisive trends.

The political system, however, did generate types of conflict which erupted in periodic violence. General elections were followed by violent attacks on the defeated party. The role of a democratic opposition itself was not fully integrated into the system. With political power went an extensive system of political patronage which reached down to the village level and divided the population sharply across social strata, vertically, according to party affiliation and loyalty. The abuse of power by government and the accumulation of grievances by the opposition found expression in widespread post-election violence in 1965, 1970, and 1977.

The most deep-seated conflict which has threatened the country's integrity and the viability of Sri Lanka as a unified society is the ethnic conflict between the Sinhala majority and the Tamil minority. The Sinhala community comprises approximately 74 per cent of the population; the indigenous Sri Lanka Tamils, approximately 12.6 per cent. In this brief survey it is not possible to present the full complexity of the problem, even in broad outline. The implications for planning are discussed further in a later section (see p. 96). At this point what is important to note is the progressive deterioration of relations between the two communities and the problems it poses for the political stability of the country. The process of democratization itself, which resulted in mass political mobilization and provided greater opportunity for participation in government, had the effect of bringing to the surface the latent conflicts between the two groups. The Sinhala majority began to assert their cultural identity and set in motion a process which sought to redress what it saw as disadvantages imposed on it during the colonial period. This applied in particular to the Sinhala Buddhist community, the preponderant majority of the country. These adjustments were disadvantageous to the Tamil minority, which had enjoyed a share of élite positions and employment in government administration visibly greater than its proportion of the population. Many of the developments which took place in regard to language, employment, education, and new agricultural settlements affected the Tamil minority adversely. The policies that were being pursued by the Sinhala majority were perceived by the Tamil minority as seriously discriminatory, threatening their culture and ethnic identity.

The political and administrative structures that emerged from the colonial period were also not conducive to the solution of the problems. The structures remained highly centralized and were not readily amenable to the sharing of power or the decentralization and devolution of governmental responsibilities, all of which could have helped to create conditions which could have contained the conflict. On the other hand, the democratic framework allowed for a non-violent solution, but several efforts at such a solution were aborted, mainly on account of the pressure from Sinhala extremist groups. By 1976, the main Tamil political party had declared its intention of establishing a separate state, and a militant youth group had begun to use violent means to defy state authority and wage an armed struggle for separation.

Implications for National Planning

This brief overview of the development experience of Sri Lanka has attempted to draw attention to several critical problems and issues of relevance to the present study. We turn now to an examination of how the national planning process was related to these issues; the key considerations may be summarized as follows:

1. There is first the problem of managing an economy highly dependent on an external sector which is facing sharp short-term fluctuations together with a long-term declining trend in the terms of trade. The strategies for major structural adjustments to this situation could be regarded as among the highest priorities of a national planning process.
2. The welfare system, the political imperatives pertaining to it, and the trade-offs between social goals and objectives of growth and productive investment seem to have been issues of overriding importance that should have been taken into account in designing and steering a development strategy. To what extent did these enter into the calculations of planners and how were they handled within planning, if at all?
3. In the conditions of uncertainty which beset the balance of payments and the government budget, the efficient management of current affairs of the economy had to be closely linked to the formulation and implementation of programmes of investment. It is necessary to examine how the tasks of economic management were combined with investment planning and implementation of development programmes. This includes the handling of the key problems relating to the growing constraints and deficits in the external account on the one hand and the government budget on the other.
4. How did the national planning process deal with critical problems such as massive unemployment among educated youth or the urgent need for policy initiatives and planning in the field of population? Was it structured and oriented to anticipate, identify, and respond to the major issues and problems?
5. The changes of government and the accompanying alternations of policy posed a serious problem to national planners. This problem was linked to the special character of the mixed economy and the ideological disposition of different governments to the relative roles of the public and private sectors.
6. Finally, the youth insurrection and ethnic conflict bring into focus the pre-

cedential importance of the political foundation for economic growth and development. They raise fundamental issues concerning the manner in which planning is related to the political context in which it operates.

The Evolution of the Planning Process in Sri Lanka

The Initial Efforts at Planning, 1947–1956

At the time Sri Lanka gained independence, the government was already making efforts to plan its activities and investments within a time frame which mobilized resources for achieving certain development goals. The policical party which assumed power at the time of independence was the UNP. It was conservative in orientation, advocated change within the democratic system, clearly favoured private enterprise but envisaged a major role for the state in development and social welfare. The UNP leaders, while holding office in a system of limited responsible government, advocated and implemented a series of far-reaching welfare measures which included free education, free public health, and subsidized food.

The first attempt at the preparation of an investment programme for government activities was a document entitled "Post-War Development Proposals for 1946." This document contained a number of government programmes, both ongoing as well as those which could be undertaken in the future in the various sectors of the economy. It provided a large inventory of projects and programmes on which the governments that followed were able to draw when formulating their investment programmes.

The first two budgets that were presented after independence were published as a six-year plan. A document published in 1950 entitled *Ceylon Today — A Government by the People* contained a section with the heading, "The National Plan."[10] This gave in broad outline the objectives of the government budgets that had been presented from 1947 to 1949. These were still incipient and very rudimentary efforts at planning, but they recognized that "future progress must be according to a well-defined plan devised to secure an equally well-developed objective."[11] However, its claim that what it had in the collection of budgets was a "National Plan for the economic and social development of the country covering a period of six years"[12] was certainly exaggerated. Even so, some of the explicitly stated objectives of "planning" in this initial phase defined some of the limits within which the planning process that followed would have to operate.

The Six-Year Plan identified several broad areas of action. First, there were the wet-zone crops, tea, rubber, and coconut. Already at this time one observes that the attention given to the plantation and export sectors was limited. The wet zone is seen "as fully exploited"[13] and the resources available capable of generating its own momentum. The external trade of the country was still in surplus. No serious pressure existed for either diversification of the export sector or strengthening of its existing assets — a situation which was to have disastrous consequences by the beginning of the 1960s and turn the economy around to face an increasing trade deficit.

Second, the programme placed emphasis on import substitution in both agriculture and industry. In agriculture, this implied the development of the dry zone for food production, particularly rice. Politically, the agricultural policies enhanced the importance of the rural electorate. Economically, the agricultural sector grew in importance; its efficiency became a critical factor for the country's balance of payments. The plan envisaged the development of an area of 113,000 acres during the six years.

In industry, the Six-Year Plan underscored the need to develop the capacity "to supply as far as possible the goods that are imported."[14] It aimed at a rough target for import substitution in the region of Rs 100 million. Textiles and manufactures amounted to approximately 40 per cent of the import budget during this period — that is, approximately Rs 400 million. The target of Rs 100 million in manufactures was, therefore, an ambitious one. The government recognized the major role the state would need to play in industrial development and announced that "certain basic industries should be State-owned."[15] In this pronouncement, the government defined its commitment to the mixed economy. The implications of this commitment to the planning process are examined in a later section of this paper.

A central feature of the Six-Year Plan was the place given to state welfare in government outlays. Free mass education, food subsidies, and free public health services made up the most important components of the welfare package. In the period 1950–1953, the welfare component absorbed an annual average of approximately 47 per cent of the total government current expenditure.

Last, the development of the economic infrastructure, power, transportation, and posts and communications was also given an important place in the government's capital outlay.

Thus, the government programme during this period broadly covered the main sectors of the economy and attempted to provide some balance between investments in the commodity-producing sector, agriculture, and industry on the one hand and the social and economic infrastructures on the other.

As mentioned, the main thrust in the commodity-producing sectors was in the direction of import substitution. The growth sectors that were identified were in food production and selected industries intended to contribute to import substitution. At the same time, the high proportion of resources devoted to social welfare was becoming a matter of concern to policy-makers. The need to balance the competing claims of welfare and growth was being stressed.

The political presuppositions of the plan were also made very explicit. The process of change the government envisaged was clearly one which had to take place through "the exercise of legitimate powers that democracy had vested in it." It rejected what it described as "a bloody advance along a broad front of social advancement."[16]

The main objectives of development and the concomitant problems of economic management that emerged during this period were to remain constant elements in the development strategy over a long period. They assumed different combinations and underwent varying shifts of emphasis but continued to remain at the core of both the development effort and development constraints for nearly three decades. Planning, or the role of government in directing the economy, was placed within the political framework of a social democracy at an early stage of development.

The plan of the first UNP government, however, did not have the technical form or content which we associate with the formal planning exercise. It related the proposed government outlay to the national income in very broad terms, providing no macro-economic framework showing how resources were to be mobilized and how the main aggregates — savings, consumption, and investment and gross domestic product — were expected to grow during this period. While it gave the broad magnitudes of government revenue, it did not set the budget within a macro-economic framework and show its relationship to the total development effort and investment that was expected. Neither did it define the expectations in regard to external resources and the balance of payments. The availability of such resources and a relatively favourable balance of payments was taken for granted. Any minor disequilibria were to be settled through borrowings from the IMF. Finally, the proportions of public- and private-sector investment were estimated and set in such a way as to give the state the principal role in investment. Private investment was expected to make its contribution without any special encouragement and promotion from the state. There was no clearly defined, systematic drive to stimulate and direct private enterprise to new investment fields.

The absence of a well-formulated macro-economic framework meant that the tasks of economic management were carried out on a somewhat *ad hoc* and pragmatic basis. Policy responses were, therefore, of a short-term character, geared to problems as they arose. The national income data available were inadequate and consequently unreliable for constructing a macro-economic framework which could have been useful for policy analysis and forecasting.

The first systematic effort at programming public investment within a medium-term framework was the Six-Year Programme of Investment 1954/1955–1959/1960, prepared by the Planning Secretariat and published in July 1955. The programme could not, however, be implemented in the form contemplated as the government changed in 1956. The preparation of the Six-Year Programme, however, took the process of national planning a step further. First, a formal planning body in the form of a Planning Secretariat was established and attached to the cabinet. The programme also, for the first time, required ministries and departments to undertake a disciplined exercise of phasing its ongoing projects and future investments over a period of six years. This compelled all government agencies to make fairly realistic estimates of the total capital resources required over a six-year period and to plan project implementation. The exercise "established a general system of financial allocations, secured the type of data pertinent to an overall public sector programme, ensured the consistency of this data with the annual budgetary provisions and generally integrated and aggregated individual projects and programmes to a single whole."[17]

But the government clearly indicated that the programme did not "add up to the total of investment in the economy and that, therefore, owing to its partial coverage it did not constitute an overall plan for the economy as a whole."[18] The Planning Secretariat was unable to undertake the exercise as "neither the data available nor the machinery of planning was adequate for the task."[19] But in undertaking the programme for the public sector, the government argued that capital formation in the public sector was still in excess of the private sector and that, therefore, the government was still the major actor in the development scene. A well-formulated public-sector investment programme was, therefore, expected to take the lead toward economic growth and facilitate the development of the private sector.

The thinking behind the Six-Year Programme of Investment, the decision to confine the planning exercise to the public sector and express this in terms of concrete programmes and projects, continued to provide the basis for many of the planning efforts of the UNP government in the later period. Such an approach put the emphasis on formulation of sectoral programmes and individual projects and on the phasing of such programmes in terms of a feasible estimate of resources and, finally, concentrated on the implementation of the programme.

The New Ten-Year Phase in Planning, 1956–1965

A new Left-oriented government was voted to power in the general elections of 1956. The political front which opposed the UNP and defeated it consisted of a coalition of parties, led by the SLFP. The SLFP could be regarded as a party of the centre, with economic policies favouring a mixed economy in which the state assumed a dominant role. The new government included smaller parties which were Marxist in their approach and wanted the country to move more decisively in the direction of a socialist system. This coalition was, however, short-lived. Policy differences aggravated by personality conflicts led to the withdrawal of the Marxist group from the government in 1958.

The period immediately following the change in government marked a major change of direction in national planning in Sri Lanka. The government made it clear that it was firmly committed to the formulation of a comprehensive national plan which was to be the main instrument for directing the development of the country. A National Planning Council was established by an act of parliament, with the prime minister as chairman, the minister of finance as deputy chairman, and professionals drawn from various fields both in the public as well as private sectors as additional members. It was serviced by a Planning Secretariat manned by economists and other professionals who included those who were responsible for the preparation of the Six-Year Programme of Investment. The head of the Planning Secretariat under the UNP government continued as such under the SLFP.

The National Planning Council was conceived essentially as the agency for the formulation of a national plan. Preparation of the plan took three years. According to the mandate given by the prime minister, the chairman, the council was to undertake its work as a scientific, professional body examining the problems of the economy in depth and planning for structural changes in the economy in a manner which would be of lasting value to whatever government was in power. Planning was thus defined primarily as an intellectual and technical task. The tone and substance of the preface to the Ten-Year Plan given by the chairman underscore the character of the work. The plan represents, nevertheless, a further maturing of the planning process, particularly since the publication of the Six-Year Programme of Investment.[20]

The preface studiously refrains from linking the plan ideologically with the government in power. For example, no mention is made of the political objectives of the government and its much-publicized socialist goals. The objective was to give a continuity to the planning process and enable it to deal with the essential problems in a manner which would provide an indispensable technical resource for all governments. The National Planning Council was, therefore, not vested with any executive responsibilities. Its work was cast in an advisory role. This "separation of functions" could have been effective had there been mechanisms providing for the council to be a summit advisory body on economic and development decision-making. The system could have been so designed as to give the council a stature which could have made such an advisory role quite powerful and influential. Such a link between planning and economic management was not established, and the council itself was far removed from the processes of decision-making. This may explain, to some extent, why the plan document conveys the impression of being remote from the far-reaching socio-political and economic changes which were taking place during the period of its preparation.

The preparation of the plan was intensive and the methodology included most of the elements which had been absent in the earlier exercises. The Ten-Year Plan has been recognized internationally as a professionally competent document and in many ways a pioneering exercise for small developing economies.[21] The plan envisaged an increase in the rate of investment from 12.9 per cent of GDP in 1957 to 21.1 per cent in 1968. The national income over the period was expected to increase at an annual average of 5.9 per cent and per capita income at 2.9 per cent. The plan projected significant changes in the sectoral composition of GDP, with the manufacturing industry increasing its share from 7.6 per cent in 1957 to 13.7 per cent in 1968 (according to the data available to the planning agency). With the assassination of the prime minister in 1959, the plan lost the support of its main political protagonist, who had expressed a profound conviction concerning the intellectual validity of a national plan which transcended the changing fortunes of political parties and governments. Parliament was dissolved in 1960, and after a brief tenure of power by the UNP, the SLFP returned to power in July 1960. At the same time, developments in the economy belied some of the basic premises on which the plan had been formulated. There was a grave deterioration in the balance of payments together with a worsening budgetary situation in which the current account surplus was turning into a widening deficit. The flows of both external and domestic resources were falling far below plan expectations, making a critical part of the macro-economic framework of the plan irrelevant in the emerging situation. Various other factors of a political nature also intervened at this stage, leading to changes in the organizational framework as well as the personnel of the planning agency. The National Planning Council was replaced with a National Planning Department under the prime minister.

With the establishment of the National Planning Department, the planning process became more actively associated with the choice of investments in the public sector and the approval of programmes and projects for inclusion in the government budget. The change in the country's economic prospects demanded a reappraisal of some of the basic assumptions in the Ten-Year Plan. To meet these needs, the government prepared a Three-Year Implementation Programme 1962–1964. In its analysis of the development problems in Sri Lanka, the document saw the growing unemployment and stagnation of the economy as arising largely from shortcomings of past investment policies which resulted in "the imbalance between investment in physical and human capital."[22] It formulated a programme which emphasized investments with quick-yielding returns and reallocated resources away from projects with longer periods of gestation, such as major new irrigaion projects. It set more modest targets for the programme, reducing the growth targets of 5.2 per cent per year to 4.8 per cent. Yet even for this programme, the forecasts of budgetary and external resources that were required left significant unfinanced gaps for which the programme provided no clear answer. The programme was, however, tied more firmly to the government budget.

During this period, the country's efforts to cope with its balance-of-payments crisis led to an elaborate system of exchange controls resulting in the rationing of foreign exchange. This activity became crucial for any meaningful development planning. The Ministry of Finance set up machinery to manage the allocation of foreign exchange for both the public and private sectors. An important feature of the Three-Year Programme was the preparation of a portfolio of projects for which external assistance was being obtained. The Three-Year Programme, therefore, focused on a component of economic management and planning which was to become critical in the years to come and act as the key determinant of economic growth — namely, the external sector of the economy.

The Three-Year Programme was essentially conceived in the form of an implementation programme. Thus it had the character of an action-oriented programme which had to be implemented in the short-term. The plan suffered an initial political setback when the finance minister, who was the principal sponsor of the plan, resigned when his budgetary proposals for the reduction of the subsidy were not accepted by the cabinet. The plan, however, remained an important frame of reference for decision-making.

Macro-economic Management and Sectoral Planning, 1965–1970

In 1965, the UNP was voted back in to power. National planning underwent major changes and adaptations both in organizational form and content. The head of the planning organization during the period 1954–1960 was brought back as the professional head of a newly created ministry which took over the portfolio for national planning. The prime minister became the minister of planning and economic affairs. This change in structure was a response to the changing character of the economy and to the new and complex problems that had emerged in the first half of the 1960s.

At the outset, the planners defined for themselves a set of tasks and responsibilities in which the formal exercise of preparing a national plan in the manner of the Ten-Year Plan had low priority. The secretariat expressly indicated its intention not to devote its time to writing a plan decument. It approached its new responsibilities on two levels: It set up four planning committees at the sectoral level to examine and evaluate ongoing public-sector programmes and future proposals in relation to short-term and long-term needs and to prepare phased programmes of public-sector investment for the period 1966–1970. At the macro-economic level, it drew up a strategy for "economic recovery" which aimed at mobilizing and augmenting external resources, restoring supplies, improving the depreciated capital stock in key sectors such as transportation to get the economy working at capacity, and increasing the efficiency of public-sector investment. The main elements of planning during this period comprised the mobilization of foreign aid, the management of the foreign exchange budget, and the preparation and supervision of the government capital budget in terms of sectoral programmes.

To perform these tasks, the Ministry of Planning and Economic Affairs took control of a few key decision-making levers. The concerns of foreign aid and foreign exchange budgeting were transferred from the Ministry of Finance to the Ministry of Planning and Economic Affairs. All important proposals of sectoral ministries had to receive the comments of the Planning Ministry before they could be considered by the cabinet. The government capital budget, both

·at the stage of formulation and in connection with negotiation of budgetary allocations and implementation, came under close supervision of the Planning Ministry. The ministry was thus actively involved in obtaining as well as allocating the key resources of the economy, on a continuing basis. It consequently acquired considerable decision-making power and authority over execution.

In this process, however, the short-term tasks of economic management and resource allocation took precedence over long-term planning. During this period the Planning Ministry had a division concerned with perspective planning. It attempted to prepare an input-output matrix for the economy and develop a planning model, but this remained at the experimental level and never became an instrument for short-term forecasting or medium-term planning and decision-making. The division and its work had little influence on the central concerns of the ministry.

In the 1965–1970 period, the planning process acquired several new elements which would influence and define its future role in the total structure of national decision-making. Organizationally, the planning apparatus was brought to the centre of economic decision-making, and the conventional planning functions, such as programming of investment, were linked firmly to economic management. This was reflected in the designation of the ministry itself — Planning and Economic Affairs. It also introduced new disciplines of project evaluation for improving the efficiency and productivity of the public-sector investment programme and established systems of progress control for monitoring plan implementation. Some of its sectoral programmes were quite successful, particularly the programme in domestic agriculture. The organizational changes during this period transformed planning from the advisory role that had been envisaged for it in the National Planning Council to one of active involvement in resource mobilization and allocation. The structure that was set up had some of the features enumerated by Nicholas Kaldor when he criticized the purely advisory role of the National Planning Council and recommended a planning committee of the cabinet.[23] The 1965–1970 government established a Cabinet Planning Committee which became the apex institution for discussion and decision-making in economic matters.

The period also witnessed the entry of new major determinants of economic policy — external aid and foreign borrowings, with the consequent increase in foreign indebtedness and the continuing reliance on flows of foreign aid and foreign loans to finance the gap in the balance of payments. The external resource gap, which was Rs 323 million in 1964, rose to Rs 1,235 million in 1969, amounting to nearly 40 per cent of the total import payments. The major part of this gap was financed by short-term and long-term borrowing from abroad. This meant a set of adjustments to external factors very different from what was required in the period prior to 1960. The presence of international institutions and the disciplines and policies promoted by them, which included non-inflationary budgets and realistic exchange rates, became increasingly important. The adjustments to short-term fluctuations in external transactions became an overriding demand. The implementation of medium-term plans in a relatively stable environment was no longer a realistic prospect.

The 1965–1970 period also emphasized the differences in the economic policies between the UNP and the SLFP. The strategy of the UNP was directed towards creating conditions for a better functioning of the market mechanism: a dual exchange rate was introduced with this objective. The response of the economy to this approach was fairly positive. The improvement in supplies and the flow of external resources resulted initially in a spurt of economic growth. But after achieving a high of 8 per cent in 1968, the growth rate fell to 5.1 per cent in 1969 and 4 per cent in 1970. There were inherent contradictions in policies directed at liberalization and implemented at a time when the balance of payments was worsening that could be overcome only if drastic corrective measures were taken to reduce demand. The planning process was caught in the dilemma of applying deflationary policies to meet short-term problems on the one hand and sustaining an adequate rate of economic growth in the long-term on the other. At the end of the period, the government was formulating a strategy which would have imposed greater austerity on the economy if the government had been returned to power. It was, however, defeated in the general elections.

The planning process during this period was also grappling with another set of problems which were peculiar to the nature of the sort of mixed economy that had grown. A large part of the economy, in both services and production, was managed by state enterprises. This constituted an administered part of the economy. Policies which were intended to make greater room for the operation of market forces were not entirely effective in the case of public-sector enterprises. The mixed economy and the coexistence of two systems of economic enterprise — the state and the private sector — each requiring a different set of incentives and policies, posed a host of complex problems for planners and economic managers which were not fully understood nor clearly conceptualized for the purpose of policy-making. The public sector was recognized as a liability, as it were, by the government which favoured private enterprise. On the other hand, the private sector became the stepchild of the government with socialist objectives. A lack of a firm commitment to a mixed economy in which both the public and private sectors had well-defined roles hampered the process of long-term investment and tended to demoralize both sectors. Some of these problems became more pronounced moving into the 1970s.

The Alternations in Planning in the 1970s

The 1970s once again witnessed the oscillation of political power between the two major parties. These had their expected repercussions on the planning process. In 1970, a coalition of parties with the SLFP as the dominant partner assumed power. The Planning Ministry continued as a separate body, under the prime minister, but with a new designation, the Minstry of Planning and Employment. As in the case of the previous SLFP coalition governments with broad socialist ideals, the secretariat of the Planning Ministry commenced the preparation of a formal plan document for a period of five years. It mobilized the available government machinery for the purpose through sectoral com- mittees and working groups. Unlike in the past, these groups were informal in character: the main task of preparing the sectoral programmes fell to the secretariat.

If in the 1965–1970 period the dominant problem which preoccupied the government and planners was foreign exchange, in the first half of the 1970s unemployment became the critical issue. The manner in which the problems emerged to dominate the national decision-making process might itself be re- garded as a symptom of the ineffectiveness of the planning process. The process was not able to identify in time the magnitude and severity of the problems and to design strategies to avert a major crisis. In each case, the problem had already begun to assume crisis proportions before the planning process could deal with it adequately. This situaion is examined in some detail in a later section (see p. 95). As a result, the entire planning activity had to be conducted in crisis conditions in which the basic assumptions required for medium-term plans could not be made with any degree of certainty.

By 1970, unemployment had reached proportions which threatened the en- tire social system. The unemployment rate had risen to nearly 15 per cent, and a large proportion of the new entrants to the work-force who were coming out of the free education system were without employment. The Five-Year Plan had, therefore, to give a central place to employment creation. An emergency em- ployment programme preceded the preparation of the plan, and many elements of the emergency programme were incorporated into the plan itself. The other major problem the plan needed to address was foreign exchange. For the first time, export diversification became a major objective, and an export-promotion plan was included as a major component. The Five-Year Plan was thus in many ways more problem-oriented than previous plans. As it was directly related to major aspects of the prevailing crisis, the plan could have become a useful instrument of decision-making. However, this did not happen.

In many respects the fate of the Five-Year Plan resembled that of the Ten- Year Plan. The unsettled conditions in the world economy in the fist half of the 1970s, the world food shortage, the devaluation of the dollar and the steep rise in energy prices rendered the macro-economic framework totally irrelevant immediately after the publication of the plan. The sectoral programmes were, however, pursued within the limits of available resources. The outcome of the development effort during this period was far short of plan expectations. The impact on employment was negative. Unemployment continued to rise, to about 24 per cent by the mid-1970s. Growth rates, targeted for an annual average of 6.1 per cent, only reached an average of 2.5 per cent.

There were many reasons why the Five-Year Plan did not become an effective instrument for policy-making. Some are to be found in the inadequacies of the plan itself. It lacked a well-defined policy component for macro-economic management in changing international conditions. As the international economic crisis gathered momentum, the plan's framework for resource-allocation became irrelevant. There were no alternatives built into the plan which would have made an orderly change of direction possible. The political environment was also not favourable. Within the government, the Marxist partners wanted more decisive action in terms of nationalization and socialist transformation. The plan offered little to satisfy these political objectives. The plan's commitment to a mixed economy did not have the full consensus of the coalition. These policy differences became more acute, leading eventually to the withdrawal of the Marxists from the coalition in 1974. Furthermore, with the youth insurrection in 1971, the social and political crisis became the centre of attention of the government. In this regard, the medium-term strategy of the plan did not draw the involvement of policy-makers as had been expected.

Personality conflicts also played a part in reducing the effectiveness of planning during this period. The finance portfolio was held by two strong and powerful ministers, and the relationships between the ministries of finance and planning were not always complementary and supportive. Finally, the Planning Ministry weakened organizationally with the creation of several centres of co-ordination and authority. A separate co-ordinating secretariat, directly under the prime minister, gave special attention to the agriculture programme, independent of the Planning Ministry. The functions of plan implementation were taken away from the ministry and vested in a different ministry, the Ministry of Plan Implementation. As a result of these changes, the rationality in the allocation of functions was somewhat impaired.

In 1977, the political pendulum swung again to the Right, and the UNP returned to power. Soon after it assumed office, the government began rearranging the planning organization to bring it in line with its plans for liberalizing the economy. A series of policy measures, discussed previously, were taken to restore the functioning of the market mechanism. As a result of these policy changes, the planning process too had to undergo considerable adaptation.

The UNP governments had demonstrated an approach to planning which had generally avoided the centralized planning exercises of the socialist governments. This approach reflected policies which placed greater reliance on the market and private enterprise and which applied the planning process selectively to public-sector programmes and to specific sectors. These features in the planning approach became more pronounced in the post-1977 period. The tendency in the government was to decentralize decision-making to enable ministries and agencies to assume greater responsibility. The intervention of a planning agency in policy-making and investment tended to get diminished in the process. Agencies set up for specific programmes such as the Mahaweli Development Authority and the Greater Colombo Economic Commission as well as the sectoral ministries themselves acted with greater autonomy and obtained their mandates directly from the cabinet. A committee of secretaries from the development ministries and a committee of cabinet ministers became the co-ordinating organs within the government for evaluation and approval of development programmes and policies. Within this set-up the role of the planning apparatus was considerably reduced. Planning became part of the Ministry of Finance, redesignated as the Ministry of Finance and Planning. Planning activities and the government budget were brought under this ministry. While this helped to make planning a service to the ongoing decision-making of the government and to be closely associated with the government budget and financial management, it pushed into the background the formal exercise of plan formulation and with it some of the essential tasks of planning, such as defining medium-term perspectives for the economy and ensuring the internal consistency of programmes and policies beyond the short-term.

The main planning instrument in the post-1977 period was the Five-Year Public Investment Programme, which was revised annually. These rolling plans, however, did not have the formal structure or the comprehensive coverage of national planning documents. They concentrated on public investment programmes, which were presented in summary form. Five programmes were prepared during the period 1979–1983, each for a five-year span and each revising the previous plan and taking it one year forward, and thus it was possible to make adjustments in response to changes. The government was able to mobilize resources to embark on a public investment programme of massive proportions and to step up the total investment in the economy to levels which rose to as much as 31 per cent of GDP. The programme thereby had an impact on the total economy greater than any before. It concentrated on three lead projects, which absorbed the bulk of the investable resources. The implementation of the major river diversion project — Mahaweli — was accelerated. A free-trade zone was established, and foreign investment mobilized. A large urban development and housing programme was undertaken.

The initial response of the economy to the change of policies and the dramatic increase in investment was favourable. The rate of growth of GDP rose to an average of approximately 6.5 per cent in the period 1977–1981. Unemployment fell from the inordinately high rate of 24 per cent in the mid-1970s to about 13 per cent in 1980. This was not, however, the outcome of an elaborate planning exercise, but rather a package of policies designed to stimulate the economy and release the market from the rigidities which the regulatory system had imposed. The implication of this for planning techniques and economic management will be examined in greater depth in the succeeding sections.

The experience of the 1978–1982 period, however, brought to the surface a number of shortcomings and imbalances in both the investment programme and the management of the economy. These had serious macro-economic consequences for both the government budget and the balance of payments. The diminution of the role of planning and the relative absence of a centralized, well-defined, and internally consistent framework, with accepted national and sectoral targets, certainly contributed to this situation. Private consumption and investment in the liberalized regime were at times wasteful of scarce resources and neglectful of the long-term interests of the economy. Despite considerable adaptations of the planning machinery and the planning process, the system of decision-making in force at this writing has not been able to evolve the right mechanisms which would impose the discipline of planned development in a mixed economy in which the market is expected to play a dynamic role. This was a recurrent problem in both the UNP and SLFP governments. As we saw, in each case the source of the problem was different. In one case, the problem arose as a result of the system veering too much towards an administered economy and, in the other, moving too far away from central directing towards the "market." An understanding of the various implications of this problem requires some analysis of the political economy of planning in Sri Lanka. An evaluation of the effectiveness of national planning requires this wider context.

The Institutionalization of the Planning Process

Planning in Sri Lanka, both in its substance as well as in the institutional forms it assumed, lacked the continuity found in that of many other developing countries. Sri Lanka cannot point to medium-term plans which have been produced with relative regularity as in the cases of India, Nepal, Pakistan, or Bangladesh. Sri Lanka's planning organization occupied different positions in the national decision-making system at different times according to the priority and importance assigned to planning. Planning did not, therefore, acquire the stability of a national organization which retained its main features over a considerable period of time and thereby accumulated knowledge and developed and strengthened its professional competence and expertise. The major changes which took place at different times often resulted in some loss of personnel, skills, and the organizational capabilities which had been developed in preceding periods.

As against this, however, the lack of continuity allowed for a great deal of institutional flexibility and adaptability which had some positive features. The planning organization was periodically restructured to meet the needs of the succeeding governments and in so doing, to make good some of the omissions and inadequacies of earlier phases. But on the whole, planning tended to move from one approach to another without adequately incorporating what was of value in the preceding period. This is illustrated, for example, in the frequent shifts in priority between long-term planning with formal plan preparation and short-term economic management. As a result, the institutional capability developed in one planning phase was not retained and strengthened in the next.

In the sections that follow, the institutional framework for planning that evolved is examined in relation to the issues that have arisen in the course of these changes. One set of issues concerns the location of the planning agency within the total system of decision-making, its links with and access to the highest political level, and its influence and control over the system of resource allocation. Another set of issues relates to the institutional links which the planning agency was able to forge with the sectoral ministries in order to develop planning capability within the ministries and create an effective planning system for all important sectors. A third set of issues deals with the machinery for regional and district planning. Fourth, the planning organization has to provide the institutional framework which enables the private sector and various interest groups to participate in planning. Finally, some of the more recent institutional developments which have created new centres of planning, such as the Central Environment Authority, the Mahaweli Development Authority, the National Aquatic Resources Authority, have added a new dimension to planning.

The Planning Organization at the National Level

It is possible to delineate three distinct phases in the organizational changes that were made in the planning system after independence. For most of the period between 1948 and 1965, the planning agency had an organizational status which was less than that of a ministry. In 1965, planning responsibility was vested in a separate ministry, and during the period 1965–1977 the portfolio for planning was held by the prime minister. In 1977, the Ministry of Planning was amalgamated with that of finance under an enlarged Ministry of Finance and Planning.

In the years immediately following independence, no identifiable institutional form was given to planning, although government policy statements underlined the need for national planning. At this initial stage, the government annual budget was the main instrument for allocating resources in the public sector and for co-ordinating the programmes of the different ministries. During this period, therefore, there was no organizational unit or professional cadre specially assigned to the task of plan preparation.

On the recommendations of the World Bank Mission in 1952, an Economic Committee of the Cabinet was established in 1953, consisting of seven ministers, with the prime minister as chairman, and serviced by a small Planning Secretariat. After a few months, however, the seven-man committee became defunct as the head of the secretariat was transferred. In the following year, the cabinet decided that the Economic Committee should be served by the whole cabinet, that the entire cabinet should assume responsibility for planning, and that the Planning Secretariat should be strengthened and placed under the Ministry of Finance. This planning unit was responsible for the preparation of the Six-Year Programme of Investment, 1954–1960. After its publication, an attempt was made to bring in the private sector by establishing a Development Advisory Board as recommended by the World Bank, but the proposal was not implemented.

The location of the planning apparatus from its very inception within the total system and its link with the resource-allocating and decision-making centres — the Ministry of Finance and the cabinet — became key issues in the institutionalization of planning. In the early efforts at institutionalizing planning, the government regarded planning as an activity closely linked to the government budget and to the process of resource allocation by the Ministry of Finance. In the normal course, this could have strengthened planning and enabled it to play a decisive role in government policy-making. This would have been possible, however, only if the minister of finance had had a long-term interest in planning and the Cabinet Planning Committee had become a regular decision-making body. In practice, however, the Finance Ministry devoted most of its time and energy to its normal functions relating to the government budget. Individual ministries tended to formulate their sectoral programmes without much central guidance or direction, and in the competition for resources, ministries with forceful and dynamic ministers who had political weight were able to obtain cabinet approval for their proposals. The investments in public sector industrial projects during this period are an example. The Six-Year Programme of Public Investment was therefore largely an integrated presentation of the proposals initiated by the different ministries. The Planning Secretariat provided the guidelines and the format for the phasing of the investments.

With the change of government in 1956, there was a firm commitment to planning and the preparation of a comprehensive national plan. The planning machinery was accordingly adapted to fulfil these objectives and underwent major changes. The National Planning Council Act No. 40 of 1956 set up a National Planning Council of 12 persons, including 5 ministers and 7 "leading citizens." It was presided over by the prime minister, with the minister of finance as the deputy chairman. The council was serviced by the secretariat functioning as its secretary. The Planning Secretariat of the council was the first formal planning organization to be set up at the national level as an independent unit. However, as stated earlier, neither the council nor the secretariat had any clearly defined supervisory or decision-making functions and powers over governmental programmes and policies. Its role was essentially an advisory one and its main function was the preparation of national plans. In the words of Oscar Lange, who was one of several eminent economists invited to advise the government, "the planning system had no operative centre responsible for the realisation of the plan."[24]

The change of government in July 1960 was accompanied by changes in the planning organization. The council ceased to exist and the overall responsibility for planning was assumed by the Cabinet Committee on Planning, under the chairmanship of the prime minister. The Planning Secretariat was converted into the Department of National Planning and brought under the direct supervision of the prime minister. The Cabinet Committee on Planning included the ministers of finance and of all development sectors. The director of national planning functioned as its secretary. The Department of National Planning was expected to co-ordinate the plans and programmes of the individual ministries and departments and to integrate such plans into consistent development programmes.

The changes effected in the planning organization after 1960 had mixed consequences. On the one hand, because the planning body was linked more closely to the short-term programme and budgetary exercises, closer attention was paid to problems of implementation. Since the minister of finance acted as the parliamentary secretary to the prime minister, there was greater scope for centralized decision-making and for consultations on economic planning and plan implementation. On the other hand, there was a definite diminution in the role of the planning agency in defining goals and planned objectives for the national economy, formulating plans for their achievement, and guiding their implementation. As a department, it was less than a ministry and did not enjoy the political stature of the council. Many of the proposals for strengthening the planning machinery contained in the interim reports of the planning council were not pursued. In fact, an IBRD-IDA mission to Sri Lanka noted in its report to the meeting of the Aid Ceylon Group in March 1968 that even the existing planning organization "fell into disuse and disintegrated in the early sixties."

It was with the change of government in 1965 that the planning agency acquired the status of a full-fledged ministry. As a ministry with the prime minister holding the portfolio and a secretariat headed by a permanent secretary of planning, the planning organization acquired the administrative status which enabled it to exercise its functions with greater authority and power than it had under the previous organizational forms. The ministerial structure brought it into the direct line of command in the government system and clearly established its supervisory and co-ordinating role. A Cabinet Planning Committee, consisting of the minister in charge of finance and ministers with major development portfolios such as the ministries of state, lands, and industries, was set up, chaired by the prime minister and serviced by the Ministry of Planning. This committee met at fairly regular intervals. The Ministry of Planning and Economic Affairs which had been created was provided with its own staff, consisting of a permanent secretary, a senior and three junior economic advisers, while the three departments added in 1966 — namely, the departments of national planning, foreign aid, and plan implementation — were serviced by directors, deputy directors, and research officers.

It was during this period that the Planning Ministry acquired specific functions of resource allocation through the control of the foreign exchange budget and the government capital budget. The Ministry of Planning was required to make observations on all cabinet papers which had planning or economic implications before cabinet decisions were taken. This was a key procedural arrangement which ensured that the Ministry of Planning would have an overview of activities and proposals of the sectoral ministries. As a result, the planning role was transformed from an essentially advisory one to one which involved it in national decision-making on all important economic issues.

A special Plan Implementation Division was established within the Ministry of Planning and Economic Affairs, with a committee consisting of the permanent secretaries of the major development ministries, that met regularly to review the progress made in the most important development projects. Under the division's direction, detailed operational programmes with quarterly targets were prepared for all the programmes and projects of the government and public sector corporations. Ministries were requested to prepare operational plans giving the breakdown of programmes into quarterly components, with a time schedule for the completion of the total programme. The ministries themselves were required to install an effective system of progress control based on this programme and to submit quarterly reports to the Department of Plan Implementation. Quarterly reviews of progress and performance were submitted by the Committee of Permanent Secretaries to the Cabinet Planning Committee. All these measures improved plan implementation. An information centre at the national level called the National Operations Room displayed the progress data for all important programmes, and this succeeded in compelling ministries to install a system of progress control and review to improve their efficiency in implementation. To enable ministries to prepare viable projects and investment proposals, improved techniques of project formulation were introduced which estimated the commercial profitability of projects as well as their total social costs and benefits in terms of each project's contribution to the country's import capacity, its impact on employment, and its use of scarce resources and skills.

The change of government in May 1970 brought about further changes in the institutional framework for planning and implementation. The Ministry of Planning and Economic Affairs was redesignated the Ministry of Planning and Employment. This designation emphasized the priority assigned to employment as one of the principal objectives of planning at a time when unemployment had reached levels then threatening the stability of the entire system. The new ministry, however, continued to retain the basic organizational framework of the previous Ministry of Planning and Economic Affairs, with the exception of the Employment Division, which was set up along with the Bureau of Graduate Employment. The foreign exchange budget and the government capital budget continued to remain under the control of the Ministry of Planning.

For purposes of implementing the Five-Year Plan (1972–1976), sectoral committees were set up in the Ministry of Planning and Employment both to review plan performances as well as to take corrective measures whenever necessary. The Planning and Progress Control Division was responsible for the overall supervision of the implementation of the plan. The government, however, decided that the two functions of plan formulation and plan implementation should be separated. Consequently, a new Ministry of Plan Implementation was set up in June 1973. As a result, the close links that had existed between project evaluation, monitoring of project implementation, and control of financial allocations were broken. Deprived of the functions of evaluation and management of the capital budget, the task of progress control became less effective. The reorganization was accompanied also by the setting up of a Co-ordinating Secretariat under the prime minister's office which was serviced by the officers of the National Planning Division of the Ministry of Planning and Employment. This unit undertook a trouble-shooting function at a high political level, as it functioned directly under the prime minister. The distribution of functions in this manner was not conducive to a well-defined division of responsibility and exercise of authority. The relations between the Ministry of Planning, the Co-ordinating Secretariat, and the sectoral ministries deteriorated, with the newly formed Ministry of Plan Implementation performing tasks which were somewhat peripheral to the important tasks of national policy formulation and decision-making.

When considering the formal structures of planning, it could be argued that the administrative apparatus for planning during this period was better equipped for imposing the discipline of a plan over the entire government machinery. In practice, however, it failed to exercise the co-ordinating authority and the influence on strategic decision-making which the Ministry of Planning and Economic Affairs had exercised in the 1965–1970 period. This was largely due to the different political environments in which planning operated in the two periods, the relationships which developed between the main actors in the planning scene, and the commitment to planning at the highest political level. Despite the fact that the 1965–1970 government was a coalition, the UNP was the dominant partner and gave the government the homogeneity which enabled it to function effectively. The coalition government of 1970 soon developed differences of approach which were reflected in pulls and pressures felt in the whole system, including the Cabinet Planning Council and its sectoral committees. The relationship between the Ministry of Planning and the Ministry of Finance seriously deteriorated. The secretary of planning was an ex-member of the party of which the minister of finance was the leader — the Lanka Sama Samaja Party (LSSP) — and had joined the SLFP. The two ministries were unable to establish a working relationship of collaboration and mutual confidence which was crucial to the success of the coalition government's programme. The Ministry of Planning did not have the measure of acceptance by the sectoral committees to enable it to play its proper role as a national planning organization. The relationships between the head of the Planning Ministry and the Co-ordinating Secretariat were also fraught with problems. Given these overriding personal elements, the structures themselves were unable to fulfil their objectives. Several important constitutional and institutional changes took place at all levels of planning administration when the UNP government came into power in 1977. The presidential system which was established replaced the prime minister as the chief political executive by a directly elected president who exercised power as head of state, chief of the cabinet, and executive head of administration. Thus, the political and executive co-ordination of sectoral ministries was effected at the president's office and the cabinet.

For the first time since independence, a new cabinet portfolio of finance and planning was created in 1977. The Ministry of Planning was joined with the Ministry of Finance. The planning division of the new ministry took over many of the functions of the Ministry of Planning. There was, however, a significant diminution in the role of planning in terms of both personnel and the scope of work. An organizational structure which combines the two functions of finance and planning under one ministerial head and one secretary will inevitably give greater weight to current critical issues of economic management and accord lesser priority to the tasks of long-term planning. Nevertheless, the new structure linked the planning division more closely to the short- and medium-term tasks of annual planning, budgeting, and forecasting.

The new government retained the Ministry of Plan Implementation and enhanced its functions. The portfolio is held by the president. In addition to its function of monitoring the implementation of annual plans, it established a Regional Planning Division which assumed responsibility at the national level for the formulation and implementation of regional plans, such as the integrated Rural Development Project and district development plans under the decentralized budget. In addition, special intersectoral programmes, such as those concerning population and food and nutrition, were located in the ministry. It also became the focal point for national programmes and policies relating to women and children. The ministry therefore acquired control over a significant cluster of issues and activities which were interrelated and provided scope for undertaking an important component of planning and policy formulation.

At this writing, the co-ordinating machinery for planning consists of an Economic Committee of the Cabinet, comprising the ministries with important development portfolios, presided over by the president. At the official level, the highest co-ordinating body is the Committee of Development Secretaries, chaired by the secretary to the cabinet. The Planning Division within the Ministry of Finance and Planning services the Committee of Development Secretaries. As in the past, the Planning Division is required to study and make its observations on all investment proposals made by sectoral ministries and acts in collaboration with the divisions responsible for budgetary management and control. The secretary to the Ministry of Plan Implementation is a member of the committee. The committee, therefore, becomes the main instrument for the management and co-ordination of the government development programme. However, the committee's functions are primarily focused on the annual plan and budget, and its very heavy agenda devoted to current affairs has left little time for it to assume the responsibilities germane to planning. As mentioned earlier, the planning function has become part of a much larger ministry which is responsible for the annual budget. Thus planning has lost some of the status, independence, and power it exercised as a separate ministry under the prime minister in the earlier system. This organizational change reflects the government's new orientation to planning and its role. It has had consequences, both positive and negative, discussed earlier and to be commented on further later in this section.

The Machinery for Sectoral Planning

The need to develop the planning capability of sectoral ministries as part of the national planning system received the attention of the government during the early stages of planning activity. However, for the period when the Six-Year Programme of Investment and the Ten-Year Plan were prepared, the operating ministries did not have sectoral planning units. Nevertheless, the key ministries, such as the Ministry of Agriculture and the Ministry of Fisheries, did get involved in the preparation of plans for their respective ministries. The first Agricultural Plan, for example, was drawn up by the Ministry of Agriculture and Food in 1958, independent of the Ten-Year Plan.

For the preparation of the Ten-Year Plan, sectoral committees were appointed to help in the formulation of the sectoral components of the plan. These were composed of members of the National Planning Council, heads of the implementing institutions, as well as persons with the relevant expertise drawn from both the public and private sectors. Lange, in his critique of the planning machinery, argued that adjustments are necessary in the organizational structure of the ministries responsible for implementing the various components of the plan. He added that "all Ministries to whom part of the national plan of economic development is assigned for implementation should have a special planning division responsible for implementation of the plan in the fields assigned to the Ministry. Such planning divisions should be attached directly to the Ministry."[25]

The *First Interim Report of the National Planning Council*, published in July 1957, discussed the need for appropriate planning arrangements within the ministries. The report recommended "establishment of distinct units within ministries to serve as focal points for all work connected with the programme and related measures of these ministries." The recommendations, however, were not pursued.

It was during the 1965–1970 period that the proposal to establish planning units in the main development ministries was implemented. A cadre of planning officers was established. Programming divisions with suitably qualified personnel were formed in a number of ministries, including Agriculture, Lands, and Industries. In short, together with foreign experts about 50 officers were active in the national planning apparatus as a whole, including the sectoral ministries. A programme of training was organized for officials in sectoral ministries and in the Ministry of Planning for development of the required skills in planning, sector programming, and project evaluation. The performance of these sectoral units was, however, uneven. Their work was often hampered by a shortage of qualified staff. The units were not readily accepted and adequately supported by all the ministries. The motivation and leadership provided to them at the sectoral level also varied widely. As a result, they were not always drawn into the centre of decision-making.

Many of the sectoral programming units which were set up in the late 1960s have continued to function within the ministries. But within the present planning system where ministries enjoy a considerable degree of autonomy in the preparation of their sectoral programmes and proposals, these units and the Central Planning Agency do not seem to constitute a closely co-ordinated network in which there is constant feedback and collaborative effort from the early stages of programme and project formulation. As a result, the approval of programmes and projects and the co-ordination of sectoral activities devolves mainly to the Development Secretaries' Committee. The decision-making at this level, however, is not always preceded by an adequate process of project formulation and evaluation in which the planning agency and sectoral ministries work closely together. Such a process would provide for more prudent and cautious decision-making. While the committee has the necessary technical servicing and support from the ministries, the pressures which reflect the relative political strength of the various ministries can be an important factor in the decision-making. This is illustrated in the allocations that have been made to several programmes and projects, such as the programme of house construction in the 1977–1982 period or the foreign loans approved for the state enterprise managing the national airline. The Ministry of Finance and Planning has continued to experience great difficulty in maintaining budgetary descipline and holding sectoral programmes to the framework of resource allocations that has been planned.

Participation in Planning

Participation in planning as used in this context refers to the process by which the planning system is able to interact with groups outside the formal system in government decision-making. Such groups include business groups in the private sector, the trade unions, employers' associations, and other interest groups such as farmers, small-scale producers, and ethnic minorities. In the early stages of planning, there was, however, little recognition of the need for an institutional framework which would provide scope for greater social involvement and participation in the definition of plan objectives and the formulation and implementation of plans and programmes. The National Planning Council, established in 1957, had a membership which included leading citizens with professional experience and knowledge who could contribute to the work of the council and the secretariat, but this was not specially designed to promote a dialogue between the government and other important actors in society; neither did it attempt to forge a broad-based social commitment to a plan and its implementation.

In the early 1960s, a committee comprising representatives of the Chamber of Commerce, the Development Finance Corporation, and the Development Division of the Ministry of Industries was formed under the auspices of the Department of National Planning to act as a co-ordinating agency between the private sector and the planning organization. It was not, however, until the period 1965–1970 that a more formal link between the government and the private sector was established. This was the Development Advisory Committee, consisting of permanent secretaries and 18 representatives of business organizations. The Private Sector Affairs Division in the Ministry of Planning serviced the Committee and organized a continuing dialogue with the private sector on relevant economic issues and policies. However, this remained but an exchange of views and ideas, not leading to a collaborative process of planning for the private sector.

The Development Advisory Committee as an apex institution for private sector participation and collaboration in planning ceased to function effectively after 1970 with the change of government. There has been no attempt since to create a similar body. Co-ordination between the government and the private sector now takes place through a variety of devices, such as advisory bodies set up for specific purposes, as in the case of export promotion. The committees which have been set up to approve private sector investments, both foreign and local, are the main instruments through which the government is able to establish priorities and give some direction to private sector development.

At a different level, there have been various institutions which have been created to enable local communities, and particularly the farming community, to participate in local development as well as in the planning and management of agricultural activity. These include rural development societies, cultivation committees, agricultural productivity committees, and, more recently, the representative institutions such as Gramodaya Mandalayas (village councils), Pradeshaya Mandalayas (divisional councils), and district development councils. The rural development societies have been concerned mainly with the improvement of the rural infrastructure. On the whole, these continue to function as important village-level institutions which have been able to mobilize resources that are then matched by government grants for various types of infrastructure improvement, such as roads, bridges, culverts, and public buildings. In the recent past, an effort has been made to train rural development workers and use the societies as instruments for village-level planning.

Two institutions which attempted to activate farmer participation were the Cultivation Committee and the Agricultural Productivity Committee (APC). The Cultivation Committee was replaced by the APC in 1972. The Agricultural Productivity Law which established these committees was an ambitious effort to create an institutional framework for the planned development of agriculture from the village level upwards. The array of functions assigned to these committees ranged from the provision of agricultural services and credit facilities to the preparation and execution of agricultural development programmes and employment creation. The APC was, therefore, a village-based institution designed for co-ordinating agricultural planning and development. The committees, however, were bodies nominated by the minister, and the nature of their composition was therefore not designed to elicit broad participation from the farmer community. During the period that followed their formation, the committees could not avoid a high degree of politicization, which introduced factionalism and reduced their effectiveness as development institutions.

The foregoing survey indicates that the country has not yet been able to develop a well-designed structure for participation in planning at different levels. The multiplicity of institutions that have grown, while providing scope for initiative and leadership in diverse fields, have also led to rivalries and overlapping of responsibility that have been harmful to a process of constructive popular participation. To bring about a participatory system, there would have to be considerable rationalization of the existing institutions and structures.

New Institutions and Their Implications for Planning

The National Planning Council, established in 1957, drew attention to the need for creating several new institutions to deal with planning problems that could not adequately be covered by the normal sectoral structures. One such area that was selected for special institutional arrangement was the agricultural development of the dry zone. The council recommended the establishment of a central survey organization which should be independent of ministries and should undertake a comprehensive survey of the dry zone and provide inputs to the sectoral programmes and projects of this region undertaken by the various ministries. Similarly, it recommended setting up permanent technical working groups for atomic energy and the export sector, among others. In making these recommendations, the council was drawing attention to some of the limitations of the prevailing structure, where the planning activity was organized on sectoral lines through the available sectoral ministries. Some of the planning problems cut across sectors and called for an intersectoral approach which would bring the relevant sectoral agencies together in a more integrated effort. These recommendations, however, were not implemented in the planning phases that followed. It was the familiar vertical structure of planning that prevailed. The isolated exceptions were the areas under development authorities involved in the planning and development of large river-basin projects.

In the early 1970s, the Export Development Board emerged as an intersectoral body which was required to identify the export potential and promote planned export development in a number of sectors, ranging from agriculture to manufacturing. In the post-1977 period, however, a variety of intersectoral agencies were set up under special legislation as statutory bodies and vested with responsibilities in defined areas which cut across sectoral boundaries. These authorities are different from government departments and enjoy a higher degree of autonomy. Both their structure and their extent of responsibility make them relatively autonomous, important centres of planning. These include the Mahaweli Development Authority, the Urban Development Authority, the Greater Colombo Economic Commission, the National Aquatic Resource Authority, the Central Environment Authority, the National Health Council, and the Export Development Board.

Most of these agencies have responsibilities of a multisectoral character and, by the very nature of these responsibilities, need to prepare plans and programmes encompassing a wide range of development issues. They thus become important components of the total planning system. They can bring new dimensions to planning by focusing national attention on newly emerging priorities and areas that have been relatively neglected in the conventional sectoral framework. The positive aspect of these institutions is that they are autonomous centres of planning and can introduce a creative and innovative element to national planning. Yet, the autonomous character of these institutions can create problems of co-ordination and result in the pursuit of policies and institutional goals which are mutually conflicting and also not in accord with national interests. The present institutional framework for planning is not equipped to have an overview of the entire system and harmonize the diverse initiatives taken in different parts.

Methods and Techniques of Planning

Typology of Plans

We have seen that Sri Lanka's planning effort has run the full spectrum — a long-term ten-year plan, medium-term five-year to six-year plans, a short-term three-year plan, and five-year rolling plans (or perspectives) with annual programmes. As already mentioned, these were not parts of a simultaneous exercise. The planning activity moved from one to the other, based on the experience of past planning as well as the ideological preferences regarding the type of planning entertained by the government in power.

Apart from these national planning exercises of varying time-spans, there were other planning efforts independent of the national planning effort. These include a number of sectoral programmes, mainly those which were prepared in the 1965–1970 period in the absence of a formally prepared national plan. In the period before this, two sectoral programmes prepared in this manner were the Agricultural Plan, prepared prior to the Five-Year Plan, most of which was later incorporated into the Ten-Year Plan, and the Five-Year Fisheries Plan prepared in 1964. The Fisheries Plan brings out the intrinsic weakness and danger in the preparation of independent sectoral programmes. These programmes tend to give the sector concerned priority much above what might have been given within the discipline of a national plan; they tend, therefore, to make excessive claims on available resources and demand policy changes which are inconsistent with national objectives.

Another innovative development was the effort to prepare special plans relating to major development problems facing the economy. Planning of this type moved out of the conventional categories of national and sectoral plans and dealt with major macro-economic issues such as employment or diversification of export which cut across sectoral boundaries. In almost all phases of planning in Sri Lanka, the need for multisectoral plans of this type was recognized. The specialized plans were instruments which directed effort on a national scale in selected areas or in relation to urgent problems. The Ten-Year Plan's proposal for the development of the dry zone was oriented towards this type of planning. In 1970, when the new government assumed office, an emergency employment plan was prepared which was later implemented in various sectors. A less detailed plan for a new export sector followed.

The planning activity in the post-1977 period includes a few examples of this type of planning. The Food and Nutrition Strategy, for example, which, at this writing, is being further developed, goes beyond a conventional sectoral plan and attempts to co-ordinate a wide range of policies and other inputs from different sectors. Likewise, the Central Environment Authority is proposing an examination of alternative development scenarios in relation to the management of the environment and its "carrying capacity." The Plan Implementation Ministry has sponsored and co-ordinated the preparation of a National Science and Technology Policy Plan. These various initiatives reflect the new direction in which the approaches and methodologies of planning are moving. In each of these exercises, conventional plan components are restructured and organized on a multisectoral basis in relation to specific development goals.

Another type of plan which arose in the 1970s was the regional integrated development plan. The initiative for this type of planning in Sri Lanka was taken by IBRD. This type of plan was prepared independently of national plans. The planning effort was focused on a selected district, and a package of development projects identified in the main sectors of production in the district as well as in other sectors to bring about improvements in health, education, housing, roads, and electricity. These plans thus differed in their orientation from national and sectoral plans; they brought the planning activity down to the regional level and identified development needs in the local context. Nevertheless they did not depart from the up-down technocratic approach. There was little effort to involve the beneficiaries in the identification of needs and the formulation of proposals through processes of consultation and participation. The plans themselves were also not integrated in the sense of promoting the structural transformation and the social well-being of the region as a whole. Instead, they identified specific projects in the region which benefited parts of it. This could have been satisfactory if they had been part of a long-term programme of development which progressively covered the entire region, but they were not. These regional planning exercises have been the subject of numerous evaluations which bring out both their advantages and shortcomings. Despite their inadequacy, they have introduced a much needed regional component to planning and prepared the ground for a more effective planning process which provides for interaction in planning at the regional, sectoral, and national levels.

Tools and Techniques of Planning

Even at the time the Six-Year Programme of Investment was prepared, planners recognized the need for more effective techniques of macro-economic planning than were applied in that exercise. Part of the document contains a stimulating discussion on the process of development and the technique of programming. In the section on technique of programming, the document presents a relatively simple forecast of growth based on population projections and the doubling of per capita income by 1980. The projections are based on assumptions of consumption and investment and capital output ratios.

The Ten-Year Plan was based on a much more detailed framework of macro-economic aggregates which forecast the balance of payments, the government budget, and the consumption and savings in the economy. It undertook the various steps which are part of the conventional techniques of national planning. It started from the demand side, examining population growth, the expansion of the work-force, and the future demand for productive employment. Then it examined the prospects and potential of the economy in relation to those needs. It then proceeded to develop a macro-economic framework which defined the overall magnitudes of national income, consumption and investment, the resource mobilization in terms of both domestic resources and the balance of payments. It also apportioned the contribution expected from the public and private sectors. The plan went on to work out in detailed disaggregated form the sectoral composition of the investment in the public sector in terms of programmes and projects and the phasing of the investment year by year for the period 1959–1968. The framework provided a handle on macro-economic variables and, with more detailed technical elaboration, could have been developed as a tool for macro-economic management. This was not done, however; the macro-economic framework was prepared only to derive a set of assumptions on which the investment programme could be based. The national planning exercise itself, however, employed the required techniques that made possible an internally consistent plan in which projections of resource availability, investment, population, and work-force were tied together. The sectoral composition of investment and output was worked out in detail to yield the planned rates of growth.

The national plans that followed did not attain any further degree of sophistication. There were efforts to prepare an input-output table for the economy in the 1965–1970 period and to develop an econometric model. These did not, however, become tools either for the planning exercise or for policy formulation. Work on elaborating the input-output table has continued, and although it has not become an important operational tool, it has been used for more limited purposes in depicting the intersectoral linkages and relationships of the economy and contributing background information for other analytical exercises.

What is of greater relevance is the effort to develop a framework of macro-economic accounting which is helpful for the management of key variables. In the 1965–1970 period, the Perspective Planning Division of the Ministry of Planning prepared a plan framework based on a set of national accounting and macro-economic tables; the framework sought to bring out the interrelations and behaviour of these variables. These tables included an account for resources and their utilization for the whole economy, the income, expenditure, and capital accounts for the private and public sectors, and a consolidated current and capital account for external transactions and its links with the behaviour of the domestic variables. This set of tables was directed to the problems of economic management and was not merely a forecast to substantiate the investment plan as was the macro-economic framework in the Ten-Year Plan. If the work begun in this area had been carried further, it might have been possible to develop a set of tools which could have had some predictive capacity for the management of the economy. The 1970–1977 period, however, saw a change in emphasis. The Ministry of Planning concentrated on the Five-Year Plan. A strong finance minister took over the main tasks of economic management, and the Ministry of Planning had little incentive to pursue the initiative it had taken in the 1965–1970 period.

Entering the post-1977 period, the strong incentive for developing effective tools of economic management gains in urgency. With the introduction of new economic policies which favoured an open, liberal economy, a large part of the regulatory system was dismantled, and market prices were allowed to operate more freely. Consequently, the management and monitoring of macro-economic variables — the government budget and the financing of deficits of the budget, the balance of payments and its key components, the monetary aggregates, and the flow of funds in the economy — all assumed critical importance. In the 1982–1986 programme of investment, the Ministry of Finance and Planning used the "flow of funds" format to depict the various transactions in the economy. In setting out the macro-economic accounting matrices, it pointed out "that the presentation assures internal consistency in the basic policy document used for short- and medium-term financial and economic programming, namely, the government budget, the balance of payments and the monetary system accounts, thus increasing their usefulness for analysis; it generates a private sector account; it provides an overall view of the transactions taking place within the economy and helps to show the effect of a change in the exogenous variable upon the system as a whole." The document on public investment, 1983–1987, claims that one of the most useful exercises that can be undertaken with the matrices is to trace the repercussions of alternative policies on variables that enter into the system; it goes on to state that it is possible to work out a series of matrices corresponding to alternative policy specifications. This brings in an important element regarding the techniques of planning in an environment of uncertainty. A major shortcoming in the planning exercises in the past was their lack of flexibility to deal with changing situations. There was no attempt to prove alternative forecasts or plans for selected contingencies. In the case of most plans, forecasts of resources went seriously awry. The plans themselves did not provide a guide or reordering of priorities with the contraction of resources. This critical challenge to planning was discussed by this writer in 1972:

The national plan has to be formulated as a succession of annual plans if its implementation is to be most effective. When the plan is presented in clearly defined annual segments, performance as well as measurement of performance is clearly identified, the preparation of the implementation budget within which activities are disciplined is facilitated and above all the revision of plans, shortfall in resources, or performance becomes easier. The annual Plan must, of course, cover the whole economy and include targets for the macro-economic aggregates, the outputs of the public and private sector, and performance objectives for each department and public sector enterprise.

Arising out of this observation, we could consider another major problem which affects plan implementation. This is the sharp fluctuation in the availability of a critical resource such as foreign exchange which can seriously disorganise implementation. Here again the formal structure of the plan could take account of this vulnerability, and as far as possible provide variants related to different levels of resources, so that where there is an unforeseen drop in resources, one layer of the plan could be removed or deferred without serious injury to the high priority core of the Plan. Each Ministry and Department would have to formulate their programmes in this manner and organise their implementation in such a way as to enable them to excise the low priority items without serious dislocation of their activities. . . . The flexible implementation strategy geared to this problem will be very different from the implementation programmes organised on the basis that the allocated resources will be definitely available.[26]

The formulation of alternative scenarios and the preparation of plan variants which can help the reordering of priorities offer a set of tools adapted to the conditions of variability which, in the context of Sri Lanka, needs to be explored to improve economic management and to make planning more relevant.

One of the analytical tools which has received attention recently in Sri Lanka is the social accounting matrix. This has been developed by World Bank experts in collaboration with local scholars. The social accounting matrix is capable of taking the macro-economic matrix to a further level of disaggregation and identifying the impact of the main transactions of the economy on different socio-economic groups. Such a social accounting matrix can often serve as a valuable instrument for tracing the social outcomes of macro-economic policies and for integrating economic planning with social planning. It can provide the framework for guiding development policies in relation to desired social goals. However, further work has to be done to improve the data base for such a matrix as well as to identify the levels of disaggregation which would be meaningful for policy formulation.

Sectoral Planning

The Ten-Year Plan itself contained a number of well-formulated sectoral programmes. These included the programmes for plantation crops — tea, rubber, and coconut — the paddy production, and fisheries. These sectoral programmes served as the framework for policy-making, investment, and the development effort as a whole in the relevant sectors and were heavily drawn upon when more elaborate and detailed sectoral programmes came to be prepared. A model sectoral programme in the Ten-Year Plan was the Fisheries Programme. It set realistic goals for fish-import substitution, worked out in detail the expansion and mechanization of the fishing fleet and the improvement of fisheries infrastructure, for example anchorages, harbours, and ice plants; it spelt out the extension services and other assistance required by fishermen, supported the programme with a research component and prepared the financing plan and, further, identified the main organizational structure needed for implementation. The entire programme was broken down in great detail in all its components, year by year, in the form of clearly defined targets of implementation in terms of which performance could be monitored. The main elements of the programme continued to provide the basic framework for policy and investment in the sector despite changes of government and thereby demonstrated the value of a well-prepared sectoral plan.

However, it is in the 1965–1970 period that the approach to national planning made sectoral programmes the main instrument of planned development. The difference in approach between the Ten-Year Plan, the Six-Year Plan of Investment, and the Short-Term Implementation Programme on the one hand and the exercises in the 1965–1970 period on the other was that, in the latter, there was no conscious attempt to prepare these sectoral programmes as part of a comprehensive national plan. This does not mean that the broad internal consistency of the investments taken together was entirely neglected. As might be expected, the sectoral programmes themselves were based on assessments of markets and resource availabilities which took account of the macro-economic environment. What was relatively new was that these sectoral programmes were formulated in much greater detail and prepared for implementation. They included, therefore, not only a well-defined project component, phased annually, but spelt out the ingredients essential for fulfilling the plan targets — that is, the policy framework, the critical inputs (in the case of paddy, seed material, fertilizer, credit requirements, etc.), and the administrative machinery for implementation.

A broad analysis of two sectoral programmes will illustrate the evolution of sectoral programming and its place in national planning. It will be seen that in some of the more successful programmes, the initiative and direction came from the political level and the role played by the national planning agency was of a supportive character. This was true of both the paddy subsector and tourism. The sectoral paddy programme had a unique combination of characteristics which secured for it a commitment at a high political level from all governments. These characteristics include social, economic, and political objectives which all converged to give the programme high priority. Paddy production was the important economic activity of the rural peasantry, which was one of the largest political constituencies. The agenda of any political party had to cater to the interests of this group if it was to acquire substantial political support, given the multiparty democratic system which was in operation. Socially, a programme which increased the earning capacity of this segment would at the same time be promoting a more equitable pattern of development and integrating the backward parts of the economy into the process of development and modernization. The structural changes resulting from such a process would initially help to reduce the dichotomy and imbalance created during the colonial period. Economically, self-reliance in the country's staple food considerably strengthened the economy as a whole; it diversified the agricultural sector, reduced the country's import dependence, and contributed to the long-term stability of its balance of payments. The paddy programme also had political appeal of a more profound character which reached out to the country's historical heritage and stirred deeper national sentiments. A major component of the paddy programme was the resettlement of the dry zone of the country, the seat of its ancient civilization. It had been served by a technologically efficient system of irrigation reservoirs and canals which, however, had fallen into disrepair over the centuries but which was still in a condition capable of speedy restoration. In the context of the paddy programme it was an extremely valuable capital asset. Therefore, from its inception, the sectoral paddy programme became the centre-piece of the development programmes of succeeding governments. The main elements of the programme were already in place before the national planning exercises were begun.

The programme on tourism and the way in which it was initiated and formulated were very different from the formulation of the paddy programme. Here again, the initiative came from outside the Ministry of Planning. The programme took definite shape in the 1965–1970 period in the Ministry of State. The programme involved very different actors from those of the paddy programme — the organized private sector, which had to undertake large investments for tourist accommodation, transport, and other services; the state, responsible for improving the basic infrastructure; and foreign investors and marketing agencies necessary to make the programme a success. In this sense, it was one of the few programmes where there was private sector involvement in the formulation of the investment plans. The government obtained the services of foreign consultants to prepare an initial long-term prognosis and plan. This approach ensured a fair degree of consultation with the important interest groups involved in tourism, both locally and abroad. The programme thus included the necessary components which made it an effective instrument for policy formulation, financing, and monitoring of implementation. The plan contained incentives for tourists and for investments in tourism, in the form of premium exchange rates and tax incentives for both investment and income. The financial allocations were identified and made available. Most important of all, these were tied to a strategy of tourist development which identified the special attractions of Sri Lanka in terms of locations and the tourist itinerary, so as to ensure that investments were directed to the appropriate locations and to the essential supporting services.

Lessons from Sectoral Planning

There are several lessons that can be learnt from the successful sectoral programmes. First, they enabled the government to select a manageable component of economic activity which had high economic and social priority, concentrate on it, and mobilize the needed resources. This selective effort also made it possible to develop an integrated programme of action in which the techno-economic aspects, the policy framework, and the administrative machinery and manpower could be organized and co-ordinated. The way in which sectoral plans evolved and were developed helped the sectoral agencies and interests to identify themselves fully with the programme and take a leading role. The plans were not seen as emanating from a central agency which assumed direction, control, and initiative.

Second, the important sectoral programmes acquired a national momentum of their own, for social, political, and economic reasons which transcended the professional planning effort. We saw this in regard to the food drive. They acquired the character of "lead" programmes. This was best illustrated in the post-1977 period, when the entire national development effort was dramatized, as it were, in a few "lead" projects — the multipurpose Mahaweli River Valley Project, the Free Trade Zone, the Greater Colombo Development Programme, and the Housing Programme — which dominated the economic scene and covered the agricultural, industrial, urban infrastructural, and social sectors. Once they acquired this character, they were immediately elevated to the highest political decision-making levels and received the commitment of the entire system. Mobilization of the required resources and motivation of the administration for implementation then became a relatively smooth process which cleared the different bureaucratic hurdles without the usual obstructions. The programmes gained a national prominence which animated the sectoral actors who were involved.

These factors greatly helped the implementation of a particular programme; nevertheless, there were corresponding disadvantages: A programme could become "politicized," the professional content and the disciplines it involved sometimes being overridden for political objectives. The more restrained and calculated decision-making processes of the professional planners played a diminished role in this situation. This resulted in over-investment and costly errors, while the implementation of the programme itself went on unimpeded. If the planning disciplines had been more active in these sectoral programmes, they could certainly have been more cost effective. This could describe parts of the irrigation programme and the tourist programme, or the housing programme during the period 1977–1981, when the government undertook a costly programme of urban and rural housing.

Project Planning

The 1965–1970 period, when projects had to be presented for aid, saw the introduction of new techniques of project evaluation, such as discounted cash flow with the internal rate of return or net present worth and the social cost-benefit analysis with shadow prices. These brought new discipline to the selection and evaluation of investments. It was observed that the poor performance of the national plan was to a large extent due to the deficiencies in project formulation and evaluation. The new project planning helped appreciably to correct this shortcoming. Project planning also had its impact on the planning process as a whole and directed attention to the complexity of development in a way which the macro-economic planning processes seldom had.

An in-depth study at the level of the project is in many senses a study where the interrelations of technical, economic, social, managerial, and other elements are manifest. It is in project studies of this nature that the major externalities come to the surface — the impact of the project on the environment, on skill formation, on the whole process of modernization. Project studies may reveal the need for institutional changes in a sharper light than any general analysis; they may uncover the irrationalities in the economy in such areas as pricing or the rate of exchange; they may help to recast priorities in regard to investment. Project planning thus has to be one of the basic disciplines in the whole planning process.

However, certain limitations arose in the evaluation techniques that were introduced. They approached projects as incremental investments which make marginal additions to existing capacity. They thus focused on the profitability of the investment, whereas all major development projects in a developing economy almost always result in far-reaching structural changes which make the externalities of the project critically important for the evaluation. The evaluation techniques were most often not able to capture these externalities. To do so, the project would have had to be inserted into a dynamic model and its social and economic effects traced throughout the system.

The Planning Experience — Constraints and Limitations

The three preceding sections have given a brief account of the evolution of the planning process — the scope and content of planning, the institutional changes during different periods, and the methodologies and techniques of planning. This section attempts to provide a summary evaluation of the performance and impact of national planning and examines some of the problems and lessons to be derived from the planning experience in Sri Lanka.

The Predictive Capability of Plans

Growth and Capital Formation — Targets and Performances

We can begin with a straightforward comparison of the plan targets with performance for the various planning exercises that were undertaken. The relevant planning exercises are the Ten-Year Plan 1959–1968, the Three-Year Implementation Programme 1962–1964, the Five-Year Plan 1972–1976, and the Public Investment Programme 1979–1986. In the case of the Ten-Year Plan, we have to take into account the fact that the plan was not accepted for implementation following the changes in government in 1960. An evaluation of performance is, therefore, not strictly relevant in the case of this plan. It is possible, however, to comment on its predictive capability and the quality of its analysis and forecasting of broad sectoral trends by comparing some of the targets with the eventual outcome after the ten-year period. We could examine whether divergences are due to shortcomings in the formulation of the plan and miscalculations regarding the major constraints facing the economies or to managerial and political failures to implement policies and programmes prescribed in the plan. In the case of the other three plans, the governments responsible for the formulation of the plans remained in power during the plan periods, and no major internal changes relating to the planning agency and the allocation of responsibility occurred during the periods to disrupt the implementation of the plans.

The national targets for the growth of GDP set in the Ten-Year and Five-Year plans were significantly above the actual performance of the economy during these periods. The annual average growth of GDP planned for 1959–1968 was 6 per cent, while growth during this period actually averaged 4.2 per cent. We should, however, exclude the exceptional performance for 1968, when GDP grew at approximately 7.8 per cent, as the growth during this year followed on policy changes and resource flows which were part of a framework of economic management distinctly different from that of the Ten-Year Plan. Thus, the average rate of growth drops to 3.4 per cent for the nine-year period 1959–1967. The performance during the 1972–1976 period was much more dismal. Against a target of 6.1 per cent given in the plan for the period 1970–1976,[27] the actual growth was 2.7 per cent. The performance relevant to the other two planning exercises was much closer to the targets. In the case of the implementation programme, the plan target was a reduced 4.8 per cent per annum. Against this target, a rate of 4.5 per cent was achieved. The rolling plans for the post-1977 period set targets which varied marginally from year to year, ranging from 5.5 per cent in the 1979–1984 plan to 6 per cent in the 1982–1986 plan. The eventual out-turn reflected a growth rate of approximately 5.8 per cent for the period 1977–1982. In all the plans, the sector where the gaps between targets and performance were largest was the industrial sector. The Ten-Year Plan targeted for a growth rate of approximately 10 per cent per annum, but the actual achievement was only 5.4 per cent. Similarly, the Five-Year Plan also targeted for a growth rate of 10 per cent, while only a marginal growth of 1.5 per cent was reached.

The relative success and failure of different sectoral programmes enable us to examine whether the causes are to be found in the quality of sectoral planning and programming. This aspect was dealt with in the preceding section. Regarding the Five-Year Plan, paddy production in 1975 and 1976 had fallen below the 1970 level owing to two consecutive years of severe drought and crop failure. Both the shortfalls and excesses reflect not only the imponderable elements which result in performances that diverge widely from the target but also the shortcomings in the target setting exercise itself. In the two decades of the 1960s and 1970s, all plans tended to set very high targets for paddy production, spurred on by the desire to achieve self-sufficiency in rice as speedily as possible. These targets often proved to be unrealistic, but the shortfalls in the targets detracted from the positive quality of the performance itself. The paddy sector was in fact one of the most vigorous growth sectors in the economy and recorded steady rates of increase in output and productivity. After the lean years of 1975 and 1976, it recovered and rapidly moved closer to self-sufficiency.

Therefore, comparison of performance with targets alone is not a reliable measure of the quality of the development effort that has taken place. There is also an implicit bias to set targets at a level somewhat higher than what might be possible to achieve in order to stretch capacities and spur the implementing agencies to greater effort. From the viewpoint of management and implementation, target-setting can thus serve a variety of objectives. And yet if the targets are completely out of keeping with what is realistically achievable, they are likely to be totally ignored and fail to serve as a frame of reference for policy formulation and implementation. This was in fact the case in the Ten-Year and Five-Year plans.

Forecasting the Behaviour of Macro-economic Variables

The performance measures in terms of GDP and sectoral output, however, do not reflect some of the more strategic issues relating to the capacity of the planning process as it functioned during this period. A more illuminating comparison which throws light on these issues would be that between forecasts of major economic variables such as the balance of payments and the government budget and the eventual outcome. The plans make their projections on constant prices derived from a base year — 1957 in the case of the Ten-Year Plan and 1970 in the case of the Five-Year Plan. Consequently, they do not take into account either the variation in terms of trade or inflation. As the projections are those of real output, it is assumed that the economy would have found the means of adjusting itself to the behaviour of these crucial variables. In such an approach, the effects of the terms of trade and inflation are assumed away and removed from the plan frames. The plans do not, therefore, consider or directly address the problems of adjustment.

At constant 1957 prices, the Ten-Year Plan forecast a net current account deficit of Rs 151 million, after a merchandise surplus of Rs 128 million. It anticipated increases in the export volume of all export products, including an increase in manufactures by 121 per cent on a very small volume of such exports in 1957. The actual performance varied widely from these targets.

The plan anticipated that total government revenue would increase from an average of Rs 1,346 million in 1959–1961 to Rs 2,460 million in 1968. The actual accrual of revenue fell short of this figure by 12 per cent, or approximately Rs 300 million.[28] Total recurrent expenditure had increased to Rs 2,186 million, leaving a current account deficit of Rs 30 million. Capital expenditure, according to the plan, was to have been Rs 1,121 million; the actual expenditure, however, was Rs 714 million, a shortfall of 36 per cent on the planned target. The plan had expected to finance the entire budget, both recurrent and capital, from non-inflationary sources which included, besides current revenue, receipts from loans and grants. The non-revenue component was expected to realize 18.4 per cent of the total in 1968, or Rs 456 million. The actual budgetary performance was very different. Total borrowings rose to Rs 722 million in 1968, of which about Rs 302 million consisted of direct borrowing from the Central Bank.

The Short-Term Programme of Implementation was much closer to reality in its three-year forecasts because the time-span was more manageable. But the Five-Year Plan, as we saw in the previous section, failed disastrously in its forecast of the external accounts. The débâcle of the Five-Year Plan, however, occurred in exceptional circumstances arising from global disequilibria which could not have been easily foreseen.

It was not that the plans were unconcerned with the crucial macro-economic variables. The Ten-Year Plan, in fact, devoted sections to a discussion of its assumptions on the budget and the balance of payments. But it made assumptions which reveal to us the limitations of the state of planning at the time. It also reflects another more fundamental shortcoming — that is, a lack of a proper appreciation of the basic structural weaknesses of the economy, its vulnerability resulting from the highly unstable external sector. It is surprising that in discussing the balance of payments, the plan regards 1957 as an unusual year concerning the out-turn on the merchandise account, which showed a deficit for the first time since 1953. This year was, in fact, the beginning of a long-term decline in the terms of trade and of a persisting adverse trade balance, a trend which was interrupted only for a single year, in 1977.

It is equally surprising that eminent visiting economists did not draw sufficient attention to this aspect, besides making general cautionary remarks. They failed to highlight the problems of planning in an environment of instability and uncertainty — an indicator of the confidence and enthusiasm that existed at the time concerning planning and its capacity to accelerate growth in developing countries. The national planning agency in Sri Lanka, therefore, did not perceive of its role as one which required it to provide a framework for management of the crucial macro-economic variables. The management of these variables was not conceived of as a basic condition for the success of a plan. If it had been, the main elements in the management of these variables would have been better identified, and the framework of economic policies relating to strengthening the balance of payments and managing the budget on a long-term, stable basis would have been more clearly formulated. As it turned out, the behaviour of the variables was assumed away in a few broad hypotheses, and attention was drawn to the fact that if they behaved differently, the expectations of the plan would not be fulfilled. There was a tacit assumption that the task of economic management had to be performed elsewhere. Economic management and planning consequently remained separate functions, in both the minds of the planners as well as in the institutional arrangements governing the allocation of functions.

The Problems of Planning in Uncertainty

The Structural Characteristics Producing Uncertainty

The foregoing discussion has attempted to indicate, in broad terms, some of the underlying structural features which create the environment of uncertainty in which planning operates. More specifically, there is the instability arising from Sri Lanka's dependence on external trade based on a particular composition of exports and imports. This has already been examined at some length in the preceding sections. The assumptions regarding the availability of resources were altogether falsified at the very beginning of both the Ten-Year and Five-Year plans. In the case of the Five-Year Plan, almost simultaneous to the document's release, the world economy began moving into a prolonged crisis. The world food shortage, the devaluation of the dollar, the changes in the exchange rate system, and the steep escalation in the price of oil followed in sequence. They rendered the macro-economic framework and the forecasts of resources, particularly the balance of payments, totally inapplicable. The Five-Year Plan, therefore, ceased to be a meaningful frame of reference for either resource allocation or for the management of the investment programme, never mind the key macro-economic variables.

Another basic element of uncertainty were the climatic variations. In each of the plan periods, prolonged droughts had severe adverse impact on agricultural production. The problems were most acute in the case of paddy, which was heavily dependent on water, but they also affected all other crops, including the export tree-crops tea, rubber, and coconut. Sri Lanka's economy, one which contained a large share of agriculture in its GDP — approximately 40 per cent in the early 1950s, declining to 30 per cent by the end of the 1970s — these variations had grave repercussions on its entire development effort, and seriously interrupted and retarded its growth. This is clearly seen in the trends in paddy production. Paddy output increased steadily from 36.5 million bushels in 1959 to 50.5 million bushels in 1964, and then dropped below 1959 levels in 1965, to 35.6 million bushels. Again, having risen to 77.4 million bushels in 1970, output dropped to 62 million in 1972 and 1973, rose to 76.8 million in 1974, and declined below the 1972 level, to 55.3 million, in 1975 and to 60 million in 1976. Paddy production and the extent of import substitution achieved were a key factor in the mangement of the balance of payments. Decline in output meant higher imports of rice. Very often, crop failures in Sri Lanka coincided with rising international prices for rice. The cycle of unfavourable weather affected many rice growing areas in Asia generally and resulted in a reduction of exportable surpluses and a contraction of supply to the world market — a situation which occurred in 1973.

The third element of variability and uncertainty resided in the political process. Social and political instability are endemic in development, which engenders a process of rapid structural change. Demographically, populations are rapidly expanding, there is greater geographic mobility — particularly from rural to urban areas — all of which break down traditional structures of control. They are not replaced fast enough with new structures that impart stability to the total system. Socially and economically, many of the advancements, such as higher rates of literacy and better infrastructure, which provides improved access to backward areas, help in drawing an increasingly large mass into the political process, accentuate conflicts of interest between various social and ethnic groups, and add to the political instability. Sri Lanka's post-independence development has been marked by two major political upheavals — first the youth insurrection of 1971, which was a major set-back for the development programmes of the government elected to office in 1970, followed by the ongoing ethnic conflict, which has erupted in widespread violence, creating conditions of instability that are adversely affecting growth and investment in a number of sectors (such as tourism). Moreover, resources have been diverted to military expenditures on a massive scale.

Apart from these major upheavals which threaten the system as a whole, the type of social democracy in Sri Lanka has led to sharp alternations of power between the two political parties. This has resulted in discontinuities in development policy which have not been conducive to effective planning.

Instruments and Strategies for Coping with Uncertainty

In this context, the options open to planning for coping with uncertainty are limited. It is possible to identify several elements in the planning efforts of the 1960s and 1970s which attempted to adjust to the problems of uncertainty. First, the Three-Year Implementation Programme, for example, was a result of the recognition of the problems of the long time-span for purposes of planning and therefore worked within a much shorter time-span in which forecasts could be made more realistically and in which the focus would be on implementation. The programme also envisaged the preparation of annual rolling plans. The government which came to power in 1977 adopted the annual rolling plan within a five-year perspective framework as its main planning instrument. This was a much more flexible device for coping with uncertainty. On the one hand, it kept in sight medium-term goals and a macro-economic framework which was consistent with them. On the other, it worked out the annual short-term component, taking account of the most recent developments and making the necessary adaptations and revisions.

To cope with the uncertainty arising from the country's external transactions and the government budget, the planning process had to be firmly tied in with the tasks of economic management. The main inadequacy of most of the planning exercises, particularly of the Ten-Year and Five-Year plans, was that they neglected this essential link between economic management and investment planning. They did not identify the major policy issues relevant to plan implementation nor proceed to the next step of defining in adequate detail the policy framework within which a plan would have to operate, particularly the framework for the management of the key maro-economic variables related to the balance of payments and the government budget. We saw that during the 1965–1970 period, the Planning Ministry concentrated on the short-term management of the balance of payments and the government capital budget, but even then, its control and monitoring of budgetary operations as a whole were partial. It did not get adequately involved in the macro-economic tasks of managing the financing of budget deficits and analysing the behaviour of aggregates such as money and overall prices. This was corrected to a large extent in the post-1977 period, when finance and planning became parts of one ministry and when indicators such as the current account surplus in the budget and the government capital budget, as proportions of GDP, were carefully watched in relation to planned targets. The burden of debt servicing and the dependence on external borrowing were also monitored in relation to planned magnitudes.

It cannot, however, be said that the post-1977 effort was wholly successful in combining the exercise of short-term economic management and planning with the longer-term exercise of engineering the required structural adjustments and changes to overcome the deep-rooted instabilities and weaknesses of the economy. For example, it has not been able to reconcile the import substitution and export promotion efforts in the industrial sector with its strategy of a liberal, open economy nor to come up with an effective industrial policy. This gap is also evident in the management of the floating exchange rate: Sri Lanka allowed the rupee to depreciate against the dollar and appreciate against other convertible currencies, seriously impairing its international competitiveness in non-dollar markets, which were of great importance for its export drive. The long-term structural adjustments needed to narrow the trade deficit, diversify exports, and adjust smallholding agriculture to the emerging self-sufficiency in rice have also not received adequate attention. This is due partly to the fact that serious perspective planning has not been accorded its rightful place in the total planning process.

Coping with Political Instability

The third factor which has been discussed is the uncertainty arising from political instability and changes of government. While sound planning contributes indirectly to a stable political environment by accelerating economic growth and distributing its benefits equitably, its capacity to contribute directly to the resolution of political problems is somewhat limited. Even so, national planning has to be sensitive to and take account of the political forces shaping the development process in the country. First, it has to set development goals which will meet the socio-economic aspirations of the mass of the people and, for that purpose, balance growth with equity. Second, it must perceive specific problems in the system which have a high potential for political conflict and upheaval, identify the economic elements which contribute to them, and address itself to the removal of those elements, thereby helping in the resolution of the conflicts.

In all the national plans, the definition of the main development goals showed, as might be expected, explicit concern for the satisfaction of the basic needs of the people and followed what could be described as an equity-oriented strategy. It must be mentioned, however, that the equity-orientation in the plans was not a specific and conscious contribution of the plans. The plans took over and incorporated the programmes and policies that were already being pursued by the state from the early 1940s. The incorporation of these elements enabled the plans to balance objectives of social welfare with those of growth. Nevertheless, it cannot be said that the planning process was adequately sensitive to the interplay of political forces and the ideological conflicts that were being generated. These were having an important impact on areas of national policy such as nationalization, expansion of the public sector, the role of private enterprise, and foreign investment. The planning process had no regular means of handling and responding to these problems — many of which came in the wake of changes of government. The efforts of the MEP (People's United Front) government in 1957 — in particular the view of national planning held by the then prime minister — might have been able to create an institutional frame and a focus of activity which would have transcended partisan politics. The government sought to establish national planning and its outcomes as resources that would be available to all governments. This proved to be unrealistic, however, in the context of the deep ideological conflicts dividing the political parties.

It could be argued that national planning would have worked best where there was a basic national consensus on the broad social, economic, and political goals relating to economic growth, distribution, the nature of the mixed economy, and a common commitment to democratic processes and structural changes and reforms. There was a possibility of achieving such an overarching consensus, which is to be found in social democracies, in the case of Sri Lanka as well. The failure to achieve it is due to a combination of factors, including the quality of political leadership and the way in which political parties evolved in Sri Lanka. A discussion of these aspects is outside the scope of this study. What is relevant for us is the fact that the processes of social democracy did not lead to such an overarching consensus on societal goals.

Major National Issues and Planning

An inadequacy of another kind was the failure of planning to anticipate and give attention to national problems which had an intensely disruptive potential for the entire political fabric of the country . Two examples are the problem of youth unemployment and unrest, leading to the insurgency of 1971, and the ethnic conflict which resulted in the armed struggle and widespread violence after 1977.

Unemployment

The preceding section included a brief discussion of the growth of unemployment in the 1960s and the failure to grapple effectively with this problem. The Ten-Year Plan approached the problem in relatively conventional terms, seeking the solution in accelerated industrial growth. Little attention was paid to the special character of the unemployment problem in the context of development as it was taking place in Sri Lanka. The links between the system of education, the skills and expectations it generated, on the one hand and the manpower needs on the other were not clearly appreciated and acted upon. Sectoral programming in the area of education was quite effective and successful in terms of the sectoral indicators themselves, such as participation in the system at the primary and secondary levels, the teacher-pupil ratios, classroom space, and availability of and access to educational facilities. But the relevance of the system to the pattern of development and the skills of the work-force and their appropriateness to the demands of the various sectors did not receive adequate attention. As a result, the educational output and the expectations generated did not match with available or potential employment opportunities.

At another level, no serious attention was paid to the choice of technology and its impact on employment. The Ten-Year Plan expected a rapid increase in employment during the ten-year period, an annual rate of approximately 3.1 per cent, outstripping the rate of increase of the total work-force. This expectation proved totally unrealistic: the employed work-force grew at only about 1.7 per cent. Furthermore, industry, which was expected to yield as many as 230,000 additional jobs, appears to have provided at best about 100,000 jobs. The cost of employment creation in industry appears to have been quite high. Most of the large-scale industrial investments which took place in the public sector were highly capital intensive. The expectations of the plan that industry would be the major growth sector for new employment were negated. The critical issues pertaining to employment and its links with education and technology began to receive adequate attention in plan formulation only after the problem had reached crisis proportions. The ILO mounted a mission in 1971 with specific focus on an employment-oriented development strategy for Sri Lanka. By then, however, the youth insurrection had already broken out. When the Five-Year Plan was being prepared and the lessons had already been learnt at a high social cost, the planning agency gave a central place to employment creation in the choice of investments, in pattern of technological change, and development priorities in the Five-Year Plan. The performance of the plan, however, as we saw earlier, fell far short of its targets as a result of the external and internal developments which radically altered its basic assumptions.

The Ethnic Problem

The other critical issue which threatened the political and economic stability of the country was the ethnic conflict. Although the root causes of the conflict cannot be explained in terms of economic processes which came within the ambit of planning, there were many issues crucial to its resolution, to which a sound national planning effort could have contributed. These included major grievances of the Tamil minority which had grown round the questions of access to higher education, employment in the public sector, the establishment of new agricultural settlements which threatened to alter seriously the ethnic balance in areas populated mainly by the Tamil minority, and, most important of all, the decentralization of the administration and the devolution of power.

Every one of these questions impinged on national and sectoral planning. The problems of higher education arose from the increasing demand, created by the system of free education, for higher education which was not adequately met by a proportionate expansion of educational facilities. This was particularly true of the disciplines most in demand, such as the physical and life sciences, and the professional disciplines of medicine and engineering, which offered the best chances of employment. In the fierce competition for entry into these disciplines, the ethnic composition and the language medium became major issues causing serious dissatisfaction and frustration among Tamil youths. One important means of relieving the tensions in these areas would have been a realistic long-term programme for the expansion of higher education.

National land policy should have addressed itself more directly to the question of land settlement and its impact on the ethnic problem. Later studies indicated that a careful analysis of the long-term prospects for new settlements and the implications of different scenarios could have helped in evolving a pragmatic approach which would have removed many of the causes of conflict.

The key issue of decentralization and devolution draws attention to one of the major deficiencies in the methodology that governed planning. National planning remained a highly centralized exercise throughout the period under review. Efforts at decentralization of planning occurred only in the 1970s, in the wake of changes in the administrative system. These changes transferred a limited measure of political authority to the district level. But political and administrative systems reinforced each other in maintaining a centralized decision-making process. Had a greater effort been made to initiate development planning from below and secure a greater degree of popular participation through elected and representative agencies at the subnational levels, the planning process would have created an environment more congenial for a system of devolution. This would probably have facilitated a pattern of decentralized government and devolution of political power, which have constituted one of the main issues in the ethnic conflict.

Nationalization and the Food Subsidies

There were other strategic development issues which had become so indissolubly linked to the political agenda that most often planning itself was bypassed and could not bring to bear any independent influence on the decisions affecting them. Nationalization and the food subsidy were two such issues. Nationalization was related to the role of the state and the relative position of the public and private sectors in the economy. The food subsidy and its benefits concerned the social goals and the nature of the welfare state which could be supported by the country. Both issues and the approaches to them were related to the management of the special variant of mixed economy that had evolved in Sri Lanka.

The SLFP governments, during both the period 1956–1965 and 1970–1977, undertook large-scale programmes of nationalization. In the first period, omnibus transport services, banking, insurance, and important items of import trade such as milk products were taken over by the state. The government went on to take over the import and distribution of petroleum products. The election manifesto of the coalition which won the elections in 1956 declared that "all key industries must be run by the State . . . , all essential industries, including foreign-owned plantations, transport, banking and insurance, will be progressively nationalised." The declaration held out the prospects of an economy in which the private sector would progressively contract and play a diminishing role.

Such an approach did not accord with a commitment to a mixed economy. It was inspired essentially by the objective of a socialist economy in which the state would play the predominant role. In this sense, it was different from the role which Indian leaders assigned to the state. The state in the future economy of India was to be in control of the commanding heights in industry and other modern sectors, but the different fields of enterprise for the public and private sectors were fairly clearly demarcated. In the case of Sri Lanka, no such clear demarcation was made. The economic objectives of nationalization were distinctly subordinate to the political goals. The parties which stood for nationalization saw the organized private sector and large-scale private enterprise as being inveterate supporters of the UNP. Nationalization and expansion of the public sector was a means of reducing the existing concentration of economic power in the hands of a group which was politically hostile to the UNP. They thus hoped to promote a system which they could control more effectively when they were elected to power. In this political context, planners were reluctant to involve themselves actively in working out the appropriate balance between the public and private sectors and providing an objective analysis of all the implications of specific strategies and decisions on issues of nationalization. The Ten-

Year Plan contained a brief analysis of the issues and discussed some of the implications but refrained from indicating how the conflicts of development goals inherent in them could be handled and resolved.

The management of the food subsidy during the period 1948–1977 also illustrates how critical economic issues were bypassed in the planning process. The food subsidy scheme was first introduced in 1942 and consisted of the untargeted distribution of a ration of rice at subsidized prices through an extensive network of co-operatives set up by the government. The food subsidy became a major budgetary problem for all governments. Ministers of finance from almost all political parties advocated cuts in the food subsidy. The UNP removed the food subsidy in 1953, and this led to widespread rioting. The SLFP minister attempted to impose a cut in the rice subsidy in 1962, and in 1972, the LSSP coalition government finance minister made a similar effort. Both faced serious opposition from the government rank and file and had to abandon their proposals. The political parties themselves adopted contradictory positions on the issue. Parties in opposition advocated the food subsidy and opposed its reduction. These same parties, when they assumed power, attempted to control or reduce the food subsidy in their effort to manage the economy and balance revenues with expenditures. In the early period of the food subsidy, there was no attempt to analyse the full economic and social implications of the subsidy or to modify it so as to achieve clearly defined objectives of welfare. The subsidy remained an untargeted universal scheme, providing the same benefits to all segments of the population irrespective of their income levels or needs. The entire philosophy of the food subsidy was never clearly defined in terms of its social and economic objectives. It was only towards the late 1960s and 1970s that the government began to consider the possibility of targeting the food subsidy to certain income groups which required some form of income support.

Conclusion

The planning experience in Sri Lanka lacks the continuity to be found in many other developing countries, where the national plan was adopted as a central instrument of decision-making and where comprehensive medium-term plans (mainly five-year plans) were produced in regular and uninterrupted sequence. (This applies to most of the countries in the South Asian region — Bangladesh, India, Nepal, and Pakistan.) In the case of Sri Lanka, the planning system did not have the benefit of such a regular process of plan preparation and the progressive accumulation of experience and technical expertise within a stable institutional framework.

This lack of continuity in the planning process derived from a variety of factors. First, an economy which was heavily dependent on imports and exports imposed severe constraints on medium- and long-term planning. Many of the basic macro-economic variables, such as the balance of payments and the government budget, were subject to such major fluctuations and uncertainties that the few formal long-term and medium-term planning exercises which Sri Lanka undertook lacked the minimum of stability and predictive capability essential for planning. Second, many of the changes that took place in the planning system itself had their source in more significant changes which were occurring at the political level and in the differences in the ideological approaches to planning adopted by alternating governments.

Sri Lanka's planning attempted to cope with these problems and uncertainties in a variety of ways. This study has described how the planning activity in Sri Lanka alternated between long-term and medium-term exercises, with targets of economic growth and structural change, on the one hand and short-term economic management and partial development efforts in selected sectors on the other. Comprehensive national plans with well-developed sectoral components were prepared in the 1956–1965 and 1970–1977 periods. In the period 1965–1970, Sri Lanka avoided the preparation of formal plan documents; it concentrated on short-term adjustments and on selected sectors, with specific objectives, such as import substitution in rice and tourism. This reorientation of approach and change in plan priorities can be attributed partly to the recognition that the earlier medium- and long-term planning had been unproductive.

In the post-1977 phase, the approach to planning underwent further modification. The government adopted the device of rolling plans, which were adequately flexible to take into account the constantly changing macro-economic situation, and organized development around several lead projects. The rolling plans enabled the government to adjust the annual and medium-term plans to the changes as and when they occurred.

These changes in approach, however, were due not only to the perceptions of planners regarding the inadequacies of planning in a given phase; they were primarily the outcome of changes of government and the different approaches governments took to planning. While the socialist-oriented governments favoured a more central role for the state and a more centralized direction of the economy through such instruments as a comprehensive national plan, the Rightist governments favoured an approach which concentrated on the management of the economy and the implementation of policies and incentives which stimulated growth through the market system. This study has examined in some detail the dilemma planning faced in the context of Sri Lanka's particular type of mixed economy and the proportions of public and private sectors. The fact that there was no broad political consensus regarding the mixed economy as a system weakened the capacity of planning to create the right framework of incentives which would stimulate growth in both sectors. The shifting frontiers of public and private sectors in the Sri Lankan economy contrasted sharply with the fairly clear definition of the relative role of the public and private sectors in the Indian economy.

The lack of continuity in Sri Lankan planning is also reflected in the numerous changes that have taken place in the institutional framework for planning in Sri Lanka. These changes illustrate the way in which the government experimented with the different combinations of roles for planning, ranging from an advisory role distanced from the decision-making process to one centred in the policy-making process. These experiments again illustrate some of the ambiguities which have characterized the attitude of governments towards the planning process and its proper role. In the effort to link planning to the tasks of economic management and decision-making, there was a tendency to neglect long-term planning. The planning process itself was not successful in mastering the problems in this area. It did not acquire the capacity to combine the task of coping with short-term problems of management with that of engineering the long-term structural adjustments in the economy which were needed if the very conditions of uncertainty and instability which plagued the planning process were to be effectively contained and overcome.

The planning experience in Sri Lanka demonstrates the inadequacy of planning where the various components of planning, such as the long-term, medium-term, and short-term aspects, are not present together in a comprehensive planning system. In the case of the Ten-Year and Five-Year plans, the absence of short-term and annual plans resulted in a failure to adapt to the changing resource situation and adjust the decision-making instruments, such as the government budget and the foreign exchange budget. The implementation of the development plans themselves were thus not related to the short-term and medium-term management of the key macro-economic variables. On the other hand, in the case of the post-1977 period, the absence of a long-term plan chartering the broad directions of the economy impaired the quality of the short-term effort and tended to divert attention from some of the long-term structural problems.

If these elements had coexisted, the planning exercise in its totality would have been very different. In Sri Lanka in any given phase of planning most of the effort went primarily into one of the elements. In a combined effort, the emphasis on each element would vary according to the perception of priorities in any given period. In periods of crisis, the greater effort would go into the short-term adjustments and annual plans for grappling with urgent problems; at the same time, adequate attention would be given to other medium-term and long-term components in order to give direction to the short-term adjustment and accelerate the process of development and structural change.

This study has also drawn attention to the way in which planning has responded or failed to respond to the broader social and political issues critical in shaping the development process itself and forming the planning environment. The successful responsiveness of planning to these overriding issues depended on two important conditions. First, the professional content of planning itself had to acquire an interdisciplinary approach according due place to the other disciplines — in this case, those of the social sciences, such as sociology and political science. Planning within the government system became very much the prerogative of economists and economic planners. Development planning as a concept which included societal changes and went beyond economic planning had not gained acceptance for most of the period under review. Development planning required a body of interdisciplinary knowledge and analytical tools which was more than the sum of the separate disciplines and which would identify the critical linkages in development and act on them in a systematic way.

Second, the planning activity had to be institutionalized in a manner which established links between professional planning and national decision-making at the highest level. The planner's vision of the optimal path of development had to interact with the politician's vision of a good society and the politically viable path towards it. Neither the relationships which had grown between political decision-making and planning nor the formal planning tasks themselves led to a disciplined study and analysis of the problems which had major political and social implications. Cited in this study as examples are the issues of nationalization, food subsidies, unemployment, and the ethnic conflict. Planning failed to make any significant contribution to an objective understanding and appraisal of these problems and to the long-term effect of political decisions that were being taken. Most of the decisions on these critical issues bypassed the planning process. Even the social goals relating to welfare programmes were defined largely in terms of a social and political process, and planners tended to accept these as given parameters within which they had to work. As a result, planning was fitted into the system as a subordinate, technocratic task. The important responsibility of defining social and economic goals was not one in which the planners were able to participate intellectually.

The experimental nature of Sri Lankan planning, however, resulted in a flexibility which provided scope for a variety of planning innovations and approaches. Attention has been drawn to the responses by planners to special problems requiring urgent attention. In 1970, for example, the Planning Ministry produced an emergency employment plan. The Export Development Plan, which was incorporated as a component of the 1972–1976 plan, was prepared as an independent exercise. The decentralization of planning that appears to have taken place in the 1970s and 1980s, particularly in the post-1977 period, has resulted in a number of initiatives of this nature where plans have concentrated on clearly defined clusters of problems. The food and nutrition strategy is an illustration. The tendency towards this type of decentralized planning has been reinforced by the institutional changes that have taken place. A number of new public agencies that have been established, such as the Central Environmental Authority, the Export Development Board, the Urban Development Authority, and the Mahaweli Development Authority, have acquired powers which cut across a wide range of sectors. The issues they deal with involve several sectors, and these agencies therefore need to undertake planning exercises of an intersectoral nature. The agencies and their programmes draw attention to the importance of intersectoral or multisectoral planning and underscore some of the limitations of the conventional planning structure, which is organized on vertical and sectoral lines. These various initiatives, however, have to be brought together in an overarching national planning system which can give them coherence and consistency. At present, there is a tendency for these "autonomous" centres of planning to function in a manner which leads to contradictions and inconsistencies at the national level. The task of evolving a planning and decision-making system which balances the desired degree of autonomous planning with national consistency is, therefore, of the utmost importance.

In this connection, a recommendation recently made by the Sub-Committee of the National Science Policy Committee which dealt with the social infrastructure has special relevance. The Sub-Committee states: "Somewhere in the national system there has to be a capacity to project and define future scenarios of development based both on current trends as well as desirable norms." The report argues that current methodologies of scenario building provide an effective means of bringing together the diverse planning efforts and enable the whole range of relevant disciplines to participate in assessing current trends, defining the desirable social goals, and evolving appropriate development strategies. There have been a few efforts to begin work on long-term scenarios which depict alternative futures for Sri Lanka by the year 2000. These efforts, although they may yield some valuable insights, are, however, most likely to be partial and impressionistic, given the resources made available for such exercises. If they are to be effective, the work on future scenarios will have to be organized on a national scale with the full support of the entire planning apparatus.

An activity of this nature could also fill a gap which has been evident throughout the planning activity in the past. This relates to the relationships of planning to the people and interest groups outside the public sector. This study has pointed out that, despite various initiatives that have been taken to institutionalize consultations with the private sector as well as grass-roots level organizations, these have not added up to a well-conceived institutional framework of popular participation in development planning and implementation. Such a framework would obviously serve several important purposes. First, it could play a major role in building a consensus among all the important actors on development goals and programmes in different sectors. Its role of education and persuasion could have the far-reaching impact of enhancing an understanding of the relevant development issues among the various interest groups. It would provide the forum for an informed exchange of ideas which could provide feedback to the planning agencies on the expectations and responses of the people. What has been said earlier in regard to future scenario building has special relevance for the type of broad-based social participation in planning which is envisaged. It can provide both the organizational framework as well as the motivation.

Notes

1. GDP at cost at 1959 prices increased by Rs 1,657 million during 1959–1965. After adjustment for the effects of the terms of trade, the increment was reduced to Rs 1,348 million (Central Bank, *Annual Report 1970* [Colombo, Central Bank of Ceylon], table 6, appendix II).
2. Central Bank, *Annual Report 1970*; *Annual Report 1980*.
3. Central Bank, *Annual Report 1980*.
4. In a recent revision of the national accounts, adjustments in the sectoral allocation of value added in relation to export duties result in a significant change in the shares of different sectors. According to the adjustments, the share of agriculture in 1950 is 29 per cent of GDP and that of services 58 per cent. On these changes in the sectoral composition of GDP, the shares of industry and manufacturing increased respectively from 14 per cent and 9 per cent in 1950 to 21 per cent and 11 per cent in 1980. Agriculture and services declined to 24 per cent in 1980.
5. World Bank, *Economic Adjustment in Sri Lanka: Issues and Prospects* (Washington, D.C., IBRD, 1982), p. 9.
6. Central Bank, *Annual Reports*.
7. World Bank (note 5 above).
8. This section relies heavily on the analysis contained in my *Changing Needs of Children* (Colombo, Ministry of Plan Implementation, 1982).
9. UNICEF Sri Lanka, *The Social Impact of Economic Policies during the Last Decade* (Colombo, UNICEF, June 1985).
10. Department of Information, *Ceylon Today: A Government by the People — The National Plan* (Colombo, Ministry of Finance, n.d.), pp. 15–46.
11. Ibid., p. 15.
12. Ibid., p. 43.
13. Ibid., p. 17.
14. Ibid., p. 23.
15. Ibid., p. 27.
16. Ibid., p. 46.
17. The Planning Secretariat, *Six-Year Programme of Investment, 1954/55 to 1959/60* (Colombo, Government Press, 1955), p. 15.
18. Ibid., p. 10.
19. Ibid.
20. National Planning Council, *The Ten-Year Plan* (Government Press, 1959), p. 111.
21. Gunnar Myrdal, *Asian Drama* (London, Pelican Books, 1968); Donald Snodgrass, *Ceylon: An Export Economy in Transition* (The Economic Growth Center, Yale University, 1966), p. 112.
22. Department of National Planning, *The Short-Term Implementation Programme* (Colombo, Government Press, 1962), p. 15.

23. National Planning Council, *Papers by Visiting Economists* (Colombo, Government Press, 1959), p. 11.

24. O. Lange, "The Tasks of Economic Planning in Ceylon," in National Planning Council (note 23 above), p. 79.

25. Ibid., p. 84.

26. G. Gunatilleke, "The National Plan: Its Formulation and Implementation," in *Report on the Second Seminar on the "Role of Audit in a Developing Country"* (Colombo, Government Press, 1971), pp. 1–15.

27. 1970 has been selected as the base year for the plan, as the latest year for which national accounts were available at the time of plan preparation was 1970.

28. The revenue figures apply to the budget year from 31 October 1967 to 30 September 1968.

Select Bibliography

Plan Documents

Ceylon, Ministry of Finance. 1948. "The budget speech 1948–49," delivered by Hon. J. R. Jayewardena. Colombo, Govt. Press, 54 p. Includes the Six Year Plan, 1947/48–1952/53.

Ceylon, National Planning Council. 1959. *The ten-year plan.* Colombo, Planning Secretariat, 490 p.

Ceylon, Planning Secretariat. 1960. *Six-year programme of investment 1954/55 to 1959/60.* Colombo, Govt. Press, 510 p.

Ceylon, Department of National Planning. 1962. *The short-term implementation programme.* Colombo, Department of National Planning, 346 p.

Ceylon, Ministry of Planning and Economic Affairs. 1966. *The development programme 1966–1967.* Colombo, Ministry of Planning and Economic Affairs, 52 p.

Ceylon, Ministry of Planning and Employment. 1971. *The five-year plan 1972–1976.* Colombo, Ministry of Planning and Employment, 137 p.

Government of Ceylon. 1946. *Post-war development proposals.* Colombo, Govt. Press, 221 p.

Sri Lanka, Ministry of Finance and Planning, National Planning Division. 1980. *Public investment 1980–84.* Colombo, Ministry of Finance and Planning, 95 p., tables.

———. 1981. *Public investment 1981–1985.* Colombo, Ministry of Finance and Planning, 112 p.

———. 1982. *Public investment 1982–1986.* Colombo, Ministry of Finance and Planning, 143, xxvii, vii p., maps, tables.

———. 1983. *Public investment 1983–1987.* Colombo, Ministry of Finance and Planning, 232 p.

———. 1984. *Public investment 1984–1988.* Colombo, Ministry of Finance and Planning, 183 p., tables.

———. 1985. *Public investment 1985–1989.* Colombo, Ministry of Finance and Planning, 223 p., tables.

Sectoral Plans and Subsidiary Documents

Ceylon, National Planning Council. 1957. *First interim report*. Colombo, Planning Secretariat, 192 p.

Ceylon, Ministry of Agriculture and Food. 1958. *Agricultural plan: First report of the Ministry of Planning Committee*. Colombo, Ministry of Agriculture and Food, 381 p.

Ceylon, National Planning Council. 1959. *Report of committee and technical working groups*. Colombo, Planning Secretariat, 102 p.

Ceylon Fisheries Corporation. 1965. *Draft 10-year plan for the development of the fishing industry*. Colombo, Ceylon Fisheries Corporation, 111 p.

Ceylon, Ministry of Planning and Employment. 1965. "The five-year plan: Agriculture sector programme [including fisheries]." Colombo, Ministry of Planning and Employment, 108 p. Mimeo.

Ceylon, Ministry of Agriculture and Food. 1966. *Agricultural development proposals*. Colombo, Ministry of Planning and Economic Affairs, 351 p.

Ceylon, Ministry of Land, Irrigation, and Power. 1966. *Plan of development of Ministry of Land, Irrigation and Power, 1966–70*. Colombo, Ministry of Planning and Economic Affairs, 302 p.

Ceylon, Planning Committee on Industry. 1966. *Report of the Planning Committee on Industry*. Colombo, Ministry of Planning and Economic Affairs, 17 p.

Ceylon, Planning Committee on Economic Overheads. 1967. *Report of the Planning Committee on Economic Overheads*. Colombo, Ministry of Planning and Economic Affairs, 40 p.

Ceylon, Planning Committee on Education, Health, Housing, and Manpower. 1967. *Report of the Planning Committee on Education, Health, Housing and Manpower*. Colombo, Ministry of Planning and Economic Affairs, 107 p.

FAO. 1968. *Report of the irrigation programme review — Ceylon*. Colombo, Ministry of Planning and Economic Affairs, 117 p.

ILO. 1971. *Matching employment opportunities and expectations: A programme of action for Ceylon — Report of the inter-agency team*. Geneva, ILO, 2 vols.

Regional Development Plans and Projects

FAO, Investment Centre. 1981. *The Sri Lanka Badulla Integrated Rural Development Project Preparation Report*. Rome, FAO, 2 vols.

ILO. 1981. *A five-year integrated rural development programme for Mannar District, Sri Lanka*. Bangkok, Asian Regional Team for Employment Promotion, 134 p.

IRDP. 1982. *Integrated Rural Development Programme, Nuwara Eliya District: A summary*. Nuwara Eliya, IRDP, 1982, maps.

Marga Institute. 1980. *A development plan for the Gampaha District*. Colombo, Marga Institute, 365 p., tables.

Sri Lanka, District Ministry Jaffna, Planning Division. 1980. *Integrated rural development plan, Jaffna District*. Jaffna, District Ministry, 173 p., tables.

Sri Lanka, Kachcheri, Batticaloa. 1979. *Batticaloa integrated rural development project, 1979*. Batticaloa, Kachcheri, 26 p., tables.

Sri Lanka, Kachcheri, Kalutara. 1979. *Kalutara District integrated rural development programme*. Kalutara, Kachcheri, 217 p., maps, tables.

Sri Lanka, Kachcheri, Kandy. 1980. *Integrated rural development project: Kandy District preliminary report*. Kandy, Kachcheri, 74 p., annex.

Sri Lanka, Ministry of Local Government, Housing and Construction. 1978. *Colombo central area: Colombo master plan project*. Colombo, Ministry of Local Government, Housing, and Construction, 77 p., maps.

Sri Lanka, Ministry of Plan Implementation. 1979. *Integrated rural development plan (draft report): Matara District, 1980–1984*. Colombo, Ministry of Plan Implementation, 355 p., maps, tables.

Sri Lanka, Ministry of Plan Implementation. 1979. "Integrated rural development programme for the Puttalam District." Colombo, Ministry of Plan Implementation 67 p., tables. Typescript.

————. 1979. "Integrated rural development project for the Hambantota District." Colombo, Ministry of Plan Implementation, 16 p. Typescript.

Sri Lanka, Ministry of Plan Implementation, Regional Development Division. 1978. *Integrated rural development project for Kurunegala District. 1975–1983*. Colombo, Govt. Press, 40 p., maps, tables.

————. 1979. *Integrated rural development programme, for Mullaitivu District*. Mullaitivu, Ministry of Plan Implementation, 30 p.

Sri Lanka, Ministry of Plan Implementation, Regional Development Division. 1979. *Moneragala District integrated rural development project situation report and project proposals*. Colombo, Ministry of Plan Implementation, 49 p., appendices.

————. 1982. *Sri Lanka: Kegalle District Integrated Rural Development Project: Development plan 1984–1988, prepared by the Regional Development Division, Ministry of Plan Implementation and the Inter-agency Committee on Integrated Rural Development for Asia and the Pacific*. Colombo, Ministry of Plan Implementation, 356 p.

UNDP. 1978. *Colombo metropolitan region: Sri Lanka regional structure plan: Report prepared for the United Nations acting as executive agency for the UNDP*. Colombo, UNDP, 4 vols.

4

TOWARDS EFFECTIVE PLANNING IN MALAYSIA: SOME STRATEGIC ISSUES

Lai Yew Wah and Tan Siew Ee

Social, Political, and Economic Background

Malaysia, comprising Peninsular Malaysia (formerly the Federation of Malaya, which achieved independence in 1957) and East Malaysia (Sabah and Sarawak states) was formed in 1963. The 1957 constitution determines the nation's political systems and the legislative powers for the whole federation as well as for the individual states. It also specifies the respective concerns of the federal government and parliament, besides delineating the power distribution between the legislature, executive, and the judiciary.

The bicameral parliament consists of a House of Representatives (Dewan Rakyat) and a Senate (Dewan Negara). Election to the House of Representatives takes place once every five years, which is also the duration of each parliament. Malaysia practises a system of parliamentary democracy modelled on the British example. The constitutional monarch, the Yang Di Pertuan Agong, appoints the prime minister, his cabinet, and the judges of the land. This system has been in force since 1957, excepting a brief interruption in 1969 when parliament was suspended because of racial riots. For this brief lapse the National Operations Council was set up to administer the country. Since the first election in 1959, the Barisan Nasional (National Front) — an alliance of several political parties — has been the ruling party. This has provided political stability in the country, which is an essential factor for effective planning.

Malaysia has essentially a free-enterprise economy. Although state intervention in many areas of enterprise is becoming more evident, the private sector still dominates. In the past, public participation in entrepreneurial activities was negligible, but because of the peculiar nature of the socio-political problems confronting the nation, interventionist policies were inevitable. This problem is easier to comprehend when it is noted that in multiracial Malaysia, issues such as poverty and wealth distribution are usually laced with racial overtones. Hence, government policies are shaped by the overriding objective of achieving national unity and harmony.

Demographically, Malaysia is a plural society with a colourful mixture of races, cultures, and religions. In 1965, the total population was 9,421,000, with 8,052,000 (85.6 per cent) residing in West Malaysia. In 1985, the population had reached 15,655,000. In other words, the rate of population growth was nearly 2.7 per cent per annum over the period, which is among the highest in the world. In terms of racial identities, the Malays made up 56.4 per cent of the population in Peninsular Malaysia, whereas the Chinese and Indians made up 32.8 per cent and 10.1 per cent respectively. Despite this high rate of population expansion, the country is fortunate in that with rising productivity and high levels of exports, as well as a very diversified economy, Malaysians were still able to experience increasing per capita consumption and per capita income levels. Latest figures place the real per capita income levels at US$1,740 in 1985, compared to US$374 for 1965. The unemployment rate, although quite high at approximately 7.0 per cent of the labour force, is fairly good when compared to the rates in many other developing nations. However, in view of the disproportionately high share of youthful population below 15 years of age in Malaysia — 37 per cent or more — and the equally large number of labour-force entrants into the job market — 3.2 per cent each year in the 1970s and early 1980s — it could be said that Malaysia will have to be judicious in its choice of employment-related policies if the nation is to avoid a massive backlog of unemployment in the difficult years to come. The current labour force is 5,947,000, out of which 371,200 are unemployed. Thus, with a high economic-dependency ratio, on account of the large number of the school-age population, it is to be expected that substantial demands will be made in the near future on public expenditures, especially for education, health, and welfare, and that, in turn, will impinge on the national resources that could otherwise be channelled towards savings and productive investments.

Table 1 lists key economic indicators for the country for various bench-mark years. As indicated earlier, Malaysia possesses bountiful natural resources which have enabled its population to enjoy a relatively high standard of living. The country has been the world's leading producer and exporter of major commodities such as rubber, tin, palm-oil, pepper, and, lately, even highly sophisticated electronic components. The high proportion of exports is evident in table 1, where it is shown that, in all the years surveyed, about one-half or more of the nation's GNP was sold overseas. Correspondingly, the share of imports, mainly industrial products, is high. Owing to the resilience of the economy, the country was able to maintain a consistently high (20 per cent or more) ratio of gross savings as well as partake in high-level gross investments (as high as 33 per cent

TABLE 1. Key economic indicators of Malaysia

	1960	1965	1970	1975	1980	1983
GNP at current price (M$)	6,649	8,637	12,155	21,606	49,880	63,888
GDP at current price (M$)	5,220	7,830	10,708	15,315	51,838	67,480
Share of exports in GNP (%)	55.0	49.8	47.7	47.1	61.5	57.5
Share of imports in GNP (%)	45.1	45.8	44.4	46.6	58.4	62.3
Share of savings in GNP (%)	21.0	17.8	20.5	22.2	27.2	22.8
Share of gross consumption in GNP (%)	75.5	81.5	78.0	77.0	71.6	77.1
Share of gross investment in GNP (%)	15.0	16.3	20.3	23.8	29.6	33.3
Share of private investment in GNP (%)	11.9	9.0	12.0	13.5	18.5	20.6
Share of public investment in GNP (%)	3.1	7.3	5.7	10.3	11.0	12.7
Share of agriculture in GDP (%)	37.8	31.5	31.4	29.8	23.8	22.4
Share of manufacturing in GDP (%)	8.6	10.4	13.6	14.3	18.6	17.9

Sources: Compiled from various data sources.

in 1983). However, much of the recent public investment was the result of intentional deficit-financing (especially for achieving restructuring objectives). This aspect will be discussed in greater depth later, but for now it suffices to add that quite a substantial restructuring of the Malaysian economy has occurred over the last two decades. In 1980, the share of agricultural output in GDP was 23.8 per cent, compared to its high, 37.8 per cent, share in 1960. Much of the restructuring was in favour of the manufacturing sector, which increased its share from 8.6 per cent in 1960 to 18.6 per cent in 1980. In terms of export shares, manufactured goods have increased in importance, rising from 6.5 per cent in 1965 to almost 30 per cent in 1984. Within the agricultural sector itself, rubber exports have declined in importance in favour of palm-oil. Nevertheless, the top five resource-based commodities, including rubber, palm-oil, timber, crude petroleum, and tin, contributed no less than 60 per cent of all export revenues in 1984.

The high ratio of exports to national output is a source of instability to the economy, as recent incidents have clearly demonstrated. In 1980–1982, the world recession affected Malaysia badly, as commodity prices for rubber as well as palm-oil plummeted. The price for crude petroleum also fell during this period, leaving the Malaysian economy open to the destabilizing effects of export fluctuation. Thus, despite careful planning and agricultural diversification programmes, Malaysia was not able to escape the effects of world-wide recession, owing to its large export sector. It is obvious that agricultural diversification will not be the solution to such problems of economic instability, and greater efforts will have to be made in intersectoral transformations. To this end, the government has given priority to expanding the manufacturing sector.

As shown in table 2, there was substantial economic diversification between 1960 and 1985, whereby the primary sector's share of GDP fell drastically from 43.7 per cent to 26.6 per cent. The share of mining in GDP would have been even lower had it not been for the inclusion of crude petroleum in this sector. This is because the output of tin shrank perceptibly between 1960 and 1985. As mentioned earlier, the manufacturing sector has increased its share in GDP significantly. In the early 1970s, the strategies to support the rapid growth of manufacturing encompassed mainly import-substituting measures such as the granting of tariff protection, tax rebates and investment credits for capital investments and machinery imports. Consequently, import substitution industries, particularly in food manufacturing and textiles, expanded rapidly.

Starting in the late 1970s, the orientation of industrial development planning shifted towards exports. Hence, greater industrial and product diversification became more evident as other, non-traditional products such as electrical machinery, appliances, and electronic parts featured more prominently in total industrial exports. In fact, by 1983 these products constituted 52 per cent of all manufactured exports. Chemicals and petroleum products took up 9.7 per cent, followed closely by the traditional textile (9.3 per cent) exports. It is expected

TABLE 2. Sectoral distribution of gross domestic product for selected years: Malaysia

Sector	Shares for selected years							
	1960[a]		1970		1980		1985[b]	
	$	%	$	%	$	%	$	%
Agriculture (including livestock, forestry, fishing	1,976	37.8	3,432	32.1	6,255	24.6	7,673	21.8
Mining and quarrying	306	5.9	613	5.7	1,171	4.6	1,696	4.8
Manufacturing	453	8.7	1,307	12.2	4,875	19.2	6,534	18.5
Construction	158	3.0	481	4.5	1,209	4.8	2,090	5.9
Electricity, gas, water	70	1.3	245	2.3	605	2.4	933	2.6
Transport, storage, communications	189	3.6	606	5.7	1,803	7.1	3,153	8.9
Wholesale, retail trade, including hotels and restaurants	817	15.6	1,423	13.3	3,529	13.9	4,757	13.5
Finance, insurance, real estate, business services	71	1.4	836	7.8	2,041	8.0	2,971	8.4
Government services	339	6.5	794	7.4	3,202	12.6	4,533	12.9
Other services	841	16.1	874	8.2	720	2.8	914	2.6
Statistical discrepancy	—	—	97	0.8	—	—	—	—
Gross domestic product @ factor cost in 1970 prices	5,220	100.0	10,708	100.0	25,410	100.0	35,254	100.0

Source: Compiled from various Malaysian plans.
[a] For West Malaysia only
[b] Estimated

that the export-oriented strategy will be intensified, so that the base of the Malaysian economy will be further strengthened. Overall, it could be said that, judging from table 2, a remarkable degree of structural transformation has occurred in Malaysia, and if the manufacturing sector can maintain its high rates of annual growth — estimated at 11.4 per cent per annum between 1971 and 1980 — by the end of this century Malaysia will be able to join the ranks of the so-called developed industrial nations.

Table 3 shows the growth rates of selected indices that reflect Malaysia's large capacity for growth. Despite the constraints of external dependency and world recession problems in the early 1980s (1981–1983), Malaysia was still able to achieve a 6.2 per cent annual rate of growth in its GDP. Tracing through the other periods coinciding with the implementation of the various Malaysian development plans, one can see that the most vigorous phase of economic growth took place in the 1970s. In all the periods when development plans were implemented, the annual rates of growth of GDP exceeded 6 per cent. As a result of the country's vast natural resources, significant growth in output led to continued increases in real per capita consumption and income levels. The golden years are reflected in the period of the Third Malaysia Plan (1976–1980), where real per capita income grew by 4.8 per cent annually. National savings, which rose continuously in the 1960s and 1970s, dropped precipitously, however, in 1981–1983, when, for the first time, a negative real savings rate was recorded. As discussed earlier, the emergent problems of deficit budget financing, together with the rising balance-of-payments deficits that were not found in earlier plan periods, have finally caught up with the Malaysian economy. Malaysia was fortunate, however, to be able to generate sufficient job opportunities every year to accommodate the expanding labour market and manage to keep the rate of unemployment at around 6 per cent per annum. In recent years, the emphasis on employment creation appears to have diminished somewhat as industrial investments have become increasingly capital-intensive.

Table 3 also provides glimpses concerning the nature of investment in Malaysia. Economic development in many of the plan periods was stimulated largely by public sector expenditures for investment. The public sector investments, especially from the Second Malaysia Plan period (1971–1980) onwards, also provided counter-cyclical impact on the economy, especially when exports were weak and private sector investment was lethargic. This was observable, for instance, in 1971–1975 under the Second Malaysia Plan, when public sector investments grew by 17.6 per cent per annum as compared to the 1.9 per cent per annum under the First Malaysia Plan (1966–1970). During the early phase (1981–1983) of the Fourth Malaysia Plan (1981–1985), this situation was repeated when public sector investment grew at 12.5 per cent per annum to compensate for the slack in private sector investment that arose due to the severe slow-down in export earnings and the weakening of the private sector demand. However, the offsetting investment exercise of government investment imposed

TABLE 3. Growth of gross domestic product and selected indicators during selected plan periods (%)

Period	Rate of growth (%)						
	GDP	Gross investment	Private investment	Public investment	Gross savings	Real per capita income	Employment
Draft Development Plan 1950–1955	1.4	14.6	NA	NA	NA	neg.	NA
First Malaya Plan 1956–1960	2.9	5.7	18.1	12.1	NA	0.9	NA
Second Malaya Plan 1961–1965	6.4	11.5	5.1	27.6	4.1	2.7	3.0
First Malaysia Plan 1966–1970	6.0	6.4	9.6	1.9	6.9	2.2	3.2
Second Malaysia Plan 1971–1975	7.1	11.0	7.2	17.6	8.9	1.6	3.4
Third Malaysia Plan 1976–1980	8.3	8.4	9.9	6.2	10.5	4.8	3.7
1981–1983	6.2	10.0	11.0	12.5	neg.	2.9	2.9
Fourth Malaysia Plan 1981–1985*	7.6	8.7	8.0	-1.4	2.7	4.8	3.2

Source: Compiled and computed from various Malaysian Five Year Plans and V. Banerji Rao, *National Accounts of West Malaysia*, Singapore, Heinemann Educational Books (Asia), 1976.
*Expected rate of growth

a heavy burden on the public coffers, such that by 1984 the government had to announce drastic cut-backs in investment spending. Thus, for the first time ever, public investment is expected to be negative for a planning period (1981–1985). Even then, by 1983 the public sector had accounted for almost 38.2 per cent of total investment, which is significantly higher than the comparative figure for the Second Malaysia Plan (1971–1975) period (32 per cent). Overall, however, in a mixed economy such as that of Malaysia, the private sector is still expected to lead in the quest for greater economic diversity and growth, and, in this, it is guided by the principle of profitability. In Malaysia, with the expected cut-back of public sector involvement in investment activities and the increased emphasis on privatization, it is likely that private investment will in time become more important as the stimulus to development.

A discussion concerning the impact of investment on the growth of the Malaysian economy behooves us to look into the subject of ownership of private investment equity. In fact, this is a central issue in Malaysia because of the sensitivities involved. Perhaps Malaysia is unique in the sense that ownership of share capital is linked to racial inequalities and inter-ethnic differences, and the statistics in table 4 do not appear to dispute this. In 1970, foreigners owned 63 per cent of the nation's entire corporate wealth, leaving the residual to the locals. Of the latter proportion, the Bumiputras ("sons of the soil") laid claim to a miniscule 2.4 per cent. Thus racial identities become entangled with unequal distribution of wealth. Pressure by Malays for immediate rectification of such an anomaly began to build, and government reaction found its expression in the form of the restructuring strategies as incorporated in the Second Malaysia Plan. In fact, the policies and programmes of this plan were specifically designed to restructure Malaysian society so as to correct the imbalance in ownership and control of wealth, employment, and income distribution. The planning and implementation machinery of the government has thus aimed at creating economic balance in the broadest sense so that a harmonious Malaysian nation could be achieved.

Specifically, as set out in the Second Malaysia Plan, by 1990 30 per cent of all commercial and industrial enterprises must be Bumiputra-owned, and the employment in all categories and sectors should reflect the racial structure. This restructuring motive, or the "New Economic Policy," forms the operational basis of all subsequent plans. In practice, however, it has proven to be extremely difficult for Bumiputra individuals to own the targeted shares. Hence, in 1983, although foreign ownership of equity had been greatly reduced (to 33.6 per cent), the Bumiputra community owned only 18.7 per cent of the corporate equity, and a great deal of this was in the hands of trust agencies. These trust agencies are set up with initial financial support from the government, and their aim is to enable an eventual transfer of shares to Bumiputra individuals. Examples of important trust agencies are the Amanah Saham Nasional (National Unit Trust Scheme), Permodalan Nasional Berhad (PERNAS, National Equity

TABLE 4. Ownership of share capital in Malaysia 1970–1985

	1970		1980		1983		1990*	
	Value	%	Value	%	Value	%	Value	%
Malaysian residents	1,952	36.7	18,493	57.1	33,011	66.4	52,194	70.0
Bumiputra trust agencies (a + b)	126	2.4	4,051	12.5	9,275	18.7	22,369	30.0
(a) Bumiputra individuals	84	1.6	1,880	5.8	3,762	7.6	3,891	5.2
(b) Bumiputra trusts	42	0.8	2,170	6.7	5,512	11.1	18,477	24.8
Other Malaysians	1,827	34.3	14,443	44.6	23,736	47.7	29,825	40.0
Foreign residents	3,377	63.3	13,927	42.9	16,698	33.6	22,369	30.0
Share of Malaysian companies	—	—	7,791	24.0	9,054	18.2	NA	NA
Net assets of local branches	—	—	6,135	18.9	7,643	15.4	NA	NA
Total	5,329	100.0	32,420	100.0	49,708	100.0	74,563	100.0

*Data are estimates from the Fourth Malaysia Plan, p. 176.

Corporation), and Majlis Amanah Rakyat Malaysia (MARA, or Council of Trust for Indigenous People). It has often been asked whether the restructuring targets are practical, but as 1990 draws closer, the call for more aggressive efforts to achieve a more equal distribution of equity among the various communities has become increasingly vigorous. However, it can be stated without reservations that the equity control of foreign investors will be greatly lessened by 1990.

Equity control need not, however, be equated with control over the nation's wealth, as the capacity of investments to generate income is dependent upon the manner in which the share capital is put to use. In Malaysia, while foreign-controlled companies have dwindled since 1970, they are still a potent force as far as their shares of the total sales of limited companies are concerned. These foreign companies accounted for 39.5 per cent of all sales of limited companies in Malaysia in 1980, which is certainly more substantial than their shares of equity would suggest. If the usual assumption that foreign companies are better organized and tend to yield higher profit ratios is correct, then the dominance of the foreign sector is hardly diminished.[1] In fact, in the period 1971–1980, the value of foreign-owned corporate stock trebled from $M4 billion to $M13 billion, and their sales grew by 17 per cent per annum.[2] It is apparent, then, that the locally controlled companies have much to gain from the example of their foreign counterparts.

We now come to one of the most crucial problems of Malaysia, namely poverty. Just as with the unequal distribution of wealth among the different racial groups, poverty in Malaysia is also easily identifiable with ethnicity. While restructuring was one of the platforms of the Second Malaysia Plan, the eradication of poverty amongst *all* races constitutes the other basic goal of all development efforts. Unfortunately, however, as poverty affects the Malays and other indigenous groups most, strategies to uplift their status become necessarily discriminatory.

In table 5, an indication of the level and incidence of poverty in Peninsular Malaysia for 1970 and 1983 are given. Although poverty is a relative concept that changes over time, the structure of the incidence of poverty in Malaysia has changed little. For example, in 1970, when the New Economic Policy was about to begin, poverty was rampant in the agriculture (68 per cent), construction (37 per cent), and transport (37 per cent) sectors. Within the agricultural sector, the majority of the poor were rubber smallholders, paddy farmers, and estate workers. In absolute terms, the largest number of poor households was found in agriculture (74 per cent), and this is followed by the trade and services sector (14 per cent). Overall in 1970, nearly one-half of the households in Malaysia were defined as poor. Has the situation changed much in 1983, after 13 years of uninterrupted development and high rates of economic growth? Superficially at least, the incidence of poverty has declined, to 30.3 per cent. However, strict comparisons are not possible in view of the undisclosed figures for the compo-

TABLE 5. Incidence of poverty in Peninsular Malaysia 1970–1983 by economic sectors*

Sector	1970			1983		
	Total households (000)	Poor households (%)	Distribution (%)	Total households (000)	Poor households (%)	Distribution (%)
Agriculture	852.9	68.3	73.6	906.6	54.9	69.4
Mining	32.4	34.3	1.4	5.2	41.0	0.3
Manufacturing	150.2	32.3	6.1	222.2	12.6	3.9
Construction	35.0	36.6	1.6	38.0	13.7	0.7
Transport and utilities	74.1	36.6	3.4	92.3	15.6	2.0
Trade and services	461.4	23.8	13.9	1,106.4	30.1	23.7
Total	1,606.0	49.3	100.0	2,370.7	30.3	100.0

Source: Compiled from p. 163 of Third Malaysia Plan and p. 80 of Mid-Term Review of the Fourth Malaysia Plan.
*In Malaysia, poverty is officially defined in relation to an undisclosed poverty-line income which is adjusted annually for changes in the Consumer Price Index. Three major components are used in computing the poverty-line income, namely (a) food, (b) clothing and footwear, and (c) non-food components such as rent, transport, etc. The actual figures on these components are, however, not disclosed.

nents for the computation of the poverty line income.[3] In terms of profile, however, it appears that, owing to the massive injections of development funds and manpower into the rural economy, some slight improvements have occurred in the lives of poor farmers and other small agriculturalists. As the data show, in 1983 the percentage of poor households in the agricultural sector had fallen to 55 per cent. On the other hand, the number of poor households in the trade and services sector rose significantly, to 30 per cent, corresponding to the large increases in the population of the non–primary trade and services activities. The manufacturing sector recorded the lowest incidence of poverty. Thus between 1970 and 1983, the situation changed for the better in all sectors except the mining and trade and services sectors.

The policies to eradicate poverty in the agricultural sector essentially emphasized land and rural development, *in situ* development, or the provision of productivity-raising facilities and the dissemination of advanced knowledge relating to agricultural production. This will be elaborated upon in our discussion on agricultural development planning below. For the other sectors, especially the urban-based economy, the provision of greater job opportunities, housing, welfare, and health amenities constituted the major focus of public sector expenditures. As a result, the incidence of urban poverty fell from 25 per cent in 1970 to 11.1 per cent in 1983. The corresponding figures for rural poverty was 58 per cent for 1970 and 42 per cent in 1983.[4]

In the foregoing, we have highlighted and discussed some of the most important development planning issues of Malaysia. These ranged from the problems of poverty, economic diversification, commodity and trade dependence to unemployment, public investments, and ownership restructuring. Obviously, not all issues have been covered, as, for example, the growing national debt problem or the balance-of-payments problems. However, the discussions made so far will at least provide a good overview of the nature of the Malaysian economy and the difficulties Malaysians are facing. Similarly, too, this overview will serve to enhance the reader's appreciation of the many constraints that development planning will have to meet.

History and Nature of Planning in Malaysia

Malaysia has had quite a long experience with development planning. In fact, the country's experiments with macro-economic planning stretches back to the early 1950s, when the British colonial administrators drew up the Draft Development Plan of 1950–1955. To date, a total of seven development plans have been implemented, each spanning a period of five years. In addition to the Draft Development Plan, there were the First Malaya Plan (1956–1960), the Second Malaya Plan (1961–1965), the First Malaysia Plan (1966–1970), the Second Malaysia Plan (1971–1975), the Third Malaysia Plan (1976–1980), and the

Fourth Malaysia Plan (1981–1985). Incorporated within the Second Malaysia Plan is an Outline Perspective Plan 1971–1990, which mapped out the strategies of the government to alter the structure of the economy a well as to solve the socio-economic ills of the nation within a period of twenty years. The Fifth Malaysia Plan (1986–1990) was being drafted at this writing. For each of these plans, there were accompanying mid-term reviews, whose purpose is to assess the achievements and problems of each plan at the half-way stage of implementation. The first two plans were very simple documents which were mere aggregations of the annual budgets of the various government departments. The over-riding goals of these plans were to achieve balance between revenue and expenditures of the respective government agencies.

Over the years, however, the level of sophistication involving planning techniques and their application has increased considerably. For example, in the Second Malaya Plan, an aggregate Harrod-Domar (ICOR) model acted as the basis for estimating the investment required to achieve a certain target rate of output growth for the entire planning period. Although this planning model has its limitations, it represented at that time an improvement over the previous methods used; it was more objective and it enabled plan targets to be quantified.

The various plans employed common strategies to assist the economy to develop in the desired direction. These strategies included specifically the infusion of capital and advanced technologies, as well as improving the institutional structures throughout the economy. Further, efforts to inculcate attitudes that enhance productivity were stepped up. The diffusion of such resources was to be attained mainly through foreign trade, investment, and aid mechanisms. Besides these strategies, the development plans of the early 1960s and 1970s also stressed the need for integrating the rural sector with the modern sector, chiefly through advanced technologies from the developed nations. Thus, one central feature of the early plans is that they were all based on the notion of economic dualism and that only through the integration of the traditional, underdeveloped sectors with the dynamic, modern sectors would economic development and modernization in Malaysian society be attainable. Although it has been argued that this dualistic notion of the coexistence of a modern sector and an underdeveloped periphery is erroneous for Malaysia,[5] it nevertheless continues to be accepted by most Malaysian planners. Hence, it is possible to observe that in all the plans implemented to date, reference is always made to the existence of the low productivity, stagnant, and backward sectors or activities and the more organized, capital-intensive, and highly productive urban sectors. Further, the planners often perceive the existing dualistic whole as comprising a dominantly Bumiputra traditional sector and a predominantly non-Malay modern sector.

Basically, most of the plans implemented in Malaysia are of the "partial" or "indicative" type, whereby targets concerning the desired rates and quantum of economic growth, investments, savings, etc., are issued to the private sector through the plan documents. This is in spite of the fact that partial planning has two major limitations, namely the uncertainty of the private sector achieving targets and the non-concurrence of investments with desired social-political goals even if the targets are met.

As explained earlier, the Second Malaysia Plan incorporated a New Economic Policy because of the existence of widespread poverty and income and wealth ownership disparities between the Bumiputras and non-Bumiputras. The plan proposed that the inequalities be reduced drastically so that greater unity could be achieved. One of the ways to do this, apart from rural and urban development, would be to promote regional development rather than maximizing growth. Thus, whereas in earlier plan periods it was hardly mentioned, from the second Malaysia Plan onwards, regional development gave plans a new direction and impetus. The rationale for emphasizing regional development was to achieve closer integration among the various regions of the country as well as to achieve a more equal distribution of incomes. To supplement this strategy, four basic methods were relied upon by the planners; they include new-land or resource-frontier development, industrial dispersion, in-situ development in rural areas, and the creation of new growth centres. These strategies will be discussed in greater detail in later sections. Basically, the planning strategy's primary aim is to achieve higher rates of productivity by diverting growth to less developed regions. Because of its redistributive potential, regional development planning has been singled out as one of the best means to reduce the high degree of regional economic disparity in the country, and it is likely to remain as one of the most crucial instruments of planning.

When development plans were first introduced into the country, the principal objective of the colonial masters was to strengthen their own economic position, which had deteriorated considerably as a result of the Second World War. In the late 1940s and early 1950s, they also faced severe balance-of-payments difficulties, and one way of reducing this problem was to assist British investors to increase their exports so that they could repatriate greater sums of profits home. Hence, the priority of development planning in colonial Malaysia was the provision of good and sufficient infrastructural facilities such as roads, railways, electricity supplies, and other public sector investments that would favour the foreign-controlled economy. Increased social services such as health, educational, and welfare expenditures were accorded low priority, especially when, at that phase of development, the political threat from the communist insurgents was at its gravest. Thus it is not surprising that in the Draft Development Plan, more than 92 per cent of total development expenditures were spent on the economic services, whereas only 8 per cent of the budget went towards meeting social needs. The situation improved during the First Malaya Plan period, when social services were provided with a slightly higher (14 per cent) allocation of the development budget. Altogether, during the 1950s the priority of planning was on the provision of economic services and non-economic services that tended to favour the British investors, especially those in the rubber and tin-mining industries. Apart from this, the achievement of internal stability during an era of disruptive communist upheaval also acquired top priority.

By the 1960s, however, the government had taken more control over planning matters, and even though the highest possible rate of economic growth represented the government planners' top priority, a higher commitment to the eradication of poverty could be detected. Although the state continued to support the interests of the foreign capitalists and the growing class of local, overwhelmingly Chinese, entrepreneurs, it also committed itself more fully to the reduction of poverty among the rural Malay populace. The main vehicle for attaining this goal is the Federal Land Development Authority (FELDA), whose function is to open and develop massive tracts of land for the poor and landless. Connected to the land development programmes, extensive efforts were made in crop diversification, such that higher-income-yielding crops, such as oil-palm, were to be substituted for rubber. It was also in the 1960s that steadily rising proportions of public development expenditures were incurred for the provision of social services and education. Notwithstanding these policy shifts, the priority at this stage of planning still rested with the provision of good and adequate infrastructural amenities which will contribute towards higher rates of economic growth.

As far as the industrial sector was concerned, during both the 1950s and 1960s, the government did not participate directly in profit-making activities in the manufacturing sector. Private investments (especially foreign) were given strong encouragement in the form of a liberal range of incentives, from tax holidays, investment credits, to tariff and non-tariff protection, etc. With such generous public support, it was not surprising that the rates of growth achieved by the manufacturing sector, compared to other activities, were highest during the 1960s and early 1970s. But it must be pointed out that behind this façade of rapid growth lay certain weaknesses. For example, local economists[6] have pointed out that the industries engendered by the industrial strategies of that planning phase were often those with low value-added contributions, low-labour absorption capacities, negligible inter-industry linkages, and so on. Further, being mainly import-substituting industries, their potential for future growth was limited.[7]

In the aftermath of the severe race riots of 1969, it was apparent to planners that the time for an overhaul of development priorities had come. The relative neglect of the poorer strata of society, together with the higher incidence of interregional and interracial inequalities, forced the planners to direct more attention to these problems. Although rapid economic growth remained a top priority of development planning, it was made to share the limelight with the eradication of poverty and the reduction of interracial inequalities in income and wealth ownership. The growing disenchantment of the Malays and other

Bumiputras with their status, and the fact that the benefits of capitalist development have largely passed them by, pressured the policy-makers to make drastic
adjustments to the planning priorities. Instead of development for growth, the
philosophy of planning in the 1970s now became growth with equity, and this
has become the underlying rationale for all planning exercises in Malaysia
since.

Some background information concerning income inequalities may be useful
here. Between 1957 and 1970, the trend in income distribution was one of
increasing disparities. According to Snodgrass,[8] during this period there were
increasing income inequalities, whether measured in terms of household or personal income, or in terms of different ethnic groups and different regional strata
(rural or urban). Further, in spite of all the development efforts undertaken
since 1957, the Malay households continued to earn less than half of the total
income of non-Malay households. This evidence of rising income disparities
was also recorded in the study by Lim Lin Lean.[9]

Summarizing this section, it could be said that this phase of planning was one
in which the priority was the accelerated pace of injecting Malay participation
into modern economic activities in order to achieve greater unity amongst the
different races. As things stand at the moment, private sector enterprise and
initiative will be paramount, but public sector incursions will become increasingly more commonplace.

The Machinery for Development Planning

Before we set out to review the various development plans, some brief description should be made of the administrative machinery of planning and how it has
changed over the years in Malaysia. When the Draft Development Plan was
first drawn up, the planning and selection of projects rested basically with the
Treasury, although at that time the Economic Development Committee, under
the chairmanship of the colonial Economic Advisor, wielded considerable influence, especially when the choice of priority projects was involved. During the
First Malaya Plan period (1956–1960), the Treasury maintained control over
planning matters, even though during this phase of planning the Economic
Secretariat was the agency which actually drafted the plan, under the guidance
of an Economic Committee. This Economic Committee was in turn subordinate
to the Federal Executive Council, which was composed of all the ministers from
the ruling party and representatives of the colonial government. Thus, for this
period of planning, the Treasury's role was paramount, because all projects that
were proposed by the various departments operating under its auspices had to
be scrutinized by the top Treasury officials prior to their incorporation into the
plan. With the sort of financial prudence required under the early system, it was
not surprising that the targets of the early plans were modest and unambitious.

For the drafting of the Second Malaya Plan, a National Development Planning Committee (NDPC) took over from the Economic Committee the major responsibilities of formulating, budgeting, and evaluating plans. While in the latter the various ministries were represented, the NDPC members were usually the top civil servants from the ministries. The NDPC chairman was the secretary of the Treasury. It must be mentioned that prior to the formation of the NDPC, a Central Working Committee (CWC), comprising representatives from the financial and economic departments, was responsible for the drafting of the plan. At this time too, the influence of foreigners in plan formulation was still quite significant, as two "experts" from the International Bank for Reconstruction and Development (IBRD) were assisting members of the economic section of the CWC to look into technical aspects of planning. Following the upgrading of the CWC to the NDPC, the economic section was also expanded to become the Economic Planning Unit (EPU). The EPU itself was composed of top planning officials from the Treasury, the ministries of Agriculture and Education respectively, and the Central Bank, and it retains today its foremost position as the most important planning agency in the country. The EPU works very closely with other planning agencies, such as the State Economic Planning Units (SEPUs), the Socio-Economic Research Unit (SERU), and a host of other planning organizations. Beginning with the Second Malaysia Plan, the structural set-up of the planning machinery appeared as illustrated in figure 1.

The administrative machinery for planning in Malaysia has become increasingly complex. While only four departments or ministries were involved

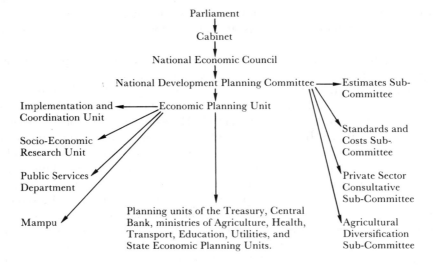

FIG. 1. Organizational structure of planning machinery in Malaysia

directly in plan formulation prior to the 1970s, under the present arrangement, almost all the planning units of key ministries are represented in the drafting stages of a plan. In addition, while the colonial administrators and their technical advisors were influential in the past, the control and influence has now shifted to local planners, including both politicians and bureaucrats. One other noteworthy feature of current planning practices is the inclusion of private sector representation in the form of the Private Sector Consultative Sub-Committee. Under the new planning scheme, the National Economic Council, which is made up of ministers under the chairmanship of the prime minister, first issues the directives on development policy. These are then acted upon by the various departments directly concerned with plan drafting and implementation. The plan proposals are then considered by the specific ministerial committees before the final approval is given by the cabinet and parliament. Within this hierachy, the EPU takes on the foremost position as far as co-ordination and presentation of issues and policies are concerned.

The EPU is located in the nation's capital and operates within the prime minister's department itself. Other agencies besides the EPU that undertake planning at the national level include the Malaysian Administrative Modernization and Manpower Planning Unit (MAMPU), SERU, and the Implementation and Coordination Unit (ICU). Some of the tasks of planning are also undertaken by the planning units of the Central Bank, the treasury, and key ministries (see fig. 1). Further, to co-ordinate planning activities between the various ministries, Inter-Agency Planning Groups (IAPGs) have become fashionable. At the state levels and parallel to the IAPGs are the SEPUs, whose major function is to co-ordinate planning activities carried out by federal and state governments, particularly with regard to the formulation and implementation of land development projects and other programmes in the respective states.

It might be mentioned that in the context of Malaysian development planning, foreigners have, for a long time, exerted considerable influence. In fact, one could identify three distinctive phases of planning in Malaysia in terms of the degree of foreign influence. These phases may be classified as the colonial phase, the phase of foreign (DAS/HIID, Development Advisory Services/Harvard International Institute for Development) consultants, and the phase of local planning. In the 1950s, the Draft Development Plan was almost entirely the conception of the British bureaucrats serving in the economic and financial secretariats. In that phase of planning, locals hardly had a role to play in the formulation of plans, except perhaps for the Treasury, which wielded ultimate control over the allocations for the various development projects proposed in the plans. Similarly, the First Malaya Plan was heavy with foreign influences in the form of IBRD experts' advice in the drafting of the plan. Subsequently, the Second Malaya Plan and First Malaysia Plan also had a substantial injection of American and Western European advice. Between 1964 and 1971, the Ford

Foundation, through the DAS of Harvard University, offered technical consultants to the EPU. These technical experts, besides advising the Malaysian government and its planning agencies on major aspects of industrial and agricultural planning, also invariably involved themselves in the activities of plan formulation or project identification at the EPU. Specifically, between 1966 and 1971, both the DAS consultants and other foreign advisors were deeply involved in preparing policy papers relating to all aspects of industrialization and trade. In fact, it has been estimated that roughly 50 per cent of the First Malaysia Plan was prepared by foreign consultants. As for the payment of these foreign experts, the practice then was for the Ford Foundation and World Bank to finance as much as 80 per cent of the expenditures incurred in the provision of such advisory services.

Since 1970, foreign control and influence in planning matters have diminished significantly, and local planners have now taken almost full control over the responsibilities of planning at both the state and national levels. In addition, following the usual bureaucratic set-up of many public sector bodies, there has been a rapid emergence and proliferation of planning institutions and agencies entrusted with plan formulation, implementation, monitoring, and evaluation.

A Review of Malaysian Development Plans — Their Objectives, Strategies, and Achievements

Draft Development Plan 1950–1955

The Draft Development Plan was an attempt to define the objectives of social and economic policy for the period 1950–1955, to balance them in relation to each other and to plan them within the range of the resources available to finance them. The plan itself was divided into four sections, covering social services, national resources and utilities, trade and industry, and a description of the sources of finance. However, the allocation of public development expenditures was very lopsided — 91.9 per cent was for the economic sector, serving colonial interests. Indeed, planning under the Draft Development Plan was determined mainly by the need to protect British interests in Malaysia, specifically in the plantation and mining sectors. Expenditures on social services programmes were negligible because they were regarded as being not productive. The preference was for public investment in sectors such as infrastructure that could enable the foreign investors to further enlarge their profits. Expenditure for agricultural development involved mainly the setting up of "new villages" for resettlement of the Chinese living on the jungle fringes so that supplies to the communist-led insurgents could be reduced. This was in response to the needs of the Emergency which threatened colonial interests. In total, the expenditures on defence and internal security took up a substantial portion (40 per cent) of all federal expenditure, totalling $M680.6 million during this period.

In terms of target fulfilment, the rate of success was obviously higher in the infrastructural and agricultural development sectors than in others, since so much priority had been accorded the former. Manufacturing industry was hardly supported in the Draft Development Plan. Overall, it can be said that the overriding concern for British welfare and British conservative fiscal policies in Malaya led to a very unambitious programme in the Draft Development Plan.

First Malaya Plan 1956–1960

The First Malaya Plan was based on a report of an IBRD mission which had come to Malaysia in 1954, at a time when the Emergency had reached its peak, to explore ways to accelerate the economic development of the country. The findings of this report indicated that Malaya already had a well-developed infrastructure for the export industries (mainly rubber and tin). The main recommendation of the report was that greater efforts should be channelled into developing the poor, and predominantly Malay, rural sector. Also, in view of the phenomenal growth of the synthetic rubber industry, the report recommended a massive replanting scheme in order for the rubber industry to increase its competitive edge.

The plan was a vast improvement over the Draft Development Plan in that it covered more comprehensively the problems and needs of all sectors of the economy. The plan supported the recommendation of the IBRD report on the rubber replanting schemes and the emphasis on rural development, and it also recommended that priority should be given to the oil and mining industries, as well as to industrial development. Infrastructural and agricultural development obtained the highest allocation of public expenditure (54 per cent and 23.6 per cent respectively). Financial assistance in the form of replanting subsidies on smallholder planting of rubber contributed to the rapid expansion of high-yielding acreage in the later years, thus enabling the commodity to be competitive in the world market. However, it must be mentioned that the subsidies handed out so generously during this period benefited the smallholders less than the foreigners who owned large estates. This was due to the fact that the estates, being larger, were able to replant in stages and thus reap more of the benefits of the replanting subsidies. Additionally, industrial investment, particularly private sector investment, was given a boost with the passing of the Pioneer Industries Ordinance of 1958. Notwithstanding the emphasis on the overall development of both the agricultural and industrial sectors, as reflected in a high, 98 per cent fulfilment, of set targets, the plan was dominated by the concern over the defence and security problems. Overall, a growth rate of 4 per cent for GDP was recorded for this period.

Both the Draft Development Plan and the First Malaya Plan were basically concentrating on capital formation in the public sector and were not based on any theoretical framework.

Second Malaya Plan 1961–1965

In contrast to the Draft Development Plan and the First Malaya Plan, the Second Malaya Plan, formulated with technical assistance from the World Bank, was theoretically more refined as it was based on the Harrod-Domar model. The plan was systematically organized, with objectives and strategies clearly spelt out. The plan document was presented in four separate chapters, with the first reviewing the progress made under the First Plan, the second outlining the problems and economic objectives of the present plan, the third describing the size of capital expenditure required, distribution of capital outlay, and intended results, and the last dealing with the methods of financing. The objectives of the Second Malaya Plan were to:
— improve the standard of living in the rural sector;
— provide more job opportunities;
— achieve an accelerated rate of economic growth;
— diversify agriculture activities and promote industrial growth;
— improve and expand the social services, including education, health, housing, and utilities.

To attain such goals, the government basically adopted a *laissez-faire* development strategy which unwittingly favoured the British interests and helped consolidate the position of the local businessmen, predominantly Chinese. There was minimum government interference, except to maintain a sound monetary policy to ensure rapid capital formation. Non-government interference was not the case, however, in the rural areas. Vigorous attempts were made to provide facilities to help raise the standard of living.

In general, the plan succeeded in achieving the established targets. Actual public development expenditure, for example, amounted to $M2,651.7 million, exceeding the target by over $M500 million. Of the 66.5 per cent of public development expenditure that went to the economic sector, 47 per cent was devoted to infrastructural development, 18 per cent to agricultural development, and 2.2 per cent to industrial development. Social services, including education, health, housing, and other services, were allocated 15.6 per cent of total expenditure. The balance was spent on public administration (6.3 per cent) and security (11.6 per cent).

In terms of specific objectives, the annual growth rate of output was 6.4 per cent, exceeding the targeted 4.4 per cent. Per capita income grew at 2.7 per cent annually, which was high by international standards. At the same time, the number of jobs created, at 344,000, was well in excess of the target. In the rural development programme, emphasis was placed on land development, rubber replanting, and drainage and irrigation. Land development expenditure surged from $M17 million during the First Plan to $M130 million during the Second Plan. This was during the period when FELDA first began to actively engage in land development schemes. From 4,300 hectares opened up in 1960, FELDA had developed more than 48,910 hectares by 1965. Apart from new land settlement schemes, substantial investment was also made in drainage and irrigation schemes to improve the productivity and income of farmers.

To reduce the dependence on rubber and tin, the government also embarked on a diversification programme which emphasized the planting of oil-palm. In the industrial sector, diversification was pursued mainly by adopting an import-substituting policy. Various incentives, including tax holidays and a protective tariff structure, were generously offered under the 1958 Pioneer Industries Ordinance. Import substitution had taken place only in a few sectors, such as cigarettes and tobacco, biscuits, soap, bicycle tubes, and cement. It was clear, therefore, that there were still ample opportunities to accelerate private investment efforts in import-substituting industries in view of the high level of demand for consumer goods.

First Malaysia Plan 1966–1970

The First Malaysia Plan was the first plan incorporating the development needs of East Malaysia since the formation of Malaysia in 1963. The plan itself was basically similar to the Second Malaya Plan in terms of planning techniques and objectives. Before the plan set out to list the objectives, it addressed itself to the main socio-economic problems, which were over-dependence on rubber and tin, a high rate of population increase, an uneven distribution of income, and a relatively low level of human resource development. The problems of population growth and disparity of income distribution had not been recognized in the previous plans, where the main emphasis was on economic growth.

In recognition of the undesirability of promoting economic growth based on the then twin pillars of the economy, rubber and tin, which were subject to price unpredictability in the world market as well as the problem of depletion of resources in the case of tin, the main strategy adopted in the plan was diversification of economic activities. The core of the economic programme of the plan was thus the promotion of traditional and new export opportunities, including rubber, tin, palm-oil, and timber, to stimulate domestic food production, specifically paddy, and, lastly, to exploit fully the possibilities of industrial production.

Agricultural diversification was to be achieved by the promotion of oil-palm planting, especially through FELDA-sponsored schemes, as well as increasing productivity in the rubber industry through improved methods. Industrialization was pursued vigorously with the aim of replacement of imported consumer goods by domestic production. Results in these two areas were satisfactory. By 1970, for example, about 92 per cent of estates and 63 per cent of smallholdings were under high-yielding rubber. Output of rubber increased 6.9 per cent annually. Similarly, output of timber and palm-oil increased significantly over the period, the former growing by an annual rate of 12.7 per cent and the latter by 24.1 per cent. Dependence on rice imports also diminished considerably, mainly as a result of better irrigation schemes. Manufacturing, on the other hand, grew by an annual rate of 10.4 per cent annually during the plan period. Substantial import substitution took place in foodstuffs, beverages, tobacco and petroleum products, cement, rubber and plastic goods, fertilizers, textiles, and steel bars. To complement the import-substitution policy, the plan also advocated an export-oriented industrialization strategy encouraging labour-intensive industries, notably electronics, to generate employment opportunities in addition to increasing export revenue.

The strategy to achieve the objective of redistribution of income and wealth was to provide better rural infrastructural facilities and to open up new land development areas. Here it must be noted that, beginning with the First Malaysia Plan, there was a tendency for the state to incur budget deficits in order to meet the massive public outlays on infrastructural facilities and development programmes in the rural sector.

In terms of target fulfilment, actual investment was $M8,204 million, or roughly 16 per cent below the planned investment levels. The shortfall in total private sector investment was slightly higher, at 18 per cent, despite the government's hope that the private sector would be the "engine of growth" for the economy. In comparison, government expenditure fell short by 7 per cent. Notwithstanding these shortfalls, the rate of real GDP growth was 6 per cent per annum, exceeding the target growth of 4.9 per cent per annum, due mainly to the fact that commodity prices did not decline as much as was expected. However, the number of job opportunities created fell short of the targeted 377,000 by 27,000. Consequently, the rate of unemployment went up from 6.0 per cent in 1965 to 8.0 per cent in 1970. This happened in spite of the fact that in 1968, in order to promote employment in the industrial sector, the Investments Incentives Act was legislated.

Second Malaysia Plan 1971–1975

The Second Malaysia Plan was formulated based on the overriding concern of national unity, an objective made more urgent in the aftermath of the civil disturbances of May 1969. With this plan, the government partially discarded its basically *laissez-faire* policy towards development and began to play a very active role in ensuring the achievement of objectives. Through the formulation of the National Economic Policy (NEP), the government sought to directly influence the rate and pattern of investment in order to eventually eradicate poverty and to restructure the Malaysian economy so as to eliminate the identification of race with economic functions. This process involved the modernization of the rural community, a rapid and balanced growth of urban activities, and the creation of a Malay commercial and industrial community.

In specific terms, the NEP, which was to be implemented over a 20-year period from 1971 to 1990, stated that, by 1990, at least 30 per cent of all corporate ownership of capital should be held by the Bumiputras and that employment by sector and at all levels should approximate that of the racial composition of the population, which was 54 per cent Bumiputras and 46 per cent non-Bumiputras. In implementing the NEP, a growth, rather than a redistributive, policy would be adopted. In other words, efforts to eradicate poverty and restructure society were to be undertaken in the context of an expanding economy rather than a stagnating one.

The goal of eradicating poverty was to be achieved by a strategy of increasing infrastructural development in the rural areas, establishing more land development schemes, and providing a wide range of free or subsidized social services. In the urban sector, programmes aimed at alleviating poverty took the form of greater public amenities, such as low-cost housing and utilities. To achieve the objective of restructuring society, the government participated directly by establishing entreprises for Bumiputras through such statutory organizations as PERNAS and MARA. The private sector, too, was expected to play a positive role and complement the government's efforts in achieving the objectives. Additionally, the rural sector would be modernized, regional imbalances corrected, opportunities for education provided to more Bumiputras, and urbanization stepped up.

At the macro level, GDP was expected to grow by 6.8 per cent annually, with planned investment at a level of $M12,150 million, of which public investment would amount to $M4,307 million. Public development expenditure was targeted at $M7,250 million and private development at $M7,101 million. Employment was projected to increase by 596,000 jobs, which meant an annual growth rate of 3.2 per cent. To help achieve this employment target, the Labour Utilisation Relief was introduced in 1971 to encourage greater employment in industries.

In evaluating the plan, it could be stated generally that reasonable progress was achieved in respect of the specific objectives of eradicating poverty and reducing economic imbalances. There was overall economic development in terms of growth and employment generation, despite the uncertainties of the international economic situation. GDP grew by 7.4 per cent per annum during the period, against the targeted rate of 6.8 per cent, although it fell short of the revised, mid-term review target of 7.8 per cent. The shortfall was attributed to the impact of the world recession of 1974/1975. The agricultural sector managed to grow by 5.9 per cent per annum, due mainly to the phenomenal growth of palm-oil (which registered a 24.7 per cent per annum growth rate), and remained the predominant sector in the economy. Transport and manufacturing grew by more than 10 per cent annually during the period. Economic growth during this period was largely the result of public investment and consumption, which also provided a counter-cyclical impact during periods of weak exports and private investment. In terms of employment, the number of new jobs created was 588,000, slightly short of the target. The rate of employment growth was highest in the manufacturing sector, which registered a rate of 6.6 per cent annually.

Insofar as the eradication of poverty is concerned, the strategies of establishing new land schemes, infrastructural development, and providing social amenities had taken their effect. The incidence of poverty dropped in the rural sector from 68.3 per cent in 1970 to 63.0 per cent in 1975. This decline in rural poverty was achieved at a price however, and it was in the form of an escalation in the public sector budgeting deficit. But, since the Malaysian economy was as yet still highly resilient and buoyant in view of the impeccable state of the nation's external finances, scant attention was paid by the government to the emerging fiscal problems. In the urban sector, where the strategies were to provide public services and greater urban employment opportunities mainly by stimulating the manufacturing and construction sectors, the incidence of poverty dropped from 21.3 per cent to 19.0 per cent. Unfortunately, the success in reducing poverty was accompanied by an increase in the inequality of income distribution, especially within the Bumiputra community.[10]

As a result of the restructuring policies of the government, which included preferential treatment of the Bumiputras in education, financial assistance in the form of easy credit facilities, training and advisory assistance, and so on, there was substantial improvement in the racial structure of employment as well as ownership of share capital. The percentage of employment of Bumiputras in all the main sectors increased considerably, and all the rates of growth exceeded the overall rates of growth of employment. Progress in restructuring ownership of share capital was somewhat slower. Nevertheless, the proportion of foreign holdings of share capital in the corporate sector declined from 63.3 per cent in 1970 to 54.9 per cent in 1975, with a corresponding increase in Bumiputra ownership from 2.4 per cent to 7.8 per cent. In terms of the non-corporate sector of modern agriculture, the Bumiputras increased their share of acreage from 13 per cent in 1971 to 19 per cent in 1973, reflecting the achievements of the land development programmes of FELDA, FELCRA (Federal Land Consolidation and Rehabilitation Authority), and other government agencies. During the early 1970s, the number of public sector enterprises (wholly or in joint-venture-ship with the private sector) that were established multiplied rapidly. A fair amount of these were trust agencies.

Third Malaysia Plan 1976–1980

The Third Malaysia Plan constituted the second phase in the implementation of the NEP and it therefore essentially continued with the same programmes initiated in the Second Plan to eradicate poverty and restructure the economy. Expecting increases in export demand up to 1978 due to world economic growth, the plan targeted a growth rate of 8.5 per cent per annum. In contrast to the Second Plan, when the public sector investment played the major role, the impetus of economic growth was expected to come from private sector investment in addition to the strong export demand. Direct government participation in investment through joint ventures with the private sector as well as wholly-owned public enterprises were also expected to play an important role. Of the total investment target of $M44.2 billion, 59.7 per cent was expected to be undertaken by the private sector, channelled mainly towards manufacturing and construction. An average 10 per cent annual growth rate was predicted. In contrast, 25.5 per cent of the public sector investment would be in the agricultural sector, and 36.5 per cent for infrastructural development. The manufacturing sector was expected to play a significant role in creating new job opportunities, thereby reducing the unemployment rate to 6.1 per cent in 1980.

In terms of target achievement, there was significant success in alleviating poverty. The incidence of poverty fell from 43.9 per cent to 29.2 per cent between 1975 and 1980. In the rural sector, it dropped drastically from 63 per cent in 1975 to 46.1 per cent in 1980. In comparison, urban poverty dropped from 19.0 per cent to 12.6 per cent. With regard to the restructuring objective, about 12.4 per cent of corporate capital ownership was held by Bumiputras in 1980, falling short of the targeted 16 per cent. However, in relative terms, the rate of growth of corporate ownership by Bumiputras and government trust agencies for this period was very high, accounting for 23.5 per cent and 39 per cent per annum respectively. Overall, approximately four-fifths of all development funds allotted by the government for commerce and industry during this period was for restructuring purposes. However, in view of the widening intra-ethnic income disparities, it is likely that the economic base for the Bumiputras created by public sector interventionist policies tended to affect those Bumiputras who had already become established in the circle of entrepreneurship. In terms of employment, total employment in 1980 was 4,816,900, exceeding the targeted number of 4,670,500. The unemployment rate was 5.7 per cent, which was better than the targeted rate of 6.1 per cent. In spite of this, however, the racial composition of employment did not meet the intended objective. By 1980, the Bumiputras were over-represented in agricultural and primary sector activities but were under-represented in the high-earning and skilled professions.

The economy, on the whole, achieved a growth rate of 8.6 per cent per annum, exceeding the targeted 8.4 per cent. As expected, the engine of growth came from private sector investment, which grew by 13.6 per cent over the period. In contrast, public sector investment grew by 9.3 per cent.

Fourth Malaysia Plan 1981–1985

The Fourth Malaysia Plan did not deviate from the long-term goals of poverty eradication and the restructuring of the economy as laid out in the Second Malaysia Plan. Despite an anticipated slow-down in the world economy at least until 1983, the plan predicted bright prospects for the economy, based in part on the nation's resilience and its strong resource base and its ability to maintain the tempo of growth through fiscal and monetary policies expected to be of a counter-cyclical nature. The private sector was again called upon to mobilize its resources and play a leading role in meeting the targets. The bulk of private investment would be in the manufacturing and the construction sectors. Expansion of manufacturing would be concentrated on resource-based industries such as rubber and timber, integrated production of the electronics industry, and the manufacture of ancillary products by the engineering industries. The agricultural sector, as usual, was accorded the highest priority. Also, surprisingly the government decided to establish and encourage the growth of heavy industries, spearheaded by the Heavy Industries Corporation, which is wholly owned by the government.

In specific terms, the GDP was projected to increase by 7.8 per cent per annum, considerably lower than that achieved in the previous plan. Domestic prices, which hitherto did not cause much of a problem, were a major concern in this period as the government strived to keep the increase within 6–7 per cent a year. About 860,000 new jobs were expected to be created during the period, thereby reducing the unemployment rate from 5.7 per cent in 1980 to 4.9 per cent by 1985. The manufacturing sector would continue to be a major source of growth and employment in the plan period, since it was expected to provide for 31 per cent of the total new employment.

In comparison with all the other development plans, the Fourth Malaysia Plan failed disappointingly. The uncompromising conclusion of the Mid-Term Review of the Fourth Malaysia Plan was that by the end of 1983 the plan had already spent 94.4 per cent of the allocated budget but had not achieved its targets. The economy was expected to grow by 7.6 per cent, but in the first three years, only a 6.2 per cent growth rate was achieved, although by international standards it was commendable. Employment grew by only 2.7 per cent per annum compared to the targeted 3.1 per cent; 34 per cent of the new jobs created came from the public sector. The overall incidence of poverty even increased slightly, from 29 per cent in 1980 to 30.3 per cent in 1983, an increase of 81,700 poor households. In restructuring patterns of employment, Bumiputras were still under-represented in manufacturing and commerce and other high-earning professional jobs. In terms of equity restructuring, Bumiputra owner-ship went up from 12.5 per cent in 1980 to 18.7 per cent in 1983, due mainly to acquisitions by government trust agencies. The domestic rate of inflation, however, rose more slowly than anticipated: it rose 4.3 per cent per annum instead of the expected 6–7 per cent per annum.

The private sector was expected to be dominant in investment and provide the catalyst for growth, but, due to the adverse effects of world recession, private sector investment was listless. The public sector was therefore forced to take up the slack, contributing 48.9 per cent of total investment by 1982 instead of the targeted 27.8 per cent.

The Mid-Term Review blamed the failure of the plan on the world-wide recession, which made the assumptions on which the plan was based invalid. The government, to counter the recessionary effects, adopted a counter-cyclical approach in spending, which worked remarkably well in the 1960s and 1970s. But this time around, the prices of all the commodities fell, rendering the government's diversification programme ineffective.

Following the alarming situation at the half-way point of the plan, the Mid-Term Review, instead of reviewing the progress of the economy, adopted a completely different approach. It focused on the structural problems of the econ-omy and suggested adoption of new strategies to ensure continued prosperity. In other words, it assumed the role of a plan itself. The review's basic points were that the economy had to break away from the dependence on government spending to spearhead growth, on exports to generate wealth, and on govern-ment subsidies to eradicate poverty. Public sector spending would be trimmed. The government would no longer increase public sector investment to support sluggish investment in the private sector. The private sector would be expected to contribute significantly to economic growth. The government would also aggressively promote the concepts of privatization and "Malaysia Incorporated." Under the Privatization and Malaysia Incorporation Programme announced in 1983, the government and private sectors would no longer be regarded as separate entities; they were to complement each other for the overall benefit of the nation. In keeping with these concepts, the government was to hand over selective public services and industries (e.g. television, telecommunication, public utilities) to the private sector. Also, civil servants could apply to move over to private sector employment. All these moves were to enhance the restruc-turing objective of the NEP. In specific terms, most of the original targets of the plan were considerably scaled down. The projected 7.6 per cent growth rate was revised to 6.7 per cent. With the adjustments, the review hoped that the econ-omy would return to fiscal discipline.

As table 6 shows, it is apparent that since the implementation of the NEP, considerable progress has been achieved in attaining the objectives of economic growth, reducing unemployment, restructuring society, and eradicating pover-ty. Although in the Fourth Malaysia Plan the counter-cyclical policies did not

TABLE 6. Summary of development plans since the implementation of the NEP

	SMP 1971–1975 (%)	TMP 1976–1980 (%)	FMP 1981–1985 (%)
Economic growth (GDP)			
Projected (% per annum)	6.8	8.4	7.6
Revised (Mid-Term Review)	7.8	8.3	6.7
Actual	7.4	8.6	6.2*
Unemployment rate			
Projected	7.5	6.1	4.9
Actual	7.6	5.7	5.8*
Bumiputra share ownership			
Projected	1.9	9.0	21.9
Actual	NA	12.5	18.7*

Incidence of poverty	1970 (%)	1975 (%)	1980 (%)	1983 (%)
Rural	68.3	63.0	46.1	41.6
Urban	21.3	19.0	12.6	11.1
Total	49.3	43.9	29.2	30.3

Sources: Second Malaysia Plan, Third Malaysia Plan, Fourth Malaysia Plan, and the respective Mid-Term Reviews.
*Figures for 1983

have their intended impact, the Second and Third plans generally performed satisfactorily.

System of Control and Monitoring of Planning Implementation

Effective plan implementation requires constant monitoring evaluation. In Malaysia, the responsibilities of monitoring the progress of plan implementation are undertaken by several government agencies. But to ensure coordination and implementation at the national and inter-departmental levels, the ICU (Implementation and Coordination Unit) — a unit within the prime ministerial department — is solely responsible. In addition, the ICU and the Treasury are responsible for monitoring the financial requirements and progress of all development projects. The ICU has computerized data storage and retrieval facilities which enable it to keep track of all the projects.

Amongst the various agencies involved in planning control, the National Operations Room was probably the most established and effective. Initiated during the Second Malaya Plan, this is a unique and remarkably effective technique for reporting and controlling operations related to development in Malaysia. In the

Operations Room are current, complete, and uniform reports on progress in public development programmes at the federal, state, and district levels. The Operations Room, equipped with the latest audio-visual and computer systems, keeps tabs on the project status relative to previously set targets. The information in the National Operations Room is kept up to date by the various ministries and departments, each being responsible for reporting its own activities, expenditures, successes, and problems.

At the state, district, and village levels, there are also Operation Rooms which are organized along similar lines. Each state, district, and village has its own Rural Development Committee, involved in the planning process, just as is true of the National Development Planning Committee at the federal level. The link between the village committee and the national committee is the "Red Book." Suggestions for development from the villages are passed on from the village headman (Penghulu) to the district officers, until they reach the national level. Discussions, negotiations, and amendments are made along the way. Approved large projects are then incorporated into the national development plans, while small projects at the village level (e.g. rural roads) termed "Red Book Plans," are implemented by the district officers with funds from the ministry.

The Operations Room technique was revamped and updated from the Third Malaysia Plan. New feedback techniques were introduced, especially with regard to problems and progress experienced by the less-developed states.

The successful implementation of any plan depends also on whether the public sector has the capacity and trained manpower to properly administer the implementation process. The shortage of skilled manpower which impeded the programmes of the Second Malaysia Plan, for example, was recognized, and in the Third Malaysia Plan, MAMPU (Malaysian Administrative Modernization and Manpower Planning Unit) was established (in 1977) to improve the administrative machinery and the process of manpower planning. New management techniques and innovations were developed to increase the effectiveness in the system of development implementation and decision-making at all levels of government. In addition to MAMPU, the National Public Administration Institute, known as INTAN, established in the Second Malaysia Plan, also expanded its training programmes in regional and project planning to upgrade the administrative capacities of the public sector for plan implementation.

An integral and essential part of successful planning and policy formulation is the evaluation of the impact of development planning, which then provides the feedback for planners. In Malaysia, evaluation is being done through the compilation and analysis of regularly collected and published statistics, as well as special surveys and research studies undertaken by the Socio-Economic Research and General Planning Unit (SERGPU). Many of these studies aim to assess the impact of development planning on the various socio-economic groups, particularly those in the lower income strata. SERGPU is also currently undertaking an in-depth study on the effectiveness of government policies, in particular, the NEP.

Besides SERGPU, INTAN, and EPU itself, other research agencies, for example the Rubber Research Institute of Malaysia, the Malaysian Agricultural Research Development Institute, the Palm-Oil Research Institute of Malaysia, the Institute of Medical Research, and the various universities, also undertake important research activities which contribute to a better understanding of the effectiveness of current development programmes and help provide a framework for improving the planning efforts.

All of these research efforts, and planning evaluation in general, call for the provision of reliable and timely data. The Department of Statistics, established during colonial times, bears the main burden of collecting, analysing, and presenting data to the various users. Since the Third Malaysia Plan, a National Integrated Data System, initially operating on a regional basis in Penang, has been developed as a data bank tailored to the needs of planning, monitoring, control, and evaluation of public and private sector development activities.

The achievement of the objectives and targets of the various plans obviously requires the close co-operation of the government, the private sector, and the general public. To obtain such co-operation, interaction between the government and the public is essential. Dissemination of information from the government to the public as well as the reverse, in the form of proposals and reactions to government policies, is accomplished mainly through the mass media. Besides the mass media, other channels which offer opportunities for suggestion are the parliament debates, the political parties, and voluntary organizations such as consumer groups, workers' and social groups. A Private Sector Consultative Sub-Committee was also established to provide a channel for consultation and suggestions for planning implementation. Consultation with the public also took place in the form of pre-budget dialogues held every year (since 1982) in which the Ministry of Finance and other government departments involved in annual budget preparation held separate sessions with various interest groups — for example, banking, industry, academics, consumer groups — to solicit their suggestions and opinions.

Another system of monitoring to ensure successful implementation of planned programmes were the various mid-term reviews of plans, employed since the First Malaysia Plan. (There was also an Interim Report of the Second Malaya Plan, undertaken in December 1963.) The mid-term reviews are usually assessments of economic progress. After taking stock of the economic performance, the reviews come out with a set of revised targets and recommend measures to achieve such targets. However, the Mid-Term Review of the Fourth Malaysia Plan was more than a mere assessment of economic progress. It was a complete revision of the plan, undertaken due to the adverse effects of the world recession on the Malaysian economy. The mid-term reviews, just as in the case of the original plans, are prepared by the EPU, with assistance on monitoring macro-economic performance drawn from the Treasury and the Central Bank. The performance of various sectors of the economy is also monitored through group discussions among officials from various agencies. Altogether, there are 12 inter-agency planning groups, one for each sector of the economy, with representatives from relevant ministries. Each session is chaired by the EPU, and discussions are usually comprehensive, covering methodology, strength and weaknesses of each sector, alternative strategies, and policy implications. Where necessary, EPU also holds more detailed discussions with private sector representatives of the various subsectors, for example, textiles, electronics, and others. Reviews prepared by the EPU are submitted to NPDC and, subsequently, to the National Planning Council (NPC), where senior ministers of the cabinet are present.

Sectoral Planning in Malaysia

Agricultural Development Planning

In line with the expected structural change in the economy, the relative importance of the agricultural sector in the country's economy has gradually been reduced over the last decade. This can clearly be seen from a comparison of its share in GDP, contribution to foreign exchange earnings, and employment in the 1970s and 1980s. Notwithstanding its declining relative importance, the sector nevertheless continues to play a dominant role in the economy and forms a major component in the overall development programme of the country. In view of the high incidence of poverty (for definition, see note to table 5) in the rural areas, the preoccupation with agricultural development is not only an economic necessity for the government but a political one as well. The main emphasis of the agricultural programme in the last 15 years, in line with the NEP, has been to increase the income of farmers through raising productivity levels, expanding employment opportunities, and creating a dynamic economic and social environment. This, in turn, is intended to facilitate the modernizing of traditional agriculture and eventually integrating it with the other sectors of the economy.

In view of this overriding concern, it is not surprising, therefore, that planning for the agricultural sector has been comprehensive and detailed, comprising numerous sectoral and planning programmes. Steps were taken by the various federal ministries, departments, and statutory bodies, which account for much of the work done on sectoral and project planning, to increase their effectiveness in formulating sectoral strategies and policies and in undertaking the identification, preparation, monitoring, and evaluation of projects. For instance, the Ministry of Agriculture undertakes sectoral planning on a continuous basis on the important crops, such as rubber, oil-palm, and cocoa. Similarly,ꞏ the Ministry of Lands and Regional Development is responsible for planning for the new land development schemes and *in-situ* development.

New Land Development Schemes

The new land development schemes form the most important sectoral planning strategy under Malaysia's rural development programme. It aims to create employment opportunities in the rural sector, thereby stopping the rural-urban migration flow, to increase farm productivity, and to produce viable farming communities. These schemes concentrate on the cultivation of commercial crops such as rubber, oil-palm, and cocoa. Such schemes are operated by public agencies such as FELDA, FELCRA, and RISDA (Rubber Industries Smallholders Development Authority), and fringe alienation schemes (land alienated for rural development), state government agencies, and joint-venture estates between the private sector and state governments (e.g. DARA, Pahang Tenggara Regional Development Authority), among others. An impressive result of these schemes, and FELDA schemes in particular, is that not only have they attained the objectives of creating employment, providing ownership of optimal-sized holdings and a capacity to earn higher incomes, but they have also developed technology and group organization through management inputs to raise efficiency and productivity up to the level of many private estates.[11] The efficiency in planning formulation, organization, and implementation resulted in a high rate of achievement, contributing greatly to the objectives of eradicating poverty and the redistribution of wealth. FELDA is the most important land development authority in Malaysia and is by far the most efficiently organized. Established in 1956 with the designated aims of clearing jungle areas for agricultural development and settlement, by the end of 1983 it had resettled 79,900 families and developed 477,874 hectares of land for the cultivation of commercial crops such as rubber and oil-palm. The cultivated acreage forms 41 per cent of the total land development under the various schemes. The FELDA schemes are very comprehensive. They reduce the pressure on the existing farming areas, resettle whole families, and provide them with economic-size holdings. A class of landowning farmers is created in this way. Settlers start repaying the FELDA loans only after the first harvest of their crops.

The success of the FELDA land development programmes led to the formulation of numerous other land schemes, with the main initiatives coming from the various state governments. A useful lesson that can be drawn from this sort of project planning is that programmes which hold the highest priority in terms of political, economic, and social necessities are able to extract full commitment in formulation, monitoring, and implementation, which in turn ensures success. This commitment is also a result of the fact that the approach is politically acceptable to all the major ethnic groups and interests. It is a more realistic and effective approach than a direct one, which would generate more strains on the various ethnic groups. Though the majority of the settlers are Malays, other groups, for example the Chinese, also benefit, since the emphasis on output provides more contracts and purchases, which are handled by Chinese. Another reason for the success of such planning techniques is that organization and control is centralized. Without a multiple number of agencies involved, formulation and implementation are smooth. Coupled with political necessities, the schemes hardly fail.

Notwithstanding the successes of the FELDA schemes, they are not achieved without some set-backs. Firstly, the cost of resettlement in the schemes is very high, due in part to expensive infrastructural and management development programmes. It is estimated that the average expenditure on each family settled in FELDA schemes was $M51,200 in 1983, and it continued to increase due to the greater remoteness of the areas, the increased cost of labour and other, general expenses. Secondly, the benefits accrue to only a small percentage of people. In relation to the number of peasants, the number settled in the schemes is insignificant. Thirdly, settlers joining FELDA schemes are not always landless peasants, and even if they already have land, they are not required to dispose of it before joining the scheme. As a result, the landless may be deprived of the opportunity to participate in the scheme. Fourthly, each individual state serves its own interests first; it resists accepting settlers from other states, giving preference to its own residents, even when these people already have land.

In-Situ Development Planning

While new land development strategies are significant in the agriculture sectoral planning programmes, *in-situ* development aimed at increasing productivity in existing depressed rural areas is given equal emphasis. *In-situ* development programmes are mainly in the form of specific project plans, referred to as Integrated Agricultural Development Projects (IADP). This type of project planning involves the provision of necessary infrastructure, inputs and service support, institutional development, extension and training facilities — all of which are integrated into a package focusing on the development of specific potential areas. By 1983, a total of 15 IADPs were being implemented, covering an area of about 847,500 hectares and expected to benefit 480,100 farm families. The success of the completed schemes is phenomenal, achieving income growth rates ranging from 23.6 to 197 per cent per household and productivity increases ranging from 23 to 103 per cent.

Other *in-situ* development programmes carried out by the various departments have not, however, been as successful. These include drainage and irrigation schemes, replanting and rehabilitation programmes, fisheries, and livestock and forestry development programmes.

Institutional Development

A third component in sectoral planning in agriculture is the provision and improvement of institutional facilities. These facilities include the training and extension programmes provided under the National Extension project and credit and subsidy schemes, offered by the Agricultural Bank. Agencies such as RISDA, MARDEC (Malaysian Rubber Development Corporation), LPN (National Paddy and Rice Authority), and FAMA (Federal Agricultural Marketing Authority) extend processing and marketing services to ensure stable and fair prices for the farmers.

Overall, it can be said that agricultural development planning has always been given prominence in the various five-year plans since the First Malaya Plan. Planning for this sector assumed a new sense of urgency in the aftermath of the civil disturbance of 1969, leading to the formulation of the New Economic Policy. Although considerable success has been achieved since then in land development schemes such as those of FELDA and *in-situ* development schemes such as the IADPs, there is still much to be done if the policy's targets are to be achieved by 1990. In view of the limitations in the agricultural strategies described above, a National Agricultural Policy (NAP) was announced in January 1984.

National Agricultural Policy

The National Agricultural Policy (NAP) was formulated to ensure a balanced and sustained rate of growth in the agricultural sector *vis-à-vis* the other sectors of the economy. The NAP, in the form of a 13-page Green Book, set out the principle for agricultural development up to the year 2000. The basic objective of the NAP was to maximize income from agriculture through the efficient utilization of the country's agricultural resources. To achieve this aim the current strategy, that is land development schemes, *in-situ* development, provision of support services and institutional development, would be continued, but modified and improved. The NAP proposed that agricultural sector activities would be grouped into two categories, food production and industrial crop production. For food production, the main emphasis was to be on rice, while for industrial crop production, the cultivation of oil-palm, cocoa, and tobacco was to be encouraged.

The NAP identified the constraints facing the agricultural sector as follows:

1. Current agricultural policies are too commodity-oriented and are independent of one another and lack co-ordination.
2. Holdings are of uneconomic size, producing crops that yield low returns.
3. Traditional methods of production are restrictive and of low productivity.
4. There is inadequate access to assistance and support services.

5. There is a shortage of labour, leading to abandonment and under-utilization of cultivable land and the need to import workers from neighbouring countries.

The NAP was formulated because planners recognized that existing approaches to agricultural planning lacked co-ordination among the numerous ministries, departments, agencies, and state authorities involved. Also, a lack of flexibility in the approach resulted in non-responsiveness to world market conditions. Being a long-term comprehensive policy, the NAP aimed to remove the constraints of the present short-term agricultural policies and thus help revitalize the sector.

The NAP was first proposed in 1974, and its announcement 10 years later was a real disappointment. The main architect of the policy, the Ministry of Agriculture, had prepared a 700-page draft containing all the facts and figures. Hacking it down to a 13-page booklet gave the impression that piecemeal plans regarding crops and problems had just been lumped together without any co-ordination. In any case, the NAP did not address the important issues concerning the viability of the agriculture sector, its linkages with other sectors, poverty eradication, and problems relating to the availability of land. Problems regarding the sector as a whole and objectives of the policy were spelt out, but it offered no new ideas and failed to grapple with the causes of poverty and declining growth. Instead, it recommended the current practice of *in-situ* development and land development schemes be continued. It also failed to mention the overlapping jurisdiction of the different ministries and myriad agencies concerned with agriculture and how they could be co-ordinated.

Added to the policy's extreme brevity, it was drawn up without any extensive discussions with the private sector or other interest groups. Without such participation and the accompanying support information, the NAP can, in all aspects, be considered a bad case of planning.

Industrial Development Planning

Industrial development planning has generally been recognized as being remarkably successful since it was first mentioned in the Second Malaysia Plan. In 1957, the manufacturing sector, which consisted largely of the processing of estate-type agricultural products in factories, contributed only 8 per cent of GDP. By 1984, however, its share had risen to 18.6 per cent, only slightly lower than the 21.1 per cent GDP share of agriculture. In the decade of the 1970s, manufacturing output grew at a phenomenal annual rate of 12.5 per cent. This was a result largely of the implementation of several policy measures which, favourable to industrial development, aimed at bringing about major structural changes in the economy. Soon after independence, the government began to pursue and implement its industrialization programme in earnest through an import-substitution policy. Various tax incentives and an elaborate system of tariffs were implemented to protect the local industries. Toward the end of the 1960s, it was realized that import substitution, as a source of growth, could not expand indefinitely (especially in a small developing economy such as Malaysia's).[12] It was also apparent that the import-substituting policies did not fulfil the objective of employment creation with great success, although it generated substantial growth.

In view of the above, the government subsequently embarked on a policy promoting export-oriented industries, particularly industries that use labour-intensive methods of production. Exporters of manufactured foods were accorded special incentives in terms of tax grants, subsidies, and other credits. Free-trade zones were established in many regions of the country, the most successful of which was in the Bayan Lepas area in Penang, where the electronics factories had, by 1983, become the world's leading exporters of electronic components — especially integrated circuits and microchips. The policy measures in the 1970s continued to actively encourage private foreign investments to stimulate growth in the sector. The task of identifying and implementing manufacturing projects was left to the private sector, while the government was responsible for the provision of the basic social and economic infrastructures. Apart from rapid growth and expansion within the sector, the policies that continued into the Fourth Malaysia Plan were expected to help solve problems related to unemployment, rural-urban migration, industrial concentration in specific areas, and regional economic disparities. Other major objectives included achieving the NEP objectives, dispersal of industries, diversifying the manufacturing base, promoting high-technology precision-based industries, small-scale industries, and establishing heavy industries.

In evaluating the industrial policies, a striking feature is the government's firm commitment to free-entreprise principles that left industrial development in Malaysia determined largely by market forces and reasons of comparative advantage. Planners and policy-makers set out broad policy objectives without exerting much effort to organize and promote specific industrial sectors. It was up to the private sector and foreign investors to decide the sort of industries they would like to invest in. In the early stages of industrialization, it was mainly the foreign manufacturers who made the investments; some had the objective of maintaining their share of the market by their own foreign firms which had been exporting to Malaysia, while others wanted to take advantage of the various incentives and the cheap labour. Local investors, on the other hand, tended to be cautious about investing in manufacturing industries, preferring to engage in retail trade, plantation industries, or property development.

The large inflow of foreign capital in the earlier years enriched the economy. However, following the implementation of the NEP, the liberal policies pertaining to foreign investments were scaled down. Although there is still a need for foreign capital and technology, preference is now given to those that would help establish resource-based export-oriented industries. A direct result of the practice of *ad-hoc* industrial policies in the past has been the narrow base of the sector. More than 60 per cent of Malaysia's export earnings from manufactured goods were contributed by the electronics and textile industries. There was, therefore, an urgent need to expand and diversify the manufacturing base in order to sustain the sector's growth.

Insofar as policy implementation is concerned, the agency responsible for the promotion and co-ordination of industrial development is MIDA (Malaysia Industrial Development Authority). It also functions as an advisor to the Ministry of Trade and Industry on the formulation of industrial policies to be included in the development plans. In addition, it undertakes feasibility studies of industrial possibilities. It provides facilities for exchange of information and also acts as the co-ordinating agency among institutions engaged in industrial development. Evaluation of applications for pioneer status, for tax exemptions from local and foreign investors is also dealt with by MIDA.

The Industrial Master Plan (IMP)

In an effort to have a comprehensive industrial policy to ensure continuing growth in the industrial sector, the IMP was, at this writing, in the process of being drawn up, having first been initiated in 1982. This plan, undertaken by MIDA with assistance from the United Nations Development Programme, will form the basis for industrial policies in the Fifth Malaysia Plan and in plans up to the year 2000. The IMP will cover in detail the sectoral and subsectoral activities that will optimize the allocation of resources and ensure an efficient linkage between sectors and a more balanced industrial growth among regions. In particular, the plan will identify small industries for implementation. The examples of Japan and Korea, where industry was supported by small industries, will serve as a model for promoting small-scale industries in Malaysia. Emphasis will also be given to export promotion, as well as to development of a second round of import substitution and heavy industries, which is a departure from the previous policies of import replacement of consumer goods.

Sectoral studies related to the plan include food processing, palm-oil, rubber, wood, metal, chemicals, pharmaceuticals, machinery, transport equipment, shipbuilding, building materials, electronics, and textiles. With such studies, the plan will identify which industries have potential for growth and which are declining. This information will help investors decide where to invest. The plan is also to include policy options, technological needs, and projected manpower requirements, related administrative, social, and economic infrastructure, the role of research and development, and raw material resources.

In ensuring the successful implementation of the IMP, the mistakes which occurred in drawing up the NAP should not be repeated. Private sector inputs should be solicited before actual implementation takes place. As it is, the planning of the IMP was done primarily by Korean and Japanese planners, with only a few local planning agencies involved.

Constraints and Issues of Planning in Malaysia

The preceding sections have brought to light several issues of planning under Malaysian conditions. First and foremost, the political and socio-economic realities have set some constraints on the direction of planning objectives and implementation. Secondly, planning in Malaysia takes place under conditions of great uncertainty, mainly because of its large external sector. World economic conditions have a significant impact on the success or failure of any planning strategy. Thirdly, in view of having to operate under uncertainty, a major issue would concern the capability of planners to adjust to change. Another issue concerns the lack of control over cost effectiveness of programmes in the public sector. Lastly, the planners should also be concerned with the issue of integrating research and technology into the planning process.

Political and Socio-Economic Effects on Planning

The political and social realities of the society in terms of the disparity among the various ethnic groups have had a heavy influence on Malaysian planning since the Second Malaysia Plan. Prior to the Second Malaysia Plan, the plans were basically formulated on free-enterprise principles, which tended to favour and promote capitalists' interests, that is, the large estate plantations, which were mainly foreign-owned. There were government attempts at promoting rural development of course, but they proved to be fairly ineffective. However, the civil disturbance of 1969 changed the whole premise of planning in Malaysia. The formulation of the NEP, which aimed at eradicating poverty and restructuring society, represented a new chapter in planning. Planning was now based on growth with redistribution and not on growth alone.

In the drive to achieve the objectives of the NEP, however, a number of strategies — strategies based on the principle of optimal utilization of resources — were not implemented. For example, the numerous land development programmes aimed at providing land and resettlement for landless peasants, thus raising their standard of living, did not really solve the existing structural weaknesses of the agrarian economy. The FELDA scheme, the most prominent land scheme in the country, had become too rigid and expensive. As a result, the number of peasants settled in FELDA schemes was — and is — insignificant relative to the total number of landless peasants in the country.

In the corporate sector, where the Bumiputras are expected to own 30 per cent of equity by 1990, present policies may not be able to achieve the target.

The low income of the Bumiputras and their consequent low prospensity to accumulate capital has meant that most of the equity shares intended for Bumiputras has not been taken by private individuals but have had to be held in trust by statutory bodies. Thus, the restructuring exercise appears more in terms of Bumiputra trust agencies than of Bumiputra individuals. Such political and social considerations have undoubtedly had a profound impact on the effectiveness of planning in Malaysia. For this reason, economic planning concepts and implementation measures and strategies are always interlaced with non-economic factors. Similarly, past implementation strategies and measures are rarely evaluated by means of a strictly economic yardstick. A good example is the Fourth Malaysia Plan. It was mentioned earlier that by the end of the first three years of the Fourth Malaysia Plan, 94.4 per cent of the total allocation for public development expenditure had already been exhausted, almost all of which was financed out of external and domestic borrowings. As a result, Malaysia's external debt of \$M37 billion by the end of 1984, equal to almost 51.7 per cent of GNP, had become a serious problem. The large foreign borrowing and high spending to finance the development projects under the plan for the first three years were blamed squarely on the counter-cyclical public sector policies during this period, a period that is now defined as a structural world recession. Yet, even when the Fourth Malaysia Plan was first written, UN agencies, such as the World Bank, had already noted the impending recession as structural, but the planners did not seem to take notice. Nevertheless, counter-cyclical policies per se were not at fault, rather, it was the application of such policies to structural problems that was inappropriate. It is apparent that the pressures of the NEP objectives of eradicating poverty and restructuring society had resulted in increased allocations and spending based on counter-cyclical policies, leading to an amassing of a large foreign debt.

In seems at times, too, that planning policies are really not analysed carefully in terms of economic benefits and cost. Political considerations and nationalism appear to be the over-riding determinants. The establishment of the Heavy Industries Corporation of Malaysia (HICOM) is a case in point. Despite the numerous criticisms as to the wisdom of including projects in heavy industries, (such as the Malaysian Motor Car Project, criticized in terms of economies of scale, inadequate skilled manpower, etc.), the government has proceeded with such projects, knowing full well that they are not going to help reduce the growing deficit problem.

The preceding observations suggest that inputs and views from the private sector as well as other interested parties, for example, academicians, consumer groups, etc., which are often solicited through the Private Sector Consultative Sub-Committee on national planning or the annual pre-budget dialogues, are not necessarily taken into account. Targets drawn up for the private sector often do not conform to the preferences or tendencies for investment of the private sector and are thus unrealistic and unattainable. For example, the National Agricultural Policy and the Industrial Master Plan, which are supposed to lead the economy into the next century, have been roundly criticized for not having sufficient private sector input in their formulations. The government should allow the private sector more say in the planning process. Consultations should be carried out right up to the time the plans are being finalized.

Planning Methodologies under Uncertainty

Tracing the planning techniques used in development planning in Malaysia revealed that in the first two plans rudimentary techniques were used. These plans were basically programmes for public sector development, formulated without worry about internal consistency. Also, there did not appear to have been any attempt to estimate the investment requirements of either the private or public sectors to meet target levels of income and employment.

The next two plans, the Second Malaya Plan and the First Malaysia Plan, utilized the basic Harrod-Domar model to estimate the level of investment required to achieve predetermined target growth rates.

Although the actual results obtained from these two plans were satisfactory in relation to the targets, they were achieved not by virtue of accurate predictability of the plans based on the classic Harrod-Domar model. The use of such a model in planning is quite irrelevant for a country such as Malaysia, which has a large export sector and which is subject to a high level of uncertainty. The model assumes a given incremental capital-output ratio. But in Malaysia, as in many other developing countries, technology changes so rapidly that it is impossible to have a constant incremental capital-output ratio. The forecasting capability of a plan thus formulated would leave much to be desired. But, fortunately for the two plans that were based on this model, the error in forecasting was unimportant as the actual performance exceeded the targets.

No mention of the Harrod-Domar approach was recorded in the subsequent plans. To cope with the problem of uncertainty caused by a large external sector, the government invariably implemented counter-cyclical policies to offset the slack in private investment due to poor external demand. Thus, for example, in the Third Malaysia Plan, the first two years were marked by a slow growth in private investment due to weak export growth, but economic growth was sustained through increased public investment and consumption. However, as was explained in the previous section, counter-cyclical policies do not work if the underlying cause of the world recession is structural rather than cyclical, and, in this case, the nature of the problem necessitates a strategy of stimulating private sector investments instead of compensatory public investments on a large scale.

Capacity of Planning for Adjustment

In spite of the seemingly well-organized structure of control on planning formulation and implementation, in reality co-ordination efforts among the different planning agencies left much to be desired. There are just too many agencies involved in the planning process — departments, agencies, statutory bodies, ministries, state and district development agencies, economic boards, and more. There is too much duplication. On paper, the Economic Planning Unit and the Implementation and Coordination Unit are in charge of co-ordination to ensure that policies are properly implemented. But the task of ensuring that the juris-dictions of the myriad agencies do not overlap is immense. As a consequence, planning in Malaysia suffers from inflexibility and cannot respond quickly to changing economic conditions.

This inability partly accounts for problems such as accumulating external debts and over-spending of public allocations. The rigid approach in planning is also borne out by the impossibility of the system to transfer funds originally allocated to one agency or department to another agency which has more press-ing needs. For example, funds allocated to the Public Works Department could not be transferred and used for waterworks, even though the needs for the latter were more pressing. In the face of a global recession, this sort of inflexibility could hamper development efforts.

Inefficient Costing of Public Sector

The inflexible approach mentioned in the preceding paragraph is also partly a result of the lack of consciousness of cost effectiveness in public agencies. A perennial public sector problem is that its departments and agencies are not functioning as operational cost centres. Against the cost of funds going into projects, the costing of benefits from the projects is poor. In other words, there is a lack of financial discipline and a cost-conscious approach in the implementa-tion procedures. The inefficient costing approach has led to the fast-growing rate of borrowings, not only in the normal government departments and agencies but also in the off-budget agencies, which contributed more than one-fifth of the nation's total foreign debt. There is an urgent need to extend the authority of the auditor-general to scrutinize the accounts of the off-budget agencies, which have hitherto been outside his purview.

Integration of Technological Change in Planning

One of the integral components of planning for rural development in Malaysia is the introduction of modern technology to replace traditional farming, to in-crease productivity and, consequently, income levels. In this regard, however, it has failed in its objective, for, as stated elsewhere in this paper, the incidence of poverty in the rural sector is still very high and, in fact, increased during the period 1980–1983. The problem of technology development in the rural sector is that it may increase productivity, but this is not reflected by rising income levels, especially during the last few recessionary years, when price declines tend to offset any gains in profits due to enhanced productivity. Thus, price fluctuations are more important in the determination of income changes than productivity. This is especially so for poor rural groups such as the paddy farmers, fishermen, rubber smallholders, and estate workers. In the estate sector, the situation is not as bad. Any increase in income due to rising productivity as a result of increased mechanization is reflected in the gains in profit of the corporations controlling the estates.[13] In cases of worker demands for higher wages, the government has tended to side with the estate management, which claims that higher labour costs would erode the competitiveness of the products in the world market. Consequently, estate workers received income not commensurate with their productivity.

Technology development may have led to another problem: the declining employment opportunities for the small farmers, resulting in significant rural-urban migration. The rural sector, which employed more than 50 per cent of the working population in 1970, now employs only 30 per cent. Obviously, other factors need to be considered to complement technology development so that both higher productivity and higher income are achieved.

As stated earlier, the industrialization programme has resulted in a narrow base of the manufacturing sector, dominated by the electronics and textiles industries, which, unfortunately, use low levels of technology. It was estimated that in 1984, whilst exports of integrated circuits was $M4 billion, value added amounted to only $M400,000. It is hardly surprising, as the electronics industries in Malaysia were more concerned with assembling of parts than manufacturing. To compound the problem of a low technology level, the capacity of the sector to absorb and adapt foreign technology is also grossly underdeveloped. There is, therefore, an urgent need for rational planning to build up indigenous industrial technology to complement the fairly adequate technology in the agricultural sector. The government should identify research and development projects for future opportunities and for allocating resources to anticipate, counter, or integrate competitive technological innovations and advancement.

Vital to the ability to absorb rapidly changing technology is the need to have a good system of economic data collection and dissemination. This is sadly lacking in Malaysia. As the planners of the Industrial Master Plan complained, the importance of economic data is not fully appreciated.[14] There is little creation, distribution, and consumption of up-to-date information, although so essential to ensure successful planning and implementation.

Policy Suggestions and Conclusions

In the foregoing section the crucial issues of planning in Malaysia have been put forth. These issues are not easy to resolve, especially in view of the fact that in multiracial Malaysia, planning is not dictated by economic principles alone.

Concerning the issue of the predictive capacity of macro-economic planning in Malaysia, it is necessary to reduce the margin of error in forecasting. This is especially so in a situation where the external sector is significant. We have suggested that one way to achieve a more precise forecasting capability is to shorten the period of the various development plans to a more manageable three-year period. A shorter period is more suitable as it is more definite and lessens the degree of inconsistency between planned targets and achievements. Perhaps the planners could choose a three-year ruling plan with detailed annual reviews — the way planning is usually done in a big private corporation. The current practice of holding pre-budget dialogues annually with the private sector, interest groups, academicians, and so on, could be exploited so as to provide a source of input to the annual reviews. In addition, this method of shorter-term planning would be consistent with the concept of Malaysia Incorporated. For indicative purposes, it would be possible to retain a long-term planning device, such as one covering seven or more years. The present system of reviewing development plans at their mid-points is not effective, as is shown by the Mid-Term Review of the Fourth Malaysia Plan.

The effectiveness of short-term planning as proposed above could also be enhanced by adopting a more rigorous approach based on sectoral planning. The formulation of the recent Industrial Master Plan is a step in the right direction.

Concerning the problem of the lack of co-ordination among the numerous bodies involved with either plan formulation or implementation, theoretically there already exist various systems of control and monitoring. In reality, however, co-ordination breaks down regularly somewhere along the line. The Implementation and Coordination Unit is the premier co-ordinating agency, but, because of the myriad agencies involved at the district, state, and federal levels, it faces enormous problems in co-ordination. In announcing the National Agricultural Policy in 1984, the deputy prime minister admitted to this problem of co-ordination but offered no effective solutions. What can be done then to streamline the co-ordination efforts to improve planning efficiency?

One possible way would be to restructure the whole organizational machinery of planning. Considering the huge number of agencies involved, perhaps it would be necessary to use a system of decentralization, instead of the current system of the ICU co-ordinating each and every agency. There is also the need to re-examine the amount of duplication of efforts in the different agencies. Obviously, with less duplication in the work of planning agencies, co-ordination efforts will be facilitated, apart from achieving substantial savings on public expenditure. At the moment, Malaysia supports more than 880,000 public servants, and, given the relatively small size of the total population (15 million), it is indeed a very heavy burden for the nation to bear. For every dollar that the government spends, 46 cents go towards paying the public servants, and it is logical that such a situation must be remedied. The ongoing privatization programme involving major government agencies such as the Telecoms Department will certainly help reduce the heavy burden of supporting the huge public sector. Such programmes should be intensified.

With regards to the rigidity in planning, by which funds allocated to one agency are not transferable to another, even though needs in the latter are more pressing, the government has now decided to adopt a more flexible approach. It has been announced that under the new approach, funds will be freely transferable between agencies, depending on priorities. This new measure came into being because it was found that in the past many agencies were embarking on low-priority projects because funds were freely available, while those which had viable projects failed to implement them because of the lack of funds. In such circumstances, they invariably turned to borrowing — mainly from external sources. Cost-effectiveness of projects was seldom the guiding principle of investment spending. Here the auditor-general's office should be expanded so that there will be sufficient manpower to scrutinize expenditure of the numerous agencies.

Planning as is practised in Malaysia has never had much in the way of built-in checks and balances to ensure the efficiency of the public sector. There are numerous examples of inefficiencies and financial losses incurred by the state economic development corporations and other public sector agencies, as well as uncontrolled spending by off-budget agencies (e.g. Petronas, UDA, etc.). The solution evidently lies with more stringent controls on spending. The purview of the auditor-general's office has recently been extended to cover also the OBA's off-budget agencies. In this connection, it could be noted that the move towards greater privatization could help to reduce the problem of public sector inefficiencies. This is by virtue of the fact that privatization involves a motive of profit, thus ensuring that projects are cost-effective.

Regarding the critical issue of planning under conditions of uncertainty, in a country such as Malaysia, where external shocks arising from changing world-market conditions are inevitable, some of the proposals suggested above will help, to a certain extent, alleviate this problem. While it is not possible to totally eliminate conditions of uncertainty, countries such as Malaysia may be able to reduce them significantly by adopting the following policies:
— promote import-replacement of goods, for which Malaysia has comparative advantages
— upgrade and broaden the service sector in order to improve the balance-of-payments position
— expand local markets for agro-based products as well as manufactured products

In Malaysia's case, a start has been made to expand the local market by promoting the "Buy Malaysian Campaign."

These measures would help to reduce the over-dependency of Malaysian production on world markets and would therefore facilitate planning. However, given that uncertainty is still a major constraint, solutions in addition to those proposed above must be sought.

The Malaysian government has admitted that the piecemeal results of current policy planning could impair domestic production and investment and incur heavy external debt. One suggestion to help erase the uncertainties of economic planning is to use detailed indicators as the basis for fiscal and monetary policies. With better indicators, evaluation of projects will be facilitated. For example, the country has to make a choice between foreign debt and equity participation and any decision made as well as any strategies implemented should be based on precise indicators. The relationship between plan formulation and end results would then be clearly established. In this regard, the cabinet has recently recommended an economic review using this approach to erase uncertainties in planning.

The lack of participation in the planning process of the private sector and interest groups also increases the element of uncertainty in planning. The current practice of soliciting input for planning formulation through the Private Sector Consultative Sub-Committee is apparently not sufficient. Either the planners have not taken into consideration the private sector preferences in investment decisions or government priorities have been ignored by the private investment decisions that are based more on business instructions. Private sector involvement should therefore be carried right up to the point when a macroeconomic plan is finalized. In this connection, the Industrial Master Plan, touted as a dynamic sectoral plan, still fails to measure up as far as private sector participation is concerned.

On the problems associated with technology development in the rural sector, one of the ways to alleviate such problems is to increase efforts directed to the production of crops for local consumption, thereby reducing the overdependence on export crops which are subject to volatile price fluctuations. Also, as rising income arising from productivity increases tends to be restricted to the well-planned land development schemes, there is an urgent need for wider participation in such schemes. Provision of economic-size landholdings should also be made to the rubber smallholders and other poor farmers, so that costs of production can be reduced through economies-of-scale and productivity increases.

On the issue of accommodation of industrial technological change in the planning process, the problem has now been recognized. Plans are being drawn up to set up several infrastructural projects to upgrade technological development and also bring about closer co-operation between the public and private sectors in research and development. Such projects include setting up various technology resource centres to promote industrial diversification, a technology transfer centre, which would be a source for technological information as well as to determine the suitability of foreign technology, and, lastly, a national centre for computer assisted design and manufacturing, which would train and provide facilities to the private sector. These are all in the planning stages and hopefully the qualified professionals from the industrial sector will be requested to participate actively to ensure sound planning and implementation.

In this paper, an attempt has been made to examine the nature of planning in Malaysia and the issues arising therefrom. In analysing the process of planning, it is evident that political factors, more than any other, exert the greatest influence. The National Economic Policy was formulated as a result of such political constraints, and the pursuit of priorities as stipulated by the NEP have determined the course and pattern of planning policies. As a result, planning in Malaysia is not based totally on economic concerns (which is usually the case in most developing countries with a monolithic culture). However important the political motive for planning is, it cannot isolate itself from the financial constraints caused by external uncertainties.

Despite having to face various constraints, planning in Malaysia has enabled the country to achieve one of the highest standards of living in the developing world. Recent attitudes toward planning in the government indicate the adoption of a more pragmatic approach, which will serve to enhance the effectiveness of planning.

Notes

1. M. Kulasingam and Tan Siew Ee, *Changing Patterns of Foreign Investments in Malaysia: Determinants, Issues and Implications*, Discussion Paper Series, School of Social Sciences, Universiti Sains Malaysia (Penang, 1982), p. 23.
2. ESCAP/UNCTC, *Transnational Trading Corporations in Selected Asian and Pacific Countries* (Bangkok, ESCAP, 1985), p. 266.
3. Zainal Aznam Yusof, "Poverty and Poverty Eradication Policies," in K. S. Jomo, ed., *Malaysia's New Economic Policies* (Kuala Lumpur, Malaysian Economic Association, 1985), p. 53.
4. David Lim, "The Political Economy of the New Economic Policy in Malaysia," in David Lim, ed., *Further Readings on Malaysian Economic Development* (Kuala Lumpur, Oxford University Press, 1983), p. 16.
5. Shamsul A. Bahruddin, "Theoretical Orientations of the Second Malaysia Plan," in Cheong Kee Cheok et al., eds., *Malaysia: Some Contemporary Issues in Socio-economic Development* (Kuala Lumpur, Malaysian Economic Association, 1979), p. 6.
6. David Lim, *Economic Growth and Development in West Malaysia 1947–70* (Kuala Lumpur, Oxford University Press, 1973), p. 153.
7. Fong Chan Onn and Lim Kok Cheong, "Investment Incentives and Trends of Manufacturing Investments in Malaysia," *The Developing Economies*, 23 (December 1984): 417.
8. Donald R. Snodgrass, *Inequality and Economic Development in Malaysia* (Kuala Lumpur, Oxford University Press, 1980), p. 85.

 9. For exact figures on income disparities, see Lim Lin Lean, *Some Aspects of Income Differentials in West Malaysia*, Monograph Series on Malaysia Economic Affairs, Faculty of Economics and Administration, University of Malaya (Kuala Lumpur, 1971), p. 99.
10. David Lim, *Further Readings* (note 4 above), p. 12
11. Zulkifly Hj. Hamzah, "Agricultural Development Strategies under the Fourth Malaysia Plan," in K. S. Jomo and R. J. G. Wells, eds., *The Fourth Malaysia Plan: Economic Perspectives* (Kuala Lumpur, Malaysian Economic Association, 1983), p. 99.
12. Lai Yew Wah and Tan Siew Ee, "Industrialisation Patterns and Unemployment Growth in Malaysia," in Philip M. Hauser, Daniel B. Suits, and Naohiro Ogawa, eds., *Urbanisation and Migration in Asean Development* (Tokyo, National Institute for Research Advancement, 1985), p. 294.
13. Toh Kin Woon,"Rural Development Planning and its Impact on Poverty Eradication," *Consumers Association of Penang Seminar on Problems and Prospects of Rural Malaysia* (Penang, Consumers Association of Penang, 1985), p. 12.
14. "Wanted: Relevant Info for Business," *New Straits Times*, 24 Feb. 1986, p. 12.

Select Bibliography

Anand, S. 1977. "Aspects of poverty in Malaysia." *Review of Income and Wealth*, vol. 23.

Bettelheim, C. 1959. *Studies in the theory of planning*. Bombay, Asia Publishing House.

Central Bank of Malaysia. Various years. *Annual reports*. Kuala Lumpur, Kum Printing Sdn Bhd.

Dubois, P. "The use of projections for indicative planning in developed countries: The French experience." *Journal of Development Planning*, no. 4.

Federation of Malaya. 1950. *Draft development plan of the Federation of Malaya, 1950–1955*. Kuala Lumpur, Government Printer.

———. 1956. *A plan of development for Malaya 1956–1960*. Kuala Lumpur, Government Printer.

———. 1961. *Second five year plan 1961–1965*. Kuala Lumpur, Government Printer.

Hoffmann, L., and Tan Siew Ee. 1980. *Industrial growth, employment and foreign investment in Peninsular Malaysia*. Kuala Lumpur, Oxford University Press.

Ho, R. 1965. "Land settlement projects in Malaya: An assessment of the role of the Federal Land Development Authority." *Journal of Tropical Geography*, vol. 20 (June).

H. Osman-Rani, K. S. Jomo, and Ishak Shari. 1981. *Development in the eighties*. Kuala Lumpur, Malaysian Economic Association.

Huang, Y. 1975. "Tenancy patterns, productivity and rentals in Malaysia." *Economic Development and Cultural Change*, vol. 23, no. 4 (July).

Johari b. Mat. 1983. *Regional development in West Malaysia — A comparative effectiveness study of Jengka, Dara, Kejora and Ketengah*. Kuala Lumpur, National Institute of Public Administration.

Kenessey, Z. 1978. *The process of economic planning*. New York, Columbia University Press.

Khor Kok Peng. 1983. *The Malaysian economy: Structures and dependence*. Kuala Lumpur, Marican & Sons (M) Sdn Bhd.

Lim, David. 1975. *Readings on Malaysian economic development*. Kuala Lumpur, Oxford University Press.

Lim Sow Ching. 1976. *Land development schemes in Peninsular Malaysia*. Kuala Lumpur, Rubber Research Institute of Malaysia.

Malaysia. 1966. *First Malaysia Plan 1966–1970*. Kuala Lumpur, Government Printer.

————. 1971. *Second Malaysia Plan 1970–1975*. Kuala Lumpur, Government Printer.

————. 1973. *Mid-term review of the Second Malaysia Plan 1971–1975*. Kuala Lumpur, Government Printer.

————. 1976. *Third Malaysia Plan 1976–1980*. Kuala Lumpur, Government Printer.

————. 1979. *Mid-term Review of the Third Malaysia Plan 1976–1980*. Kuala Lumpur, Government printer.

————. 1981. *Fourth Malaysia Plan 1981–1985*. Kuala Lumpur, Government Printer.

————. 1983. *Mid-term review of the Fourth Malaysia Plan 1981–1985*. Kuala Lumpur, Government Printer.

Malaysia, Ministry of Finance. Various years. *Economic report*. Kuala Lumpur, Government Printer.

Ozbekhan, H. 1969. "Towards a general theory of planning." *Perspectives of planning*. Paris, OECD.

Rudner, M. *Nationalism, planning and economic modernization in Malaysia: The politics of beginning development*. New York, Stage Publications.

S. Husin Ali. 1981. *The Malays: Their problems and future*. Kuala Lumpur, Heinemann Asia.

Tan Siew Ee, and Lai Yew Wah. 1983. "Protection and employment in the West Malaysian manufacturing industries." *Weltwirtschaftliches Archiv* (Review of world economics), vol. 119, no. 2.

Thillainathan, R. 1976. "An analysis of the effects of policies for the redistribution of income and wealth in West Malaysia, 1957–75." Ph.D. diss., London School of Economics and Political Science.

Todaro, M. 1977. *Economic development in the third world*. London, Longman.

5

THE CHANGING NATURE OF ECONOMIC PLANNING IN COLOMBIA

Miguel Urrutia

The Post-War Development Experience

The Political and Institutional Setting

Colombia has been an independent nation since 1819 and has had an elected president for most of the time since 1821. At present the country's political system is determined by a constitution framed in 1886, which brought to an end the extreme federalist experiments of the 1860s and 1870s.

The present constitution establishes the classical division of power between the executive, legislative, and judiciary branches of government. The president has a four-year term and cannot serve two consecutive terms. In this century only Alfonso Lopez Pumarejo has been elected for more than one term, although other presidents have run for a second term. In the same period, only one president, General Gustavo Rojas Pinilla, came to power by unconstitutional means, and the military handed back the reins of government to a civilian elected government within a relatively short time.

Since the 1850s, power has alternated between the Conservative and the Liberal parties. Although all parties are legal, new parties seldom obtain significant electoral support. The Communist party, probably the best organized minor party, usually can only obtain about 2 per cent of the total votes. On various occasions, after periods of national crisis, the Liberal and Conservative parties have organized coalition governments.

Both parties support a mixed economy and state intervention in the economy, but both have been reluctant to establish state enterprises outside of the so-called public services sector and the sector exploiting natural resources. The

156

TABLE 1. Public consumption as a proportion of gross domestic product (1981) (%)

Kenya	21	Sweden	30
Malaysia	21	United Kingdom	22
Mexico	15	Fed. Rep. of Germany	21
Nigeria	12	United States	18
Colombia	8	France	16
Sri Lanka	7	Japan	10

state owns mineral deposits and owns or participates in the management of companies that exploit them. It has also gradually bought out the private sector in the area of public utilities and administers the railroads, water, electricity, and telephone companies. In the financial sector, there are both private and public commercial and investment banks. There are, however, few state enterprises in industry, agriculture, or services. The government, then, has direct control over a rather small proportion of the national income. In Colombia the proportion of public consumption in GDP is lower than that in the average developing economy and far below that in any industrialized nation. Table 1 gives some comparative figures.

The Economic Growth Record

The Colombian economy grew very slowly, with little increase in per-capita income in the first 100 years of independence. Since about 1923, however, the country has experienced sustained economic growth.

Table 2 shows some rather rough estimates of economic growth since 1925. The figures for the period before 1950 are very rough estimates, but they probably reflect the real general trends in the economy.

The rate of growth in per-capita income, while not spectacular, is fairly constant. Until the crisis of the 1980s, the country had not experienced any recession since World War II which caused decreases in per-capita income for more than one year.

This constant rate of economic growth has produced the structural changes in the economy that one would expect: Colombia is no longer an agricultural nation, and the majority of the population lives in towns and cities. In fact, Colombia is more urbanized than other developing countries with similar levels of per-capita income. While Côte d'Ivoire has 41 per cent of its population in urban areas, the figure for Costa Rica is 44 per cent, for Turkey it is 47 per cent, for Tunisia 53 per cent, and for Colombia it has reached 64 per cent.[1]

The country has a fairly efficient agricultural sector, and its food imports are not important. Agriculture accounted for 34 per cent of GDP in 1960 and 27 per cent in 1981. Mining accounts for a very small proportion of total production,

TABLE 2. Average economic growth rate of Colombia

Period	Growth of GDP	Growth GDP/capita	Growth GNI	Growth GNI/capita
1925–29	7.4	5.3	6.7	4.7
1930–34	3.2	1.2	3.4	1.4
1935–39	4.4	2.3	4.1	2.0
1940–44	2.3	0	1.3	−0.9
1945–49	5.9	3.6	7.5	5.2
1950–54	4.7	1.9	6.2	3.4
1955–59	4.0	0.7	4.0	0.7
1960–64	4.8	1.5	4.7	1.4
1965–69	5.1	1.8	5.0	1.7
1970–74	6.7	3.3	6.9	3.5
1974–78	5.5	3.5	6.1	4.1
1978–82	3.2	1.2	NA	NA
1979	5.1	3.1	3.2	1.2
1980	4.0	2.0	NA	NA
1981	2.5	0.5	NA	NA
1982	1.4	−0.6	NA	NA

Sources: Miguel Urrutia, *Cincuenta Años de Desarrollo Economico Colombiano*, Bogotá, La Carreta, 1979, p. 16; Banco de la República, *Cuentas Nacionales*, for 1974–1979; Fedesarrollo, *Coyuntura Economica*, various issues, for estimates for 1980–1982.

and manufacturing, which accounted for 17 per cent of GDP in 1960, comprised only 21 per cent in 1981.

Another peculiarity of the Colombian case is that foreign investment has not played an important role in the development process. There is today virtually no foreign investment in the agricultural or export sectors. In the period of import substitution, some foreign investment took place in protected sectors such as chemicals and pharmaceuticals, but one can safely say that currently Colombian industry is predominantly in the hands of local entrepreneurs.

Between 1923 and 1929, foreign loans were an important proportion of foreign exchange receipts, but since then foreign capital inflows have not been particularly impressive. Since the 1950s, the country has had access to loans from official bilateral and multilateral agencies such as the World Bank and Inter-American Development Bank, and in the late 1960s, aid funds coming from these sources and from USAID helped the country over a rather serious balance-of-payments crisis. In general, however, Colombia has borrowed less than most Latin American countries. Table 3 gives an idea of the current account deficit for the last 18 years and of the net inflow of external funds for the public sector. The last column shows that the government has used foreign credit in moderation.

TABLE 3. External current account balance and the public debt

Year	Current account in the balance of payments[a] (millions of current $)	External public debt (current $)[c]		Utilization of external public credit[d]		Service of the public debt[e]	Net inflow of external funds for public sector
		(billions of current $)	(annual rate of growth)	(used in the year)	(balance utilized)		
1960	−79	0.31	—	17.8	67.5	82.9	−65.1
1961	−132	0.34	9.7	88.7	145.8	70.8	17.9
1962	−161	0.44	29.4	160.5	258.9	74.3	86.2
1963	−127	0.51	15.9	137.0	295.1	87.0	50.0
1964	−122	0.60	17.6	170.2	306.8	103.9	66.3
1965	−11	0.66	10.0	137.8	369.3	97.5	40.3
1966	−280	0.74	12.1	162.2	350.0	112.3	49.9
1967	−67	0.85	14.9	186.3	406.0	107.3	79.0
1968	−160	1.00	17.6	232.9	495.3	114.4	118.5
1969	−175	1.16	16.0	223.9	655.5	107.2	116.7
1970	−302	1.35	16.4	273.1	719.9	128.1	145.0
1971	−453	1.51	11.8	261.1	835.9	148.5	112.6
1972	−191	1.77	17.2	358.8	801.5	164.4	194.4
1973	−56	2.08	17.5	444.0	867.6	218.0	226.0
1974	−351	2.26	8.6	424.3	710.3	339.6	84.7
1975[b]	−80	2.53	11.9	424.6	715.5	278.1	146.5
1976[b]	222	2.64	4.3	296.9	982.8	314.6	−17.7
1977[b]	455	2.84	7.6	408.9	1,104.6	349.4	−17.7

TABLE 3. *Continued*

Year	Current account in the balance of payments[a] (millions of current $)	External public debt (current $)[c]		Utilization of external public credit[d]		Service of the public debt[e]	Net inflow of external funds for public sector
		(billions of current $)	(annual rate of growth)	(used in the year)	(balance utilized)		
1978[b]	386	2.90	2.1	327.0	1,527.0	402.0	−75.0
1979[f]	566	3.46	19.3	977.0	1,946.0	649.0	328.0
1980[f]	104	4.18	20.8	1,018.0	2,476.0	542.0	476.0
1981[f]	−1,722	5.17	23.7	1,299.0	2,740.0	668.0	631.0
1982[f]	−2,885	6.08	17.6	1,291.0	3,718.0	936.0	359.0
1983[f]	−2,826	6.96	14.5	1,342.0	3,682.0	980.0	362.0
1984[f]	−1,870	8.09	16.2	1,764.0	4,402.0	1,182.0	582.0

[a]David Morawetz, *Por qué el emperador no se viste con ropa colombiana?* Bogotá, Fedesarrollo, 1982, p. 14.
[b]Gabriel Turbay M., "El Crédito Público Externo y el Desarrollo Colombiano," in Alkbrecht von Gleich, Diego Pizano Salazar, *Colombia en la Economía Mundial*, Bogotá, Carlos Valencia Editores, 1982, Cuadro 2.
[c]Turbay, *op. cit.*, Cuadro 4.
[d]Ibid., Cuadro 5.
[e]Ibid., Cuadro 6.
[f]Banco de la República, *Deuda Externa de Colombia — 1970–1985*, Agosto, 1985 y Revista, Octubre, 1985.

For most of the time since the 1930s, the country has had exchange and import controls. Except for the decade of the 1970s, the lack of foreign exchange has been a serious constraint on growth and the main economic policy problem of the government. This problem exists because exports have been dominated by agricultural commodities which have had limited and fluctuating world markets. In the 1960s, 78 per cent of exports came from the agricultural sector, and 86 per cent of the agricultural exports were accounted for by coffee,[2] which, due to the low income and price elasticities of demand for it in the world market, cannot easily generate growing export revenues. In the twenty years between 1960 and 1980, primary commodities (excluding fuels, minerals, and metals) held their share of total exports constant.[3]

Due to continuous balance-of-payments problems, the state has intervened fairly extensively in foreign trade since the 1930s, when exchange and import controls were instituted. In the 1930s, protectionist tariffs were introduced for industry, and the tariff structure has changed little since then. As a result, the sector of manufactured consumer goods has received substantial protection, while the agricultural sector and the sectors of exports and capital goods have been discriminated against.

The state has also often intervened in price determination through price controls. The justification for this is the desire to avoid monopoly profits in view of Colombia's strong protectionist import policies which limit competition in certain industrial sectors.

Finally, a word about income distribution. Income has traditionally been quite concentrated in Colombia. The Gini coefficients of concentration are high by international standards, although normal by Latin American standards. Around 1964, 10 per cent of the labour force received about 50 per cent of the total national income.[4] On the other hand, there is very good evidence that income concentration has not increased during the processs of economic development.

Although the distribution of income might have become more uneven during the 1940s and 1950s, by 1964 it was probably fairly similar to what it had been in the late 1930s.[5] A study I have recently finished concludes that in the 15 years after 1964, the distribution of income did not deteriorate, and, further, there is some evidence to suggest an improvement at the end of the 1970s.[6]

In summary, since the country has experienced fairly stable economic growth, and the income distribution has not deteriorated, all sectors of society have improved their standard of living. The improvement has been substantial, as is illustrated by table 4. Some social indicators also suggest not only an improvement in the general welfare of the population but also, as shown in table 5, a more widespread penetration of the benefits of growth than is the case in other developing countries.

The picture of Colombian society given above may seem to be too rosy and therefore smack of propaganda. Outside of the country, most people know little

TABLE 4. Comparison between per-capita GDP of the USA and Colombia using the purchasing-power-parity exchange rate (US = 100)

	1960[a]	1970[b]	1975[c]	1980[d]
Colombia	12.1	18.1	22.4	24.3
USA	100.0	100.0	100.0	100.0

[a] I. B. Kravis, "A Survey of International Comparisons for Productivity," *The Economic Journal*, vol. 86, no. 341 (March 1976), p. 19.
[b] I. B. Kravis, A. Heston, and R. Summers, *International Comparisons of Real Product and Purchasing Power* (New York, U.N. and IBRD, 1978).
[c] IBRD, *World Development Report 1983* (New York, Oxford University Press), p. 203.
[d] *World Comparisons of Purchasing Power and Real Product for 1980* (New York, U. N. Statistical Office, November 1985), table 1.

TABLE 5. Social indicators: Various developing countries

	Per-capita income ($ 1981)	Infant mortality rate (aged 0–1)		Life expectancy at birth		Number enrolled in primary school as percentage of age group	
		1960	1981	1960	1981	1960	1980
Sri Lanka	300	71	43	62	69	95	100
Kenya	420	138	85	41	56	47	108
Nigeria	870	183	133	39	49	36	98
Peru	1,170	163	85	47	58	83	112
Côte d'Ivoire	1,200	173	125	37	47	96	76
Colombia	1,380	103	55	53	63	77	128
Tunisia	1,420	159	88	48	61	66	103
Turkey	1,540	190	119	51	62	75	101
Rep. of Korea	1,700	78	33	54	66	94	107
Malaysia	1,840	72	30	53	65	96	92
Mexico	2,250	91	54	57	66	80	120

Source: IBRD, *World Development Report 1983*.

about Colombia, and few are aware that in the northern tip of South America there is a country that has been democratic for many years, that has achieved some measure of economic success, and where income distribution has not been getting worse and substantial progress has been made in the elimination of extreme poverty.

These macrotrends, however, receive less news coverage than the costs of development incurred by the type of development model followed by Colombia.

Other aspects of Colombia's recent history tend to cast a shadow over the positive achievements elucidated above. Since the 1950s, small guerrilla groups have been active in certain rural regions. More recently urban terrorist groups have emerged; they often kidnap individuals and have carried out rather spectacular attacks on government institutions. A judicial and institutional system geared to the protection of human rights and to keeping the security force at a minimum has also meant that the administration of crime control is inadequate and the cities are therefore quite unsafe.

The weak law enforcement apparatus means that urbanization has been quite chaotic, since people can build with a complete disregard for urban norms. The result is the emergence of some very unattractive, illegally-built neighbourhoods which are often located in areas where it is difficult to provide public services.

There are beggars in the streets, and in Bogotá as many as one or two thousand children live and sleep in the streets and subsist on income produced by begging and petty theft. Although both private foundations and the public sector have attempted to create institutions which will care for these children, most of them find institutional regimentation unpleasant and return to the streets.

There is also no unemployment compensation or family allowance for very poor families. Life is indeed very hard in Colombia for people who, for some reason, cannot find productive employment. This includes abandoned mothers with children to care and provide for, handicapped persons, and people with no education or marketable skills.

The above very brief summary of the Colombian economy and of the nation's institutional framework may serve as a background for the discussion on national economic and social planning that follows.

The History of Planning

The Beginning of Planning

Among developing countries, Colombia probably has one of the longest planning traditions. A comprehensive transport plan was made as early as the 1920s, and a consitutional reform in 1945 established that congress should create the plans and programmes that should serve as the framework for public investment decisions and measures to promote development.[7] Specific sectoral plans, such as the transport plans, helped to provide continuity and rationality in public investment, but the attempts made to draw up coherent plans for macro-economic management usually did not lead even to published plan documents and had no effect on policy-making.

Before 1952, different governments set up various economic councils and gave them the responsibility for dealing with certain economic policy areas. The councils, which included the Consejo Nacional de Economía, the Junta de

Defensa Económica Nacional, the Comisión de Expertos Financieros, and the Cómite de Desarrollo Económico, were usually composed of government ministers and officials, and they limited themselves to hearing the opinions of prominent businessmen and politicians. Since none had a technical secretariat, they did not carry out serious studies of economic issues or produce technical recommendations.[8]

The first study that analysed the whole Colombian economy and made recommendations on how to improve its performance was carried out by a World Bank sponsored study mission in 1949.[9] In 1948, the World Bank was just beginning to turn its attention from the reconstruction of Europe to the problems of the developing countries. When Colombia started exploring the possibility of a loan, the bank president, John McCloy, called Emilio Toro, the executive director for Colombia, for a chat, and maybe to be provocative, asked him how the bank could judge if the project in question was really a top priority for the country. Toro told him the bank should send a mission to judge for itself. By May 1949, Robert L. Garner, vice-president of the bank, formally consulted Toro about a study mission to Colombia, and the latter was able to report that Colombian president Mariano Ospina gave his enthusiastic support to the initiative.

Garner approached Lauchlin Currie, a New Deal economist who had been assistant to the chairman of the board of governors of the Federal Reserve System and assistant to President Roosevelt, and asked him to head the study mission. Colombia was to become the first country to receive a study mission organized by the World Bank.

Currie planned a comprehensive report, with chapters dealing with the major sectors of the economy, and put together a team of 14 people, mostly borrowed from other agencies, US universities, and a few junior members of the World Bank staff. The report was published in March 1950 under the title, *The Basis of a Development Programme for Colombia*.[10]

According to Currie, the report had two broad thrusts: a progressive bias on the one hand, in that it favoured various liberal objectives such as progressive taxation, land taxes, decreasing inequality in consumption, and greater expenditure on basic needs in areas such as health, education, and public services. On the other hand, the report supported economic orthodoxy by emphasizing the need to raise productivity and the desirability of relying on the market mechanism in order to achieve efficient resource allocation. This meant the dismantling of a broad range of price and foreign exchange controls, the elimination of rationing and subsidies, and the promotion of competition. It even recommended that the government not invest directly to create a steel-producing enterprise.

In order to create a sizeable national market, which is prerequisite for a substantial increase in productivity, the report insisted on carrying out ambitious transport investments. At the time, Colombia, with a population of 11 million, was a group of regional markets with limited links between them. The topography of the country, with its three major mountain ranges extending from north to south, necessarily hindered the integration of these regional markets into a sizeable national market.

The first attempt at economic planning was rather successful. The report was widely read in government and business circles and also used in the emerging faculties of economics in the universities in the following years. Probably the greatest value of the report was that it showed the first generation of Colombian economists how economic analysis and theory could be applied to the specific problems of their own economy and introduced policy-makers to modern economics.

Some of the fiscal recommendations actually became legislation, and other recommendations were followed in the formulation of some of the proposed public administration reforms. But more importantly, in the next decade, tax measures recommended by the mission were adopted whenever a fiscal crisis led ministers of finance to search for revenue sources.

A large part of the impetus of the bank report was due, however, to the feeling common in government circles that foreign financing would be available for the implementation of the projects recommended by the mission. In fact, of course, the World Bank and other aid institutions did give preference to the projects recommended by the mission, and as a result Colombian access to foreign capital for development was enhanced.

Some of the practical force of the bank report was also due to the follow-up mechanisms set up by Currie. He promoted, as a private individual, the organization of a committee on Economic Development. The World Bank agreed to make experts available to the committee from time to time, and the government agreed to provide a national staff. Currie proposed the format of the British Royal Commission, and the president appointed members to the committee on a bipartisan basis. The task of the committee of eminent people was to study the report chapter by chapter and make recommendations.

The committee did its most productive work in the transport sector, in part because of a dynamic and willing minister of public works, but also because of the strong likelihood that the projects which the committee approved would obtain World Bank financing.

Although at the beginning of the study mission the bank approved a comprehensive approach to development, by 1952 it had decided that it could only finance "productive" projects.[11] The World Bank, by deciding not to be involved in social projects, eliminated any incentive that countries might have had to do comprehensive planning in collaboration with the bank since IBRD limited its loans to the foreign exchange component of traditional infrastructure projects. Only in the late-1960s, when McNamara again involved the bank in social projects, was an external incentive gain created for the preparation of social projects.

In summary, some of the projects and recommendations of the report were implemented largely because of an expectation by the government that doing so would generate external funds. Due to the bank's new policy of declining to grant loans for social projects, an important part of the report lost its force. From this experience, it may be inferred that foreign advice with respect to development strategies will not be effective unless it is sweetened with the offer of external funds. To substantiate this inference, it can be observed that when another mission, organized by the International Labour Organization (ILO)[12] 20 years after the Currie mission, came to Colombia and recommended a broad strategy, it had little impact on policy because the ILO was not a funding agency. (It may be pointed out that there were also other reasons for the report lacking impact, including the fact that it had many general recommendations but few concrete policy initiatives.)

To finish this survey of the first serious planning attempt in Colombia, it might be useful to tell the story of how the report led to the government's acceptance of the necessity for a devaluation. The Currie mission had concluded that the Colombian peso was overvalued and that it would be difficult to promote exports and dismantle some import restrictions without a devaluation. When the Committee on Economic Development started to discuss the issue in earnest, on the initiative of Currie, the minister of finance stopped all dealings in foreign exchange to avoid speculation. The committee then convinced the president to accept a more drastic devaluation than he had originally been willing, for political reasons, to contemplate. The devaluation came at a time when overvaluation had not yet caused serious balance-of-payments problems, and it had quite positive effects. This experience shows that one important objective of planning is to mention the unmentionable sufficiently early so as to create a policy crisis before a costly economic crisis forces the required policy change. After this currency realignment, Colombia abandoned effective economic planning, and subsequent devaluations started to take place only after overvaluation and speculation had left the country with no international reserves or international credit.

Strictly speaking, after the Committee on Economic Development finished its work and published its recommendations, the government created, in 1952, the National Planning Council. The council had three members, with Albert Hirschman and Lauchlin Currie as advisers. The main achievement of the council was to introduce Albert Hirschman to the realities of a developing economy. This has paid off handsomely, since Hirschman has written some of the most thoughtful academic works on the problems of development.

In 1958, another study on the Colombian economy, carried out by a team directed by a foreign mission, was presented to the government. This was the study carried out under the direction of Father Louis Joseph Lebet.[13] The study was important because it emphasized education and health as prerequisites for development and presented, for the first time, systematic empirical data illustrating the deficiencies in these areas, but it clearly did not have the structure of a development plan. The mission carried out scientific surveys of living standards and analysed the problems of health, malnutrition, housing, social services, and education. The influence of the study on policy-making and planning was, however, limited.

The Period of Macro-economic Planning

From 1953 to 1957 Colombia had a military government. An imaginative but arbitrary minister of finance handled economic policy. Maybe as a reaction, when democracy was reinstituted congress created a new planning mechanism.

Carlos Lleras, one of the leaders of the Liberal party and the established politician with the greatest reputation in economic affairs, presented a draft law to congress creating a planning agency as an advisory body to the president on matters of economic policy. Congress made some changes, but in 1958 it passed Law 19, creating the National Council of Economic Policy and Planning and the Planning Agency, the latter being a body reporting directly to the president. Lleras had been influenced by the planning proposals of the UN Economic Commission for Latin America (ECLA) and actually consulted with Raul Prebish, the prestigious director of ECLA, about his scheme.

In Lleras's scheme, planning decisions would be made by a council chaired by the president and made up of ministers dealing with economic affairs plus the heads of the Central Bank and the Coffee Federation. Congress made drastic changes to the draft law and created a four-man council, of which two members were appointed by the president and two by congress. The Planning Department, however, was created as an agency reporting to the president, as recommended by Lleras.

The new Planning Agency, after getting organized, set out in earnest to produce the first, and as it turned out, the last, "textbook" macro-economic plan for Colombia. The plan was drawn up following the ECLA blueprint. ECLA advisors were invited to Colombia, and with their assistance a model plan was put together. Griffin and Enos, in their textbook on planning, describe it as follows.

The document... contained a formal planning model, complete with underlying econometric projections, capital-output ratios, savings coefficients, etc. A high target rate of growth was fixed and the savings and foreign exchange gaps were calculated.[14]

The plan was presented in January of 1962 to the Organization of American States to meet the requirements of the Charter of Punta del Este. A committee of ten experts (the so-called Committee of Wise Men) set up by the charter studied the plan and, after making some minor technical suggestions, approved it. This approval gave funding agencies the green light for massive aid and foreign financing for Colombia.

Griffin and Enos have made a realistic evaluation of the usefulness of the plan:

The Plan has never been used in preparing economic policy and it became evident soon after publication that its growth target was unrealistic. . . . As a diplomatic manoeuvre for attracting foreign capital, the plan was a success.[15]

There is no doubt that the plan document helped to meet the formal conditions required for obtaining access to US aid under the rules of the Alliance for Progress. Further, the documentation of the plan made it easier for the aid bureaucracy to process Colombian loan applications. Yet, the plan may not have been as vital a condition for Colombia's receipt of external aid as has commonly been supposed in view of the following favourable conditions: (i) the country had a progressive democratic government which was embarking on land reform; (ii) President Alberto Lleras was a statesman of continental influence; and (iii) he was very influential both with President Kennedy and with the Washington bureaucracy of US and international organizations.

As Enos and Griffin mention, however, the plan was never used as a basis for economic policy. Once the formalities of presenting it to the international community were over, it was conveniently forgotten.[16] Also, once the plan was published, the Planning Agency pretty much fell apart. The councillors of the National Council of Economic Policy and Planning and the head of the Planning Department appointed by the new government were soon in conflict. The division of functions between the councillors and the head of the Planning Agency was not clear. In addition, the lack of a common criterion, due to the conflicts between the councillors and the department head, weakened the agency. These conflicts prevented the council from having effective working relations with the different ministries.

The conflict between the councillors and the head of the department was so serious that in 1963 the government felt compelled to reform the National Council. The reform followed the model proposed by Carlos Lleras in 1958. However, President Guillermo Leon Valencia did not really believe in planning, and he felt that the reform he carried out was a sufficient gesture to appease Lleras and the partisans of planning. The new council, made up of the economic ministers and the president, met only once between 1963 and 1966. The position of head of the Planning Department was even left vacant for many months.

In 1965, however, in the loan negotiations with the World Bank and the IMF, Colombia was asked to commit itself to strengthening the planning office. IBRD offered the services, at the end of the year, of its expert on planning,

Albert Waterston. During his mission, he recommended that the Planning Agency concentrate on the preparation of projects and the planning of the public sector. The staff of the department was preparing itself for this change of strategy when Carlos Lleras, elected in early 1966, became president in August.

The Period of Project Planning

President Lleras took planning very seriously. During the presidential campaign and in the months before the inauguration, he even had his brain trust introduce the concept of economic planning in the constitutional reform he hoped to propose to congress. During the long process that is required for constitutional reform, some modifications were made to his proposals, but the final articles approved established that the government should present a plan to congress and that the annual budget would have to follow the priorities set out in the plan. The constitution thus reformed even contained an article requiring that new expenditures could be voted upon only if they were adequately justified by cost-benefit project evaluations. The reform also set up a congressional commission to study the plan and monitor its implementation.

In the 15 ensuing years, however, congress has shown a decided lack of interest in the commission: it has not been able to decide upon the membership of the commission, and it has, therefore, never met.

Congress has focused its interest instead on specific legislative initiatives and cases of mismanagement of government institutions and funds rather than on the broader issues of the economic planning process and policy formulation.

The main business of congress, however, has been to create political coalitions among different factions within the parties in order to obtain majority backing for a certain presidential candidate and then to work for his election. Economic policy-making has been, therefore, almost exclusively in the hands of the executive branch. Congress intervenes only when there is the need to pass major tax legislation, although it does influence public expenditure through the discussion of the central government budget.

Despite having introduced the concept of planning into the constitution, President Lleras did not present a plan to congress until the last days of his administration. He did, however, reform and substantially strengthen the Planning Agency. The administrative structure he created in 1966 still shapes the way planning is carried out in the country today.

Lleras brought into the Planning Department a whole new generation of economists and engineers with higher degress from foreign universities and used the Planning Department as his economic policy staff. The Council of Economic and Social Policy started to meet weekly under his personal chairmanship, reorganized so as to include the ministers involved in economic issues and other key economic bureaucrats. The council would consider and act upon policy papers prepared by the Planning Department. In order to assure full discussion of the issues, the president established the practice of reading aloud the whole document, a practice that tended to give the Planning Department the assurance that the members of the council and the less friendly ministers would have to listen and consider all of the arguments. The tradition of reading policy documents prepared by the Planning Agency at council meetings chaired by the president lasted for almost 20 years and five administrations.

The director of the Planning Agency has ministerial status and attends cabinet meetings, but has few executive responsibilities. He is essentially the president's economic chief of staff. Legally, however, he has been given a series of functions which give him substantial leverage to influence economic policy in a direction compatible with the plan.

The Planning Agency is responsible for preparing the central government investment budget to be presented by the Ministry of Finance to congress. Ministries, therefore, cannot usually get approval for their investment projects without having previously justified them to the Planning Agency. The department must also give approval to all requests for foreign indebtedness made by public sector agencies, and this again assures some degree of order in expenditure commitments. Finally, the department must approve all direct foreign private investments, which gives it some influence over industrial policy.

In addition, the department head, or his representative, is a member of all the major economic policy bodies, including the board of the Foreign Trade Institute, the Monetary Board, the Tariff Council, and the boards of directors of many public enterprises. The department also regulates the prices of public utilities and operates a fund that finances investment feasibility studies for both the public and private sectors. More significant, however, is the fact that from 1970 to 1978, the head of planning had a weekly private meeting with the president to discuss policy issues and the subjects to be brought before the council. Quite logically, the heads of planning, after the reforms of 1968, did not use this structure and these powers to concentrate on the framing of formal macroeconomic plans, but rather dedicated much of their time to participating in the framing of short-run economic policy and specific investment programmes.

In fact, as has been mentioned, the Lleras government did not produce a macro-economic plan. The plan it presented to congress towards the end of the presidential period was merely a list of project priorities which reflected the work the Planning Department had been involved in during the previous three years.[17]

In 1966, the department shifted from the macro-economic modeling favoured by ECLA to the project approach recommended by Waterston, a model which more adequately fulfils the requirements of IBRD and the lending agencies. The approach was to plan projects. This meant a shift from macroplanning to micro-planning. Waterston gave a convincing justification for this shift in approach:

Experience shows that countries that have counted on well-prepared projects that have been coordinated with some budget organization and controls can do without general economic plans, at least for a time and even then maintain high growth rates.[18]

In addition, the project approach was a sensible move in Colombia in 1966 because of the foreign exchange crisis that became evident at the end of that year. The Central Bank had depleted its international reserves, and the country could not obtain credit from the New York banks because the IMF would not sign a stand-by agreement unless the peso was devalued by more than 50 per cent. President Lleras broke negotiations with the IMF, established strict exchange controls and import licensing, and instituted a system of a "crawling peg" for the Colombian peso. (The Colombian crawling peg is a system of weekly mini-devaluations of the peso against the dollar meant to keep the peso from becoming overvalued due to internal inflation.) The country had almost no foreign exchange earnings and the economy ground to a halt in the face of severe import rationing. Economic growth could take place only if foreign credit financed imports for a transition period in which new exports could be developed under the protection of a more realistic exchange rate.

Once the IMF, the World Bank, and USAID accepted the concept of the crawling peg, the main objective of the Planning Department was to produce fundable projects to generate foreign exchange. Fortunately, USAID at the time agreed to give soft loans to the coutry in which the foreign exchange was converted to local currency, and those funds were then used by the government to finance agreed-upon development projects. The USAID, IMF, World Bank, and the Inter-American Development Bank loans between 1968 and 1971 allowed the country to break the foreign exchange constraint and grow while its export potential was being built up. This set the stage for a decade of rapid development which put the country into the category of a newly industrializing country.

In addition to producing fundable projects and rationalizing the public investment budget, the department also helped define many policies through the Council of Economic and Social Policy. It brought before the council issues as diverse as minimum wage policy, pricing and taxation criteria for locally assembled cars, policies with respect to foreign investment in the banking sector, analysis of whether certain roads should be built, pricing policy for public utilities, and plans for interconnecting all electric-power companies.

When the new government came to power in 1970, the Planning Department presented, and the council approved, a new plan, which brought back into the plan document some simple macro-economic models.[19] Under the influence of the ILO report, which emphasized the problems of unemployment, the model attemped to show the compatibility of the growth targets proposed and employment creation. This type of planning was not very attractive to the president, and therefore a crisis emerged between him and the head of the department, which led to the latter's resignation and that of all the departmental heads in the agency. The new team formulated a different type of plan.

Strategies for Development

The new plan of President Pastrana's government was very much the brain-child of Lauchlin Currie, the director of the World Bank mission twenty years before. Dr. Currie had stayed on in the country after the mission, married a Colombian, and had eventually become a Colombian citizen. Since the early 1960s he had been proposing a strategy of development based on massive investments in residential construction. He believed that the problem of the country was that the economy was in an underemployment equilibrium growth path and proposed that a massive programme of investment in construction could accelerate economic development.

Currie published the first version of his strategy in 1961 as an alternative to the 1960–1970 plan of the government.[20] For the next 10 years he held frequent seminars for businessmen and policy-makers and wrote articles and books on his theory. Among his converts was Roberto Arenas, a good friend of President Pastrana, who was to become his planning director.

Candidate Pastrana was quite interested in urban problems, and in his campaign he emphasized policy measures to solve the problems of unemployment. Furthermore, the opposition candidate in the presidential campaign, General Rojas Pinilla, the ex-dictator of 1953–1957, had been able to create a new political party with wide appeal amongst the urban masses. Due to the massive vote for Rojas in the cities, Pastrana narrowly won the election by about 100,000 votes. For him a development strategy based on massive employment creation in the cities therefore looked particularly appealing.

In addition, Lleras, his predecessor in the presidency, had been promoting land reform for a decade and concentrating on public investment in rural projects. President Pastrana, a conservative, wanted to differentiate his policies from those of Lleras and the previous liberal administrations; the Currie strategy, therefore, which emphasized a shift in public investment from rural to urban projects, appealed to him.

Consequently, in his first year in government, he did not lend political support to the initiatives of the administrators of the two institutes — INCORA (the land reform institute) and the Planning Department — that Lleras had built up to spearhead his development objectives. When Jorge Ruiz Lara, the Lleras-appointed planning director, resigned, Roberto Arenas was appointed and Currie started to draft the new development plan.

In the preparation of Operación Colombia (see n. 20) in 1960, Lara, working with Currie, had predicted that one of the problems with the urban construction strategy would be that the increase in aggregate demand generated would lead to an increase in demand for imports which, in turn, would result in a foreign exchange crisis. The strategy which Currie and Arenas presented to the Council of Economic Policy for consideration, therefore, had two components: massive investments in residential urban construction and a continued export promotion plan. In the council, however, Hernan Jaramillo Ocampo, minister of agriculture and an influential conservative politician and ideologue, opposed the excessive urban bias of the plan with the support of other ministers and council members, such as the heads of the Central Bank and the Coffee Federation. The result was that the government decided to include measures for increasing agricultural productivity in the plan. In addition, the fear that the construction strategy might lead to a concentration of income and the desire to attract the urban voters by increasing government expenditures in social programmes led to the addition of a fourth strategy of income distribution based on more progressive taxation and more social expenditure. The government approved these development priorities and sent a planning document to congress. It also published a book for distribution to the public. This was the first plan in Colombian history that was published as an attractive book and made available to the public. The title of the book was *Las Cuatro Estrategias* (The four strategies). Only later did the Planning Department publish a technical document in which, using an input-output table, the feasibility of the construction strategy was shown. The main document did not contain any economic models or projections and contained very few statistics.

Economic decision-making in the remainder of the presidential term promoted the original Currie objectives. The government supported export promotion efforts and, more importantly, used the crawling peg to produce an effective devaluation of the peso which promoted exports. With respect to the construction strategy, it brought about an institutional innovation which made available funds for housing construction in greater volume than ever before.

The Currie theory was built on the hypothesis that there was an untapped potential for generating savings which could be invested in housing construction because of the very high latent demand for housing. Such investment would in turn employ many unskilled workers, and this would increase aggregate demand in general and accelerate growth.

To mobilize the newly generated savings, the government promoted the creation of private housing and loan banks, which could offer a new financial instrument in the market. This was a savings deposit with monetary correction for inflation and a real positive interest rate in which funds could be withdrawn at any time. While the existing financial intermediaries could only offer fixed interest rates, often with a ceiling below the rate of inflation, the new housing corporations could offer a sight deposit with daily correction for inflation and an additional 3 or 4 per cent interest rate paid quarterly. The new instrument of offering protection against inflation was designed to provide an incentive to save.

This objective was clearly in the mind of the Planning Department, but it also wanted to shift existing savings into housing. The proof of this is that it refused to allow an increase in the interest rate in regular bank savings deposits and did not allow financial intermediaries to introduce new financial instruments that could compete with the constant purchasing power deposits (UPAC) of the housing corporations. In addition, the inflation adjustment was made tax-exempt, while all interest rates continued to be subject to the income tax. Given the attractiveness of the new financial instruments, with prompting from the Planning Department and Dr. Currie personally, the private sector set up the new financial intermediaries. To avoid opposition from the existing financial institutions, they were allowed to invest in the new corporations.

The success of this institutional innovation was impressive. The availability of funds in a sector which had traditionally been chronically short of funds stimulated many private developers to invest in construction projects, and urban residential construction increased significantly. Table 6 shows the rapid

TABLE 6. Deposits in housing corporations

Period	Constant Dec. 1972 pesos (millions)	Current (millions)
March 1973	829	884
December 1973	3,556	4,395
March 1974	5,143	6,911
December 1974	5,343	8,324
March 1975	6,763	11,304
December 1975	7,512	13,775
March 1976	8,796	17,246
December 1976	8,646	19,928
March 1977	10,194	25,891
December 1977	8,175	24,194
March 1978	10,604	33,244
December 1978	9,992	35,111
March 1979	11,400	43,825
December 1979	11,785	53,019
March 1980	14,052	66,780
December 1980	14,763	83,234
March 1981	17,001	103,537
December 1981	17,182	122,208
March 1982	19,174	145,499
December 1982	19,455	171,758

Source: L. E. Rosas, "Evolucion del Sistema Colombiano de Ahorro y Vivienda," *Desarrollo y Sociedad*, Cuaderno 6, August 1983.

growth in the availability of credit for construction in the first year of the life of the system.

Between 1970 and 1974, private construction increased by 40 per cent (number of square meters built). Given the notoriously innaccurate way savings are measured in the national accounts, it is difficult to ascertain whether total savings increased,[21] but the financial statistics suggest some increase. Unemployment in the cities decreased and GNP growth accelerated. The main objective of the plan seems to have been met, but it is hard to say how much of the success was due to the construction strategy.

By 1974, it was clear that inflation was also going up. The reason for this was a growing fiscal deficit, financed to a great extent by foreign credit, which increased the money supply. In addition, there was great pressure from the non-construction sector on the Central Bank for investment funds. The government yielded to the pressure by increasing money supply through special rediscount facilities for agriculture and industry. In addition to the excessive increase in money supply and the persistent presence of a fiscal deficit, the increases in international prices and the devaluation also contributed to the inflation.

The main weakness of *The Four Strategies* was that the non-construction sectors did not accept the policy that housing receive the bulk of savings for an extended period, and this made the growth model inherently inflationary.

To Close the Gap

The government of Alfonso Lopez Michelsen took away some of the privileges of UPAC and carried out the fourth strategy (fiscal reform) of the previous plan. In addition, the government proposed a series of policies with less of an urban bias which included large investments to modernize the rural traditional sector, the elimination of subsidies benefiting the urban middle classes, and a decrease in industrial protectionism.

The plan, published as a book titled *To Close the Gap* (Para cerrar la brecha), laid out clearly the policies that the government would follow. The blueprint was followed fairly closely during the next four years, and this gave coherence to policy-making.

Candidate Lopez had been the head of the Leftist opposition faction within the Liberal party for 15 years, and throughout this period he had attacked the industrial protectionist model followed by all previous governments and proposed instead a strategy of development which would favour agriculture and the rural and urban poor. In addition, during the campaign he had attacked the inflation record of the previous administration. Working with these ideas and following his broad directions, his economic brain trust put together an economic strategy, which was later transformed into an economic plan. The new plan contained the following elements:

1. A broad progressive tax reform to improve equity and eliminate the inflationary fiscal deficit
2. A financial reform which, through less regulation of the financial sector, would improve resource allocations, create incentives for savings, and diminish the credit demands on the Central Bank
3. A redirection of government expenditure to areas and projects which would benefit primarily the 50 per cent poorest segment of the population
4. Continued promotion of exports and a policy on foreign debt consistent with macro-economic policy

The plan document was, therefore, a policy statement containing detailed descriptions of the actual policies to be implemented. In the four years of the presidential term, the policies were in fact implemented in the way proposed. The Planning Agency dedicated itself to ensuring, through the weekly meetings of the Council of Economic and Social Policy, that the decisions of the different ministries and agencies be consistent with the framework of the plan. The president, in most cases, supported the efforts of the Planning Agency to maintain such consistency.

Surprisingly, the economic strategy was carried out: the fiscal and financial reforms became law; new projects in nutrition and for rural development in areas dominated by small farmers were started; prestige projects and public works investments were cut; and Colombia made net debt repayments, when most developing countries were increasing their foreign debts.

This last policy outcome illustrates the advantages of a policy plan as opposed to a macro-economic plan based on econometric projections. When the plan was formulated, coffee, the country's major export, commanded low prices in the international market and this determined a decrease in the international reserves of the country. All economic projections identified a serious foreign exchange constraint which limited the country's growth potential. As a result, it was logical to increase foreign debt for some years while the attempt to improve the export capacity of the country bore fruit. However, instead of setting targets for new debt inflow, the plan established the following policy guidelines:

It is fundamental to insert public external indebtedness within a general framework for policy in the area of foreign trade in order to avoid that borrowing becomes a source of inflation. In general terms, this will be achieved by avoiding the receipt of large external credits in periods in which the Central Bank's international reserves are increasing, and on the contrary, increasing indebtedness in periods of less surplus. In fact, a rational foreign exchange policy would require the net amortization of external debt in periods of rapid increases in foreign exchange. Given the present international situation, however, which presents serious difficulties for the sale of our products abroad, the Government has programmed a relatively fast increase in foreign debt.[22]

In August of 1975, part of Brazil's coffee trees were affected by a frost, and coffee prices shot up in the international market. Government policy with respect to foreign debt shifted automatically, and Colombia decreased the pace at which it contracted new foreign debt. Table 3 shows the decrease in foreign exchange inflows from foreign debt in the period of high coffee prices in 1976–1977.

It may be interesting to note that at this time Colombia's neighbours (including Venezuela, which was experiencing an unprecedented export boom due to the increase in petroleum prices) were implementing development plans that required massive foreign debt to finance ambitious investment programmes.

With respect to industrial policy, the Planning Department, collaborating with the Ministry of Development, negotiated with the private sector specific industrial sector plans affecting areas such as the paper, automobile, and cement industries. In these plans, the private sector and the government would agree on required investments; the private sector would receive a guarantee from the government that the relevant imports of machinery and foreign credits would be authorized; and an agreement would be reached with respect to a tariff structure and a liberalization of price controls if certain production targets were met. The problem with the specific industrial sector plans was that after their approval, economic conditions might change, and a new minister of development, instead of readjusting the sector plan, would disregard the agreement reached by his predecessor with respect to price policy or tariff structure. The plans were useful, however, insofar as they forced private sector companies to get together and agree on a common strategy for the sector. That is, the specific industrial sector plans forced co-ordination within the private sector.

The Planning Department was also active with respect to energy policy. The department collaborated with the Energy Ministry in pressing for increases in gasoline and electricity prices. Specific measures were also taken to diminish the barriers to foreign investment in oil, coal, and uranium development and to approve new foreign investment in the mining sector. In summary, the Planning Department reformed foreign investment regulations and price controls which constrained the development of the mining and energy sectors. These reforms were based on detailed long-term projections of demand for and supply of energy and long-term balance-of-payment projections.

The role of the Planning Department was to systematically recommend policies (e.g. price increases) which were often unpopular and to convince the ministers, local politicians, and the president of the long-term costs involved in not implementing such policies. The department also played a vital role in vetoing ambitious and élitist public expenditure projects; for example, it managed to stop for some years the construction of an underground mass transit system in the capital city.

The 1979–1982 Plan

The type of planning carried out in 1974–1978 was not popular. Tax reform, negative real growth in public investment, increases in energy prices, and a shift in expenditure on public works and services from urban projects that benefited the politically powerful middle-class to rural programmes and nutrition proved to be a strategy that failed to generate political support in the short run. Therefore, President Julio Cesar Turbay, elected largely by the local machines of the Liberal party politicians, found a shift in economic priorities necessary. The fuel required for local political machines was public works expenditure and public expenditure that generated employment opportunities that the political machine could offer to the people who supported them. Originally he was not really interested in presenting a plan, but after some criticism, he announced a plan which presented a rationale for a massive increase in public investment. Since the government chose not to risk unpopularity by increasing taxes, the expansion in public expenditure had to be financed by credit. The plan document held that using foreign credit would not be inflationary, because a projected decrease in coffee prices would generate a decrease in international reserves for some years.

This projection was reasonable, but it did not materialize. Various conditions kept internal interest rates high, and this generated a net inflow of foreign exchange to the private sector despite the decrease in coffee prices. High interest rates also promoted the repatriation of the profits being generated by the illegal drug trade. In these circumstances, the foreign indebtedness incurred to finance the public investment budget was equivalent to financing the deficit by creating money. The undesirable impact of external credit on money supply and inflation required the abandonment of the basic assumption inherent in the plan: that an increase in foreign credit for public investment was essential for growth and was non-inflationary. Yet, the assumption that foreign credit growth was needed was retained. Measures to compensate for the excessive growth in government investment abroad led to a series of economic policy decisions which created an economic recession.

However, the explicit expression of the government strategy in a plan document made possible informed public discussion of government economic policy. In fact, as soon as the plan was published, various academic experts pointed out its inconsistencies, and with time some opposition politicians and spokesmen for the private sector joined the critics. At the beginning, the private sector was quite happy with the plan's concentration on public works and promise of no tax increases. With time, however, the spokesmen for the employer associations became convinced that the prevailing foreign exchange situation would cause the increase in public investment to crowd out private sector investment. The advantage of a democratic system with a free press is that when criticism, even of a technical nature, mounts, the government reconsiders its policies. In this

TABLE 7. Foreign debt service ratio of Colombia

Year	Interest and amortization of debt as a percentage of current foreign exchange income
1970	29.3
1971	33.5
1972	30.7
1973	29.9
1974	33.1
1975	23.1
1976	19.3
1977	15.0
1978	16.1
1979	19.2
1980	17.6
1981	24.3
1982	34.1

Source: Leonardo Villar G., "Nuevas tendencias en el endeudamiento externo Colombiano," *Coyuntura Economica,* Sept. 1983, p. 253.

case, it implicitly abandoned its plan and started to moderate the pace of growth of the public works budget.

The harm had already been done, however, and foreign indebtedness increased, while the economy stagnated (see table 7). After the Mexican debt crises of 1982, new foreign credit availability to Colombia declined dramatically, and in such circumstances servicing the debt became for the first time in many years an important concern of the minister of finance.

Planning and Policy Coherence

The Colombian experience with national economic planning suggests that the type of macro-economic planning taught in universities and recommended by the UN regional commissions does not have much impact on policy-making. On the contrary, it would appear that a planning agency dedicated to framing a consistent series of economic policies to achieve the political objectives of a government may improve economic performance.

One of the problems in many developed and developing countries is that specific economic policy decisions may be inconsistent with each other, and this can lead to substantial waste in the economy. For example, a minister of labour may present minimum wage legislation which is inconsistent with the inflation targets of the minister of finance. A minister of finance may increase foreign indebtedness to finance a fiscal deficit at the same time that he is trying to control money supply through the central bank, thus crowding out the private sector or favouring public investment which has a large import component.

A national plan, which specifies how different policies (i.e. monetary, exchange, fiscal, public expenditure, pricing, and tariff) will be used to achieve a series of objectives on which there is a political consensus, will guarantee coherent management of the economy, hence eliminating waste and providing the private sector with clear guidelines on what to expect from the government.

No planning agency can guarantee the co-ordination necessary to achieve policy coherence, since governments are often characterized by the existence of very independent ministries and agencies which passionately defend their policy initiatives. Such co-ordination can only be done by the head of state, and this implies that planning will only be effective if the head of state has a clear concept of the economic strategy that the government will implement and if he maintains a permanent interest in pursuing its goals by assuring the coherence of policy decisions made by the many departments and agencies of the government.

In this situation, it would seem logical to place the planning agency directly under the head of state. Further, its director should be viewed as distinct from the other ministers in that he is the economic chief of staff of the head of state and, as such, should not have a political base of his own. For him to be able to co-ordinate various policies effectively, his recommendations must be of a purely technical nature within the context of the priorities set out by the head of state. This purely technical and politically neutral position should keep the director of the planning agency aloof from the power disputes within the cabinet, and this should enhance his effectiveness.

Aid Agencies and Planning

It is fashionable to claim that aid agencies determine the broad features of economic policies in developing countries. In Colombia it is not hard to find evidence indicating the widespread influence of the aid agencies.[23] While it has, admittedly, been greater in some areas than in others, the aid agencies have, undeniably, had an extensive influence on the planning process.

As described in a previous section, the first fairly comprehensive strategy for development was put together by the World Bank (1950). The first formal development plan, the Ten-Year Plan of 1961, was in part constructed in order to meet a condition for aid of the Alliance for Progress, and it was drafted with technical support from the UN Economic Commission for Latin America.

The reform and strengthening of the National Planning Department in 1967–1968 was related to the need to produce a large stock of projects to be funded by USAID, the World Bank, and the Inter-American Bank, as well as by German, Dutch, and Canadian aid agencies. Due to the successful strengthening of the project preparation capabilities of the Planning Department, international financing did increase substantially.

This increase in foreign credit is shown clearly in table 3 in the column on net inflows of external funds for the public sector. From a level of US$40–50 million per year in 1965–1966, external funds increased to US$120–145 million per year in 1968–1970.

The aid agencies required the presentation of projects with technical feasibility studies and technical data such as internal rates of return, estimates of costs, and financial flows. Since a substantial portion of public investment had some external financing, the Planning Department could ask the ministries and decentralized agencies for feasibility studies whenever they requested budgetary support. This probably improved the quality of public investment projects.

Previously, regional and political considerations had played a larger role in the decisions determining which kinds of projects would be funded. In the late 1970s and early 1980s, when private international bank financing grew in importance, project designs were less closely scrutinized, and, as a result, projects whose economic benefits were somewhat doubtful were funded. In the projects financed by supplier credits, where the supplier did not insist on careful project evaluation, a great deal of waste also occurred. In the health sector, for example, it was not unusual to find X-ray machines which were financed by suppliers' credit and placed in hospitals which had no technicians to operate them. The Ministry of Finance and the Planning Department had difficulty opposing foreign credits to apparently meritorious projects (e.g. equipping hospitals) on the grounds that the projects lacked sufficient technical justification.

As is shown in table 8, foreign credit has been an important proportion of public investment. But the aid agencies always require local counterpart funds for their projects, which means that a large part of local resources for investment are also assigned to externally funded projects. On the average, the multilateral banks finance about a third of a project, which means that when 20 per cent of public investment has foreign financing, those projects tie up about 60 per cent of the investment budget. The result is that funds are assigned with priority to projects that are attractive to the international agencies. In this sense, these agencies have influenced the whole planning process by determining which projects get most of the scarce government revenue.

The Planning Department has also influenced government investment through its financing of pre-investment and investment feasibility studies. During the presidency of Carlos Lleras, the government created within the Planning Department a bank (FONADE) for funding project feasibility studies. The feasibility studies financed by FONADE later become a major component of the project pipeline put forward for consideration for external financing. In this way the Planning Department can shape the future of the government investment programme.

The system, however, creates a bias towards investment in sectors that have

TABLE 8. Public investment financed by external credit (1970 pesos)

Year	Public investment (1)	Disbursements from multilateral and bilateral credit sources (2)	External credit contracted (3)	2/1 (4)	3/1 (5)
1967	9,297	2,696	1,913	30%	21%
1968	12,141	3,372	3,019	28	25
1969	12,034	3,159	4,227	26	35
1970	13,149	4,339	4,279	33	33
1971	15,417	3,433	5,669	22	37
1972	14,483	3,684	5,655	25	39
1973	15,538	3,765	5,384	24	35
1974	13,860	2,919	3,709	21	27
1975	14,154	2,466	3,935	17	28
1976	14,388	1,974	4,261	14	30
1977	14,286	1,866	4,805	13	34
1978	13,768	2,040	4,843	15	35
1979	25,910	1,952	8,610	8	33
1980	29,252	3,008	4,620	10	16
1981	33,075	3,032	6,660	9	20
1982	34,388	3,682	5,927	11	17
1983	32,231	5,149	6,698	16%	21%

Source: Hernando J. Gómez and Francisco Thoumi, "Una nota sobre la relación entre el Financiamiento Externo y la Inversión Pública en Colombia," *Coyuntura Económica*, Oct. 1986.

well-developed methodologies for cost-benefit analysis and for sectors where projects have a high unit cost. The techniques for evaluation of electricity generation investments are well developed, and one feasibility study generates a US$600 million loan. For the multilateral banks, too, it is easy to measure the progress of a hydroelectric dam investment and to disburse the loan. A loan of US$60 million for rural aqueducts, on the other hand, is a nightmare. One hundred feasibility studies have to be carried out and evaluated, and construction has to be supervised in one hundred out-of-the-way places, where hundreds of small local firms, with primitive technical know-how and accounting, have to participate.

There is thus a bias towards larger engineering projects and against important but dispersed investments in health, nutrition, or rural improvements. However, bypassing the planning mechanism or investing without the processes imposed by the aid agencies does not solve the problem. When the rural aqueducts are constructed without adequate studies of soil conditions and water sources, the investment is lost.

Although the international bureaucracies prefer large projects that are easy to disburse, the formal policies of the agencies usually express the desirability of promoting social projects. Therefore, if the planning department requests social projects, the aid agencies will approve them. The problem is that the rigid procedures associated with the control of external funds will make disbursement of social projects long and tedious. Insufficient efforts have been made in multilateral aid agencies to facilitate the handling of social projects that have many small components.

In Colombia, however, between 1970 and 1978, the Planning Department requested aid agencies to finance various social projects, and although negotiations were slow and disbursements even slower, the loans were approved. In fact, the Colombian Integrated Rural Development Programmes, which have had substantial foreign credit, are amongst the most successful programmes of this type in the world.

In summary, through its activity in the financing and promotion of pre-feasibility studies, the Planning Department has influenced the direction of public investment. This has given continuity to investment policy, despite the frequent change in ministers and heads of decentralized agencies. Although each new minister has a pet project, often to be located in his region, the project cannot be financed until it has a pre-feasibility and feasibility study. Furthermore, in the case of a large-scale project, the Planning Department can ask that it be approved by an international bilateral aid agency. This procedure has stopped the execution of expensive white elephants (e.g. the Bogotá Underground System, which many mayors have backed). Numerous dams of particular interest to certain regions have been postponed when feasibility studies revealed that other locations would generate cheaper electricity.

A careful analysis reveals that the sectors where planning has been most effective have the following characteristics:

1. They have projects that easily meet the funding criteria of aid agencies.
2. Each investment is large, and operating costs are a small proportion of total costs.
3. It is easy to carry out traditional feasibility studies.[24]

This has meant that planning has been effective in the electrical sector, in road construction, in building large secondary schools, in building irrigation systems, and airports. Most of these sectors are capital intensive, and require low recurrent expenses.

Planning has had little influence on sectors with high recurrent costs, such as education and primary health, since aid agencies do not finance recurrent costs and evaluation of the economic benefits of these programmes is difficult.

Another situation in which planning has been effective is where a sector has independent and predictable revenues. For example, there is a special payroll tax to finance workers' training through a special institute (SENA). This guaranteed income has meant that SENA can plan the expansion of its training centres, knowing that it will be able to cover the recurrent costs of teachers and materials. As a result, the workers' training programme has been better organized and has served the community more effectively than the regular educational system.

The public educational system has also improved its coverage (proportion of children with access to public schools) since the 1970s when, by a constitutional reform, the national government started to transfer a known sum annually to the local authorities for the payment of teachers. Before that, the level of transfers depended on the whims of the minister of finance or on the effectiveness of the pressures mobilized by a local politician who happened to be governor or mayor at a certain time. Before the innovation of automatic transfers for education, planning in the sector was even more hopeless than now.

Electricity, urban water supply, telephones, and mining investments are also sectors that generate their own funds to cover recurrent expenditures and debt amortization once an investment is made. This makes these sectors attractive to foreign lenders, and for that reason investments in them tend to be influenced by the planning process.

Finally, it should be mentioned that for two decades, all public foreign indebtedness has had to be approved, case by case, by the National Planning Department. Due to exchange control, no foreign lender will fund an operation without that approval. This gives the department substantial leverage in the design of public investment. It also has ensured that the department and the government have had adequate information on the foreign debt. Therefore, Colombia did not increase its public foreign debt in a rapid and haphazard way in the 1970s, when the private international banks were granting loans indiscriminately in Latin America. On the contrary, that period was marked by strict regulations on foreign lending to the private sector and numerous loan rejections by the Colombian authorities.

It is clear, therefore, that the effectiveness of planning in the area of public investment has been related to the importance of foreign loans within the investment budget. The procedures of the bilateral and multilateral agencies allow the Planning Department to require well-designed projects from most government agencies. The priorities of the aid agencies also influence investment, since it is clearly better to design projects that have a good chance of getting foreign loans. But the criteria of the donors are sufficiently broad so that the Planning Agency can design a wide range of investment programmes. In spite of a bias both in government and in the aid agencies towards large infrastructure projects, the Colombian experience during the 1974–1978 plan period demonstrates that foreign loans can be shifted towards the social sector, although there are many execution and disbursement problems.

The problem associated with many of these social programmes is that even

when they are discontinued, no crisis is generated because the intended beneficiaries are often the voiceless masses. For example, policy-makers may be
convinced of the desirability of a comprehensive nutrition programme for children of less than two years of age, but they do not experience personal incon-
venience when the programme is discontinued. Yet, those same policy-makers
create an uproar during an energy crisis if the electricity starts going off every
night in their homes. Newspaper reporters and television commentators, who
are not beneficiaries, remain silent in the face of the nutrition programme's
demise; but they complain stridently about an airport that cannot guarantee
service in bad weather.

Interestingly enough, however, the Planning Agency has been the most supportive body to many of these social programmes, which usually do not have
pressure-group or media support. The Planning Agency supports these programmes because its technical and theoretical analysis reveals a need for them.
In a country where the poor do not often participate in government decision-
making, the technocratic DNP (National Planning Department) is one of the
few agencies of the national government that defends their interests.

The Private Sector and Planning

During interviews with private sector managers,[25] the impression was obtained
that national planning had little effect on decision-making in the private sector.
Company managers seldom read the plan documents and believe that economic
policies change with each change of minister and that the plans, therefore,
rapidly become obsolete. The two plans with the clearest specific policy prescriptions, *The Four Strategies* (1970–1974) and *To Close the Gap* (1974–1978),
were taken more seriously, since it was felt they reflected the policy-line of the
president.

The employer associations take the plans more seriously, and analyse and
criticize them when they come out. Sometimes these criticisms, if sufficiently
strong and persistent, lead to slight changes in emphasis in public policy.

The economic sectors identified as leading sectors in a plan seem to be able to
mobilize support for it. For example, the Public Construction Industry mobilized support for the Plan de Integracion Nacional, which emphasized public
construction. When criticism of the growing fiscal deficit led to a slower rate of
contracting of new public works, the construction industry complained loudly
that the plan was not being carried out, and the government had to reduce the
rate of cut-back on investment in order to save face.

The residential construction industry and the association of housing and loan
corporations also defended with vehemence the housing construction strategy of
The Four Strategies plan. When the monetary authorities tried to diminish the

privileges of the housing and loan corporations, strong public opinion and political pressure were mobilized in support of the strategy set out in the 1971–1974 plan.

To cite another example of the way pressure groups and interest organizations react to a plan, when *To Close the Gap* announced the end of extremely protective import-substitution policies, the manufacturing association withdrew its support to the government.

At the level of the individual firm, the entrepreneur has had little interaction with the Planning Agency, and employers' associations have also exerted little influence. Price controls, quotas, import licenses, and credit privileges are negotiated with the line ministries or with decentralized institutes on an *ad-hoc* basis and with little reference to the plan. Employers, however, appreciated the technocratic approach of the Planning Agency, and when the ministries were being particularly unreasonable and political in their decisions, employers tried to get the Planning Agency involved in the negotiating process concerning these matters. But they were seldom successful.

Foreign enterprises, on the other hand, had to deal with the Planning Agency, since it approved all direct foreign investment. In general, the DNP has the reputation of being uncorrupted and fairly flexible within the rather strict legal framework required for approval of foreign investment.

In most administrations, the Planning Department drafted indicative industrial plans for specific sectors.[26] These plans were negotiated with industry and the relevant ministries and sometimes led to some revisions in import tariffs, price or credit policy. In most cases, however, the plans were abandoned soon after their adoption.

Interestingly enough, however, each time that the design of an indicative plan was proposed to the private sector, managers of the private sector collaborated enthusiastically in the technical discussions and negotiations with the government, because they usually feel left out of government decision-making and like to discuss their problems and possible opportunities, even if they are not certain that the indicative plan would be implemented. The discussions were also a useful means of co-ordinating investment plans and for the exchange of information among competitors who rarely communicated with each other.

In summary, the relation between the Planning Department and the private sector was limited and the private sector did not often find the national plans relevant to their activities. Those interviewed, however, responded negatively to the following question:

Given the large fiscal deficit of the government, and the need to decrease government expenditure, should the Planning Department be abolished?

Further, private sector managers expressed their view that the Planning Department had introduced order into government expenditure and that, in the negotiations between industry and government, the technocrats of the Planning Department were at times able to introduce some elements of objectivity which were appreciated by both sides.

To further ascertain whether private sector managers would evaluate other government agencies as positively, we asked whether the Ministry of Development, which is in charge of industrial policy, tourism, housing, and foreign trade, should be abolished. The majority of those interviewed answered that it should. One respondent said that as far as he knew, the ministry had never "developed" anything.

Many of those interviewed felt that agriculture was the sector where planning was most needed. This attitude was baffling to us in view of (i) the well-publicized inefficiency of the agriculture of socialist countries where intensive planning takes place, (ii) the fact that in Colombia there are thousands of agricultural production units, and (iii) Colombia's extensive state intervention in agriculture (e.g. agricultural price controls, government control over imports of agricultural products, and enforcement of absorption quotas of national production at fixed prices by agro-industries).

After giving the subject some thought, we concluded that farmers' associations fear international competition and for that reason seem to desire the protection of quotas, guaranteed prices, etc. Since such government intervention tends to be inefficient, our interviewees focus on the weaknesses of the agricultural planning process instead of on the irrationality of government intervention in agriculture.

The Impact of the Planning Department on the Public Sector

One way of evaluating the effectiveness of planning in a country is to interview policy-makers (e.g. technocrats who have worked for the planning agency, politicians, and private sector managers) concerning the planning agency. For this paper I decided to try out such a subjective evaluation, since the Colombian plans do not easily lend themselves to a quantitative and more objective evaluation.

Since I have postulated that the Planning Department is most effective when it acts as the technical staff of the president, it is useful to analyse what various former presidents think has been the role of the Planning Department.

Pedro Pablo Morcillo interviewed four ex-presidents, Carlos Lleras (1966–1970), Misael Pastrana (1970–1974), Alfonso Lopez (1974–1978), and Julio Cesar Turbay (1978–1982), about their management styles in the presidency. These interviews were compared and summarized by Rodrigo Losada in an interesting article, from which the following illustrative quotations were taken.[27]

Concerning the choices made among various alternatives of action, President Lleras gave the opinion that "a very close contact between the President and the Director of Planning is absolutely essential. . . . The deliberations of the Council of Economic Policy (CONPES) occurred only exceptionally without having discussed a technical document prepared by the Department of Planning. . . . On the basis of these documents, which contained all the essential data, and conclusions with respect to different types of problems, decisions were taken. . . . I believe this mechanism [of CONPES discussion] is very effective. . . ."

President Pastrana declared that he preferred to discuss problems directly with the relevant minister, unless the subject matter affected various sectors. In that case, if the problem was of an economic nature, it was taken to CONPES. Lopez also declared that he found that he received from his two heads of planning "very valuable collaboration." Turbay expressed that "in the specific case of specialized subjects of an economic nature, the National Planning Department carried out an admirable job. . . . I missed this type of support in other sectors, where an advisory body (such as CONPES) would have been very effective. . . . In reality the majority of the data that the President needed concerning economic and social questions originated in the Planning Department or the Ministry of Finance."

It is clear, therefore, that the chief executives in Colombia have found planning and the services of the Planning Department useful.

It may be interesting to see how former heads of the department evaluate the Colombian planning experience. It is possible to do this because the reflections of 12 former heads of the department were published on the occasion of the twenty-fifth anniversary celebration of the department.[28]

The first interesting insight that can be derived from this publication (which lists the heads of planning and their tenures) is that there was a gradual gain in stability in the Planning Department over the 25 years. Between 1958 and 1966, when planning was not very effective, there were six directors, a record which shows some instability. Between 1966 and 1985 there have been ten directors, which gives a longer average tenure than in most ministries. Furthermore, five of the ten later became ministers (in Colombia the cabinet is composed of 13 ministers). The relative administrative stability in the Department and the fact that often heads of state appoint planning directors in other ministries are indicative of the importance of the role that planning plays within the government.

In the papers presented by the former directors, the following themes recur frequently:

1. The Planning Department has contributed to the rationalization of public expenditure. Roberto Arenas (1970–1972) writes that "it is evident that in the last decades . . . its action [the department] has rationalized the policies that determine public expenditure and, in particular, the investments of the state."[29] Edgar Gutierrez (1961–1962/1966–1970), whose essay constitutes

a good summary of planning in Colombia, also emphasized the fundamental role of the department in the determination of public expenditure and investment.[30]

2. The effectiveness of the Planning Department depends greatly on the institution of the Council of Economic Policy and the opportunity the council gives the department to present papers to the president and the relevant ministers for their consideration. John Naranjo (1977–1978) wrote: "The possibility of access to this forum in a permanent manner with its own studies, in the majority of the cases well prepared and of high technical quality, constituted the real strength of the Planning Department. If it had not been for this access, the institution might have become one more institute for non-applied research, and its importance as a co-ordinating institute would have been small."[31]

It is also clear that the department is the technical staff of the president for economic affairs. Presidents Lleras, Pastrana, and Lopez met weekly with the head of the department, and the latter was often asked by the president to analyse certain problems for him, to provide information for his speeches, and sometimes even to draft speeches. Some presidents also asked the head of planning to mediate between two ministers in disagreement. As Luis Eduardo Rosas says, "the influence and the importance of Planning depends on the support that the President is ready to give its recommendations."[32] That support is enhanced if the president has a good working relationship with the head of the agency and has confidence in the judgement of the technocrats in the department.

3. Almost all of the directors, in their essays on planning, attributed the effectiveness of the Planning Department to the high technical quality of the staff of the department.

When the department was reorganized in 1968, a special agreement was signed with the Central Bank which allowed for a special pay scale, substantially above the normal standard, for the high-level personnel of the department. In addition, USAID, the Ford Foundation, and a Canadian aid agency provided postgraduate scholarships for promising staff members. These special arrangements enabled Edgar Gutierrez to bring into the department a group of economists and engineers with Ph.D. degrees conferred from U.S. and European universities.

When this generation of technocrats moved on to higher posts in the government or the private sector, they were replaced by staff members who had studied abroad with fellowships. The high reputation of the department also made possible the recruitment of the best qualified graduates of the local universities.

In our interviews, carried out in 1985, quite a few policy-makers asserted that the level of competence of the staff of the department had dropped and hence its effective role within the state apparatus had diminished by 1985.

Some of the reasons given were: (a) termination of foreign financed fellowships towards the end of the 1970s; (b) inability to maintain a salary differential in favour of the Planning Department (a privilege difficult to justify politically) and hence difficulty in recruiting a capable staff; and (c) internal management problems.

4. The Planning Department has also played the role of technical adviser to the line ministries. They have requested the department to assist them in formulating various policies, even though such ministries and institutes might have had numerous professionals with expertise.[33]

Furthermore, the Planning Department has been instrumental in ministers' efforts to bring about a change in policy. Even though ministers have access to their own bureaucracy, those bureaucrats could not render effective service to the ministers because they were often committed to the status quo.

The department also indirectly strengthened the planning sections of the ministries. Each ministry has a planning department of its own. This group is strengthened by the ministry's contact with the National Planning Department through the negotiations involved in the drafting of the national investment budget.

5. Many directors of DNP[34] expressed their regret over the failure to achieve continuity of the plans. Edgar Gutierrez, for example, wonders whether "it would not be better to achieve greater sobriety in the management of the plans so as to change them less and instead emphasize those criteria which appear uniformly in all the plans and the coincidences in economic management through time. . . . It would be preferable to show in the long-run an economic process with fewer plans and much more continuity."[35]

Even though each administration since 1968 has produced its own plan, to emphasize its own originality, in fact, economic policy has had a surprising degree of continuity in Colombia. One plan might emphasize construction, another rural development, and still another public works. The shifts in emphasis, however, do not affect the major macro-economic variables. Monetary policy, fiscal policy, and foreign trade policy are changed only marginally in order to adjust the economy to changing international circumstances. The shifts in plan do not imply shifts in the basic philosophy of government. All plans have allowed the private sector substantial freedom, and no plan has contemplated major nationalization of private enterprises.

The fact that special support for a certain sector does not outlast one administration and its plan seems to be salutary, since it has led to fairly balanced development. The result of having one type of reform per plan emphasized enables all political resources in each administration to be focused on carrying out that particular reform. Once made into law, the reform is not reversed by later administrations. As a result, Colombia has gained some land reform, a progressive tax structure, important advances in labour legislation, an exchange regime well adapted to the resource endowment of the economy, and a fairly well-developed urban infrastructure.

In summary, Jorge Ospina, who was the head of the Planning Department in 1983–1986 during the Betancour administration, is probably correct when he writes, in the introduction to the collection of essays, of his predecessors that "although it is possible to argue the contrary, in Colombia there has been a relative continuity in the development model adopted, and in the management of economic policy."[36]

We have used the opinions of former heads of planning and heads of state to identify in what way planning has been effective in Colombia. This survey confirms the impression of academic and private sector observers who concur that the most important role of the Planning Department is to give technical support to the president in economic decision-making and to help rationalize both public investment and foreign credit.

However, during the interviews with public sector executives and entrepreneurs (who were also ex-ministers or ex-directors of public agencies), it became clear that in some areas of government activity the Planning Department has achieved little. It has shown little concern toward some crucial problems such as the management of the administration of justice and the quality of public education. A former minister of education stated that there was little planning in the area of public education because of the absence of a serious evaluation of the educational system. He pointed out that the ministry was not even sure of the number of teachers employed in the public sector.

The Planning Department has also never intervened in foreign affairs or in coffee policy. Since coffee has been 50 per cent of total exports, this is surprising. Coffee growers, however, carry tremendous political weight and have a powerful organization of their own which plans development in the areas where coffee production is important. The Coffee Federation has elected local committees active in each coffee region, and its own financial resources. It discusses coffee policy with the president and the minister of finance only. Coffee policy, which has tremendous macro-economic consequences, has never been included in a plan or discussed in the Council of Economic Policy.

Various heads of planning also complain that some crucial aspects of economic policy are not within the mandate of CONPES or the department. Such is the case of monetary policy, which is handled by the Monetary Board, and foreign trade policy, which is handled by the Consejo Superior de Comercio Exterior. However, the head of planning is a member of these bodies and could exert influence if sufficiently well briefed. If a disagreement occurs with the minister of finance, he could temporarily veto a policy and mobilize support for his point of view from other ministers or the president. In monetary policy, however, it is clear that the technocrats of planning must compete with the equally qualified and more numerous technocrats of the Central Banks, who provide advice and expertise to the minister of finance.

Historically, the Planning Department has been particularly effective when working in tandem with the Ministry of Finance. Co-operative action, however, has not always been the case. Finance ministers and planning directors have almost come to blows in sessions of the Monetary Board. The Planning Department has often favoured more expansionary policies than the Finance Ministry, and when the Finance Ministry does not support the Planning Department (and vice-versa) the co-ordinating capability of the latter is greatly weakened.

Finally, it is useful to comment on the issue of bottom-up planning. Colombia is one of the few countries which has been able to successfully implement Integrated Rural Development Projects. One of the reasons for this is that the responsibility for co-ordination of these projects was given to the Planning Department, and it included a local planning component in the projects. In each locality where an investment was to be made, local committees were organized to determine investment priorities. These priorities were filtered by Planning Office representatives at the regional level and then included in the national budget.

Dario Bustamante, deputy director of the Planning Department in 1985, had been a regional co-ordinator of an Integrated Rural Development Project eight years before. We asked him to evaluate the effectiveness of planning from below as opposed to planning from above. He gave a high evaluation of the experience of having the local community participate in the planning process, because it made government investment more responsive to perceived needs. However, he also saw a disadvantage: once it became clear that micro-level expenditures were the responsibility of the DNP, politicians and delegations of local groups started to appear in the offices of the National Planning Department. This tied up the staff in these small decisions, and more global and long-term activities suffered as a consequence. Furthermore, the DNP ran the risk of becoming politicized, thereby losing its reputation for objectivity. These are interesting reflections on some of the positive and negative aspects of bottom-up planning in a highly political setting such as that in Colombia. In the Betancur government, the Integrated Rural Development Project was taken out of the Planning Department and put in the most political of all the ministries, the Ministry of Agriculture.

The Experience of Planning in Some Specific Sectors

A greater in-depth analysis of the effectiveness of national planning in various sectors having different characteristics was also attempted. José Fernando Isaza[37] studied investment in highways and electricity, two sectors which have received substantial foreign credit and in which it is believed planning has been fairly effective. Jorge García[38] studied the management of foreign trade, a macro-economic policy which many people in Colombia believe has not been given adequate attention in the plans.

An analysis of the plans since 1967 led Jorge García to conclude that a surprising degree of continuity has persisted in the area of foreign trade because the plan documents of all administrations proposed essentially the same external commercial policy. He concludes that "one important aspect that needs to be stressed in all these development plans is the continuity of objectives and the consensus as to how the various tools of commercial policy should be used to achieve these objectives." He then goes on to say that, although progress was slower than one would expect from reading the statements made in the different plans, trade policy did move permanently towards a more liberal trade regime that would discriminate less against exports.

In summary, despite the slowness of the process, it appears that trade policy, one of the most crucial macro-economic policies, did move in the direction stated in the plans and that the different administrations adopted and implemented fairly consistent trade policies, despite substantial opposition from powerful interest groups.

A similar study with respect to monetary policy would probably also find continuity, some progress towards less direct controls of credit and interest rates, and a growing use of indirect controls of money supply. Tax policy has also followed fairly closely the policy statement of the plans. In summary, macro-economic policy has followed the principles stated in the plans. Such explicitly stated principles have made more difficult the frequently attempted *ad-hoc* deviations from a consistent macro-economic framework.

The Isaza analysis of infrastructure investment concludes that in the road and electricity sectors planning has been effective also. However, because these sectors lend themselves to highly technical project evaluation which is more readily accepted by foreign funding agencies, there might have been over-investment in the road and electricity sectors. This over-investment, no doubt, entailed under-investment elsewhere, such as in social sectors, where it is methodologically and technically difficult to calculate conventional economic rates of return and where expenditure has less of an import content which can be financed through foreign credit.

He also casts doubt on the efficiency of allocation of government funds among various sectors. According to Isaza, planning has not given serious consideration to this problem. For example, planning has not addressed the issue of allocation of funds between the electricity sector and the health sector, although it has developed good methodologies for choosing between different hydroelectric projects.

Conclusions

Development planning in Colombia in the last two decades has not emphasized macro-economic targets. None of the plans adopted by recent governments follows closely the methodologies recommended by the development textbooks.

Rather, the Planning Department has concentrated on improving the quality of government decision-making in the areas of public investment, foreign aid and credit, investment in the mining and energy sector, foreign investment, minimum-wage policy, and economic integration policy. The initiatives of the Planning Department have been particularly effective when the organization acts as the technical staff to the president and when it monitors the diverse activities of the state apparatus to ensure policy coherence. This co-ordinating role can be played effectively only if the head of state is strongly committed to a particular strategy of development and if he is willing to pay the political cost of vetoing those projects that the Planning Department identifies as incoherent with that strategy.

In Colombia political power is dispersed, and the political cost of maintaining policy coherence is high. Let us give an example. If a minister of public works from a certain region makes a proposal to invest in a road that benefits his region but that does not have a low cost/benefit ratio, it is hard to veto the inclusion of the road in the budget because the minister might resign and cause a cabinet crisis. This threat makes vetoing a regional initiative costly. The Planning Department may be able, through technical arguments, to make possible a veto at a lower political cost by making it clear that opposition to a project does not call into question a minister's political power.

Foreign aid and credit have given authority to the Planning Department because many of the larger investment projects have to be approved by the DNP for presentation to the external financing agencies. If the socio-economic evaluation of the project is not good, the Planning Department does not veto the project; it just states that it cannot be financed, since the multilateral financing agencies would not accept it. On the other hand, it can identify projects that meet the criteria of a plan and convince the executing agencies that if they agree to carry out such projects, they will obtain national and foreign financing. The role of the Planning Department then consists of convincing the line ministries and foreign aid or multilateral agencies to approve the projects that meet the criteria of a plan. The Colombian Planning Department, through the quality of its project preparation, has often managed to convince the foreign agencies to finance even somewhat unorthodox projects, particularly in areas such as education, agriculture, nutrition, and health.

As was pointed out in the first section, the Planning Department was not very effective between 1958 and 1968, when it was involved in textbook macro-economic planning. The Planning Department became influential and effective after 1968, when it changed the nature of its activity and started to work towards the improvement of the information and criteria provided to the president and the cabinet in the process of economic decision-making. This led the DNP to concentrate on the preparation of specific public sector projects and policy documents related to very specific decisions. The Planning Department thus focused on the short-run and on projects.

The cost entailed in the short-run micro-economic approach in planning has been that no agency in the government has been concerned with the long-run. This approach was aggravated by the fact that each administration has a four-year time horizon. Although short-run economic decision-making is usually framed with the long-run in mind, the pressing day-to-day business has not allowed the Planning Department to do much research into medium- and long-term issues. The Planning Department has not even developed an econometric model of the economy, nor has it invested in the compilation of economic statistics that would make some long-run modeling and simulations possible.

The lack of research and effort put into long-run analysis has also meant that in Colombia no national consensus has been developed about general development goals or strategies. This gives the private sector and even the informed citizen the impression that government policy is capricious, erratic, and unstable. It also leads to more disagreement and conflict than necessary with respect to specific policy decisions, since these are not put in the context of an agreed-upon long-run development strategy.

In other words, the planning process has not been used as a tool for consensus building with respect to economic policy. Without abandoning short-run economic decision-making, the Planning Department could try to produce some degree of national consensus with respect to economic policy by periodically carrying out a long-term planning exercise which would involve participants representing various sectors of society. The role of the Planning Department in mobilizing public opinion behind a broad strategy of development, through a process of consultation and discussion with many sectors of society, has been important in Japan and could have important consequences in Colombia.

The Colombian experience with "planning from below" in the case of Integrated Rural Development Projects suggests that greater continuity in this direction would enable policy-makers to adapt projects to more effectively benefit low-income families. Not all government expenditure at present, however, lacks citizen participation. The political process at the local level has already been facilitating popular participation, particularly with respect to the provision of public services in urban areas. Therefore, the National Planning Department should refrain from creating competing participatory mechanisms.

Finally, it would seem that the techniques of planning and policy analysis should be introduced into sectors that have been outside the planning process. Such sectors would include the administration of justice, the administration of basic police protection, the organization of public administration, the administration of public education, and perhaps even the administration of the quality of education.

The capability of the Planning Department to expand its expertise to include these additional services hinges on the sustained existence of high-quality staff which, in turn, will require greater pecuniary incentives as well as greater training opportunities than are currently available. The effectiveness of Colombian planning in the past has depended on the ability of the state to attract qualified technocrats to the Planning Agency.

Notes

1. IBRD, *World Development Report 1983* (New York, Oxford University Press), table 22.
2. Roberto Junguito, "El Sector Agropecuario y el Desarrollo Colombiano," in Fedesarrollo, *Lecturas sobre Desarrollo Económico Colombiano* (Bogotá, Fedesarrollo, 1974), p. 583.
3. In 1960, these commodities accounted for 79 per cent of exports and in 1980 for 77 per cent; see IBRD (note 1 above), table 10.
4. Miguel Urrutia and Albert Berry, *Income Distribution in Colombia* (New Haven, Yale University Press, 1976), p. 51, table 2A.1.
5. Ibid., ch. 4, pp. 87–123.
6. Miguel Urrutia, *Winners and Losers in Colombia's Economic Growth of the 1970's* (New York, Oxford University Press, 1985), p. 5.
7. Quite inaccurately, Griffin and Enos talk about a development plan produced in 1945, when what happened was that in that year congress introduced the concept of planning into the constitution. See Keith B. Griffin and John L. Enos, *Planning Development* (London, Addison-Wesley, 1970), p. 201.
8. See Antonio García, "La Planificación en Colombia," *Trimestre Económico*, vol. 20, no. 3 (1953), p. 453.
9. For the story of this mission see: Lauchlin Currie, *The Role of Economic Advisers in Developing Countries* (Westport, Conn., The Greenwood Press, 1981), chap. 5.
10. IBRD, *The Basis of a Development Programme for Colombia* (Baltimore, Johns Hopkins University Press, 1952).
11. In 1952, it rejected a Colombian loan application for investment in a water works project in Barranquilla because the project did not have an economic purpose but a social one.
12. OIT, *Hacia el Pleno Empleo* (Geneva, OIT, 1970).
13. Presidencia de la República, Comité Nacional de Planeación, *Misión de "Economía y Humanismo," Estudio sobre las Condiciones del Desarrollo de Colombia* (Bogotá, Aedita Editores, 1958).
14. Keith Griffin and John Enos, *Planning Development* (note 7 above), p. 201.
15. Ibid.
16. One by-product of the plan was the introduction of Colombia to one of the ECLA advisers, Carlos Diaz Alejandro, an economist who has since written thoughtful academic works on the Colombian economy as well as on problems of development in general.
17. Departamento Nacional de Planeación, *Planes y Programas de Desarrollo 1969–1972* (Bogotá, Planeación Nacional).
18. Albert Waterston, "Una mirada escrutadora a la planeación del desarrollo," *Finanzas y Desarrollo*, vol. 3, no. 2 (June 1966) (translated by the author).
19. DNP, *Plan de Desarrollo Económico y Social 1970–73* (Bogotá, Planeación Nacional).
20. Lauchlin Currie et al., *Operación Colombia: Un Programa Nacional de Desarrollo Económico y Social* (Barranquilla, Cámara de Comercio de Barranquilla, 1965).
21. The national account figures for the savings rate (family savings as percentage of national income) changed as follows: 1970, 0.022; 1971, 0.008; 1972, 0.038; 1973, 0.039; 1974, 0.060.
22. DNP, *Para Cerrar la Brecha: Plan de Desarrollo Social, Económico y Regional 1975–78*

(Bogotá, Banco de la República, 1975), p. 20.

23. Gaviria Cesar, "La Visión Política del PIN," in CEDE and FENALCO, eds., *Controversia sobre el PIN* (Bogotá, 1981), p. 121. Nevertheless, the influence of the IMF, IBRD, BID, AID, etc., can be exaggerated by scholars who use the agency sources as a basis for their research. Obviously World Bank or AID experts will claim that their agencies views have been influential. If they did not, they might lose their jobs or their agencies might not be funded by congress or the relevant ministry. See also Londoño y Perry, "El Banco Mundial, le Fondo Monetario y Colombia: Análisis Crítico de Sus Relaciones," *Coyuntura Económica* (Oct. 1985): 209–243, and Gómez y Thoumi, "Una Nota sobre la Relación entre el Financiamiento Externo y la Inversión Pública en Colombia," *Coyuntura Económica* (Oct. 1986): 196–203.

24. This section is based on the conclusions of a special study made for this project on the successes and failures of planning in the transport and energy sectors. See José Fernando Isaza, "Planeación Sectorial: Obras Públicas y Energía" (Bogotá, July 1985, Mimeo).

25. The interviews were carried out in mid-1985 by the author and Monica de Sarmiento. See M. Urrutia and Monica de Sarmiento, "Opiniones sobre Planeación" (Bogotá, June 1985, Mimeo).

26. For example, the following indicative plans were presented for approval by CONPES: October 1981, the tobacco manufacturing industry; September 1981, an indicative plan for the plastics products industry; March 1982, an indicative plan on potato production; April 1982, an indicative plan on housing construction. In the period of the plan *To Close the Gap*, various indicative plans were negotiated, including those for the paper and pulp, steel, cement, glass, automobile, and the electronics industries. For example, in the case of the pulp and paper industry, the credit conditions negotiated for reforestation projects were accepted by the monetary authorities, import tariffs were decreased from 25 per cent to 15 per cent as agreed, and an agreement on absorption quotas of nationally produced pulp was implemented. See Nota del Editor, *Revista de Planeación y Desarrollo*, vol. 9, no. 1, Enero-Marzo 1977.

27. Rodrigo Losada, "Cuatro Estilos de Administración Presidencial en Colombia." *Gerencia al Día* (Dic. 1984): 33–39.

28. DNP, *Revista de Planeación y Desarrollo*, vol. 15, no. 4. (Dic. 1983).

29. Ibid., p. 32.

30. Ibid., p. 84.

31. Ibid., p. 56.

32. Ibid., p. 47.

33. This aspect was pointed out by Dario Bustamante, subdirector of the DNP in 1985. (He felt these functions took up too much of the time of the DNP staff.)

34. DNP are the initials of the Department of National Planning.

35. DNP, *Revista de Planeación y Desarrollo* (note 28 above), p. 87.

36. Ibid., p. 4.

37. José Fernando Isaza, "Planeación Sectorial: Obras Públicas (Carreteras) y Energía (Electricidad)" (Bogotá, Julio 1985, Mimeo).

38. Jorgé García García, "Commercial Policy in Colombian Development Plans between 1967 and 1982: Theory and Practice" (Bogotá, Nov. 1975, Typescript).

6

DEVELOPMENT PLANNING IN KENYA

Leopold P. Mureithi

Introduction

During the colonial era at the dawn of the twentieth century, the British built a railway from Mombasa to Lake Victoria in order to control the head-waters of the Nile, combat slave-trade, and establish legitimate commerce. To make the "lunatic" express profitable, systematic settlement of immigrants was mounted by the Colonial Office, and the addition of planned large-scale farming and trade, accompanied by planned massive drafting of African labour, completed Kenya's initiation into planning at the national level.

Further impetus to early planning was given by: (1) the outbreak of the First World War, with its need to organize supplies using the "carrier corps" in Kenya; (2) the onset of the Great Depression, which saw idle manpower and capital in Britain ready for deployment in the colonies; (3) the Second World War, which increased the need for self-reliance and total mobilization of resources on an East African (Kenya, Uganda, Tanzania) basis and which resulted in the institution of the Kenya Industrial Management Board (KIMBO); and (4) the Marshall Plan, wherein the United States insisted that the recipient European countries draw up four-year recovery programmes that included their overseas territories.

The greatest propeller of peace-time planning, however, was the Colonial

The author wishes to acknowledge research assistance by J. M. Konzolo and useful comments by M. Urrutia, S. Yukawa, and J. K. Kinyua and two anonymous referees, who are all absolved of the personal views expressed and any shortcomings contained herein.

198

Development and Welfare Act of 1945, which made provision for financial assistance to overseas territories for aiding and developing agriculture and industry, with a view to promoting commerce and industry in Britain. The Colonial Office asked territories to draw up ten-year plans.

Kenya's first 10-year plan was published in 1946. It was followed by 3-year plans[1] from 1954 to 1963. These plans were not comprehensive, since they were primarily lists of capital projects from the public sector with essentially no incorporation of the private sector. The notable exception in this regard was the overwhelmingly dominant agricultural sector. As early as 1954, the government had issued the famous Swynnerton Plan[2] to intensify the development of African agriculture by initiating demarcation of communally held land, consolidating scattered fragments of land, registering land titles and by granting permission to Africans to grow crops previously reserved for Europeans, such as coffee, tea, and pyrethrum. Although the typical colonial development plans[3] were carried out by civil servants who were little accustomed to planning, the learning effect was tremendous: independent Kenya inherited the practice of planning as an accepted function of government.

Growth of the Economy

The economy of Kenya is characterized by, *inter alia*, (1) a dominant rural (agricultural) sector in which about 85 per cent of the people live and from which they derive their livelihood; (2) a small but dynamic manufacturing sector whose primary undertaking is import substitution; (3) dependence on external markets, which results in a high degree of openness; and (4) an expanding public sector.

Since attaining independence in 1963, GDP showed an average annual growth rate of 5 per cent[4] in real terms up to 1983. These two decades, however, exhibit a distinct break in 1973. GDP grew annually by 5.9 per cent between 1964 and 1973 but dropped to 4.1 per cent per annum thereafter. With population growth rate averaging about 3.5 per cent in the first decade and 3.9 per cent in the second, per capita income increased at an annual rate of 2.4 per cent in the early period but hardly increased in the later period. After a depressed year in 1984, essentially due to widespread drought conditions, the economy picked up to grow at 4.2 per cent during 1985 — thanks to the world-wide downturn of oil prices and the miniboom in coffee prices. With oil imports taking 50.6 per cent of Kenya's foreign exchange earnings and coffee being the leading export, such an improvement in terms of trade was a salutary turn around for the economy. This has proved to be a transient respite, since coffee and tea prices declined in early 1987.

The rapid economic growth in the first decade occurred in an environment of stable prices (a creeping inflation rate of around 3 per cent per year), manageable budgetary deficits, averaging 6 per cent of GDP, and tolerable deficits in the balance of payments (around 3 per cent of GDP). The second decade experienced double-digit inflation of about 14 per cent per year, runaway budgetary out-turns of about 10 per cent of GDP, and a gaping balance-of-payments deficit averaging 9 per cent of GDP.

The year 1973, considered to be a turning point, marks the onset of the oil crisis and the subsequent prolonged recession in industrial countries. Despite the occurrence of a temporary respite in 1976 caused by the coffee and tea boom, given Kenya's participation in external trade — 29 and 39 per cent of GDP constituting its exports and imports, respectively, by 1981 — the worsening world economic environment dealt it a severe blow.

Sound economic policy is supposed to address itself to such problems and institute remedial measures. Therefore, the major objectives of this paper will be to investigate whether the country's planning agencies addressed the problems, to examine the economic, social, political, and administrative constraints they encountered, and to assess the degree of success their remedial measures achieved.

Kenya's economy has undergone considerable structural transformations. It has become increasingly monetized, with non-monetary production declining from 26 per cent of GDP in 1963 to 5 per cent in 1983. The centre of gravity has gradually shifted towards industry, with the share of agriculture in GDP declining from 38 per cent in 1963 to 35 per cent in 1983. Urbanization is evident, with the urban population rising from 7 per cent of the total population in the 1962 census to 15 per cent in the 1979 census. The economy has become increasingly dependent on international trade, with the total volume of trade (exports plus imports) rising from 64 per cent of GDP in the 1963–1973 decade to 73 per cent in the 1973–1983 decade. There is evidence of the crowding-out effect, with government services claiming 13 per cent of GDP in 1964 and 15 per cent in 1983.

Of central importance to this paper are the answers to such questions as: (1) To what extent has development planning been instrumental in the observed structural transformations? and (2) Did the observed economic development and the prevalent economic characteristics occur because of or in spite of the development planning practised? Before tackling these questions, however, we shall first examine both the strand of government policy and the main strategies propounded since the attainment of political independence.

Perspective on Policy

The First Decade

The policy of the Kenya government with respect to certain economic objectives is to be found in various statements, declarations, and publications. All these sources have announcement effects. Among the key documents are the manifesto by the ruling party — The Kenya African National Union (KANU) — as issued in 1963; the Parliamentary Sessional Paper Number 10 of 1965 on African Socialism and its application to planning in Kenya; and the development plans issued periodically (five years being the frequent practice) by the government.

The Sessional Paper of 1965 puts these objectives as: universal freedom from want, disease, and exploitation; equal opportunities for advancement; and high and growing per capita incomes, equitably distributed among the population. A sense of mutual social responsibility was to be the guiding principle, and a mixed economy was to be the economic regime — two key essentials of "African Socialism." To concretize the declared policy, the planning machinery has produced a number of development plans.

The struggle for independence was fired by the relative deprivation of the African population, Kenya's largest racial group, in terms of land, education, and employment opportunities. A land resettlement programme, as a beginning step, became politically mandatory. In addition, education, increased employment, higher productivity, and improved services (e.g. health, housing, etc.) were emphasized.

The "Red Plan" (so-called in reference to the color of its cover) was supposed to span the years from 1964 to 1970. Hurriedly drafted, in order to have a plan for the onset of the republican status of the country, and characterized by incomplete analysis resulting from the use of inadequate data, it was soon replaced by the Green Plan, covering the years 1966–1970. It seemed at the time of launching this plan that a conscious decision had been made to have rolling plans in preference to completely new ones every five years. However, the Green Plan, even though it corrected some of the more glaring omissions of its predecessor, was simply an expanded version of the Red Plan. Its greater scope, more systematic analysis, and growth targets had (with the notable exception of agriculture) little in terms of project content — again repeating the pattern of the colonial plans.

Agricultural policy was aimed at acquiring large farms previously owned by white settlers and subdividing them among landless Africans. At that time, this policy was more a political move than one to promote economic growth and development, but today the small-farm sector produces more than 50 per cent[5] of the marketed agricultural output in Kenya and is a major foreign exchange earner.

Population growth (at that time slightly over 3 per cent p.a.) was considered a key factor circumscribing economic growth. Industrial development strategy was defined as import substitution and industrial ventures (which were foreign exchange earners/savers, labour intensive, resource based, etc.) were strongly encouraged. GDP was targeted to grow at 6.3 per cent per annum.

In September 1966, a conference, which turned out to be a landmark in Kenya's economic history, was held at Kericho. It was attended by members of the academic community, policy-makers, administrators, and representatives of aid agencies. The proceedings of the Kericho conference were published in 1967 as a book entitled *Education, Employment and Rural Development*.[6]

A major emphasis at the conference was a call to give more attention to equipping people with requisite and relevant human skills and to institute measures for the development of rural areas in all spheres — agriculture, industry, services, infrastructure, etc. It was in the light of this shift in attitude that the next five-year plan was formulated.

The Second Development Plan (1970–1974), the Blue Plan, was a more comprehensive document, with extensive coverage of local government activities, private sector targets, rural development, etc. It excelled the previous plans in project specificity.

The immediate objective in this plan was to achieve more prosperity and better living conditions in the agricultural and range areas, where resettlement of Africans on small farms was being effected. It was noted that even though the economy had grown rather rapidly during the preceding five years, the growth had been sectorally imbalanced: the key sectors (agriculture and manufacturing) had grown less than building and construction, services, etc. — a pattern of growth that was less desirable. This had to be corrected.

The government, setting itself as the catalyst to increase production and income, made the following plans: expand education and training institutions and health services; improve agriculture, particularly husbandry practices, marketing, credit facilities, and land registration; extend roads, especially feeder roads, to enable farmers to get their produce to markets in all seasons; develop a rural water-supply programme on a nation-wide scale; build more facilities for rail, water, and air transport; improve and extend tourist facilities throughout the country; and expand industrial and commercial activity, particularly in the rural areas.

To accomplish these plans, government expenditure (recurrent and development) was to increase by about 11 per cent per annum during the plan period. The targeted growth of the economy was to be 6.7 per cent per annum, emphasis being placed on rural development. With agricultural production to grow at 6 per cent per annum, while rural population was to grow at 2.7 per cent per annum, the prospects for rural improvement were steady and realistic.

This plan document did not lose sight of one important fact: a development plan is a set of choices which are intended to get the most results in all spheres within the limited amount of resources there are to utilize. But the plan is also a guide in a spelt-out direction and must of necessity be flexible, particularly in the face of unpredictable events in the world economy or in natural circumstances (e.g. weather). The government's central role would continue to be the same: to provide and maintain a favourable climate for investment, to guide and assist investors, and to supply necessary infrastructural facilities. In addition, on large projects, the government was prepared to participate financially as a shareholder.

At this juncture, a backward look reveals that Kenya's development plans have remained consistent while simultaneouly becoming more detailed and specific over time. There has also been an apt readiness to adopt prevalent thinking in the economic sphere. In this connection, it is worth noting that the International Labour Organization launched the World Employment Programme[7] in 1970. This year was also the beginning of the second UN development decade, which targeted a blanket growth rate of 6 per cent per annum — a percentage above the rate targeted for the first UN development decade.

During the first decade, there was evidence of rapid growth in GDP, but manifest failure of the "trickle-down effect" (i.e. there was widespread unemployment and an emerging class of the "working poor," whose incomes were so low — defined as below KSh 200/per month — that they could not afford a modest minimum standard of living). In 1972, an inter-agency mission was sent to Kenya by the ILO and the UNDP. Its report[8] emphasized the need to rectify the imbalances by promoting greater equality among regions, districts, and individuals with regard to income, health services, physical infrastructure, education, and land-use. This was to be done in the context of continued growth and expanded production in every sector; hence, the proposed strategy of "redistribution from growth."[9]

Economic Crises and Recovery

During the *Third Five-Year Development Plan* (1974–1978), emphasis was placed on employment creation, redistribution of income, district planning for rural development, family welfare, science, and appropriate technology. This planning period was to be the most challenging since independence.

Although overall growth was targeted at 7.4 per cent per annum during the plan period, this implied an employment growth of only 3.2 per cent per annum. The high population growth during the plan period seemed to indicate that, all things being equal, the number of people joining the labour force would equal the number of new jobs created.

Agriculture was to continue to be the main source of employment, with 22.3 per cent of the development budget going to this sector. In allocating funds for agricultural development and for technical assistance and credit, greater attention was to be paid to the less-developed agricultural areas and to range lands as a way of improving income distribution. The development strategy was to concentrate on extension services, training, research, and provision of credit, as well as improved supplies of farm inputs, markets, and co-operatives — all aimed at improving, *inter alia*, rural employment and agricultural output.

The manufacturing growth rate target was 10.2 per cent per year. So far the strategy had been import substitution, but it was starting to be quite clear that emphasis had to shift to an export-promotion industrial strategy. Greater emphasis continued to be laid on small-scale industries, even though the problem of managerial skills was recognized.

The plan had some significant improvements over the previous plans. First, it carried a five-year forward budget for each ministry. Previously projected public expenditures were set forth in broad categories that did not correspond to the budgetary items; as a consequence, it was hard to ascertain whether the plan was being correctly implemented. New efforts were made to see to it that annual budgetary allocations were made according to plan priorities. Second, a project registry was set up to record essential data on each government project. Third, a complete set of national product accounts was, for the first time, projected, and there were new estimates on investment, consumption, and savings. All these endeavoured to bring control over the functioning of the plan.

However, the high growth targets, based on the previous excellent growth of the economy, were short-lived. By 1975 the global recession set in motion by the 1973–1974 oil crisis had made itself strongly felt in Kenya. Import prices rose, export receipts fell, and finances from the international capital markets became dearer. Further, the drought of 1974 adversely affected agricultural output. The government was forced to go into deeper borrowing from multilateral and bilateral aid sources.

Real GDP was dampened to a growth of 4.6 per cent per annum. Moreover, the extra costs of imports over export receipts reduced the purchasing power of what was produced, so that growth in real income barely exceeded 1.0 per cent per annum. Adjusted for population growth, real income in 1974 fell by about 2.3 per cent. These "lows," coupled with the highest inflation rate since independence — about 16 per cent per annum — clearly announced that soft development options were over.

The planning machinery was jolted into reacting quickly to the changing circumstances. A sessional paper[10] was issued in 1975. It contained a strategy to keep domestic price increases to no more than half of the increase in import prices; to hold wage increases and increases of other non-import costs of production to less than domestic price increases; to restrain imports; to promote exports; to stimulate domestic production, both in import substitution and export promotion; to choose policies that reinforce the long-term objectives of promoting growth, employment, and equitable income distribution.

It was clear that national resources would be strained to capacity in the ensuing years. It was therefore urgent to fully and efficiently utilize the resources available to raise output. Most expectations and projections as envisaged in the 1974–1978 plan were revised and considerably changed.

Unexpected events (e.g. the commodity boom of 1976–1977) appear to have gone unnoticed by our planning machinery. It was necessary to have an unambiguous policy to deal with the sudden expansion in money supply, which resulted in the rocketing of domestic prices due to demand-pull inflation. But the policy of controlling the rise in domestic prices was defeated. While it would have been salutary to harness those incomes for socially productive investments, in actuality a large portion was channelled into private use (i.e. conspicuous consumption — large cars — and speculative asset acquisition — real estate). It would have had a long-term stabilizing effect if those reserves had been sterilized by the Central Bank and released in moderate and steady instalments. Hopefully, the lesson has been learned for future windfall gains.

The Development Plan for the Period 1979–1983 had as its major theme the alleviation of poverty and better income redistribution. It was inspired by the basic needs strategy propounded by the World Employment Conference held in Geneva in 1976. The alleviation of poverty was to be pursued by creation of income-earning opportunities and by the provision of basic needs, including nutrition, health care, basic education, water, and housing. Because greater poverty exists in the rural areas, the plan placed strong emphasis on policies, programmes, and projects for rural development.

Poverty is a two-dimensional concept: inadequate or inequitable income is one dimension and uneven accesss to basic services is the other. At the time of writing the plan, 49 per cent of the people were identified as having low incomes and limited access to basic services. Employment was regarded as the greatest single challenge the planners had to face. Between 1972 and 1976, the GDP had grown on the average at 2.9 per cent per annum, while the labour force had been growing at about 3.5 per cent per annum. The forecast GDP growth rate for 1979–1983 was 6.3 per cent per annum.

Towards the end of 1979, the global economy tilted into a deep recession. This had a profound effect on Kenya's small open economy. Projected growth rates were never achieved, and for the period 1978–1981, the GDP grew on average at 4.2 per cent per annum — a performance that is commendable under the circumstances.

One of the major thrusts of this plan was an increased accent on rural development along the same lines as the previous plans — although, in addition, emphasis was laid on the importance of increasing rural participation in planning at the district level.

Sessional Paper Number 4, a 1980 policy paper, set the target rate of GDP growth at 5.4 per cent per annum up to 1983. The actual aim of this paper was to highlight new guidelines designed to reduce the impact of soaring import prices on Kenya's economy by allocating the scarce foreign exchange to priority development needs as part of a larger structural adjustment. But even these policies were undermined by shortfalls in the foreign exchange required for necessary imports.

The theme of the 1984–1988 development plan is "mobilising domestic resources for equitable development." This plan was made against the background of a global recession, with Kenya experiencing balance-of-payments difficulties while carrying a heavy debt-serving burden. In recognition of this reality, GDP is projected to grow at 4.9 per cent a year during the plan period. This is a sobering lowering of sights.

The basic long-term objectives remain the same, namely growth, employment promotion, equality of opportunities, and equitable income distribution. The government, playing the central role of facilitator, intends to enable Kenyans to help themselves individually and collectively; to improve the quality and distribution of government services by sharing the cost of existing services with those who benefit; to provide suitable incentives for production and investment; to share the costs of development through an equitable taxation system; to control and regulate the private sector activity as necessary.

As important new emphasis is on the consumer, who will have to pay more for government services. The 1984–1988 plan also promulgated the "District Focus for Rural Development," whereby responsibility for planning and implementing rural development is being shifted from the headquarters of ministries to the districts. This is meant to improve problem anticipation, project identification, resource mobilization, and project implementation at the local level — a salutary lesson from the Special Rural Development Programme of the 1970s and the Integrated Agricultural Development Programme of the 1980s.

The Mid-1980s and Beyond

In early 1986, the government issued *Sessional Paper Number 1* of 1986, which is essentially a perspective plan[11] covering the period up to the year 2000. It proposes a broad strategy and some specific measures "to renew economic growth in ways that will provide jobs for the growing labour force, prosperity for the people in the rural areas, an equitable and widespread sharing of the benefits of growth, and a continuing provision of basic needs for all."[12] A moderately rapid GDP target growth rate of 5.6 per cent a year is set for the 1986–2000 period.

Like its predecessors since 1975, the *Sessional Paper* recognizes the diminished resource base and the need to plan for maximal productivity of the scarce resources. The era of soft options — "finishing-touches" industrialization, import substitution by reproducing locally consumer goods formerly imported, extension of areas under cultivation, land transfer from foreigners to citizens, Kenyanization of personnel by mere substitution of foreign labour by citizens — is over. Hard options — diversification of industry, restructuring the same so as to export and compete internationally, integrating industry with agriculture, intensive *rather than extensive* cultivation, harnessing arid and semi-arid lands, creation of *new* jobs and work-places, production of capital and producer (intermediate) goods — must be squarely faced.

Like the 1984–1988 plan, cost sharing between the beneficiaries and the government is advocated in such areas as education, health, and water. Individuals and families must fend for themselves in the provision of food, shelter, and clothing. Greater reliance is to be placed on the private sector. Government budget rationalization is to be undertaken to reduce the share of salaries (60 to

90 per cent of the recurrent outlay in 1984/1985)[13] and increase the share of complementary resources (transport, typewriters, paper, pens and pencils) to boost productivity within government.

Budget rationalization for faster growth also entails government spending on services which are immediately or quickly productive, such as agricultural extension services, small-scale industrialization, infrastructure (roads, power, and water), to promote growth of small towns and rural areas. It also entails rational prioritizing of projects so as to maintain existing capital stock and facilities. For example, investment in new projects should be undertaken only if they have high benefit-capital ratios and if they are essential and urgent. On the other hand, essential but less urgent projects should be rescheduled, that is, postponed. A similar fate should befall merely desirable projects, while projects with low potential benefits should be cancelled. The *Sessional Paper* on economic management is to serve as the blueprint for all development plans in the coming 14 years.

Some Observations

On the whole, development planning in Kenya has been wide in scope and sufficiently comprehensive. A good foundation was laid at the start, with national goals and objectives clearly stated and consistently maintained through all the plans. Thus, Kenya is still basically on its initial growth path.

Over time, the planning machinery has demonstrated increased meticulousness, flexibility, and sharpness in dealing with unexpected circumstances (e.g. the oil crises of 1973/1974 and 1979). Policy-makers have also responded maturely and positively to changing economic perceptions. Hence, the 1964–1970 plan focused on rapid growth, in keeping with the first UN development decade; the 1970–1974 plan aimed at shifting the locale of growth to the rural areas, in line with the prevailing emphasis on *in-situ* rural development, in order to take development where the majority of the people lived; the 1974–1978 plan put an accent on employment creation in order to enable people to share directly in the fruits of production; the 1979–1983 plan emphasized alleviation of both absolute and relative poverty by adopting the basic needs development strategy; the 1984–1988 plan and the 1986 *Sessional Paper* recognize the scarcity of resources and call for the mobilization of those which are available and generative.

A look at the series of development plans in Kenya is tantamount to reviewing the recent history of the problems of underdevelopment and poverty. Globally, ways and means to solve these problems have undergone radical changes since the end of the Second World War. First, there was a "growth-and-trickle-down" approach beginning in the 1950s and lasting until the late 1960s. Then came the strategy of "growth with distribution." When redistribution proved difficult due to the structural nature of poverty, the 1970s saw the "basic needs" approach of "who gets what." In the face of fundamental changes in the economic environment, the World Bank and the International Monetary Fund have sold the idea of structural adjustment, policy planning, institutional reform, privatization, etc., as canons[14] for proper economic management. All these strands run through Kenya's economic policy and planning practice.

The frankness and adaptability of Kenyan planners is a source of strength. It has resulted in constant review of policies, programmes, targets, and projects. Coupled with the production of sessional papers on economic problems and prospects, we come as close as one could get to rolling plans.

The Planning Machinery: Structure, Process, and Problems

Before independence in 1963, Kenya's planning machinery consisted of a Planning Unit located within the Ministry of Finance, the Treasury, and staffed by a few officials of the "traditional" civil service. The implementation of projects planned by the unit rested with the operating ministries, but the Treasury exercised considerable influence through the disbursement, control, and auditing of funds.

At independence, the government established a Directorate of Planning — an expanded Planning Unit — within the Ministry of Finance and Economic Planning. It was headed by a director of planning, an economist reporting directly to the permanent secretary to the Treasury. The planning function was hived off from the Treasury, and a Ministry of Economic Planning and Development was established in 1964 under the very able late Tom Mboya. It was charged with the task of overall economic planning and co-ordination for development. This responsibility remained distinct even when the planning function was housed within the Ministry of Finance and Economic Planning (1974–1978, 1983–1985) and the Ministry of Economic Planning and Community Affairs (1979–1983). The relevant ministry is now called the Ministry of Planning and National Development.

In the beginning, the ministry was small and centralized, but by 1969 the planning machinery was extended to the provinces with the posting of provincial planning officers. District development officers were in place by 1974. Planning organization in Kenya can be represented diagramatically as in figure 1 below. This also gives the corresponding administrative set-up. At the apex is the president and the cabinet — the supreme policy-making body. In the 1960s, there was a standing Development Committee of the Cabinet, but over the years its tasks have been handled by ad-hoc committees of ministers set up to deal with specific issues. The planning function is located in the Ministry of Planning and National Development, which works in close collaboration with planning divisions in the operating ministries (Agriculture, Labour, Transport,

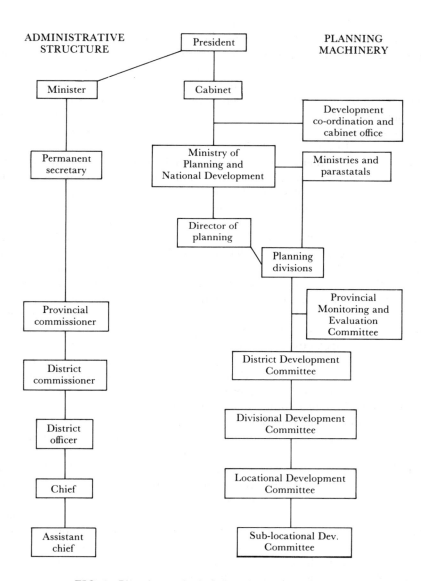

ADMINISTRATIVE STRUCTURE

PLANNING MACHINERY

President

Minister

Cabinet

Development co-ordination and cabinet office

Permanent secretary

Ministry of Planning and National Development

Ministries and parastatals

Director of planning

Planning divisions

Provincial commissioner

Provincial Monitoring and Evaluation Committee

District commissioner

District Development Committee

District officer

Divisional Development Committee

Chief

Locational Development Committee

Assistant chief

Sub-locational Dev. Committee

FIG. 1. Planning and administrative organization

etc.) through sector planning and estimates working groups and the Inter-Ministerial Co-ordinating Committee, consisting of permanent secretaries.

There are 40 District Development Committees (DDCs), comprising the district commissioner as the chairman, the district development officer as the secretary, heads of departments of operating ministries, members of parliament, the chairman of the KANU branch, the chairmen and clerks of local authorities, the chairman of Divisional[15] Development Committees, co-opted officials,[16] and representatives of non-governmental development organizations. As can be seen from figure 1, institutions have been developed to facilitate bottom-up planning, that is, local participation from the village level. DDCs issue District Development Plans.

Prior to 1983, there were eight Provincial Planning Committees (PPCs), chaired by their respective provincial commissioners, consisting of provincial administrative and professional heads of central government ministries such as agricultural, community development, veterinary, medical, and educational officers, a member of parliament, and two leading citizens nominated by the chairman. Unlike the DDCs, the PPCs never issued development plans. Although on occasion multidistrict or zonal development plans were issued by parastatals such as the Tana and Athi Rivers Development Authority, Kerio Valley Development Authority, the Lake Basin Development Authority, and the National Irrigation Board — or by the Physical Planning Department of the central government, which has issued several provincial physical development plans over the years — PPCs were simply a channelling-through agency, an intermediate stage between the ministry and the districts. In this capacity, their primary function seemed to be to increase bureaucratic red tape and delays. It was, therefore, a wise move to reconstitute PPCs into committees for the monitoring and evaluation of projects in the provinces. This watch-dog role has goaded DDCs into promptness and cleanliness in the implementation and management of development resources, programmes, and projects.

Within the office of the president, the Development Co-ordination and Cabinet Office acts as the secretariat on development affairs. This is the office that drafted the district-focus approach[17] to development in 1983. We propose that economic affairs at this level be separated from other affairs of the cabinet and that a National Economic Advisory Council (NEAC) be created and chaired by a competent, widely experienced economist who would be ranked at par with a minister and that its secretary be an outstanding economist with the rank of permanent secretary. Its core members, professional and administrative-support staff, should be minimal. Using the brainstorming approach in search of optimum development policies and strategies, the NEAC would serve as a think-tank and work closely with government officials, businessmen, trade unionists, farm leaders, outside specialists, etc. The NEAC would play an advisory role to the president on matters pertaining to the economy. The president and cabinet would formulate the policy, and the Ministry of Planning and

National Development would ensure operationalization of that policy by, for a start, incorporating it into the development plans, with a view to implementation by the substantive ministries.

Under the district-focus strategy, local initiative is exercised when compiling project and programme proposals, but final decisions are made in compliance with "policy guide-lines to be used by the district in selecting projects" issued by central government ministries.[18] Each ministry also informs each district of the level of funding available to it. These guidelines and the funding ceilings reflect top-bottom influences, the over-riding Treasury primacy, and the frequent planning-finance battles which impose real costs in terms of time and decision reversals. Subject to projects which satisfy ministerial guidelines and which do not violate funding ceilings, every DDC issues a District Development Plan that is supposed to reflect the collective will and priorities of the residents in that district.

As already elaborated, the planning machinery has become sophisticated over the years. So too has the planning cadre. In 1968, there were 6 local planning officers and 21 expatriate planning advisors. Today, however, there is almost total Kenyanization of the planning personnel, due to the attractive Scheme of Service for Economists and Statisticians, administered by the ministry in charge of planning, which covers all economists in the civil service, as well as to those entering various training programmes such as the postgraduate bachelor of philosophy programme in economics inaugurated at the University of Nairobi in 1969 and master's-degree-level training in Nairobi and abroad.

Plan formulation and construction methodologies have been rigorous, be they at the project level (Project Identification and Evaluation Unit established in 1970, New Projects Committee) for various sectors (Sector Planning Groups) or at the macro-level (Macro-Economic Models). Notable landmarks of macro-modelling are typified by the Joint Econometric Model Built for the Economy (JEMBE), in 1971, the Kenya Simulation (KENSIM) model of 1972, the World Bank models[19] built in 1975 and 1985, the Bachue[20] model done in 1977, and the current Macro-Economic Policy Model for Kenya.[21] The model, based on 1976 prices, is frequently updated for simulations and projections for key economic variables between 1982 and 1989, that is, for the medium term. It has 272 variables (36 exogenous and 236 endogenous), 54 behavioural equations, and numerous definitional relationships. A long-range planning model is on the drawing boards.

To facilitate formal modelling, a plethora of data are generated by the Central Bureau of Statistics, input-output tables are compiled (1967, 1971, 1976), and social accounting matrices published (1976, 1982). This has enabled Kenya to avoid the common pitfall of planning without facts. The pay off of adequate reliable data was clearly evident during the 1984/1985 drought, when the Integrated Rural Survey, mounted in 1974, facilitated equitable famine relief and continuous monitoring of the food situation in all areas. Data availability, in reasonable variety and quality, greatly contributes to the efficiency of the planning machinery. So too do the prevailing political stability and continuity in economic philosophy — two major factors contributing to consistency in directing the economy. The political maturity demonstrated by the smooth management of the transition from the era of the charismatic President Kenyatta (1963–1978) to the era of the dynamic President Moi has provided a salutary political infrastructure. On accession to power, President Moi promised to follow the footsteps ("*nyayo*") of the late President Kenyatta, and his Nyayo Philosophy of Peace, Love, and Unity has inspired individual, institutional, and collective commitment. A secure and stable political and economic environment is conducive to a sound investment climate.

The planning machinery could be further improved by an augmentation of the quantity and quality of data. On the former, such data as the level of unemployment, national cost-of-living and wholesale price indices, capital stock, regional GNP, etc., have yet to be generated. Among the quality improvements needed would be data on man-hour inputs by labour categories, productivity of factor inputs, land-carrying capacities, refined sectoral and intrasectoral classification of economic activities, ownership and control of firms, etc.

Over 40 per cent of the DDC personnel have no formal training in economics and statistics. It is important that such disciplines be made prerequisites for persons to qualify for these planning positions. It is also important that the planning system avoid assigning overlapping responsibilities between officers in the core Ministry of Planning and the operating ministries, say between the natural resources division and the Ministry of Agriculture, between the manpower planning unit and the Ministry of Labour or Education. For example, agricultural producer prices are set by the Ministry of Agriculture, while consumer prices are fixed by the Ministry of Finance, thus taxing interministerial integration. Friction could arise where channels of reporting are not explicit, co-ordination is not active, and/or where the various planning units are headed by officers of the same rank and seniority in service. This calls for constant vigilance and surveillance by the director of planning to ensure a smooth functioning of the planning machinery.

The district-focus strategy is an aspect of subregional planning which in turn is a subset of regional planning. The latter is operationalized through the system of trunk, major, and minor roads construction; telecommunication networks and electric-power grid system; the secondary cities programme of water and sewage installation; and the development of market and local centres. Of some assistance is the proviso of the 1976 budget that the initial investment allowance of 20 per cent be given to those newly approved enterprises that locate their operations outside the major metropolis of Nairobi and Mombasa. Coupled with lower rents, land rates, and other inputs, this has led to the boosting of "new" towns (e.g. Eldoret, Kisumu, Nyahururu, Nyeri, Bungoma, Thika, Athi River, etc.), which has in turn led to deconcentration of industries and the reduction of rural-to-capital-city migration.

This is a case of a positive response by the private sector to incentives. While direct government programmes can be effected by directives backed by budgetary allocation and expenditure, the private sector is usually induced to "toe the line" by indicative planning, a system of rewards and penalties. In Kenya, this is effected mainly through prices — exchange rates, prices of farm inputs and produce, import tariffs, interest rates, wage guidelines, etc. — and occasionally through rationing of, say, foreign exchange. There are some parastatals that are in constant direct touch with the private sector, such as the Development Finance Company of Kenya, the Agricultural Development Corporation, the Kenya Tourists Development Authority, the Coffee Board, National Housing Corporation, etc. In spite of these, the involvement of the private sector in the national planning process has been *ad hoc* (just prior to the formulation of a development plan) and informal (association of manufacturers, the chamber of commerce). The proposed National Economic Advisory Council would bring in all the parties concerned systematically and continuously.

Evaluation of Plan Performance

In this section, we shall attempt an assessment of achievement by the development plans and the planning process in Kenya. From the outset, policy-makers sought both growth and equitable distribution of income. The ultimate objective was to eliminate poverty, ignorance, and disease.

Quality of Life

During the postindependence period, per capita income grew at a higher level during the first planning period (1964–1970) than during the fourth period (1979–1983). Despite the declining rates of increase, per capita income rose at about 1.9 per cent per year over the entire period. Consequently, GDP per capita was about a quarter higher in 1983 relative to 1964. As a result, *absolute* poverty has declined — as evidenced by the proportion of households below the poverty line, having an income of KSh 2,000 per year.[22]

But *relative* poverty, as reflected by income distribution, has not fared as well. Inequalities are evidenced by the shares of GDP accruing to various income groups;[23] consumption levels which, on the average, are at least five times greater in urban areas than in rural areas;[24] intra-urban, intrarural, and urban-rural wealth (land, housing, household assets, livestock) and income differentials;[25] falling real wages and constant or rising profits.[26]

There has been, however, a policy designed specifically to alleviate poverty. The rapid diminution of the non-monetary sector has resulted in a fuller share in economic expansion by those affected. The virtually complete Kenyanization of personnel in both the private and the public sectors has meant a reduction in inequality between indigenous Kenyans, other citizens, and non-citizens. The

TABLE 1. A statistical snapshot, 1964–1983

	Planning periods			
	1964–1970	1970–1974	1974–1978	1979–1983
Planned GDP growth rate (% p.a.)	6.3	6.7	7.4–4.6	6.3–5.4
Actual GDP growth rate (% p.a.)	6.9	5.5	5.7	4.0
GDP growth per capita (% p.a.)	3.7	2.1	1.9	0.1
Kenyanization (% of personnel)	91.7	96.4	98	98.7
Gini co-efficient				
Adult literacy rate	0.43	0.52	0.60	NA
Infant mortality	20	30	45	51
(per thousand)	126	119	98	92
Life expectancy at birth (years)	47	52	54	57
Daily calorie supply (% of requirement)	103	98	86	88
Index of food production per capita	NA	100	NA	88

Sources: Kenya, *Statistical Digest* (annual), *Economic Survey* (annual), *Development Plan* (periodic); World Bank, *World Development Report* (annual) and idem, *Kenya: Growth and Structural Change*, 1983.

last two development plans (1979–1983 and 1984–1988) have singled out the seriously disadvantaged groups — the landless, the handicapped, and the unemployed — for particular attention. This task would have been easier had the targeted growth rates of GDP been achieved so that there would be sufficient increments in income to syphon off for the task. There has been, however, a widening underachievement gap in GDP growth rates. As table 1 portrays, Gini coefficients have been rising over time, in keeping with Kuznets's "law" of income distribution — that income inequality tends to increase with economic growth at relatively low levels of income.[27] This is an historic pan-national "law" that every country would like to break!

The fight against ignorance has been pursued through the provision of free primary education, adult literacy campaigns, and the expansion and multiplication of all manner of schools, colleges, and training institutions. Consequently, the adult literacy rate has jumped from a mere 20 per cent of the adult population in the 1960s to about 51 per cent in the 1980s, although this is still quite low compared with the objective of achieving 100 per cent literacy (ability to read and write in any language) by 1988.

Although primary education is free, it is not universal. The enrolment ratio for 6- to 12-year-olds was estimated at 86 per cent in 1980, and the proportion of 6-year-olds in primary schools (*access* ratio)[28] was only 73 per cent. The pupil-teacher ratio has been rising, more dramatically if only trained teachers are considered. The output of teacher training colleges has not risen to the target of 10,425 during 1983, although a concerted push to reach the 1988 target of 11,296 is in progress.[29] Adult education has been hampered by a shortage of educated volunteers and the occasional male clientele's reluctance to mix with fellow women learners. These factors exert effective constraints on mass literacy and universal education.

Memories of days when major epidemics afflicted Kenya are long lost into history. Over the years, there has been expansion of both curative and preventive medicine by way of augmentation of health institutions (hospitals, health centres, and dispensaries), health personnel (doctors, nurses, etc.), and health education in general. Primary health care (community-based health services) has been embarked upon. The Kenya Expanded Programme of Immunization (KEPI) was launched in 1982 with a target to immunize over 70 per cent of children by 1986 against six childhood diseases: measles, tetanus, whooping cough, diphtheria, poliomyelitis and tuberculosis — only 45 per cent were immunized in 1982. Reticulated potable water supply is spreading. Concrete evidence of improvement in health is the increase in life expectancy and the decrease in infant mortality.

However, there is anthropometric evidence of poverty-related protein energy malnutrition. In 1978–1979, over one quarter of the children were below 80 per cent of the standard weight-age index — reflecting stunted growth (height-age index) and a "wasted" condition (weight-height index).[30] This is not surprising when it is observed, as in table 1, that calorie supply per person has moved from over-abundance in the 1960s to a mere 88 per cent of the daily requirement (2,500 calories per adult per day) in the 1980s. Moreover, health facilities are inequitably distributed regionally, with Nairobi getting a lion's share and most rural folks living over 2 kilometres away from a health centre.

One of the more meaningful measures of economic development is the Physical Quality of Life Index (PQLI). It is a composite index of socio-economic progress that incorporates life expectancy, infant mortality, and literacy rate and serves as a gauge to measure the physical well-being of an economy at a given point in time. Life expectancy and infant survival can be seen as representing the sum of the effects of nutrition, public health, income, and general environment, while literacy is both a measure of well-being and a skill that is important in the development process. On the basis of equal weights for each of the three components, PQLI in Kenya increased by about 10 per cent between 1964 and 1983, with life expectancy at birth rising by more than one-fifth, infant mortality falling by more than a quarter, and the literacy rate more than doubling.

Targets, Policies, and Projects

An important question is why and how targets are set and projects selected. They could reflect the hopes of planners, the aspiration of politicians, or the ability of the beneficiaries. In the early days of planning in Kenya, there was little project specificity but much macro-level planning from the top. But, as we have seen, in the 1970s institutions were developed to facilitate bottom-up planning. With the implementation of the District-Focus for Rural Development, starting 1 July 1983, each operating ministry now channels project funds on a district-by-district basis. Eventually, the Treasury will be granting such funds directly to the district, which in turn will combine this with self-help ("*harambee*") contributions of money, labour, and materials for district development.

The present set-up seems somewhat patronizing. The districts are poised to depend on financial doles from the centre. Apart from the voluntary self-help monies that might be raised on grass-roots initiative and the meagre funds that local authorities raise by way of rents, rates, cess, business license fees, etc., most districts have little locally generated funds. Devolution of taxing power is called for, even if it means reintroducing the Graduated Personal Tax (GPT) as in pre-1970 or formalizing *harambee* contributions as a form of tax. To move from financial *dependence* to financial *subvention* calls for political will, since this implies power sharing (decentralization) from the centre to the periphery.

In a study on the economic effects of rural access roads,[31] the respondents within the impact areas were asked to identify the most important problems affecting their areas. The response showed that roads ranked fifth, after water, hospitals, famine, and land shortage — not a very high priority. This raises doubt as to whether the persons supposed to benefit from the construction of the roads were properly consulted about their perceived priorities. Of course, the presence of a road could help in access to medical services or delivering water, for example. But the many cases of people declining permission for a road pass through their land must have contributed to delays in implementation and, therefore, underachievement of the target.

The target for the Rural Access Roads Programme was 14,000 kilometres in 26 districts between 1979 and 1985. Only about 8,000 kilometres were completed by then — 57 per cent of the target. Apart from evidence of low priority attachment, foreign donors preferred to operate on a reimbursement-of-cost arrangement. Therefore, during times of government budgetary stringencies, the programme suffered accordingly both in terms of new construction and maintenance of the all-weather standard.

This same fate seems to have befallen the water and sewage schemes (Nyeri, Nanyuki, Kisii, Bungoma, Ndia, and Thika) co-financed by the African Development Bank and the grants given under the Lome II agreement by the European Economic Community. These projects were delayed due to "budgetary and administrative problems."[32]

One feature characterizing the Kenyan government budget is the tendency for there to be recurrent deficits in the budget and substantial shortfalls between approved estimates and actual development expenditure.[33] The 1986 *Sessional Paper* lamented that "the development budget has grown more slowly than recurrent expenditure."[34] As a proxy for the efficiency of the implementation machinery, the actual development budget — the principal vehicle of giving effect to the plan — has not fully translated the plan into reality.

Using ratios of actual to planned spending, Killick and Kinyua[35] found an achievement rate of 50 per cent for roads and 53 per cent for agricultural projects. They attributed the implementation failures to shortages in key personnel — engineers, economists, agronomists, and so forth — to plan, implement, and monitor plan progress and to inadequate and poorly maintained equipment and vehicles. Occasionally the scheduling of some projects and programmes is negatively affected by poor timing in the release of funds by the Treasury. The satisfaction of housing[36] demand is seriously constrained by rising construction costs and the insistence on building standards (e.g. ceilings, electrical and hot water installation), which are borrowed from Europe, are expensive, and are largely inappropriate in a tropical environment.

People have ways of expressing and revealing their preferences on the basis of perceived needs, costs, and appropriateness. The upsurge of enthusiasm surrounding the self-help *harambee* activities is an index of the people's *will to develop*, that is, *the will to save and sacrifice*, as is evidenced by their tremendous contributions in terms of time, money, and materials (all valued at KSh1.4 billion in 1985) to build schools, health centres, cattle dips, etc. In the beginning, central co-ordination, equipment, drugs, and qualified staff to provide the required services were absent. Consequently, some projects had to be abandoned[37] or modified to provide substandard services, resulting in wasted resources and frustrated expectations. But eventually, the plan had to follow to maintain order. This had to happen also to the informal sector housing, transport, restaurants, kiosks, etc. — all second-best alternatives which people fall to in the face of positive demand-supply gaps in the markets concerned. The plan's function is to make such undertakings viable alternatives by fostering security, reliability, sanitation, proper management, and the supply of complementary inputs.

The 1970–1974 development plan highlighted some principal difficulties in the implementation of plans, such as "weaknesses in co-ordination" and "cases where projects not included in the Plan were given preference over planned projects."[38] There are cases of national urgency that include expenditure on armaments due to the sudden worsening of the geo-military situation in the Horn of Africa in the mid-1970s; the tripartite agreements to boost employment in 1964, 1970, and 1979; the post-independence free primary education programme; and the school milk scheme of the late-1970s. When they initially demanded budgetary expenditures, these programmes were not explicitly in the development plans prevailing at the time but were of national importance and subsequent plans had to programme them accordingly.

What is a bit disturbing is the distortive effect of political brokerage. This is documented in the case of the Rural Water Supply (RWS) Programme. In selecting priority water projects, District Development Committees pay attention to such factors as the urgency of people's needs for water, the area's water needs for other development projects, and technical data on costs and water sources. According to the ILO, "the initial list arrived at in this way may be added to as a result of representation from political interests in the districts, *and these are rarely rejected*, though they tend to distort the resource allocation criteria of the RWS."[39]

Target attainment ratios in RWS range from 59 per cent in the case of number of water schemes to 67 per cent in the case of people served[40] between 1979 and 1983. During the same period, health facilities achievement[41] was 26 per cent of the targeted additional beds, 70 per cent of the proposed dispensaries, and 45 per cent of the units planned for communicable and vector-borne diseases. However, the number of beds per 1,000 of population has remained virtually stagnant at less than two. It would appear that the overall objective of attaining water and health for all by the year 2000 is quite unrealistic.

Food self-sufficiency and food security have always constituted a key concern in national policy, and that concern is now articulated in a sessional paper on food policy.[42] But vagaries of weather have, on occasion, brought about droughts and consequent diminution in supplies of grains (maize, wheat), vegetables, and other produce. At other times, limited storage facilities have militated against the carrying of sufficient strategic stocks. Total population has been growing at an increasing rate, making the target growth rate of 3.3 per cent[43] per annum by 1988 seem an elusive goal. A combination of volatile supply and an increasing number of mouths to feed have conspired to make food production per capita decrease from an index of 100 in the 1970s to 88 in the 1980s.

Perhaps the major culprit for this is government restriction on the movement of maize, which sometimes creates artificial shortages in some areas, while overabundance prevails elsewhere in the country. Added to this is price control, which invariably is at a level which does not always provide enough incentive for the farmer to produce, since "the terms of trade, in recent years, reveals that the purchasing power of farmers' incomes vis-a-vis the rest of the economy has developed unfavourably."[44] The consumer should be allowed to pay a fair proportion of the cost of producing the food. The National Cereals and Produce Board should be a buyer and seller of *the last resort*, more or less like BULOG[45] in the case of rice in Indonesia. Added to this should be a land tax to discourage the holding of idle land. But a land tax has never been a politically popular measure anywhere.

Since the attainment of independence, the government has been providing a wide range of economic and social services. In addition, it has engaged in a variety of productive enterprises. The consequence has been a rapid increase in the public sector contribution in GDP (from 24 per cent at independence to 28 per cent in 1983) and escalating budgetary deficits. Noting that this crowding-out effect is unsustainable in the long run, the Working Party on Government Expenditures[46] recommended selective divesting, retrenchment in government, and increasing privatization of the economy. This would enhance efficiency in the use of existing resources and promote better management practices.[47]

Civil servants are not trained for salesmanship, to run textile factories, or to manage slaughterhouses. Hence, for a start, there is a prima facie need for the Kenya National Trading Corporation (KNTC) to stop local distribution of manufactured goods such as bicycles, matches, spray guns, etc. These should be left to private distributors, leaving the KNTC free to concentrate on importing priority raw materials and spare parts. By so ding, KNTC might just end the prevalent over-invoicing of imports and, by getting into state trading, reduce under-invoicing of exports. This would enhance Kenya's gain in international trade. Privatization of the Kenya Meat Commission, the Uplands Bacon Factory, and even the collection of garbage in Nairobi could inject the much needed efficiency. Only policing by the proposed Prices and Monopolies Commission[48] would be necessary to ensure unrestrained trade, pure competition, and fair business practice.

Conclusions

On the whole, development planning in Kenya has been successful in guiding and directing the growth of the economy. It has been wide in scope and sufficiently comprehensive, with national goals and objectives being clearly stated. Over time, the planning machinery has demonstrated increased meticulousness, flexibility, and sharpness in dealing with unexpected circumstances, such as the oil crises of 1973–1974 and 1979.

It is important to note that today, when developing countries are plagued with economic difficulties, aid agencies (bilateral as well as multilateral) play a very important role in the design and implementation of the development plans of these countries. Most agencies' aid is conditional and often tied ("non-fungible") to specific projects irrespective of the priorities that might be assigned to them in the plan document. Occasional imposition by aid agencies cannot be overlooked,[49] even when it takes the form of a seemingly innocuous "policy dialogue."

Clearly, there are difficulties in plan implementation, some emanating from outside the nation (foreign) and others from within. Shortfalls in expected capital inflow from outside (including foreign exchange) can be a severe hindrance to plan implementation. Kenya has been a recent victim of this. The reaction of the planning machinery in Kenya to such unexpected adverse out-turns in global economic circumstances has been to come up with new policy guidelines and to revise and make more realistic the initial development targets.

Domestic causes of inadequate plan implementation in Kenya include under-utilization of the capital budget by the operating ministries, allocative distortions towards unplanned areas, lack of sufficiently qualified and experienced cadres of local professionals in the operating ministries, and a dearth of relevant data and information. While all these difficulties are interrelated, perhaps the key difficulty is the inadequacy of local executive capacity in government ministries.

Whether Kenya has developed because of or in spite of planning is a moot question. Political will to redress a land shortage in the tribal trust lands at independence brought about a successfully planned resettlement of the scheduled "White Highlands." Kenyanization and widespread primary education were vigorously planned for. But, most importantly, the plans have succeeded in making administrative bureaucracies "development conscious" and have had an "announcement effect," a conscientization of the population to actively participate. Since planning has become a way of life of the body politics, it is somewhat difficult to apply the "with-or-without" principle.

Kenya's development plans have concentrated heavily on government programmes and the public sector in general. The operations of the private sector have never been given adequate attention. This is a major weakness which should receive priority attention for the future with a view to actively involving every sector of the economy in the formation of ideas, development plans, and programmes. In this way, the strategy of relying more on the people and their organizations (co-operatives, companies, etc.) in promoting economic growth would be more readily realized.

Notes

1. *The Development Programmes: 1954–57, 1957–60 and 1960–63* (Nairobi, Government Printer, various years).
2. R. J. M. Swynnerton, *A Plan to Intensify the Development of African Agriculture in Kenya* (Nairobi, Government Printer, 1955).
3. See Barbu Niculescu, *Colonial Planning: A Comparative Study* (London, George Allen & Unwin, 1958), passim.
4. The statistics in this section are from *Statistical Abstract* and the *Economic Survey*, published annually by the Kenyan government's Central Bureau of Statistics.
5. The smallholders increased their share in total marketed agricultural production from 37 per cent in 1963 to 52 per cent in 1983.
6. J. R. Sheffield, ed., *Education, Employment and Rural Development* (Nairobi, East African Publishing House, 1967).
7. For an outline of the programme, see David A. Morse, "The World Employment Programme," *International Labour Review*, vol. 97, no. 6 (June 1968), pp. 517–529.
8. ILO, *Employment, Incomes and Equality: A Strategy for Increasing Productive Employment in Kenya* (Geneva, 1972).

9. Ibid., p. 365. See also Hollis Chenery et al., *Redistribution with Growth* (London, Oxford University Press, 1974).

10. Government of Kenya, *Economic Prospects and Policies*, Sessional Paper no. 4 (Nairobi, Government Printer, 1975).

11. Government of Kenya, *Economic Management for Renewed Growth*, Sessional Paper no. 1 (Nairobi, Government Printer, 1986).

12. Ibid., preamble.

13. Ibid., p. 32.

14. See for instance The World Bank, *Accelerated Development in Sub-Saharan Africa: An Agenda for Action* (Washington, D.C., 1981); idem, *World Development Report* (1983); and idem, *Toward Sustained Development in Sub-Saharan Africa: A Joint Programme of Action* (1984).

15. Each district is divided into administrative divisions which are, in turn, divided into locations and sub-locations headed by district officers, chiefs, and assistance chiefs respectively.

16. Usually representatives of development-related parastatals.

17. See Government of Kenya, *District Focus for Rural Development* (Nairobi, Government Printer, 1983).

18. Ibid., p. 1

19. The World Bank, *Kenya: Into the Second Decade* (Baltimore, The Johns Hopkins University Press, 1975), pp. 86–159; and idem, *Kenya: Growth and Structural Change* (Washington, D.C., 1983), pp. 529–572.

20. *Bachue* is a word meaning "fertility." See Richard Anker and James C. Knowles, *Population Growth, Employment, and Economic-Demographic Interactions in Kenya: Bachue, Kenya* (New York, St. Martin's Press, 1983), pp. 283–310.

21. Ministry of Finance and Planning, "Macro-Economic Policy Model for Kenya" (Nairobi, 1984, Mimeographed).

22. The World Bank, *Kenya: Growth and Structural Change* (note 19 above), pp. 199–201.

23. In 1976 the poorest quarter of population received only 6 per cent of the total income and the richest tenth received nearly two-fifths of the total. See E. Crawford and E. Thorbecke, "Employment, Income Distribution, Poverty Alleviation and Basic Needs in Kenya" (Geneva, ILO, 1978, Mimeographed).

24. Jennifer Sharpley, "Resource Transfers between the Agricultural and Non-Agricultural Sectors: 1964–1977," in Tony Killick, ed., *Papers on the Kenyan Economy* (Nairobi, Heinemann, 1981), p. 315.

25. See Arne Bigsten, *Regional Inequality and Development: A Case Study of Kenya* (London, Gower Press, 1983); T. Kmietovicz and P. Webley, "Statistical Analysis of Income Distribution in the Central Province of Kenya," *Eastern Africa Economic Review*, vol. 7, no. 2 (December 1975); D. M. Hunt, "Growth versus Equity: An Examination of the Distribution of Economic Status and Opportunity in Mbere, Eastern Kenya," Institute for Development Studies Occasional Paper no. 11 (Nairobi, 1975, Mimeographed); Dharam Ghai, "Stagnation and Inequality in African Agriculture" (Boulder, Colo., 1982, Mimeographed).

26. R. Kaplinsky, "Trends in the Distribution of Income in Kenya: 1966–76," Institute for Development Studies Working Paper 336 (Nairobi, 1978, Mimeographed).

27. Simon Kuznets, "Economic Growth and Income Inequality," *The American Economic Review*, vol. 45, pp. 1, 24.

28. ILO, *Increasing the Efficiency of Planning in Kenya* (Geneva, 1983), pp. 301–332.

29. Government of Kenya, *Development Plan: 1984–1988* (Nairobi, Government Printer, 1984), p. 150.

30. D. Ghai, M. Godfrey, and F. Lisk, *Planning for Basic Needs in Kenya: Performance, Policies and Prospects* (Geneva, ILO, 1979), p. 28; ILO, *Increasing the Efficiency of Planning* (note 28 above), p. 171.

31. L. P. Mureithi and B. P. Finucane, "Investment Linkages of Rural Access Roads in Kenya" (Ministry of Transport and Communications, 1982, Mimeographed).

32. See the article "Unused Money" in the magazine *Weekly Review*, Nairobi, 4 October 1985, p. 17.

33. See for example Government of Kenya, *Development Plan: 1970–1974* (Nairobi, Government Printer, 1970), pp. 56, 57.

34. Government of Kenya, *Economic Management* (note 11 above), p. 31.

35. T. Killick and J. K. Kinyua, "Development Plan Implementation in Kenya," in T. Killick, ed., *Papers on the Kenyan Economy* (note 24 above), p. 112.

36. L. P. Mureithi, S. O. Noormohammed, and J. M. Konzolo, "National Human Settlement Policies in Kenya" (Nairobi, UNCHS/Habitat, 1983, Mimeographed).

37. See Judith Geist, "Harambee Resource Mobilisation and Basic Needs" (Paper presented at the National Seminar on Employment and Basic Needs Planning in Kenya, Eldoret, May 1984), p. 7.

38. Government of Kenya, *Development Plan: 1970–1974* (note 33 above), p. 71.

39. ILO, *Increasing the Efficiency of Planning in Kenya* (note 28 above), p. 253 (emphasis added).

40. Ibid., pp. 258, 265.

41. Ibid., pp. 227, 241.

42. Government of Kenya, *Food Policy*, Sessional Paper no. 4 (Nairobi, Government Printer, 1981).

43. Government of Kenya, *Population Policy*, Sessional Paper no. 4 (Nairobi, Government Printer, 1984).

44. See Henk A. Meilink, *Agricultural Pricing in Kenya: Scope and Impact*, Report no. 11/1985 (Nairobi, Ministry of Finance and Planning, 1985), p. 32.

45. BULOG is an Indonesian acronym for National Logistic Bureau.

46. Government of Kenya, *Report of the Working Party on Government Expenditures* (Nairobi, Government Printer, 1982).

47. For an examination of the role of proper management, see P. Ndegwa, L. P. Mureithi, and R. H. Green, eds., *Management for Development: Priority Themes in Africa Today* (Nairobi, Oxford University Press, 1987).

48. Government of Kenya, *Development Plan: 1984–1988* (note 29 above), p. 64.

49. See for example David Jones, "The Involvement of Aid Donors in Recipient Country Public Policy Processes," in P. Ndegwa et al., eds. (note 47 above).

Select Bibliography

Agarwala, R. 1973. "A macro-model for projections and policy analyses." World Bank Working Paper no. 161, Washington, D.C.

Allen, C., and K. J. King, eds., 1972. *Developmental trends in Kenya*. Edinburgh, Edinburgh University Centre of African Studies.

Birgegard, L. E. 1975. *The project selection process in developing countries: A study of the public investment project selection process in Kenya, Zambia and Tanzania*. Stockholm, Economic Research Institute.

Chege, M. 1974. "Systems management and the plan implementation process in Kenya." *African Review*, vol. 3, no. 4, pp. 595–609.

Cherniavsky, M. 1965. *Development prospects in East Africa: Kenya, Tanzania and Uganda*. Bergen, Chr. Michelsen Institute.

Clark, P. G. 1968. *Development planning in East Africa*. Nairobi, East African Publishing House.

———. 1963. "Towards more comprehensive planning in East Africa." *East African Economic Review*, December, pp. 65–74.

Cohen, N. P. 1974. "Structural change in a low-income country: An econometric approach using the Republic of Kenya." Ph.D. diss., University of Wisconsin, Madison.

Dahl, H. E. 1970. *The Kenya input-output table: 1967*. Bergen, Chr. Michelsen Institute.

Delp, P. 1981. "District planning in Kenya." In T. Killick, ed., *Papers on the Kenyan economy: Performance, problems and policies*, pp. 117–126. Nairobi, Heinemann.

East African Institute of Social and Cultural Affairs. 1965. *Problems of economic development in East Africa*. Nairobi, East African Publishing House.

Edwards, E. O. 1968. "Development planning in Kenya since independence." *East African Economic Review*, vol. 4, no. 2, pp. 1–15.

Ekstrom, T. 1967. *Possible ways of speeding up economic and social development in East Africa*. Geneva, ILO.

Faaland, J., and H. E. Dahl. 1967. *The Economy of Kenya*. Bergen, Chr. Michelsen Institute.

Freeman, D. B. 1975. "Development strategies in dual economies: A Kenyan example." *African Studies Review*, vol. 18, no. 2, pp. 17–33.

Ghai, D. P. 1964. "How good is Kenya's plan?" *East Africa Journal*, July, pp. 19–28.

———. 1971. "Some aspects of social and economic progress and policies in East Africa: 1961–1971." Institute for Development Studies Discussion Paper No. 122, Nairobi.

———. 1972. "The machinery of planning in Kenya." In M. Faber and D. Seers, eds., *The crisis in planning*, pp. 120–133. London, Chatto and Windus.

———. 1974. "Unified approach to development analysis and planning: The Kenyan experience." Institute for Development Studies Miscellaneous Paper No. 52, Nairobi.

Ghai, D. M., M. Godfrey, and F. Lisk. 1979. *Planning for basic needs in Kenya: Performance, policies and prospects*. Geneva, ILO.

Godfrey, M. 1978. "Prospects of a basic needs strategy: The case of Kenya." *Institute of Development Studies Bulletin*, vol. 9, no. 4, pp. 41–44.

Granberg, P. 1977. *A numerical study of the Kenyan 1971 input-output table*. Bergen, Chr. Michelsen Institute.

Green, R. H. 1966. "Cautious growth promotion and cautious structuralism: The Kenya and Uganda development plans." *East African Economic Review*, vol. 2, no. 2, pp. 19–34.

———. 1971. "Four African development plans: Ghana, Kenya, Nigeria and Tanzania." In I. Livingstone, ed., *Economic policy for development*, pp. 387–404. Harmondsworth, Penguin.

————. 1972. "Some problems of national development planning and foreign financing." *Uchumi*, vol. 2, no. 3, pp. 1–14.

Guyllstrom, B. 1974. "Development planning in Kenya: Strategies and machinery." Department of Social and Economic Geography Report no. 12, Lund.

Harwitz, M. 1978. "On improving the lot of the poorest: Economic plans in Kenya." *African Studies Review*, vol. 21, no. 3, pp. 65–73.

Hazlewood, A. 1980. *The economy of Kenya: The Kenyatta era*. London, Oxford University Press.

Heller, P. S. 1972. "The dynamics of project expenditures and the planning process with reference to Kenya." Ph.D. diss., Harvard University, Cambridge.

Helmschrott, H. 1965. *Development and development policy in East Africa: Kenya*. Munich, IFO.

————. 1974. "Public investment in LDCs with recurrent cost constraints: The Kenyan case." *Quarterly Journal of Economics*, vol. 88, no. 2, pp. 251–277.

Hodd, M. 1974. "A design for an econometric model of the Kenyan economy." Institute for Development Studies Working Paper No. 171, Nairobi.

House, W. 1980. "Development strategy and the energy balance: An East African study." *Development and change*, vol. 11, no. 1, pp. 17–30.

Howe, C. W., and H. Karani. 1965. "A projection model for the Kenya economy: A study in development planning and comparative economic structures." *East African Economic Review*, June, pp. 21–31.

————. 1964. "A statistical model for the Kenya economy." Institute for Development Studies, Discussion Paper No. 1, Nairobi.

Hyden, G., R. Jackson, and J. Okumu, eds., 1970. *Development administration: The Kenyan experience*. Nairobi, Oxford University Press.

Iconoclastes. 1971. "Prestige Harambee projects and national development." *East African Journal*, vol. 8, no. 11, p. 2.

International Labour Office. 1972. *Employment, incomes and equality: A strategy for increasing productive employment in Kenya*. Geneva, ILO.

————. 1983. *Increasing the efficiency of planning in Kenya*. Geneva, ILO.

Kenya, Republic of. 1965. *African socialism and its application to planning in Kenya*. Sessional Paper no. 10. Nairobi, Government Printer.

————. 1964–1988. *Development plan*. Nairobi, Government Printer.

————. 1983. *District focus for rural development*. Nairobi, Government Printer.

————. 1986. *Economic management for renewed growth*. Sessional Paper No. 1. Nairobi, Government Printer.

————. 1975. *Economic prospects and policies*. Sessional Paper No. 4. Nairobi, Government Printer.

————. 1980, 1982. *Economic prospects and policies*. Sessional Paper. Nairobi, Government Printer.

————. 1963. *Growth of the economy: 1954–1962*. Nairobi, Government Printer.

————. 1983. *Guidelines for the preparation, appraisal and approval of new public sector investment projects*. Nairobi, Government Printer.

————. 1972. *Plan performance and expectations: 1969–1974. Part I*. Nairobi, Government Printer.

————. 1955. *A plan to intensify the development of African agriculture in Kenya*. (Chairman R. J. M. Swynnerton). Nairobi, Government Printer.

————. 1981. *Report of the parastal review committee*. (Chairman P. Ndegwa). Nairobi, Government Printer.

————. 1982. *Report of the working party on government expenditures*. (Chairman P. Ndegwa). Nairobi, Government Printer.

Karani, H. 1967. "A projection model for the Kenya economy: Implications of the Kenya Development Plan 1966–1970." *East African Economic Review*, vol. 3, no. 1, pp. 45–54.

Killick, T. 1976. "Strengthening Kenya's development strategy: Opportunities and constraints." *Eastern African Economic Review*, vol. 8, no. 2.

————. 1979. *Stabilization policy in an African setting: Kenya 1963–1973*. London, Heinemann.

————. 1981 "By their fruits ye shall know them: The fourth development plan." In T. Killick, ed., *Papers on the Kenyan economy: Performance, problems and policies*, pp. 97–108.

————. 1981. *Papers on the Kenyan economy: Performance, problems and policies*. Nairobi, Heinemann Educational Books.

Kinyua, J. M. 1978. "Plan implementation in Kenya." M.A. thesis, University of Nairobi.

Laubstein, K. H. 1978. "The failure of physical planning in post-colonial Kenya." Ph.D. diss., University of Toronto.

Leys, C. 1979. "Development strategy in Kenya since 1971." *Canadian Journal of African Studies*, vol. 13, nos. 1 and 2, pp. 297–320.

Lisk, F, ed. In press. *Employment and basic needs planning in Kenya*. Geneva, ILO.

McWilliam, M. D. 1963. "Notes on the economic development of Kenya." *East African Economic Review*, June, pp. 13–21.

McKim, W. L. 1974. "The role of interaction in spatial economic development planning: A case study from Kenya." Ph.D. diss., Northwestern University.

McLoughlin, P. F. 1971. "East African economic development over the next twenty years: Some forecasts about qualitative changes." *Canadian Journal of African Studies*, vol. 5, no. 2, pp. 227–240.

Masakhalia, Y. F. O. 1976. "Development planning in Kenya in the post-independence period." *Economic Bulletin for Africa*, vol. 12, no. 1, pp. 19–44.

Mboya, T. J. 1967. "Priorities in planning." In J. R. Sheffield, ed., *Education, employment and rural development*, p. xvii. Nairobi, African Publishing House.

Migot-Adholla, S. E. 1971. "Ideology and national development: Case of Kenya." *Ufahamu*, vol. 2, no. 1, pp. 1–25.

Mureithi, L. P. 1972. "Development in practice: Reflections on Kenya's experience." Institute for Development Studies Working Paper No. 53, Nairobi.

————. 1978. "Economic development, planning and employment in English-speaking East and West Africa." International Institute for Labour Studies Educational Materials Exchange, Geneva.

Mureithi, L. P., and J. O. Otieno. 1977. "Interrelations among agricultural and population policies and development programmes and achievements: Kenya." In D. Ensminger, ed., *Food enough or starvation for millions*, pp. 93–126. New Delhi, Tata-McGraw-Hill.

Murugu, J. K. 1978. "Requirement for Short-term Economic Management in Kenya." M.A. thesis, University of Nairobi.

Naiya, P. W. 1977. "Public participation in the planning process in Kenya: A case study of Githunguri Division." M.A. thesis, University of Nairobi.

Ndegwa, P., L. P. Mureithi, and R. H. Green, eds. 1985. *Development options for Africa in the 1980s and beyond*. Nairobi, Oxford University Press.

———. 1987. *Management for development: Priority themes in Africa today*. Nairobi, Oxford University Press.

Ndegwa, P., and O. D. K. Norbye. 1967. "The strategy of Kenya's development plan 1966–1970." In J. R. Sheffield, ed., *Education, employment and rural development*. Nairobi, East African Publishing House.

Nyangira, N. 1975. *Relative modernisation and public resource allocation in Kenya*. Kampala, East African Literature Bureau.

Obudho, R. A., ed. 1981. *Urbanization and development planning in Kenya*. Nairobi, Kenya Literature Bureau.

Oser, J. 1967. *Promoting economic development with illustrations from Kenya*. Nairobi, East African Publishing House.

Oyugi, W. O. 1974. "Decentralisation for integrated rural development: Some lessons from Kenya." *African Review*, vol. 3, no. 4, pp. 595–609.

Pinfold, T., and G. Norcliffe, eds. 1980. *Development planning in Kenya: Essays on the planning process and policy issues* York University Geographical Monograph No. 9, Downsview.

Seidman, A. 1972. *Comparative development strategies in East Africa*. Nairobi, East African Publishing House.

Sheffield, J. R., ed. 1967. *Education, employment and rural development*. Nairobi, East African Publishing House.

Slater, C. S., G. Walsham, and M. M. Shah, eds. 1977. *KENSIM: A simulation of the Kenyan economy*. Boulder, Westview Press.

Stewart, F. 1976. "Kenya: Strategies for development." In U. Damachi et al., eds., *Development paths in Africa and China*. London, Macmillan.

Taylor, D. G. F., and R. A. Obudho, eds. 1979. *The spatial structure of development: A case study of Kenya*. Boulder, Westview Press.

Tobin, J. 1973. "Estimates of sectoral capital output." Institute for Development Studies Discussion Paper No. 171, Nairobi.

Vente, R. E. 1970. *Planning processes: The East African case*. Munich, Weltforum Verlag.

Whitacre, R. J. 1975. "Sectoral planning in Kenya: A proposed macro-economic model." Institute for Development Studies Working Paper No. 216, Nairobi.

World Bank. 1971. *Economic development in East Africa, Vol. 11: Kenya*. Washington, D.C., IBRD.

———. 1963. *The economic development of Kenya*. Baltimore, Johns Hopkins University Press.

———. 1975. *Kenya: Into the second decade*. Baltimore, Johns Hopkins University Press.

———. 1983. *Kenya: Growth and structural change*. Washington, D.C., IBRD.

7

THE DEVELOPMENT PLANNING EXPERIENCE IN NIGERIA: EFFECTIVENESS, PROBLEMS, AND PROSPECTS

E. O. Adeniyi, A. I. Ayodele, and V. P. Diejomaoh

Introduction

Development planning is now widely accepted as the primary instrument for the effective management of a nation's economy, particularly in third world countries. Development planning enables governments to provide a sense of direction in public expenditure as well as necessary guidance to entrepreneurs in the private sector. Upon attainment of political independence, many countries in Africa, Asia, and Latin America have embarked on systematic planning of their economies with a view to achieving economic development and social transformation and to securing control of their national economies. In Nigeria, the essence of development planning has become so widely accepted that the country's 1979 constitution provides that the state shall "control the national economy in such a manner as to secure the maximum welfare, freedom and happiness of every citizen on the basis of social justice and equality of status and opportunity." In this regard, the state shall direct its policy towards ensuring "the promotion of a planned and balanced economic development."[1] This provision not only recognizes the widely acknowledged need for a planned economy in the country but also makes it mandatory for successive Nigerian governments to undertake development planning.[2]

It is therefore no surprise that national development planning, particularly since the attainment of independence in 1960, has played a key role in successive Nigerian govrnments' attempts to substantially improve the living conditions of its people. Nigeria has embarked on four different plans, usually tagged the First (1962–1968), Second (1971–1975), Third (1976–1980), and Fourth (1981–1985) national development plans (NDP) respectively. The execution of the Fourth Plan is expected to be completed at the end of 1985, and preparatory work for the Fifth National Development Plan (1980–1990) is presently at an advanced stage.

A critical examination reveals that the successive plans are progressively more ambitious not only in terms of the overall investment levels but also in terms of the number, variety, and scope of the perceived projects and pro-grammes as well as the range of socio-economic development policies, with their proposed objectives and strategies. In addition, these plans aim at "not only raising the living standards of the Nigerian people, but, also to transform the national economy into a modern, diversified and virtually self-sustaining system."[3] That is, national planning has come to be regarded as an essential and, perhaps, the main institutional mechanism for overcoming development obstacles and for ensuring sustained economic and social development in Niger-ia. In fact, development planning is seen as the most effective vehicle in which to arrive at the level of economic independence necessary to attain the objectives of political independence.

Yet, in spite of these perceptions, coupled with nearly 30 years of planning, economic performance in Nigeria, as is revealed in various recent international reports, is far from satisfactory: today the nation relies more heavily than ever before on the industrialized countries, even for its supply of food.[4] This condi-tion may be due largely to various conflicting socio-economic and political fac-tors which tend to impede the effectiveness of national development planning.

In the light of the total Nigerian experience, then, particularly since inde-pendence, our paper attempts to meet the need that arises for making an assess-ment of Nigeria's development planning strategies in order to identify the con-flicting socio-economic and political factors for rectification in future planning efforts. Attention will also be given to prospects and proposals for effective national planning in Nigeria.

The Socio-Economic and Political Structure of Nigeria

Nigeria is endowed with the vast primary resources necessary to make a country economically and politically strong. For example, there are vast areas of arable land, abundant forest and water resources, and a sufficiently varied climatic condition which favours extensive agricultural activities. Nigeria is also greatly endowed with a variety of mineral and energy resources, including crude oil, gas, coal, tin and iron ores, lead, limestone, zinc, wind and solar power, biogas, biomas, and hydroelectric resources.

The energetic private and public sectors necessary to harness these resources and to build a strong agricultural and industrial base for the long-term develop-ment of the Nigerian economy already exist. A population currently believed to be somewhere between 90 and 100 million leaves no doubt that Nigeria possesses a potentially large market for both agricultural and industrial products. Further, there is a relatively large subregional market which is currently being further enlarged on a co-operative and integrated basis by the establishment of the Economic Community of West African States (ECOWAS).

Nigeria's large population is composed of over 250 ethnic groups, whose cultures, traditions, dialects, and aspirations differ considerably. The major groups are the Hausa/Fulani in the north, Yorubas in the west, and Ibos in the east, while the smaller groups include the Edos, Efiks, Nupes, Ibibbios, Itsekiris, Urhobos, Ijaws, and Kanuris, to mention just a few.

Given this diversity, it is understandable that one major preoccupation of successive Nigerian governments has been the unification of the country into a cohesive political unit. Thus, the constitutional arrangements that have evolved into a 19-state federal structure is a political arrangement to accommodate socio-economic and cultural diversities within the country as well as to promote "even and balanced development."

Until 1967, the country was composed of four regions and a capital territory (Lagos), with the northern region dominating the federation in area, population, and politics. Between 1967 and 1970, there were constitutional crises which culminated in a series of military interventions and the Nigerian civil war. Consequently, the country has undergone considerable changes in leadership and political structural composition, which has affected the political, economic, and social developments. Despite this, the federal structure of the country has been preserved.

There has not been, however, the emergence of any specific political ideology. Although the presidential system of government was adopted within the civilian democratic framework in 1979, with the hope of keeping the country together, it has not succeeded, even though the federal structure remains intact.

Given the above resources — human and material — coupled with the social, economic, and political structure, the need arises for the evolution of an institutionalized instrument for the effective management of the economy. Since development planning provides a guideline and, of course, a sense of direction in government programmed actions, successive Nigerian governments have accepted planning as an instrument for effective development and have, therefore, embarked on a series of development plans.

The Origin of Development Planning in Nigeria

As a political entity, Nigeria, with a land surface of about 924,000 square kilometres, owes its origin to British colonial rule, which commenced in 1860. The formal promulgation of British colonial hegemony over Nigeria was the culmination of almost four centuries of contact with European nations, starting with the Portuguese in the late fifteenth century. These initial contacts with

Europe were devoted mostly to the abominable slave trade, which left Nigeria totally ravaged and depopulated by frequent internecine ethnic warfare devoted to slave raids.

Under these circumstances, no systematic development was possible given the high level of insecurity.[5] Even though British colonial rule started in the colony of Lagos in about 1860, their rule over the whole of what presently constitutes Nigeria was not consolidated until the beginning of the twentieth century, after a series of battles with various Nigerian kings and chiefs holding dominion over kingdoms or chiefdoms of different sizes in southern and northern Nigeria.

The 1914 amalgamation exercise of the protectorates of southern and northern Nigeria culminated in the origin of present-day Nigeria. This amalgamation brought together under one entity a large number of the aforementioned ethnic groups with substantially divergent cultural traditions. These cultural diversities and divergencies generated centrifugal tendencies which accentuated the difficulties of creating an integrated political, social, and economic system in Nigeria. This probably led to the adoption of a Federal constitution on which Nigeria has continued to grow up to the present.

The British colonial administration succeeded in creating a politically stable environment in Nigeria which aided its capitalistic operations to exploit Nigeria's rich resources for the development of Britain's industrial sector. Britain relied substantially on its West African colonies — Nigeria included — for the procurement of raw materials and the sale of manufactured goods. However, limited effort was made to develop the Nigerian territory and its people.

The limited economic development, stimulated by pure market forces, experienced a set-back created by the two world wars, in 1914–1918 and 1939–1945 respectively. In addition, the great economic depression of the 1930s also took its economic toll, wiping out most of what gains might have accrued from British development efforts in Nigeria. It was, thus, not until after 1945 that modern economic growth and the rudiments of development planning actually commenced in Nigeria.

In view of the foregoing socio-economic and political trends, the general feeling in Nigeria, as well as in Britain, under the more progressive Labour government, was one of aspiration for political independence through some degree of rapid economic transformation. This aspiration necessitated the formulation of conscious development plans, with the ultimate objective of greater growth and diversification of production than had hitherto existed. To this end, there was a need for private capital and enterprises, to be supplemented and in many ways led by government-programmed actions. It was apparent, therefore, that growth and development had to be stimulated through planning by the government.

The first attempt at development planning was in 1946, when, under the 1945 Colonial Development and Welfare Act, a Ten-Year Plan of Development and

Welfare for Nigeria was launched for the 1946–1956 period. Even though the main objective of this 1946–1956 plan focused on the development of the overall economy for the improvement of the people's welfare, the document did not reflect any macro or overall view of development of the economy. It was simply a public investment programme consisting of a list of public sector projects which it was hoped would accelerate overall development.

Despite this, the fast changing social, economic, and political conditions in Nigeria, arising in particular from political and constitutional changes, highlighted the difficulties of planning for a period as long as 10 years, particularly in a country as complex as Nigeria. As a result of the changes indicated above, the Ten-Year Plan was modified, and a Revised Plan 1951–1956 emerged to take care of the last 5-year period of the plan. This latter plan saw further changes in 1954, when the Federation of Nigeria came into being and the regional governments assumed responsibility for those parts of the plan coming within their respective territories.

Because of the limited scope of the 1946–1956 plan and the numerous changes it had to undergo, its actual impact on development was very limited. In spite of this deficiency, the plan was succeeded by the 1955–1960 Economic Development Programme — later extended to 1962 — which was not significantly different from the 1946–1956 plan, in terms of its being a public investment programme rather than a comprehensive national development plan. Whereas the estimated investment in the 1946–1956 plan was about ₦110 million, the 1955–1962 programme was to cost about ₦330 million. In fact, the per capita income in Nigeria during the 1946–1956 period was far less than ₦50.00.

The general weaknesses of these plans relate to the limited impact made on macro-economic performance. In fact, there had been the presumption that concentration of projects in specific areas would lead to growth, without realizing the essence of the incremental capital-output ratios of the projects concerned, particulartly in the long run, and the possible shift in policies on industrialization and the need to expand industries, as revealed in subsequent plans. Accordingly, both the 1946–1956 Colonial Development Plan, launched by the British colonial power, and the 1955–1960 plan, initiated by Nigerian leaders in the run-up period to political independence, had a limited impact on national economic development. However, it should be conceded that the public investment programmes achieved their limited target of establishing essentially a number of infrastructural facilities.

Post-Independence National Development Planning Experience

It is only natural after over two decades and four different plans of national development planning experience in Nigeria to ponder awhile and appraise development efforts thus far, to see whether or not the exercises have brought the country any nearer the age-long objectives of modernized, diversified, and self-sustaining economic growth. A critical appraisal of the various development plans and their strategies within the period will, no doubt, provide an enlightened basis for drawing any meaningful conclusion.

In addition to reaching a meaningful conclusion, such analysis will help to identify and highlight the major social, economic, and political shortcomings of development planning in the country. Therefore, an attempt will be made to examine the roles which socio-economic and political factors have played in determining the structure, scope, and relevance of past and present national development plans. To embark on this appraisal, a brief review of the various plans, particularly from 1962 to date, will be necessary.

It is pertinent to stress that a comprehensive, accurate assessment and evaluation of the achievements and failures of the successive plans is not easy. This arises probably from the rapidly changing social, economic, and political events and, more particularly, from the absence of essential and basic data to provide an empirical basis for appraisal. These problems notwithstanding, evidence suggests that there are substantial deviations from the pre-independence planning strategies in those of the post-independence era.

Whereas the pre-independence plans were conceived more as investment programmes of the federal and regional governments, each of which had its separate schemes, the post-independence plans have been more closely related to national development planning. These national plans were formulated from a comprehensive analysis of regional plans for the four regions and later 12 states established in 1967 which were subsequently subdivided into 19 states in 1976. The local governments, representing the grass-roots level, have currently been involved in the planning programmes, with their positions reflected in the national plan documents, particularly the current 1981–1985 plan.

The First National Development Plan, 1962–1968

The 1962–1968 plan was the first conscious effort by the Nigerian government after independence to set and quantify national objectives as well as ensure a common national planning framework, concerned mainly with giving concrete meaning to the newly acquired political freedom. Hence, emphasis was placed on the establishment of a "strong and virile nation" within the plan period.

In view of the above anticipation, the plan was expected to facilitate the achievement and maintenance of the highest possible rate of increase in the standard of living of the Nigerian peoples. To this end, the plan strategies were designed to create necessary conditions leading to the attainment of this goal. These envisaged strategies included the mobilization of people for public support and the provision of adequate education in order to create an awareness of both the Nigerian potentials and the expected sacrifices required to ensure meaningful national development.

In specific terms, the plan aimed at:

1. a target savings of about 15 per cent of GDP, which would be reinvested on an annual basis during the plan period;
2. an annual 4 per cent growth rate of GDP;
3. the development of agriculture, industry, and high level/intermediate manpower.

Total investments in the plan were about ₦2.2 billion, of which 50 per cent was expected to come from foreign sources, while the remaining investment was expected to be mobilized from domestic sources.

Even though the plan period had to be extended to 1970, the anticipated targets could not be attained, due mainly to a number of socio-economic and political developments within the plan period. Among these were: (1) the series of constitutional crises in the early 1960s, (2) the 15 January 1966 military coup d'etat, (3) the 1967–1970 Nigerian civil war, and (4) the inadequate investment funds from foreign sources.

Regardless of these drawbacks to a full realization of the objectives of the plan, the First National Development Plan 1962–1968/70 succeeded in laying an effective foundation for subsequent development plans, and such projects as the hydroelectric project at Kainji, petroleum refinery at Alase-Eleme, the Niger bridge at Onitsha, east-west roads, etc., were completed during the plan period. Table 1 presents statistical information concerning planned and actual targets for past plans.

The Second National Development Plan, 1970–1974

Given the extensive damage to the economy due to the civil war, the plan's major goals were to reconstruct the facilities destroyed and also rehabilitate the people displaced and impoverished by the war. The plan equally aimed at resuscitating the economy from the depression into which it had plunged during the war. In addition, the plan aimed to establish Nigeria firmly as: (1) a united, strong, and self-reliant nation; (2) a great and dynamic economy; (3) a just and egalitarian society; (4) a land full of bright and promising opportunities for all citizens; and (5) a free and democratic society.

The designers of the plan stressed the need for both the government and the people of Nigeria to seek to give concrete meaning to the objectives and thereby ensure their full realization at all times. They also stressed the need for the promotion of balanced development between one part of the country and others, and especially between the urban and rural areas.[6]

It is clear that these objectives are more political in nature than economic; they illustrate well the political nature of development planning in Nigeria.

TABLE 1. Planned targets and levels of achievement in respect to some economic variables 1955–1980(%)

Plan Period	Rate of growth GDP		Investment as proportion of GDP		Savings as proportion of GDP		Share of manufacturing in GDP		Annual rate of growth of per capita consumption	
	PT	LA	PT	LA	PT	LA	PT	LA	PT	LA
1955–1960	4.0	3.9	10.8	14.0	10.0	9.5	2.0	1.3	1.0	2.0
1962–1968	4.0	5.0	15.0	15.1	15.0	NA	10.0	7.6	3.0	NA
1970–1974	6.6	8.2	18.0	19.6	15.0	NA	12.7	4.8	3.5	NA
1975–1980	9.5	5.0	25.4	NA	15.0	15.5	16.0	8.0	10.6	NA

Source: The Development Plans of the Federal Republic of Nigeria.

Note: PT = planned target; LA = level of achievement; Some of the figures for LA are estimates.

Even today, political factors and considerations continue to affect development planning in the country.

In terms of planned investment, the plan provided for capital investment of ₦2.05 billion, as a result of windfall resources derived from petroleum production. Given the lessons from the past plan, 20 per cent of the original projected investment was expected to come from foreign sources. The economic target for the GDP was set at an average annual growth rate of 6 per cent, while the investment/income ratio was to be about 18 per cent. In the course of the execution of the plan, there was the promulgation of the Indigenization Decree of 1972, which aimed at indigenizing the private sector of the Nigerian economy. In addition, there were shifts in the industrial sector, to encourage more the intermediate and capital goods industries. Rehabilitation of infrastructural facilities, especially roads, ports, and telecommunications, also received prioritized attention.

The plan recorded significant achievements in the areas of manufacturing, transport, education, health, information, and social welfare. These achievements, however, were more the product of the windfall gains from the unprecedented inflow of oil revenue than any inherent strengths of the plan itself. Put differently, since financing did not pose any significant constraint to plan implementation, inadequacy of executive capacity could be said to be the main limitation to the plan's success.

Despite these achievements, the socio-political objectives concerning the development of a great, dynamic, and egalitarian society, as well as equal opportunities for all, were not fully accomplished. Indigenization of the private sector succeeded only partially — 60 per cent ownership of banks and greater control of the crude oil sector consequent to Nigeria acquiring controlling shares in the Nigerian petroleum industry.

The Third National Development Plan, 1975–1980

The main focus of this plan was the establishment of major capital and intermediate goods industries. It also aimed at a more equitable regional distribution of income and a more effective control of the economy by Nigerians. In the light of this, it is not surprising that indigenization of economic activities received priority attention.

The projected annual rate of growth was about 9 per cent, while the investment ratio was anticipated at about 30 per cent. Emphasis was placed on heavy industries such as iron and steel, liquified natural gas (LNG), and petrochemicals, on which feasibility reports had been conducted and accepted after considering their cost/benefit analyses. In addition, there was an emphasis on massive infrastructure — both social and economic: highways, ports, airports, expansion of educational schemes in terms of universities and polytechnics, and expansion of secondary and universal free primary eduction. With a change in the military leadership in July 1975, there were changes in the plan priorities. Emphasis shifted to social welfare objectives and agriculture. In spite of the coup, most of the infrastructural, social, and economic projects were achieved along with impressive industrial growth, largely because of the oil boom of 1979/1980. However, the LNG, petrochemical, and the iron and steel projects were not achieved, although some progress was made with the steel projects. There was significant decline in per capita agricultural output, despite an over-all investment of about ₦30 billion, which had to be raised to ₦43.3 billion before the end of the plan period. Income inequality increased during the plan period, particularly towards the end.[7]

The Fourth National Development Plan, 1981–1985

This was the most ambitious of the various plans, at least in conception. One of its main objectives was the attainment of a more equitable distribution of income among individuals as well as among states. Like the past plans, it emphasized the need realization of this was to involve increases in the real income of individuals and a reduction of the level of unemployment, which was a major focus of the plan.

In pursuance of the objectives, the annual growth rate of GDP for the plan period was anticipated at 7.5 per cent, with the growth rate of per capita income per annum to be at about 5 per cent for each of the years within the plan period. Investments in heavy capital projects (basically capital intensive) such as the new federal capital at Abuja, steel and petrochemical projects, in addition to the expansion of higher education with the establishment of six new universities of technology, were to continue. Unfortunately, these projects could not meet the employment goals of the country given their capital intensity. Total planned investment in the plan stood at ₦82 billion.

Unfortunately, the initial years of the plan period coincided with the world-wide economic recession of 1981–1983, which led to a substantial downward revision of total investment in the plan. Furthermore, GDP had declined by about 15 per cent by the end of 1983, and the GNP per capita had also declined by about 25 per cent between 1980 and 1983. In spite of the significant decline in revenue which resulted from the 1981–1983 oil glut, the Abuja project, which was of considerable political importance to the federal government, was vigorously pursued.

There has emerged, however, a significant problem of foreign indebtedness, arising from the execution of these heavy projects. With less than one year, at this writing, until the expiration of the plan period, there appears to be no prospect of substantial recovery, despite the various stringent measures taken. Inflation has reached an unprecedented high, while, concurrently, the largest number of workers ever is being retrenched daily, thereby pushing the rate of unemployment — both of university graduates and unskilled labour — to the highest level ever experienced in Nigeria's modern history. Several industries have virtually ground to a halt for lack of imported raw materials and spare parts. The Fourth Plan has, therefore, failed to achieve most of its targets, largely because of external economic developments beyond Nigeria's control. Faulty domestic economic management, irrational and political decisions, and other related major domestic policy mistakes have undoubtedly exacerbated these failures. Some of these domestic policy mistakes concern:

1. excessive expansion of educational programmes which place great emphasis on academic structures that do not necessarily fit graduates into the local environment, hence the accelerated rate of unemployment;
2. excessive import substitution industrial policy, which made most of the established industries operational directly on the basis of imported raw materials;
3. technological underdevelopment, which made Nigeria heavily dependent on the industrialized countries for equipment, spare parts, and, in most cases, personnel to operate them;
4. dependence on a monolithic economy based on petroleum, the price of which was dependent on the world market, over which Nigeria had no control;
5. more importantly, the pursuit of irrational political policies and programmes which promoted unprecedented graft, corruption, and bare-faced robbery of the public treasury by political functionaries.

Unfortunately, the various plans have, thus far, not anticipated the implications of these domestic policy mistakes, and hence, effective strategies have not been worked out to control the emerging conflicts. Worse still, it seems as if these domestic policy mistakes were never appreciated by past planners, even after the implications started surfacing. By way of a summary, table 1 briefly presents statistical information concerning the achievements and failures of the various plans in terms of their established targets and attained goals. One may note that, in spite of their noticeable shortcomings, the plans had monetary, trade, and fiscal policies, in addition to planned investments (which were disrupted by various internal and external factors, discussed in a later section).

Implications of Nigeria's Windfall Gains on Planning

National Development Plans and Windfall Gains

Every succeeding development plan in Nigeria since independence has been more ambitious in all its ramifications than its predecessors. For example, the number, variety, and scope of projects and programmes; the range of socio-economic development policies and plan objectives; and the associated strategies for the attainment of the established objectives in the Fourth National Development Plan, 1981–1985, are significantly greater than those contained in the Third National Development Plan, 1975–1980. Similarly, these variables as they stand in the 1975–1980 plan are equally well above those contained in the Second National Development Plan, 1970–1975, etc.

It is not the progressive escalation of planned investments in various development plans that matters, but the translation of the escalation into effective reality. Such a translation is possible only when the presence of some crucial factors makes finances available for development investment. Thus, given the aforementioned progressive ambitiousness of Nigerian plans, it is pertinent to examine the underlying factors.

A critical examination of the trend of events in Nigeria reveals that the discovery of crude oil, coupled with its exploitation and the significant revenue from its sales, created a development planning opportunity which paved the way for Nigeria's enhanced spending power on development projects and programmes. The increased earnings from oil acted as a catalyst in Nigeria's socio-economic and political development planning efforts. In fact, the federal government of Nigeria admitted in one of its publications — *Federal Government Economic and Statistical Review, 1978* — that the Nigerian economy has experienced profound changes since independence, but especially since the discovery and exploitation of oil and the subsequent "1973 oil price explosion."

Available statistical information attests to the dominant role of the crude oil sector in the Nigerian economy. The contributions of crude oil to GDP, total revenue, level of investment, foreign exchange earnings, etc., have shown that the oil sector is the most dynamic sector, whose development has not only been the most significant economic event but has also served as a windfall gain for national development planning efforts.

Oil accounted for about 10 per cent of domestic export in 1962. This share rose to 83 per cent in 1973/1974 — the year of oil price adjustment — and reached a peak of about 95 per cent in 1981. Its share of GDP rose from 0.5 per cent at independence to 14.6 per cent in 1970, 21.9 per cent in 1975, and about 27.1 per cent in 1980/1981. Its share of total revenue escalated from 0.8 per cent in 1959/1960 to 71 per cent in 1973/1974 and 84 per cent in 1980/1981. As a foreign exchange earner, oil accounted for 2.7 per cent of Nigeria's foreign exchange in 1960. This share rose rapidly to 57.5 per cent in 1970, 83.1 per cent in 1973, and 94.2 per cent in 1980/1981.

In the area of production, a total of about 3,000 metric tons of crude oil was produced in 1962. This rose to 107,414 metric tons in 1973/1974, but reached a height of 120,443 metric tons in 1980/1981. This is indicative of the rapid development of the petroleum sector, the impetus of which may not be unconnected with the frequent upward adjustments in oil prices in the world oil market since the early 1970s. In fact, the price of oil was below US$2.42 per barrel in the late 1960s, but reached US$12.00 in 1974, US$40.38 in 1981, and almost US$42.00 per barrel before the oil glut of 1982.

The oil price explosion which started in 1973/1974 was the result of a worldwide energy crisis — a crisis of oil supply shortages in the world crude oil market. This situation resulted in windfall gains from Nigeria's oil sales, as it generated significant revenue which reinforced the escalated planned investments in the development plans, especially after the 1967–1970 civil war in Nigeria. For example, the federal government budget was about ₦104 million in 1961/1962 and ₦200 million in 1964/1965. The annual budget escalated to ₦13.81 billion in 1979/1980. Besides, total oil revenue to Nigeria between 1977 and 1980/1981 has been estimated by the Nigerian Nation Petroleum Corporation (NNPC) as being ₦53.4 billion.

Table 2 reveals the profound changes in national development planning brought about by this windfall gain in oil revenue. The table shows the share of total investments in the various plans by public and private sectors. The 1962–1968 plan had a total of ₦2,366 million invested, with the public sector accounting for 67 per cent of this investment. This is not surprising, since the oil money had not yet been injected into planning in Nigeria.

Initially, a total of ₦3,608 million was earmarked for the 1970–1974 reconstruction and rehabilitation plan. However, because of the exploitation of oil in the early 1970s, coupled with the 1973 oil price explosion, which injected enormous amounts of oil revenue into the Nigerian economy, this plan's investment had to be revised upwards to ₦5.7 billion. That is, the oil revenue created about ₦2,092 million for additional investment in the 1970–1974 plan period. This additional investment from the government raised the share of public investment in the second National Development Plan to about 71.4 per cent of the total investment.

Given the later impressive developments in the oil sector, investments in subsequent national development plans were not only significantly high, the public share was above 70 per cent.

For example, a total of ₦45.73 billion and ₦82 billion were earmarked for investment in the Third and Fourth plans respectively, with the public share of the respective investments accounting for 71.9 per cent and 86 per cent. It is obvious that the oil sector rose in a very short period from the position of a relatively insignificant sectoral contributor to national development planning efforts to occupy a position best described as "Nigeria's engine of development planning efforts." The appropriateness of this assertion becomes more apparent with the latter developments in Nigeria's planning efforts after the launching, in January 1981, of the Fourth National Development Plan, 1981–1985, as discussed in the next section.

Development Efforts *Vis-à-Vis* the Dwindling Windfall Gains, 1980–1985

By 1980, crude oil production in Nigeria had reached a peak of about 2.5 million barrels a day, at about US$40.00 per barrel. It was widely anticipated that both production and price levels would rise further in the 1980s. Given this

TABLE 2. Planned public and private investments 1962–1985

Sector	First Plan 1962–1968		Second Plan 1970–1974		Third Plan 1975–1980		Fourth Plan 1981–1985	
	Millions (₦)	Distri- bution (%)	Millions (₦)	Distri- bution (%)	Billions (₦)*	Distri- bution (%)	Billions (₦)	Distri- bution (%)
Public Sector	1,586.0	67.0	1,976.4	54.8	32,860	71.9	70,500	86.0
Private Sector	780.0	33.0	1,631.6	45.2	12,870	28.1	11,500	14.00
Plan size (Total)	2,366.0	100.0	3,608.0	100.0	45,730	100.0	82,000	100.0

Source: 1962–1968, 1970–1974, 1975–1980 and 1981–1985 plan documents.
*Revised upwards to ₦5.7b.

anticipation, about ₦82 billion was earmarked for investment in the 1981–1985 development plan. This amount of investment made the Fourth Plan the most ambitious of all Nigerian development plans. This ambition was reflected in the annual budgets.

For example, the federal government budget in 1961/1962 was about ₦104 million. This figure rose persistently to a peak of about ₦13.81 billion in 1979/1980. However, due to the oil glut of 1980/1981, which resulted in declining oil revenues, government budgets after 1979/1980 started to decline. By 1983, the budget had fallen to about ₦10.8 billion, and this adversely affected investment planning efforts.

It may be recalled that the developing countries of the world have, for decades, been facing problems of foreign exchange reserves, especially those with which to purchase equipment and employ technical skills from abroad for the execution of development projects. Before being tentatively bailed out of the impasse by the windfall gain from crude oil, Nigeria faced identical problems.

It is against this background that the search for an efficient and effective management of the country's foreign exchange reserves became imperative in 1982, when major economic planning problems started unfolding due to the dwindling oil revenue and consequent dwindling of foreign reserves. From a peak of ₦3.7 billion in 1975, barely two years after the oil price explosion, the country's foreign reserves fell dramatically to ₦1.1 billion and ₦0.8 billion in 1982 and 1983 respectively. Export trade earnings, which is the main source of foreign exchange, declined from a level of ₦14.2 billion in 1980 to ₦8.7 billion in 1982–1983 as a result of the fall in the price and quantity of crude oil sales.

Consequently, the initial ₦82 billion investment in the 1981–1985 Development Plan became unrealistic. It had to be revised downward, and some development projects and programmes in the plan had to be cancelled or suspended. In addition, expectations of the public and private sectors of the economy were unfulfilled, and stringent austerity measures were imposed through the annual budgets.

This suggests, therefore, that the momentum generated by the exploitation and sales of crude oil had started to slow down with the downturn in the revenue derivable from oil, which had hitherto formed the main source of financing for the development plans.

Planning Machinery, Methodology, and Process

The basic objectives of development planning in Nigeria is not only to accelerate the rate of economic growth and the rate at which the standard of living can be raised but also to give increasingly more control to indigenes over their own destiny.[8] Thus, Nigeria's development planning has been a process with multiple objectives — economic, social, political, national security, ecological, etc. — most of which are not only complex but also interrelated.

Given these complexities, planning has usually embraced the joint efforts of the federal, state, and local governments, statutory corporations, and the private sector. That is, a partnership of the federal, state, and local governments in collaboration not only with each other but also with their parastatals and private business, is usually institutionalized for purposes of development planning in Nigeria. This institutionalized apparatus for planning is subject to the constant changes and developments which often affect the process, methodology, and techniques of planning. However, these changes are a function of the socio-economic and political conditions in the country.

Obviously, modern Nigeria inherited the British colonial administration, and a number of British institutions and values which have significantly influenced planning systems, particularly in the pre-independence era, but thereafter as well. There was the civilian democratic form of government, which was terminated by a series of military administrations between 1966 and 1979. Although military rule was constitutionally replaced by the presidential system of government in 1979, it was once again restored to power on December 31, 1983.

It is apparent, then, that the major planning decisions which have significantly shaped Nigeria's economy have coincided with the military era. Even though the 1962–1968 and 1981–1985 plans owe credit to the parliamentary and presidential systems of government, part of their execution, as well as the planning and execution of the 1970–1974 and 1975–1980 plans, should be credited to the military governments. However, despite some noticeable differentials in methods of government by these various systems, they possess essentially identical strategies and institutions in the area of development planning.

However, regardless of the changes in the political administration and structure of the country, there seems to be heavy reliance on the civil service, which has been powerful in the making and implementation of policy decisions of government, particularly during the military administrations. Their power and influence are derived from the political limitations of the military personnel, who require assistance and advice for effective planning.

Despite the influence of civil servants in plan preparation, planning in Nigeria could be regarded as part of the political set-up. Party manifestoes reflect programmes of action for socio-economic and political transformation intended by political parties. It therefore follows that the need for planning is usually accepted in the Nigerian system of party politics.

The hub of the planning machinery is currently the National Planning Office (NPO), called the Central Planning Office (CPO) under the 1966–1979 military administration. The NPO is the major component of the Federal Ministry of National Planning (Federal Ministry of Economic Development in the 1966–1979 period) that is responsible for plan preparation (see fig. 1a). The planning procedure involves all ministries and their agencies' parastatals at the federal and state levels as well as at the local government level.

The preparation of plans at all levels of government and state-owned com-

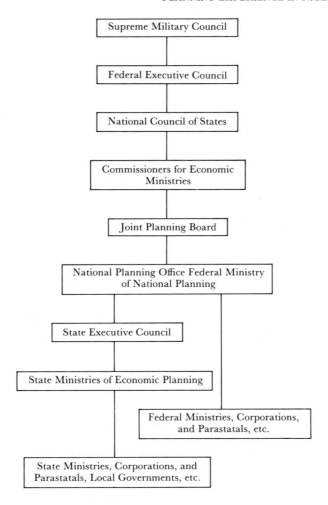

FIG. 1a. Planning machinery under the military regimes.

panies and parastatals follows a series of consultations with the NPO, after which the NPO issues guidelines. The various levels of government and their agencies thereafter submit their proposals to the NPO, which modifies and collates them in line with set-out objectives. The plan document is then sent to the Joint Planning Board (JPB) and the Conference of State Commissioners, responsible for economic planning under the chairmanship of the federal minister for national planning. Their recommendations are subsequently sent to the National Council of States (National Economic Council under civilian re-

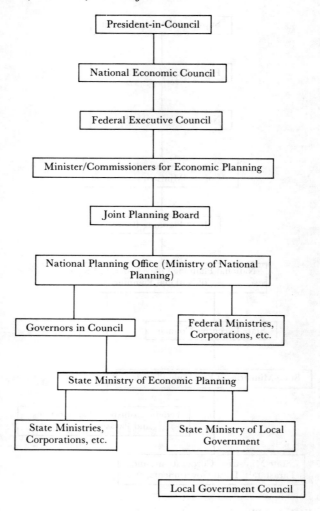

FIG. 1b. Planning machinery under the presidential system.

gimes), which is made up of state governors under the chairmanship of the head of state. The final plan document is then sent to the Federal Executive Council (FEC, made up of federal ministers under the chairmanship of the head of state), which gives final approval under civilian rule. Final approval under military rule lies with the Supreme Military Council (SMC).

The private sector is also consulted occasionally, although their investment plans are rarely integrated into the national plans, even though national plan policies and programmes influence the directions of their investment decisions. The institutionalized bodies, for purposes of discussion, modification, and approval of national development planning documents in Nigeria (see fig. 1), consist of the following:

The Joint Planning Broad

Permanent secretaries, chief executives of ministries of economic planning at the federal and state levels, and heads of the Research Department of the Central Bank, the Nigerian Institute of Social and Economic Research (NISER), the Federal Office of Statistics, and a representative of the Ministry of Finance, constitute the Joint Planning Board.

The major functions of the JPB consist of providing planning advice to the National Economic Council and preparing statements of fundamental objectives for the guidance of the various planning institutions of the federal, state, and local governments in the formulation of their development plans for each succeeding period. That is, the JPB is expected to provide a sense of direction to all institutions of the various governments in their development planning endeavours.

For example, consequent upon the establishment of the JPB, its recommendation to the National Economic Council in 1959 constituted a base for the government's decision to prepare a national development plan as an alternative to the previous regional investment programmes.

The National Economic Consultative Council

The institution is made up of federal government officials and representatives of the organized private sector, labour unions, universities, and research institutes. It is an informal body through which the government makes its policies and programmes known to the private sector and from which the government receives feedbacks on its policies and programmes of development.

Conference of Ministers/Commissioners

This is an assembly of ministers/commissioners directly responsible for economic development matters to which recommendations of the JPB are passed. The JPB is responsible for preparing the draft plan document, usually after critical discussions of the papers from the various states, federal government ministries, corporations, etc. Amendments, proposals, and recommendations are thereafter made by the conference and incorporated into a draft document which is then passed on to the next levels in the planning machinery.

President-in-Council/Federal Executive Council and National Economic Council/Council of States

The Federal Executive Council consists of the federal ministers and is chaired by the head of state; the National Economic Council of States is composed of state governors and some high-ranking government officials. Under the civilian government, the vice president was chairman of the National Economic Council, which consisted only of the state governors and the governor of the Central Bank.

The Supreme Military Council

This is the highest planning and governmental authority, with the head of government presiding over its meetings under the military governmental set-up.

This higher planning institution is expected to consider the drafted national plan or guidelines from the lower planning institutions. Once the draft is approved, it automatically becomes the planning document for the country.

A new trend in planning emerged under the 1975–1979 military administration with the appearance of a new document in the planning process — *Guideline for Development Plans* — prepared by the CPO (NPO). This document was expected to give a sense of direction to the agencies which will participate in the formulation of projected aggregates such as GDP, consumption, exports, imports, and capital formation statistics and also in the analysis of socio-economic problems anticipated for various sectors of the economy during the subsequent plan period. The production of this document, which usually follows the same procedure as that of the plan, is expected to have been critically discussed in a series of seminars, conferences, and workshops organized by universities, research institutes, ministries, and other agencies both public and private.

At the discussion stage, these various dicussion processes take the forms of seminars, conferences, or workshops lasting in most cases between one day to one week. Leadership in organizing the various fora for discussion is usually taken by NISER. For a critical discussion of the planning strategies, plan focus, level of investments, project selection, sources of plan finances, etc., participants are usually drawn from various political parties, ministries — federal, state, and local — corporations, parastatals, private and public sectors, and universities and research institutes. These representatives present position papers which stress their areas of major concern for critical discussions. The presentations are usually expected to form a basis for the formulation of policies and programmes for subsequent planning periods. Given the fundamental rationale for its production, the *Guideline* seems to have become part of the process of development planning.

It is obvious that the planning procedure in Nigeria is a co-operative venture cutting across a large number of agencies at the federal, state, and local government levels and also political, public, and private institutions. It is a tedious and time-consuming exercise due to the series of consultations and discussion and lengthy negotiations and compromises among the planning authorities and agencies submitting project proposals.

It is important to note that the effective performance of the higher planning institutions depends, to a large extent, on the quality of advice supplied by the lower planning institutions in collaboration with the associated agencies, the quality of statistics available for planning, and the willingness of the divergent sectors and states of the economy to co-operate and compromise in dealing with national issues. In this regard, it is pertinent to stress that various agencies, political or otherwise, usually attend planning meetings to defend their respective interests rather than the national objective. This has always posed a serious problem given the political differences under the presidential and parliamentary systems of government, especially during the civilian regimes. The divergence in interests are also manifested during military regimes, thereby necessitating compromises in planning objectives.

In spite of this fundamental problem of reaching a compromise between conflicting views, particularly among political parties, the highest institution for planning usually used its initiatives to take a position. Since this institution was usually composed more of the people in government, the political party or parties in power usually had their way, especially during the era of civilian government.

Development Planning and Economic Performance

The need for development planning in Nigeria, particularly within the last three decades, can be said to have been fully recognized. However, making planning machinery and programmes effective for the attainment of the established goals is equally as important as the development planning itself.

As discussed in the foregoing sections, the planning experience in Nigeria has shown that successive national development plans are usually and progressively more ambitious in terms of the levels of investments, number, variety, and scope of the perceived projects and programmes, the range of socio-economic development policies with their proposed objectives and strategies, and of course, the necessary operating machinery.

However, after over three decades of development planning endeavours in the country, there is full awareness of the obvious need for continuous planning. Despite this awareness and the various efforts in the area of planning continuity in Nigeria, it is apparent that the country is still plagued by various socio-economic and political problems which often lead to ineffective planning. An attempt is, therefore, made in this section to examine the performance of the Nigerian economy in response to the afore-discussed planning efforts.

The performance of the various development plans could be measured by an assessment of the rate of achievement of the national or sectoral objectives. It may be recalled that the most crucial goal of planning in Nigeria is the need for improved quality of the standard of living.

The attainment of this goal could be assessed in terms of the various levels of such variables as the per capita income, rate of growth of GDP, rates of savings and investment, the share of manufacturing in GDP, the rate of inflation, etc. Whereas the per capita income and the rate of inflation indicate the level of an average citizen's real income, the GDP growth rate and other variables signify the nation's wealth and its level of development. Moreover, the share of the manufacturing sector in GDP shows a fairly reliable, although crude, measure of the level of industrialization of the economy. In order to assess the effectiveness or ineffectiveness of the various development planning efforts thus far in Nigeria, the relationships between the plans' forecasts and the estimated levels of actual attainments in terms of some selected development indicators are presented in tables 3 and 4. Information on the planned targets and the actual level of achievements in respect of some selected variables is found in table 1.

Even though, regrettably, the paucity of data makes these tables incomplete, they nevertheless give an idea of the degree of success of target achievements.

It is apparent from the tables that the planned rate of growth, particularly of GDP, was achieved and even surpassed in the First and Second national development plan periods. While a growth rate of 5 per cent was attained in the Third Plan, instead of the intended target of 9.5 per cent. The expected levels of investment and savings as proportions of GDP were achieved in all of the plans. The share of manufacturing in GDP, however, fell far short of anticipated levels in all plans and continues to decline.

Although it is quantitatively difficult to determine the level of achievements in the area of the rate of growth of per capita consumption due to lack of data, it is an open secret that per capita consumption in Nigeria has, for some time, fallen below planned targets. In the case of the change in the rate of inflation, rather than negative changes, significantly positive changes have been recorded, particularly since 1980/1981, when the annual inflation rate averaged about 30 per cent. Due to the problems of inadequate and unreliable data, it is difficult to quantify in summary statistics the skewness in the distribution of income and consumption among the various groups of Nigerian citizens. Nonetheless, it is common knowledge that a large percentage of the population, particularly in the urban centres, have low levels of income. Moreover, a large proportion of people live below subsistance level; they cannot afford three meals a day and make provision for a minimum shelter from their meagre and inflation-ridden income.

In sum, the Nigerian economy is still a long way from being able to provide most of its citizens with the basic needs for an acceptable quality of life. Put differently, the plans have not attained their targets. In view of this, one wonders whether this shortfall has been due to over-optimism on the part of the planners or to the country's socio-economic and political constraints that have hampered the effectiveness of the planning machinery.

TABLE 3. Selected economic indicators: Comparison of plan forecast with current estimate 1970–1971 to 1973–1974

	1970–1971			1971–1972			1972–1973			1973–1974		
	Plan figure	Actual	Increase/ decrease	Plan figure	Actual	Increase/ decrease	Plan figure	Actual	Increase/ decrease	Plan figure	Current estimate	Increase/ decrease
Gross domestic product (at current prices)	3,485.8	5,584.4	8,098.6	3,756.4	6,851.4	3,095.8	4,110.6	7,136.9	3,006.3	4,561.8	8,329.9	3,768.1
Growth rate (%)	4.2	30.8	86.6	7.8	22.7	14.9	9.4	4.2	−5.2	11.0	16.7	5.7
Capital formation	710.0	844.9	134.9	798.0	1,234.9	436.9	836.0	1,480.0	644.0	843.0	1,745.9	897.9
Investment ratio (%)	18.4	14.8	−3.6	18.9	17.2	−1.7	18.2	19.2	+1.0	16.8	19.6	+2.5
Traditional exports	403.6	375.6	−28.0	428.4	312.9	−115.5	435.6	247.8	−187.1	455.6	319.5	−138.1
Oil exports	520.6	509.8	−10.8	659.0	980.4	+321.4	739.0	1,186.4	+447.4	792.6	1,958.9	+1,166.3
Total exports	924.2	885.4	−38.8	1,087.4	1,293.3	+205.9	1,174.6	1,434.2	+259.6	1,248.2	2,278.4	1,030.2
Imports	660.0	756.4	+96.4	725.8	1,078.9	+353.1	816.4	990.1	+173.7	939.4	1,224.8	+285.4
Current account balance	−69.2	−50.0	+19.2	−41.0	213.0	−178.0	+71.8	−317.6	−245.8	−132.0	+65.2	+197.2
Gross national savings (Nm)	328.4	794.9	+466.5	387.0	1,015.9	+528.9	341.4	1,172.4	831.4	252.6	1,811.1	+1,558.5
Savings ratio (%)	9.2	13.4	+4.2	10.0	14.8	+4.8	8.2	16.5	+8.3	5.4	22.2	+16.8
GNP as per cent of GDP	92.3	98.8	+6.5	91.5	95.5	+4.0	91.0	92.7	+1.7	91.0	93.2	+2.2
Government recurrent revenue	637.2	849.0	+211.8	794.4	1,425.9	−621.5	947.6	1,531.8	+584.2	1,140.4	2,355.4	+1,215.0
Government recurrent expenditure	571.8	786.5	+214.7	643.0	889.5	+246.5	686.0	1,120.4	434.4	718.4	1,200.7	+482.0
Budget surplus	65.4	62.5	−2.9	151.4	536.4	385.0	261.6	411.4	+149.8	488.0	1,154.7	+732.7

Source: Federal Republic of Nigeria, *Third National Development Plan, 1975–80*, vol. 1, March 1975, p. 23.

TABLE 4. Selected economic indicators: Comparison of plan forecast with current estimates 1975–1976 and 1979–1980*

Sector	1975–1976			1979–1980		
	Plan forecast	Current estimate	Increase/decrease	Plan forecast	Current estimate	Increase/decrease
Gross domestic factor cost (₦1m)	18,050.9	87,364.7	9,313.8	26,574.3	35,196.4	8,632.1
Growth rate (%)	7.2	−1.3	−8.5	11.6	8.8	−2.8
Gross fixed capital Formation (₦1m)	3,540.0	5,019.8	1,479.8	9,080.0	11,626.0	8,546.0
Investment ratio (%)	20.8	23.3	2.5	29.4	28.5	−0.9
Traditional exports (₦1m)	346.8	357.1	10.3	398.0	657.7	254.4
Oil exports (₦1m)	7,120.3	4,563.1	−2,557.2	10,633.2	10,578.3	−54.9
Total exports (₦1m)	7,467.1	4,980.2	−2,546.9	11,031.2	199.8	
Imports (₦1m)	2,270.1	3,710.0	1,439.9	7,085.1	8,468.0	1,382.9
Current account balance	3,681.4	42.6	−3,688.8	1,831.5	1,009.5	−822.0
Gross national savings	7,282.6	5,556.7	−1,725.9	11,020.6	13,307.8	2,887.8
Savings ratio (%)	42.8	85.8	−17.0	35.7	32.6	−3.1
GNP as per cent of GDP	95.5	98.6	3.1	97.6	98.8	1.2

Source: Federal Republic of Nigeria, *Fourth National Development Plan 1981–85*, vol. 1, Jan. 1981, p. 14.
*Calculated at current prices.

Major Obstacles to Planning Effectiveness

As evident in the foregoing, the past national development plans have not attained their established targets. This failure is due largely to a number of political, social, and economic factors which combine to threaten the effectiveness of the plans. An attempt is therefore made in this section to examine these factors as they affect development planning.

National Development Planning and Politics

Admittedly, development planning, especially in developing countries, enables a government to provide a sense of direction in public expenditure as well as necessary guidance to entrepreneurs in the private sector. However, the effectiveness of these provisions depends on how systematic the continuity of the directives from the government are. In turn, the systematic continuity of development planning policies and programmes hinges on the nature, characteristics, and complexities of the country's politics.

Put differently, the effectiveness of development planning efforts, especially in developing ecconomies like Nigeria, is determined by the country's political arrangements. Such political arrangements include:
— the extent of the country's political stability;
— the country's system of party politics coupled with the mode of playing that kind of party politics and the spirit of effective party coexistence;
— political leadership and the method of selection;
— political ideologies for national development (socialism, capitalism, communism, etc.).
The roles of these political factors in the effectiveness or ineffectiveness of development planning in most industrialized economies of the world are testimonies in this regard. This raises the question of the extent to which politics can affect the effectiveness of national development planning in a developing country like Nigeria.

Political Stability/Instability

Given the development planning objectives and the need for a systematic continuity in development plans and programmes, the existence of political stability in order to create an atmosphere conducive to effective and continuous planning cannot be over-emphasized. Despite the awareness of the need for political stability for the emergence of systematic and continuous planning, 25 years of Nigerian independence have installed two civil heads of state, one prime minister, and six military heads of state. Within this short period, the country witnessed five successful and one officially announced abortive military coups. During the 25 years of independence, politicians ruled the country

TABLE 5. Frequency of changes in government in Nigeria

Government	Period	Type of government	Development plan period
First republic	1960–1966	Civil rule (parliamentary)	1962–1968
First military regime	1/1966–7/1966	Military	1962–1968
Second military regime	7/1966–7/1975	Military	1962–1968, 1971–1975
Third military regime	7/1975–2/1976	Military	1975–1980
Fourth military regime	2/1976–10/1979	Military	1975–1980
Second republic	10/1979–12/1983	Civil rule (presidential)	1975–1980, 1981–1985
Fifth military regime	12/1983–8/1985	Military	1981–1985
Sixth military regime	8/1985–	Military	1981–1985

for 9 years, with the military accounting for the remaining 16 years. A summary of these changes is given in table 5.

These frequent changes in government and leadership within 25 years could be called anything but political stability. In fact, a common peculiarity of each leader was a deviation from the focus of the original plan and revision of the planning strategies and programmes of his predecessor. Besides, no two leaders are exactly identical in their programmes, strategies, and approaches to solving development problems. Thus these frequent changes can best be regarded as the nation's humps and hurdles in the path of national development planning efforts. They have inevitably limited the effectiveness of development planning in Nigeria.

Political Strategies, Party Politics, and National Development Planning in Nigeria

Various political development planning strategies abound in the world in order to give a proper focus to national development goals. Whereas capitalism as a political strategy for planning can be associated with the development strategies which originated in the West, socialism is a political development strategy which is a peculiarity of the East.

While capitalism puts a premium on national development strategies through private ownership of factors of production, socialism lays emphasis on the concentration of such factors in the public sector. Both strategies aim at rapid development of the economy, as proved and evident in the rapidity of development trends in the United States (capitalism) and the Soviet Union (socialism).

In spite of this awareness, Nigeria has not evolved a specific political ideological posture. In practical terms, Nigeria has combined both ideologies in what is usually tagged a mixed economic system. This simply boils down to a combination of complex and probably conflicting strategies for national development planning in Nigeria. The complexities arising from this combination have resulted in conflicts in the planning efforts.

For example, the failure of the 1972 Indegenization Decree and its 1976 modification can be traced to the conflicts arising from the adoption of mixed political development planning strategies. Moreover, the difficulties encountered in the implementation of the 1978/1979 Land Use Decree tell the story of the conflict in the economic system. In fact, a critical review of the various national development plans will reveal that most of the past programmes and projects have failed because no one ideology has been adopted in the country.

With regard to party politics and national development planning, Nigeria has a multiparty system. The various political parties have usually declared their commitment to accelerated socio-economic and political development of the country. Their strategies, slogans, areas of focus, and manifestos in particular, have, however, always been in conflict, one with the other. It may be recalled that political party manifestos remain important documents, containing party programmes and socio-economic activities for transforming the economy if such a party is elected.

As evident in the previous sections, planning procedures in Nigeria take a compromise form among the various states controlled by different political parties with divergent manifestos and by public and private agencies whose proposals on investments, projects, and development goals usually diverge. This compromise form of planning procedures that the parties and agencies employ constitutes the essence of politics in Nigeria and, by implication, has had a significant impact on the effectiveness (and/or ineffectiveness) of planning machineries. It is not surprising, therefore, considering the structure of Nigerian politics, that certain parties and agencies having significant influence have been able to virtually steamroller their projects through planning processes even under a military administration.

These influences also best explain why the implementation and control of laudable programmes in the development plan become ineffective. In what ways have local politics in Nigeria actually rendered development planning efforts ineffective?

It is evident in Nigeria's process of national development planning that various political considerations have, in the past, significantly influenced development project execution, estimated project investment targets, and anticipated revenue or benefits derivable from such selected projects. It is also common knowledge that undue political interference has exacerbated plan indiscipline, which has usually culminated in large-scale distortions and inevitable reversal of the original intentions of the plan.

Apart from the role that party politics have played in plan distortion, the leadership roles assumed by past Nigerian leaders — both soldiers and civilians — have often surfaced only to ultimately compound plan distortion problems. For example, if a Nigerian leader is to remain in office for long and at the same time enjoy the support and sympathy of the entire population, he has to demonstrate his concern for the people's development through positive socio-economic achievements.

Awareness of this has usually created the urge in such a leader to use available documents such as the national development plans with their associated components — annual budgets — to popularize his "concern" for the people. In most cases, such concern was usually manifested in approvals given to modified plans without recourse to the realities of the economy in terms of resource availability and with little or no attempt to express sound economic and technical judgements.

This partially explains why proposed plan targets were unrealistic and thus never achieved. In fact, Ayida — a former federal permanent secretary — once remarked that:

The published document is not the plan that planners prepared. This is the Federal Government plan approved by the NEC and expanded by the SMC into its present shape. This distinction is very important in any consideration of the financing of the plan as a whole and the state plans in particular. Some of the states' plans as augmented by the SMC are totally unrealistic either in terms of financing possibilities or executive capacities or both. . . . When I was in the Ministry for Economic Development (Federal) as a Permanent Secretary, I thought that the present scales of investment targets proposed were over-ambitious. . . . The plan revenue forecasts appeared so rosy and misleading in the harsh realities of the post-war situation.[9]

These comments by the country's foremost civil servant in the Gowon regime point to the fact that the figures presented in the plan documents were, more often than not, based on unrealistic projections. While these distortions tended to be common within the military regimes, it is not out of place to assume that they might have become a common feature under the civilian administrations. However, whether or not the interference is brazenly carried out or silently executed with military precision, the consequence is usually the same: the sterilization of the planning machinery and the invalidation and consequential ineffectiveness of the plan document.

Political leaders the world over seem to, inherently, have the tendency to modify, bend, or distort the constitutional arrangements and recommendations from lower institutionalized planning organs to suit their own political ambitions. The alarming frequency and ease with which such alterations were made in Nigeria's development process is of major concern, as Ayida's remarks indicate.

Some development projects which have fallen victim to these alterations, either in the process of their execution or pace of development, include the Abuja federal capital project, the long delayed iron and steel industry, and the Kainji hydroelectric project, to mention a few. These projects have been either delayed unduly, rushed unnecessarily, or executed in such a manner that the projects are subject to constant ineffective operations.

Another way in which politics have hampered the effectiveness of development planning in Nigeria is through the antagonistic strategies of the various political parties with their associated pressure groups. The major reason for this disparity is that Nigerian states have been polarized according to political inclinations. For example, under the last civilian administration, states controlled by the Unity Party of Nigeria (UPN) established very similar priorities among themselves, but ones which in most cases were at variance with the priorities of states controlled by the National Party of Nigeria.

A good number of development programmes have thus been harmed simply because the project priorities indicated in the plan documents, though quite similar, were not in perfect consonance with those of certain political parties. Projects which fell victim to these conflicting and antagonistic strategies include the well-applauded Green Revolution (agricultural) project of the federal government which was proposed by the NPN — the party in power — and the Free Education and Health Service projects supported in all of the UPN controlled states. Both projects were laudable, yet the antagonistic political approach frustrated their execution so that neither quite succeeded.

Nigeria's Socio-economic Conditions as Obstacles

As highlighted in the previous sections, the amalgamation of the northern and southern protectorates into one entity — Nigeria — brought together about 250 different ethnic groups with substantially divergent cultural traditions. Ethnic categorizations, in fact, formed, at least partially, the basis for state creation and boundary adjustments.

These cultural diversities have generated centrifugal tendencies which accentuate the difficulties of creating a truly integrated political, social, and economic system for effective development planning. Ethnic diversities, for example, compound the problems faced by planners who try to reconcile federal, state, and ethnic goals when attempting to determine the location and extent of development projects in different parts of the federation. They influence project determination and contract awards for project execution as well. These divergencies are also usually reflected in programmes and projects related to education.

Apart from divergent goals and traditions of ethnic groups, some sound development goals and projects have been rendered ineffective through inappropriate decisions. For example, in order to reduce the magnitude of Nigeria's deficit balance of payments and also to allow for effective Nigerianization within the industrialization programmes, import-substitution manufacturing projects were selected, defended, and vigorously pursued. At this stage in planning, Nigerian planners probably did not realize the technological limitations, inadequacy of technical manpower, unsuitability of local raw materials to the manufacturing projects, and, of course, the economic implications of the reliance on heavy importation of the machinery and raw materials needed to make the projects viable. In fact, the excessive importation of raw materials, technology, and its associated equipment and spare parts has not only compounded the deficit balance-of-payments problem but has also induced severe inflation and unemployment, the closure of manufacturing plants, and other severe consequences.

Other obstacles that could be associated with factors that hinder the effectiveness of development planning in Nigeria include:

1. heavy reliance on finances from external sources which were either unduly delayed or did not materialize at all. The 1962–1968 plan experience is a good example;
2. the scarcity of willing and competent technical partners, particularly for the development of a truly indigenous industrial sector;
3. lack of adequate local resources for development planning and plan execution, particularly feasibility studies and basic data;
4. lack of the required basic infrastructural facilities, that is, roads, water, electricity, telecommunications, etc., for effective development of the agricultural and industrial sectors.

Another crucial factor which always renders the national planning efforts ineffective in Nigeria relates to the poor perception of the concept of development with its associated focus on growth. This usually creates the problem of inappropriate indicators for monitoring and evaluating desirable goals of development. It is evident in past plan documents that planning has been evaluated on the projected rates of growth of GDP, investment levels, and import-cum-export balances, rather than on the various structural changes such as supply, infrastructural facilities, value added, and other improvements that directly relate to the basic requirements of the citizens.

Moreover, most of the projects selected for the attainment of these growth targets were not based on rigorous pre-feasibility studies which could adequately appraise such projects and sectoral linkages within the economy. In several cases, such projects led to an emphasis on the technological transfer syndrome rather than on technological acquisition. This in turn resulted in the development of "turn-key projects" which were linked neither with the local expertise nor the development — both human and material — of local resources.[10]

It is clear from the above that development planning is beset by a number of problems which limit its effectiveness. In spite of these problems, however, much has been achieved through development planning in Nigeria, and the potentialities for further achievements are quite high.

Prospects and Proposals for Effective Development Planning

The preceding section has critically examined the factors militating against effective development planning in Nigeria and it is, therefore, relevant to ask what prospects exist today for the achievement of effective development planning. The relevance of this question is underlined by the fact that the political, socio-economic, and administrative limitations identified above still exist in Nigeria. Besides, Nigeria is still a federation with development planning a concurrent subject within the jurisdiction of all levels of government — federal, state, and local. Without any attempt to de-emphasize the limitations, there is reason to believe that uncoordinated and ineffective development planning could become a thing of the past in Nigeria.

For over a decade now, the federal and state governments have continued to agree on common development objectives, and the machinery for regular consultations between the federal and state governments on development issues is being strengthened. For example, during the ongoing preparatory work for the Fifth National Development Plan, 1980–1990, the federal and state governments have agreed on common guidelines for the Fifth Plan and also on the need for their annual budgets to be linked with its projects and programmes. This agreement will, to a large extent, promote plan discipline and purposeful uniformity of approach to development issues.

It has to be emphasized that the acceptance of common development objectives is not the result of Nigeria being under a military regime; even during the now defunct civilian administration, common development objectives and guidelines were agreed upon. It must be recognized that in a federation such as we have in Nigeria, processes which bring about dynamic equilibrium between centrifugal and centripetal forces are always at work. It is clear, however, that in present-day Nigeria, adjustments are continually being made in the relationships between the federal and state governments which are in the direction of further economic integration in the country.

The institutionalization of development planning in Nigeria would provide the basis for the continuing search for effective development planning machinery. An institutional framework would no doubt provide for purposeful communication between federal and state governments in such a way as to enhance nationwide development of an administrative framework for integrated development planning.

Another factor which is likely to foster integrated development planning in the country is the increasing fiscal power of the federal government, which enhances its leadership role in all spheres of government activities, but especially

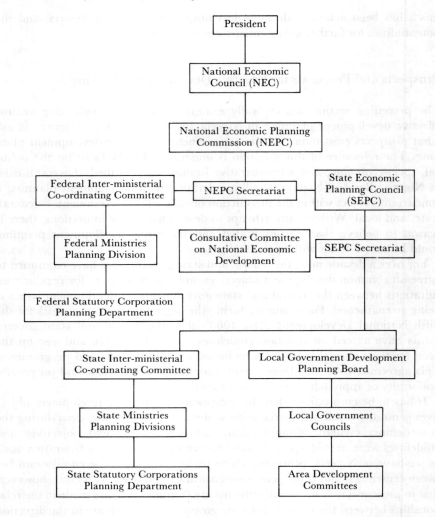

FIG. 2. Proposed institutional framework for development planning in Nigeria.

in economic planning and development matters. With a system of priority determination backed up by financial grants and directives, the federal government would be in a pre-eminent position to influence the course and effectiveness of development planning in the country.

Figure 2 illustrates the proposed framework within which such administrative machinery could be made effective in integrated development planning. At the apex of the proposed planning machinery is the president of the nation, whose ultimate responsibility it is to take decisions on the economic and social development of the country. A national development planning body known as the National Economic Council (NEC) should be set up. It should be made up of the president, the vice-president, state governors, the governor of the Central Bank, and the deputy chairman of the National Economic Planning Commission. The NEC should have powers to take decisions concerning the economic affairs of the nation and, in particular, on measures necessary for the co-ordination of the economic planning efforts or economic programmes of the various governments of the federation. It should also be required by law to meet at least thrice a year.

Given the present 19-state structure of the country, the NEC will consist of 23 members including the chairman. It may appear that by making the NEC the main planning authority in the country, the constitutional powers of the states to embark on their own planning may be limited. This need not be the case, however, as one of the main objectives of the NEC is co-ordination of development planning — an objective which could effectively be achieved through such a body in which all the heads of governments in the federation are represented. Besides, the provision of effective leadership in economic and other matters by the federal government as envisaged in this proposed machinery would enable the NEC to perform a co-ordinating and unifying role in development planning.

The responsibility for the formulation of development policies, programmes, and plans, as well as the supervision of the execution of plans approved by the NEC, should lie with a National Economic Planning Commission (NEPC). This should be a body of experts appointed on the basis of their professional competence and functional responsibilities under the chairmanship of the vice-president. An expert in development planning should be appointed its deputy chairman and should be responsible for its day-to-day administration. In addition to its chairman and deputy chairman, the commission should consist of five distinguished academicians, that is, five knowledgeable persons to represent interests in agriculture, industry, commerce, trade unions, and the professions, who would hold office for from three to five years. The *ex officio* members should consist of the director of planning and representatives of the following bodies: the Nigerian Institute of Social and Economic Research, the Institute of Policy and Strategic Studies, the Central Bank, the Federal Office of Statistics, the Federal Ministry of Science and Technology, the Energy Commission, the Federal Director of Agriculture, and the Director of the Manpower Board.

The NEPC should be charged with the responsibility for:

1. preparing statements of fundamental objectives to guide the formulation and preparation of national and state development plans;
2. formulating national development plans and providing guidance to state governments in the preparation of their development plans;
3. recommending to the NEC economic and fiscal policies and other measures

required to mobilize financial, material, and human resources for implementing development plans;

4. appraising the progress achieved in the execution of development plans and recommending needed modifications to the plans and policies; and

5. preparing studies, reports, and surveys essential for effective development planning and plan execution.

The stance of the commission should be that of a non-partisan group of experts with a long-term vision of the national economic and social development objectives.

In order to ensure full participation by various groups and interests in the national development process, a Consultative Committee on National Economic Development (CCNED) should be set up. The committee should represent a wide range of interests: the educational, agricultural, industrial, and commercial employers' associations, trade unions, professional bodies, transportation and communications, etc. The committee would serve as a consultative and advisory group to both the NEC and NEPC, as well as a clearing-house for opinions on economic and social matters of importance to national development.

The NEPC requires a well-staffed and well-equipped secretariat in order to be able to discharge its responsibilities. The existing National Planning Office of the Federal Ministry of National Planning should form the nucleus of the NEPC secretariat proposed in figure 2. The Office of Statistics and a revamped National Manpower Board should constitute integral parts of the secretariat, which should also serve the NEC and the CCNED. With the vice-president as chairman of the NEPC and a well-staffed secretariat, the NEPC should have the political backing, the expertise, and facilities at its disposal to undertake effective national development planning and monitoring.

As indicated in figure 2, the federal government should have an Inter-Ministerial Co-ordinating Committee and effective planning divisions in the various ministries to prepare and implement approved development programmes at the federal level. The federal statutory corporations which are subject to directives from appropriate federal authorities should also have planning departments to ensure that their programmes and projects are consistent with the agreed upon national objectives.

Each state government should establish its own State Economic Planning Council (SEPC) under the chairmanship of the deputy governor with membership and functions, at the state level, similar to those of the NEPC. Interministerial co-ordinating committees, planning divisions in the ministries, and planning departments in statutory corporations should also be similarly set up in each state of the federation.

Of particular importance is the proposed Local Government Development

Planning Board, shown in figure 2. The board, assisted by local governments, councils, and area development committees, is to focus on development both at the regional and grass-roots levels. Among its responsibilities would be the promotion of development at the local level through the mobilization of material and human resources as well as self-help within communities in local government areas. It should work in such a way as to promote co-operation at the local level and to ensure that people at the grass-roots level identify with the development process.

In order to ensure the effectiveness of the proposed planning machinery at all (federal, state, and local — and even parastatal) levels of government, it would be necessary to develop a cadre of professionally competent planners — specialists in the social sciences, experts in project preparation and appraisal, statisticians, etc., as well as a development-oriented civil service. There is a general shortage of planning specialists in the country, and this calls for intensive training programmes for existing officials at all levels of government and for the recruitment and training of new officials to face the challenges of development planning in Nigeria. Universities should assist in these training programmes. The Administrative Staff College of Nigeria and the Nigerian Institute of Social and Economic Research should play a particularly prominent role in this regard, because they have staff development and training programmes which are already in operation.

Conclusion

Development planning has become the major instrument for giving a sense of purpose and direction to the economy of Nigeria in promoting economic development and national integration. Nigeria has achieved much through development planning, but, as has been shown in this study, a number of political, socio-economic, and institutional factors have limited its effectiveness. It is against this background that the prospects for effective development planning in the country have been examined and proposals for effective development planning machinery have been made. The formulation and implementation of national development plans call for the development of an effective institutional framework and a political commitment on the part of policy-makers without which the country may not be able to maximize the advantages that can be derived from such plans. As Nigeria is about to embark on the fifth in its series of national development plans, it is hoped that the effectiveness of its planning machinery will be enhanced in order to ensure that the benefits of development planning will assure a steady improvement in the standard of living of its citizens.

Notes

1. Federal Republic of Nigeria, *Constitution of the Federal Republic of Nigeria, 1979* (Lagos, 1979), section 16, pp. 8–9.
2. E. O. Adeniyi, "National Development Planning and Plan Administration in Nigeria," *Journal of Administration Overseas* (London), vol. 19, no. 3 (July 1980): 160.
3. Federal Republic of Nigeria, *The First National Development Plan 1962–1968* (Lagos, Federal Ministry of Economic Planning, 1962).
4. Details appear in a number of recent reports, which include: *The World Bank Report on Accelerated Development in Sub-Saharan Africa; The Bramdt Report,* and, *The ECA Representative Study of Africa's Development 1983–2008.*
5. The effects of the slave-trade and European contacts with the Nigerian economy are discussed fully in the introductory chapters of R. O. Ekundare, *An Economic History of Nigeria 1860–1960* (London, Oxford University Press, 1971).
6. E. O. Adeniyi: "Development Planning in Nigeria," *The Nigeria Trade Journal,* vol. 25, no. 4, 1978.
7. V. P. Diejomaoh and E. C. Anusionwu, "The Structure of Income Inequality in Nigeria: A Macro-Analysis," in H. Bienen and V. P. Diejomaoh, eds., *The Political Economy of Income Distribution in Nigeria* (New York, Holmes and Meier, 1981).
8. Federal Republic of Nigeria, *First National Development Plan* (note 3 above), p. 3.
9. Federal Ministry of Information, *Report of the Seminar, "On the Second National Development Plan"* (Lagos, Federal Ministry of Information, 1971) p. 17.
10. W. F. Stolper, *Planning without Facts: Lessons in Resource Allocation from Nigeria's Development* (Cambridge, Harvard University Press, 1966).

8

ECONOMIC PLANNING AND THE MARKET ECONOMY: EXPERIENCE IN POST-WAR JAPAN

Kouichi Tani

Economic Development and the Evolution of Economic Policy-Making in Post-War Japan

This section describes the salient features of economic development in post-war Japan; Japan's post-war economic development can be divided into three phases: (1) post-war recovery (1945–1954), (2) establishment of economic self-reliance (1955–1964), and (3) economic development beyond self-reliance and extensive international interdependence (1965 to present).

These three phases can be best characterized as a change in the trade balance from a chronic deficit to a sustained surplus. The Japanese economy has achieved this epoch-making transformation through pursuing its catch-up process to an advanced stage.

World-wide economic development cannot be realized without an international transfer effect — transfer of advanced economic resources from industrialized countries to developing countries — which pervades the industrialization process all over the world. These transfers can be realized through active

Dr. Miguel Urrutia is due my heartful appreciation for his warm encouragement. I am grateful to Miss Kumiko Ishikawa and other staff of the United Nations University for their assistance, and I particularly wish to thank Professor Setsuko Yukawa of Kyoto Sangyo University for her valuable suggestions and comments on the first draft of this study. I wish to acknowledge six persons who assisted me with research in their fields: Mr. Shoichi Kojima (industrial policy), Mr. Masatoshi Sakamoto (agricultural policy), Mr. Yasutaka Nagatani (economic planning systems), Mr. Takafumi Tanaka (regional policy), Mr. Minoru Ihkura (energy policy), and Professor Gustavo Andrade (Japan's sociological background for economic development). Finally, I wish to thank the staff of the Japan Research Institute, especially Miss Sawako Takeuchi, for providing editorial assistance.

international transactions, via various channels, of a wide range of economic resources, such as physical and human resources, capital, technologies, and knowledge. This process deepens international economic interdependence.

Through international transfers, Japan has successfully achieved not only rapid industrialization but also a dramatic transition of position from an ardent recipient to a world-wide provider. The Japanese economy, at first in a passive position, coped with a seemingly endless foreign trade deficit due to its persistent and excessive demand for imports. Recently, however, Japan has made an active and positive use of its surplus in world economies which, staggering under the weight of their unfavourable trade balances, request transfers of advanced economic resources for development.

Post-War Recovery, 1945–1954

A historical review of the Japanese economy will be useful for a better understanding of its unprecedented post-war development. Japan has a long history of industrialization, beginning with the Meiji Restoration in 1868. It had become an industrial power in Asia by 1930, exporting manufactured products such as cotton and synthetic textiles. But this preliminary industrial development was decisively interrupted in 1941 by World War II.

The war, ending in August 1945, depleted the physical resources accumulated during the pre-war industrialization period and deprived Japan of more than a quarter of its national wealth. Industrial production declined sharply — almost to the level of the previous decade. Territory was diminished by nearly half. Because of military and civilian repatriation, the domestic population swelled by 6 million. Yet, so poor was the nation in natural resources, except for scanty amounts of coal and hydropower, that it could do no more for the people than to strive against starvation.

It seemed that nothing remained except a demoralized people and a devastated nation. Eventually, however, both the people and the nation played a vital role in Japan's restoration by sharing the pain of the defeat.

None of the three national sectors, the government, industry, or the household, could sustain itself at its own discretion, due to the physical deficiencies. The nation, which had accepted the Potsdam Declaration, was put under the rigorous control of the General Headquarters (GHQ) of the Supreme Commander for the Allied Powers (SCAP). The government entrusted all to the GHQ but avoided transferring its direct reign in order to preserve national integrity.

The first use the GHQ made of its predominant authority was to renovate Japanese society and to force the Japanese government to sweep away its pre-war regime. This forced renovation served as an impetus in Japanese society to implant mass democracy and to prepare an economic dynamism for its post-war development. Eventually, the Korean War, which violently convulsed the global cold war, further enhanced the industrial reconstruction of Japan. Under these favourable external conditions, Japan itself could effectively struggle to rebuild the nation.

The first post-war decade, 1945–1954, was a period of vital reconstruction which nobody could have expected or imagined while staggering under the crush of the chaotic and desperate pace of the restoration effort. The following indicators, based on the pre-war bench mark (1934–1936 = 100), clearly illustrate the main trends of the Japanese economy throughout the war and during the first decade after the war.

— Real per capita national income, which had registered 235 at the pre-war peak in 1939, fell dramatically to 110 in 1946 and revived to 225 in 1955.
— Manufacturing industry production, which had declined sharply to 29 in 1946 from the peak 182 in 1944, surged to 189 in 1955.
— Foodstuffs and clothing, which had declined to 62 and 26 respectively in 1945, recovered to 107 and 136 in 1955.

Starting from Devastation after the War

The GHQ, responsible for post-war management, began with a thorough demilitarization and democratization of Japan, not only by eliminating Japan's actual military capacity but also by rooting out the social regime which had supported the militarism. Three drastic measures were effected: dissolution of the *zaibatsu*, land reform, and democratization of industrial relations.

The first measure dissolved the ruling financial trusts which had commanded huge industrial groups and exercised monopolistic power over the entire national economy in pre-war Japan. The second liberated rural land ownership under which huge numbers of tenant farmers had been dominated. And the third gave employees the right of collective bargaining, which had been prohibited in pre-war Japan.

Besides these revolutionary reforms, the GHQ directed the Japanese government to restore a reliable economic order, without which the society would be seriously threatened by emergencies. Thus, in August 1946, the government instituted the Economic Stabilization Board as the central administrative organ. This agency, having 2,000 staff members and divided into 10 administrative bureaus, was responsible for formulating and implementing plans as well as overseeing the economic activities encompassing foreign trade, finance, production, and consumption.

In the first year, 1946, the economy was threatened by an imminent production breakdown due to poor material stockpiles. Prime Minister Shigeru Yoshida, who formed his first cabinet in May 1946, quickly set up an Advisory Council and requested an urgent deliberation of emergency countermeasures to overcome the production crisis.

The council worked out a radical economic policy programme which urged the government to integrate fragmentary policies into one geared to the reconstruction of the basic industries. The government accordingly decided, in December 1946, upon a series of intensive policy measures, called the Highest Priority Strategy for Industrial Reconstruction (to be referred to as the Highest Priority Strategy hereafter), in order to mobilize available resources for restoring basic industries such as coal-mining and steel.

Owing to the integrated policy authorized by the council, independent of particular social interests, individual policy measures were designed to be employed co-operatively, and the newly established Reconstruction Finance Bank provided preferential credit collectively for the target industries. The Highest Priority Strategy was so successfully implemented in the coal-mining industry that the target figure of 30 million tons was achieved, ahead of schedule, by the end of fiscal year 1947 (i.e. in March).

On the international scene, on the other hand, the pervasion of the cold war forced the United States to deploy power politics. The United States adopted a realistic foreign policy to strengthen the Western Allies against the Russian offensive, which led to the nullification of the non-intervention policy, one mingled with the idealism originating in the Monroe Doctrine. The United States stepped forward to enact massive economic assistance programmes designed to rebuild the industries in the Western world. With these programmes, the actual restoration of the post-war world economy started.

While the United States implemented the Marshall Plan to restore the European economies, it scaled down Japan's heavy reparation programme as well as accelerated its economic reconstruction aid to Japan. The US economic aid lasted until 1951 and amounted to as much as US$2 billion. This sum was more than enough to compensate for the current-account deficit, which was running at the level of US$1 billion. US aid relieved the Japanese economy of experiencing a crucial shortage of foreign exchange and enabled it to achieve rapid industrial reconstruction.

Japan experienced the first striking increase in industrial production in early 1948, and registered, in December of the same year, an annual expansion of 60 per cent. But this dynamic recovery of production was quickly aggravated by the rampant inflation that had reached nearly a 200-per-cent annual increase on average in terms of wholesale prices since 1945. As is often the case in an economy during a desperate reconstruction effort, there were many factors accelerating inflation: the budgetary revenue could not afford the swelling expenditures, including compensation for the military repatriates and the forced requisitions made during the war, and the economy, thirsty for production, rushed to loans from both the Reconstruction Finance Bank and commercial banks.

These factors caused monetary expansions to be dependent mainly on credit from the Bank of Japan. Thus, the outstanding bank notes rose by 89 per cent in fiscal year 1947 and by 43 per cent in fiscal year 1948. Here again, only the GHQ could take measures to remedy inflation. In December 1948, the US government, complying with the decision adopted by the National Security Council in October, sent a directive to the GHQ demanding a programme to achieve economic stabilization to be carried out by the Japanese government.

Minister Dodge, former economic advisor to West Germany, was assigned to formulate a stabilization programme. In February 1949, he presented a rigorous economic policy guideline, called the Dodge Line, which he urged the Japanese government to implement immediately. Following the Dodge Line, the government, always eager to prove its administrative competence under the indirect reign of the GHQ, decided on a single exchange rate in April and enforced a "Super Balanced Budget" for fiscal year 1949 (beginning in April).

Under a strict budgetary constraint, both public investments and subsidies were sharply reduced and the Reconstruction Finance Bank loan was suspended. Subsequently, the soaring inflation which had incessantly threatened the post-war economy was significantly curbed. The wholesale prices, which had recorded sharp annual rises of 364.5 per cent in 1946, 195.9 per cent in 1947, and 165.7 per cent in 1948, was brought down to 63.2 per cent in 1949 and 18.2 per cent in 1950. The wage rate in the manufacturing sector, which had persistently registered a 10 per cent *monthly* increase, was reduced to 14 per cent *annual* increase through fiscal year 1949.

As extra demand was being forcibly suppressed, the Economic Stabilization Board got its first chance to liberalize direct controls and to restore the market economy by gradual abolition of regulations, including price and distribution controls. The number of direct government controls diminished through fiscal year 1949 from 233 to 49 for industrial goods, from 57 to 15 for consumer goods, and from 2,128 to 531 for price regulations. Further, the adoption of the single exchange rate system (US$1 = 360 yen) eliminated trade subsidies, which had been tacitly effected in the multi-exchange rates, and exposed the economy to free market competition in the international scene.

Japan kept this exchange rate as an economic keynote for 22 years, until 1971. However, the hasty restoration of a competitive market economy, accompanied with the drastic stabilization policy, induced a severe depression. Bankruptcies counted 11,000 and job dismissals reached more than 500,000 from the beginning of 1949 to the next March, due to the severe financial pressure. The struggling economy, barely supported by government protection and controls, stumbled at the entrance to the market economy.

The Korean War and Japan's Economic Reconstruction

It was the Korean War that brought Japan an external demand of unprecedented scale, stemming from the U.S. involvement in Korea. This demand was commonly referred to as the Special Procurement. Just as World War I had a favourable effect on the US economy, the Korean War provided a buoyant lift to the depressed economy of Japan; in addition, the Korean War shook the cold war and led the United States to focus its foreign policy on a resumption of political stability in the Far East. This change in US foreign policy accelerated the pace of independence and further established Japan's role as a reliable partner in the region. Japan regained its national sovereignty under the peace treaty concluded in San Francisco in Arpil 1952.

The Special Procurement related to the Korean War, consisting of non-military battlefield supplies such as blankets, sacks, trucks, and construction materials, saved the Japanese economy, which was on the brink of overwhelming economic peril under the stabilization depression. The total amount of the procurement, which was prolonged by a reconstruction programme for post-war Korea, was estimated to have reached US$55 billion for the nine years from 1951 to 1959.

Even with this extraordinary revenue, the accumulated sum of the trade balance during the same period could barely gain a US$0.5 billion surplus. The Japanese economy was extremely weak in external competition. Japanese manufacturing industries remained infantile, as shown by the following international comparison in terms of production level in major industrial sectors in 1955: crude iron production in Japan was no more than 9.4 million tons, as against 106.2 million tons in the United States, 24.5 million tons in West Germany, 20.1 million tons in Great Britain; passenger car production of 20,300 in Japan was incomparably small against that of 7.92 million in the United States, 897.6 thousand in Great Britain, and 762.2 thousand in West Germany.

In the domestic market, however, the huge foreign demands triggered the first consumption-cum-investment boom through 1952 to the next year. There appeared several forerunners in post-war industrial innovation: As early as 1951 Kawasaki Iron and Steel embarked on an evolutionary integrated steel mill project by introducing West German technology; in the synthetic textile industry, nylon and vinylon production started in 1953, also employing foreign technology.

In the first post-war decade, despite the reconstruction chaos, the Japanese were steadily preparing for dynamic economic development in the second decade. The government, ready to eliminate direct intervention and protection, proceeded to reorganize economic policy management so as to enlarge decision-making capacity in the private sector. Combining an industrial policy and a foreign trade policy, the Ministry of International Trade and Industry, started in 1949, was to implement an industrial policy whose framework was determined by the controlled allocation of foreign currency.

In order to enhance the voluntary development of private industries under the strict restrictions of foreign exchange availability, the ministry aimed at an industrial policy management of indirect control which might reconcile competition and regulation. Therefore, the ministry was urged to involve the private sector in its policy management. The Industrial Rationalization Council, quickly instituted as a consultative organ for the ministry, consisted mainly of representatives from various industrial sectors who were appointed by the minister.

This organ was planned to enable intimate consultations between the ministry and the relevant industrial sectors, so as to form comprehensive industrial strategies which both parties could pursue.

In 1952, the year of the restoration of national independence, the Economic Stabilization Board disbanded. The board's huge concentration of administerial authority was taken over by the appropriate ministries. Inheriting the distinctive function of the above board to examine the current economic situation and to elaborate future comprehensive policy guidelines, the Economic Council Board (which, after further reform, became known as the Economic Planning Agency in 1955) was created as an independent administrative agency beyond the particular social interests of the ministries that were in charge.

This board, exclusive of all other administrative agencies, was to develop a new epoch of macro-economic policy management, beyond regulation and particular policy practices. Having this distinctive orientation, the board was charged with various aspects of comprehensive economic policy management, such as monthly and annual economic reports, current economic policy co-ordination, the elaboration of an economic plan, as well as advanced studies in its economic research institution.

Establishment of Economic Self-Reliance, 1955–1964

Extraordinary reconstruction had been achieved in the first post-war decade. However, the injury left behind by the war was so severe that the economy at the beginning of the second decade remained at the level of the peak reached in the pre-war period, nearly 15 years before. Thus, the second decade began with enormous difficulties, such as huge unemployment and the stringent situation of foreign currency, although the latter was concealed by the Special Procurement relating to the Korean War. Domestic demands, both in industrial investments and in private consumption, were swollen under the international "Announcement Effect" from the United States. They had a strong inclination to enlarge imports and to widen the deficit of balance of payment because of the deficiency in the actual domestic industrial supply.

It was the decline of the Korean Special Procurement at the beginning of the second decade that awakened the Japanese economy to the transitory nature of its indulgence in the huge additional external demand and to a realization of the urgent importance of attaining economic self-reliance. In December 1955, the first economic plan was put forth by the Hatoyama Cabinet, complying with the conclusion elaborated by the Economic Council. This plan put economic self-reliance as the primary economic target.

The plan identified industrial rationalization as a fundamental policy objective which might effectively realize economic targets and decisively overcome the volatile externalities. Meeting this objective, it successfully presented a difficult but promising future of development before the people. People could understand individually, by virtue of the economic policy guideline the plan presented, the necessity to concentrate available economic resources in industrial investments in innovative sectors. Thus, the Japanese economy was to discover that the way to realize economic self-reliance, as well as to secure employment and to enhance national welfare, was through the use of the economic principle of productivity.

Supply and Demand Gap and Restrictive Industrial Policy

Industrial rationalization necessitated nearly unlimited imports of foreign economic resources, such as machines, equipment, various technologies, and capital. But the availability of foreign currency was limited by the poor international competitiveness of the domestic industries. This essential discrepancy compelled the economic plan to elaborate an intensive policy guideline for industrial rationalization. Industry was controlled to confine vast foreign demands to those vital for the advancement of productivity. Thus, the restraint of vigorous demands from the foreign market led to the expansion of production.

It was the Ministry of International Trade and Industry that transformed this comprehensive economic policy orientation into an actual industrial policy which commanded the manufacturing industries to strive intensively to find and introduce new industrial innovations. The ministry was effective in promoting industrial rationalization, applying industrial policy measures combining beneficial finances, concessive taxation, and budgetary subsidies coupled with discriminative control on the allocation of foreign exchange based on the Foreign Exchange Budget for Imports.

The ministry, aiming at an orderly industrial development involving the voluntary dynamism of the private sector, entrusted the Industrial Council, in which representatives of key industries took part, with the elaboration of guidepost policy programmes in the short and medium term for individual strategic industries. Those programmes eventually came to be used as administrative guidelines for the beneficial and discriminative management of policy measures by the ministry.

These close consultations between the administration and private business resulted in clear strategic directions for business that enabled them to compensate for the supply-demand gaps, and they promoted intensive competition toward promising future markets authorized by the Industrial Council. The Japanese economy achieved in the second decade a striking industrial transformation and resolved the huge unemployment problem by maintaining a keen tautness between the private sector and the administration; that is, the private industrial sector with its persistent tilt toward expanding the supply capacity beyond the restrictions placed upon it by government policy and government industrial policy management with its insistence that private investment be confined within limited foreign exchange availability.

Changes in the economic indicators reveal successful industrial development in Japan in this period: Unemployment declined by half, from 400,000 in 1955 to 250,000 in 1965. The unemployment ratio decreased from 2.3 to 1.3 per cent in the same period. Reflecting rapid industrial transformation, the employment structure changed so drastically that the share of primary industry declined by 16.4 percentage points, from 41.1 per cent to 24.7 per cent, while the secondary and tertiary raised their shares by more than 8 percentage points, from 23.4 per cent to 31.7 per cent and from 35.5 per cent to 43.7 per cent respectively.

The composition of the class of workers, classified according to three categories, employee, self-employed, and family worker, underwent an unprecedented change. The employee category was expanded 1.6 times, with an 11 million increase in number. Family worker registered a reduction of 2.6 million, declining its share from 30 per cent in 1955 to 20 per cent in 1965.

The trends in macro-economic indicators in the same period illustrate miraculous features of economic growth: GNP increased by 3.59 times in nominal terms and 2.50 times, with an annual growth rate of more than 9 per cent, in real terms. The economic growth was, however, marked by sharp ups and downs. There were three phases of more than 12 per cent annual growth rate: the first two phases were interrupted by deep recessions when the growth rate decelerated by half to almost 6 per cent.

Private consumption increased by 3.16 times in nominal terms and by 2.23 times in real terms. Private investment registered the highest rise of 5.10 times in nominal terms and 4.03 times in real terms. Its annual growth rate reached 14.9 per cent in real terms, which exceeded those of GNP and private consumption.

Exports and imports, on the custom clearance basis, increased by 4.20 times and 3.31 times respectively, both of which exceeded the expansion of private consumption in nominal terms, while their expansion was less than that of domestic capital formation.

Expansion of the Home Market

In the second decade, gross capital formation expanded to the extent that its share in GNP, in nominal terms, reached around 30 to 40 per cent, while external gains by export and other means remained more or less at 11 per cent of GNP. Such a high rate of capital formation, in which the private sector, including housing construction, reached from 20 to 30 per cent of GNP in nominal terms, was supported by a high savings ratio, which expanded from 14 per cent to nearly 19 per cent in terms of average household savings ratio through the second decade. As a consequence, economic self-reliance was achieved through domestic market expansion effected by means of vigorous investments which led to extensive supply capacities. The consumer market, second only to the conspicuous growth in investment, swallowed new products one after another and made a remarkable contribution to national market expansion. Durable consumer goods, through the so-called consumer revolution, dramatically increased their diffusion ratio among households: black-and-white TV sets went from 7.8 to 95.0 per cent and electric refrigerators from 2.8 to 68.8 per cent for the eight years from 1957.

The textile industry, as a leading sector in the light industries, represents a typical industrial development where production expansion preceded the growing domestic consumer market and in which the industry conceded its leading position to the heavy and chemical industries such as iron and steel, petrochemicals, and machinery through rapid industrial transformation. During this second decade, the textile industry reduced its share in manufacturing production from 17.4 per cent in 1955 to 10.3 per cent in 1965, while machinery raised its share from 14.6 per cent to 26.5 per cent during the same period. This rapid transformation of domestic industries strengthened their international competitiveness. Thus the value of exports doubled every five years, and export composition changed considerably.

Convergence of Developing Domestic Industries on the Expanding Global Market

In the changing constitution of exports, textiles declined by half, from 37.2 per cent to 18.7 per cent in the second decade. Contrarily, heavy industries and chemicals raised their share from 38.0 per cent to 62.0 per cent. Machinery registered the highest growth, from 13.7 to 35.2 per cent in this period. As a result, Japanese exports doubled their country-by-country share in world trade from 2.4 per cent to 5.1 per cent. On the domestic scene, the export-dependence ratio of GNP remained more or less 10 per cent, showing a slight increasing trend. It was actually at a low level in comparison with other Organization of Economic Cooperation and Development (OECD) countries, except the United States.

Japanese industries rapidly expanded their share of exports in the world market, while keeping a low ratio of export dependence (i.e. the export-domestic production ratio). This feature, demonstrated by the machinery industry with its low export-dependence ratio of less than 10 per cent, even at the end of the second decade, illustrates the magnificent adaptability of Japanese industry to converge home market growth with international market expansion. A long, uninterrupted upswing in the US economy, a cheap and accessible crude-oil supply, and sustained world trade expansion in the 1960s (a striking contrast to the two world-wide upheavals induced by the monetary and energy crises of the 1970s) ensured favourable external conditions for developing the Japenese economy in the second decade, despite the painful constraint of a constant exchange rate system of US$1 = 360 yen.

Besides these conditions, there were many mutually reinforcing factors which worked to transform various restrictions into positive motivations for development. The domestic market isolation from foreign competitors made internal competition the more vigorous among newly emerged industries. Further, equal accessibility to advanced foreign technologies incited such intense competition that national industries were forced to continually provide the domestic market with newly improved products.

Behind these factors there was a series of effectively co-ordinated sectoral policies of management, complying with comprehensive economic policy guidelines contained in the economic plan of 1955. The plan defined, in macro-economic terms, the comprehensive socio-economic orientation that aimed to integrate entangling restraints and opportunities in order to create a higher standard of living, stability, and social welfare through progressive industrialization. In line with this orientation of macro-economic consistency, a variety of individual policies (e.g. industrial policies with respect to energy, steel, shipbuilding, etc., agricultural policies, and regional development policies) were formulated to guide the structural evolution in industry and agriculture in various regions. Following is a brief presentation of the development of the energy policy.

The Energy Policy and Dual Functions of the Economic Policy

The development of the energy policy can be seen in the change in the primary source of energy in the second decade, which was characterized by unprecedented economic growth. At the beginning of this decade, domestic coal supplied 45 per cent of Japan's energy. For the sake of efficient industrial development, however, the government made the crucial decision to replace this costly domestic resource with large quantities of inexpensive imported crude oil.

This change in energy policy had substantive consequences by the end of the decade: (1) total energy supply increased by three times, from 560 to 1,656 trillion kcal, in which imported fuel (mostly crude oil) soared at an increase of 8.2 times and the imported energy-dependence ratio (i.e. imported energy-total energy ratio) jumped from 24 per cent in 1955 to 60 per cent in 1965; (2) domestic coal mining labour declined from 300,000 to 110,000 workers during the decade, complying with the "Coal Mining Rationalization Program." Considering the oil crisis which occured in the 1970s and the resultant jump in energy prices, it is clear that the Japanese economy owes the success of this drastic policy decision to the favourable external conditions then in existence. This favourable international climate, however, could not have benefited Japan if the crucial decision had not been made to stake the supply of energy on external sources and, at the same time, abandon domestic sources of energy.

While pursuing intensive economic development in the second decade, it was inevitable that the government would be forced to either abandon certain domestic industries which were inferior internationally or cope with growing differentials of productivity and income. However, despite such keen discernment and decisiveness, unbalanced development emerged between industry and agriculture, large-scale and small- and medium-scale firms, and overly populated urban areas and depopulated rural areas.

Furthermore, rapid economic growth and the industrial evolution did not proceed without painful reversals regarding these so-called structural disparities. To be more specific, consider the manufacturing industry, which led the rapid economic development in the second decade. Even here there were huge income differentials among establishments of differing scale and product concentration. In 1960, the middle of the decade, the wage indices were 64.4 in medium-scale firms (200–299 employees) and 41.9 in small-scale firms (10–19 employees), as against 100 in the large-scale establishments (more than 1,000 employees). The comparative value-added productivity (productivity in large-scale firms = 100) declined from 66.1 to 58.7 in medium-scale establishments and from 29.8 to 28.9 in small-scale firms during the four years from 1956 to 1960.

These structural contrasts, to state it another way, reflected the different degrees of adjustment between those sectors which quickly adapted to the industrial transformation and those which stagnated. The former, either industrial or regional, had enough mobility to adapt voluntarily to the industrial evolution, while the latter lagged behind the development due to a deficiency in mobility. In order to offer compensation as well as support where needed, an economic policy with a dual function was employed.

It was found that the economic development policy was successful, not only in the positive adjustment policy — a forward-looking function (e.g. the concentration of available capital, human resources, and foreign currencies in promising sectors) — but also with the passive adjustment policy — a backward-looking function — of which the Coal Mining Rationalization Program stands as a typical case. A positive, direct contribution to industrial rationalization was made by importing huge amounts of crude oil, while, in a passive aspect, the Coal Mining Rationalization Program was implemented to provide intensive policy arrangements for the declining industry, including budgetary subsidies for both the closure of marginally productive mines and the survival of the relatively excellent ones, as well as employment arrangements for the displaced labourers.

Thus, the economic policy, with its dual function, was involved with many of the stagnating sectors in the economy. If the policy had neglected the passive adjustment function, the structural disparities would have induced antagonistic reactions from society against economic development. Moreover, the economy would eventually have been bankrupted from the resulting erosion of socio-economic integration. On the contrary, however, while coping with structural disparity in the various sectors (e.g. agriculture, depopulated rural areas, and medium- and small-scale enterprises), a variety of passive adjustment functions developed. They had the decisive function of mitigating income disparities through budgetary expenditures, of reallocating gains from economic growth among stagnating sectors, and, further, of enlarging the purchasing power of the domestic consumer market.

The National Income Doubling Plan

As early as the middle of the second decade, the Japanese economy was entering into a period of full-fledged high economic growth. In line with the establishment of economic self-reliance, as indicated in the first economic plan, then Prime Minister Hayato Ikeda, supported by the people's consolidated confidence in economic growth, launched the "National Income Doubling Plan" in December 1960. The prime minister, aiming at an epoch-making enhancement of national well-being, was ready to complete the final stage of economic self-reliance.

He promised the people that, by overcoming two obstacles, he would double the national income in 10 years. The first was the structural disparities described above and the other was market liberalization. The majority of society profited from the economic growth, obtaining stable employment and a steady increase in income. But there remained vast rural areas dependent on primary industry and small- and medium-scale businesses of low productivity that did not immediately profit from rapid industrialization. In the middle of the second decade, because the structural disparities were rather aggravated due to persistent economic growth, social complaints against economic growth itself became the most pressing political concern.

The Income Doubling Plan predicted that there was a high probability that the rapid economic growth would quickly encounter an unprecedented labour shortage. In actuality the unemployment rate, which had declined from 2.3 per cent to 1.7 per cent during the first half of the second decade (1955–1960), further decreased to 1.3 per cent in the next half. The plan, pressured by this tightened labour market, took the first step to involve the structural disparities issue in macro-economic policy management, not as a social policy but as an economic policy matter, incorporating idle resources into the economic development process.

To resolve the structural disparities, the comprehensive economic policy guidelines presented in the economic plan of 1960 were broken down into individual sectoral policy programmes. There were typical policy programmes in the agricultural sector and in regional development which explicitly dealt with the disparities derived from structural problems. These policy programmes played an active role in integrating the nation in economic development. The Basic Agriculture Law enacted in 1961 manifested a comprehensive orientation for Japanese agriculture to dissolve its obstinate disparities *vis-à-vis* the non-agricultural sectors. In addition, the first regional development plan, the Comprehensive Land Development Plan, was activated in 1962 with the fundamental target of reallocating industrial development opportunities all over the nation.

At the initial stage of economic self-reliance, foreign trade controls, by isolating the domestic market from foreign competitors, were the most effective policy measure for ensuring buoyant domestic demand for the domestic industries. In this context, since 1946 the foreign exchange budget had been worked out to implement discriminative trade policies. Even after becoming a member of the General Agreement on Tariffs and Trade (GATT) in 1955, Japan reserved the right of its administrative controls on foreign transactions, claiming the exception clause in the agreement which is applied exclusively to developing countries.

This protection for the domestic industries, once introduced, became too set to get rid of, even though it was clear that, logically, they were not a final target to pursue, rather an instrument of temporary advantage. The 1960 plan proceeded, however, with the task of removing the market protections under heightened foreign pressure urging the Japanese government to convert its restrictive foreign trade policy. Putting this overwhelming pressure in the forefront, the government applied a domestic market liberalization, in opposition to resisting domestic industries, while considering that the liberalization should be the unavoidable final step necessary to complete economic self-reliance.

The Foreign Trade and Exchange Liberalization programme adopted in 1960 laid down a liberalization timetable which was actually realized by October 1962, when 90 per cent of the commodities in the import quota had been eliminated. The next step was adherence to GATT Article 11 and IMF Article 8: In 1963 the Japanese government made a decisive turn toward elimination of the foreign transaction controls and abolishment of the urgent trade restrictions because of the current balance deficit. It went further in accepting liberalization on service trade and on international capital transactions when Japan became a member of the OECD in 1984.

At the end of the second decade, in 1965, the total number of employed persons expanded by 1.2 times to 47.6 million, with the employment in the manufacturing industry increasing by 1.7 times to 11.5 million during the decade. The declining burden of food and beverage expenditures, the propensity of which in the household budget — Engel's co-efficient — declined by 9 percentage points to 38 per cent in the same period, brought considerable allowances for the people in their daily lives. The successful industrial transformation expanded Japanese exports by 4.3 times, but its share of GNP remained under 10 per cent throughout the period because of the influence of a sharp rise in domestic demand.

Economic Development beyond Self-Reliance to Extensive International Interdependence: 1965 to Present

During the last two decades (beginning in 1965), before the Japanese economy had firmly established its self-reliance, it faced two huge conversions: internally, it was to experience a drastic shift from a highly growing economy to a stable one; second, an external evolution was to emerge in the balance of payments.

Throughout these decades, an annual growth rate of more or less 10 per cent in real terms was sustained until 1970, when it declined sharply to approximately 5 per cent in coincidence with the dollar crisis in August 1971 and the first oil crisis in October 1973. On the other hand, the balance of payments experienced a sustained surplus in the current account.

The two decades since 1965 can be divided into three periods:

1. 1965–1970. The last stage of the unprecedented high economic growth throughout which the Japanese economy faced a rigorous domestic-policy adjustment which was forced on the economy by the aggravated socio-economic distortions caused by sustained economic growth.
2. 1971–1982. Twelve years of world-wide upheavals induced by the floating exchange rate and the oil crisis put a decisive end to the high economic growth and invited a matured economy of 5 per cent growth. In the external scene, the economy successfully enlarged its world-wide financing activities and steadily enhanced its global competitiveness both in energy engineering technology and in the micro-electronics industries, which proved again its excellent adaptability in overcoming an unfavourable change in external conditions.
3. After 1983. The oil crisis ended and oil prices declined; Japanese industry actually emerged as a strong competitor in the international scene, with market oriented engineering technologies both in matured industries and in advanced ones. Thus, the current account has produced a huge surplus which has inspired antagonistic reactions among trade partners abroad. The Japanese government, urged to deal effectively with these foreign pressures, started an intensive struggle to rearrange the orientation of its economic policy in order to meet the goal of full-fledged "internationalization."

Socio-economic Distortions Aggravated by Rapid Economic Growth

In the period from 1965 to 1970, the Japanese economy sustained a rapid GNP growth of more than 10 per cent in real terms, coupled with an active private capital formation reaching more than 20 per cent annual growth in real terms in its upward trend. At the same time, leading manufacturing industries (e.g. steel and iron, petrochemicals, synthetic fibers, shipbuilding, motor-cycle and automobile production, and electrical appliances) became dominant in the world market. These secondary industries with high international competitiveness gained increasing surplus on the current account, which in turn facilitated a nearly 15 per cent annual wage increase.

On the other hand, the labour shortage induced by the unprecedented rapid economic growth brought about wage increases which invited typical cost-push inflation. Although it never shifted to hyperinflation with extensive supply capacity, the consumer price had increased persistently, often beyond a 6 per cent annual rate, since 1956. It was in this latter stage of high economic growth that the government was driven to examine an "income policy" in order to calm people's frustration with inflation.

The defective market, exposed by aggravated urbanization and violent environmental destruction which had been incurred by a hasty and reckless industrial development, eroded people's confidence in GNP. The press and academic circles emphasized the role of the public economy in dealing with the economic externalities and pressed the government to recognize its responsibility to make positive amends for market failures in order to protect the people from the external diseconomies.

The government put greater emphasis on its role when dealing with the public economy than when dealing with the private economy. The function of the government in relation to the public economy was eventually established in economic policy. In the areas of land use, urban reconstruction, and social infrastructure, the public economy was enlarged to the extent that the environmental issues were tackled. The Fundamental Environment Act of 1966 presented a policy framework which authorized the government to examine the various causes of pollution, to implement regulations, and to charge compensation for damages.

Conversion of the Japanese Economy in External Relations

The third decade (1965–1974) found the basic trend of the trade balance to be one of sustained surplus — a condition the Japanese had been desperately pursuing since the beginning of the Meiji Restoration a century ago. The current account, despite two oil crises which had caused a US$4.7 billion deficit, an US$8.8 billion deficit, and a US$10.7 billion deficit in 1974, 1979, and 1980 respectively, had registered rapid expansion throughout the two preceding decades. It has increased from a US$0.9 billion surplus in 1965 to a more than US$40 billion surplus in recent years.

With this external surplus, the Japanese economy has enlarged its worldwide presence in various ways. It has, for example, made extraordinary increases, directly and indirectly, in both foreign investments and economic assistance (while simultaneously facing foreign trade friction aggravated by rapidly increasing exports). During the 15 years from 1965 to 1980, an annual increase of long-term foreign assets expanded 24.2 times and the annual amount of foreign trade rose by 17.0 times, as against 11.3 times in GNP in nominal terms. The economic assistance which started permanently in 1972 has increased by 6 times during the ensuing 11 years, reaching US$3,761 million in 1983.

The Japanese economy during the third decade eventually shifted from unilateral dependence on the world economy to positive interdependence on a global scale. The former is characteristic of developing economies that can manage their development without considering international economic interdependence, while the current balance-of-payment deficit persistently restrains their economies. But in the latter stage, when the economy passes a historical turning point and is ushered onto the stage of advanced nations, it cannot continue proper economic management without seriously considering the actuality of interdependence.

In the third decade the Japanese economy entered into an advanced stage in which an outward evolution of the economy converted its position in the "international transfer" process from that of a recipient to one of a provider, as mentioned in the first part of this section. This historical conversion compelled the Japanese government to renovate its economic policy orientation and to construct a new and completely different framework for economic policy management.

The world-wide upheaval occurring in the 1970s demolished the stable foundation of the post-war world economy which the fixed exchange rate linked to the dollar and the affluent supply of cheap crude oil had supported for almost a quarter of a century. The first oil crisis at the end of 1973, accelerating world economic confusion induced by the monetary crisis, trapped the world economy in a so-called "trilemma": rapid inflation, rising current account deficits, and simultaneous recessions in the world economy.

The second oil crisis, beginning at the end of 1979, further delayed the restoration of the world economy. Every nation became exhausted trying to protect its national economy while actually being deprived of the adaptability necessary to develop a forward-looking economic policy. The Japanese economy was no exception. Finally re-emerging in 1983, it succeeded in prompt resumption of price stability and from there economic restoration.

In contrast to private industries, which displayed a remarkable capability to revive, the huge budgetary deficit, amounting to one-third of GNP, has exhausted government attempts to amend the budgetary imbalance and has retarded policy renovation. Consequently, the rising international competitiveness of Japanese industry does not adequately activate the world economy but rather accelerates international imbalance, thus further exacerbating foreign trade friction. Like most industrialized countries, current budgetary constraint has become a large obstacle to policy renovation in Japan.

This accumulated budgetary imbalance is not the only obstacle for Japan to overcome in order to convert its economic policy. The Japanese economy is now being requested to carry out global responsibilities congruent with its conversion in its "international transfer" position from a recipient to a provider. To make a parenthetical comment, Japan's current inward-looking and passive policy orientation seems similar to the position the United States was in when it adhered to the Monroe Doctrine until World War II, even though its economic power surpassed that of Great Britain by the end of the nineteenth century.

In Japan, a series of economic plans in the third decade emphasized the importance of social development and social capital formation to cope with market defects relating to urbanization and environmental problems. However, in their policy guidelines they confined their efforts to the achievement of well-balanced economic growth within the nation. In our experience during the last decade, the economic plan has not yet resulted in a policy development that might help propel both the domestic and global economies toward an extensive equilibrium.

The Role of the Economic Plan in Post-War Japan's Economic Transformation

In the first decade after the war, before the adoption of the first economic plan, the government put forward several emergency policy programmes and trial economic plans which included medium-term policy objectives. Planning was hampered, however, by the government's inability to make reliable projections of economic development, despite its full knowledge of the underlying economic constraints, because the tiny Japanese economy was overwhelmingly dependent on external conditions. Nevertheless, it was during these rather turbulent early years of devlopment that the administrative and social basis for economic planning and advancement was formed.

The first Five-Year Plan for Economic Self-Reliance was officially adopted by the Hatoyama Cabinet in December 1955. Since then, the Liberal Democratic Party (LDP) administrations have adopted ten economic plans, each of which had a time frame of five to ten years, with revisions made every three years on the average (see tables 1, 2). LDP government flexibility in revising plans to adjust targets and policy objectives to changes in internal and external conditions, coupled with careful policy management promoting industrial development, has been crucial in transforming a young market economy, which had been barely growing with protectionist government controls, into a dynamic market economy free from government protection. In addition, it may be observed that concentration on the goal of economic development (and avoiding disputes over ideology and foreign policy) has contributed to the economic dynamism of the nation.

It was the economic plans of the second post-war decade that established effective procedures for comprehensive indicative economic planning which mobilized the nation to build an independent national economy through rapid industrial transformation.

Looking at post-war Japan, it seems logical to conclude that economic de-

TABLE 1. Major policy objectives in ten economic plans in post-war Japan

Plan	Government	Policy objectives
Five-Year Plan for Economic Self-Reliance (1956–1960)	Prime Minister Hatoyama Dec. 1955	Economic self-reliance; full employment
New Long-Range Economic Plan (1958–1962)	Prime Minister Kishi Dec. 1957	Growth maximization; full employment; improvement of living standards
National Income Doubling Plan (1961–1970)	Prime Minister Ikeda Dec. 1960	Social infrastructure building; industrial transformation; export promotion and foreign aid; development in human resources and scientific research; correction of dual structure and achievement of social stability
Medium-Term Economic Plan (1964–1968)	Prime Minister Sato Jan. 1965	Rectifying socio-economic distortions
Economic and Social Development Plan (1967–1971)	Prime Minister Sato Mar. 1967	Balanced and steady economic growth to rectify the accelerated socio-economic distortions
New Economic and Social Development Plan (1970–1975)	Prime Minister Sato Apr. 1970	Construction of admirable society focusing on socio-economic balance
Economic and Social Basic Plan (1973–1977)	Prime Minister Tanaka Feb. 1973	Economic growth focusing on social welfare and promotion of international co-operation
Economic Plan for the Second Half of the 1970s (1976–1980)	Prime Minister Miki May 1976	Enrichment of quality of life and stable economic growth
New Economic and Social Seven-Year Plan (1979–1985)	Prime Minister Ohira Aug. 1979	Shift to stable economic growth path; enrichment of quality of life; contributions to world economy
Outlook and Guideline for the 1980s (1983–1990)	Prime Minister Nakasone Aug. 1983	Rectifying trade imbalance; international harmony; budgetary and administrative reconstruction; new orientation for industrial development and national life

TABLE 2. Major indicators projected by ten economic plans

Plan	Real GNP growth (%)	Unemployment rate (%)	Consumer prices (%)	Current accounts (US$100 million)
Five-Year Plan for Economic Self-Reliance (1956–1960)	5.0 (8.7)[a]	1.5 (1.5)[a]	2.0	0 (−0.1)[a]
New Long-Range Economic Plan (1958–1962)	6.5 (9.9)[a]	1.3 (1.3)[a]	3.5	1.5 (−0.2)[a]
National Income Doubling Plan (1961–1970)	7.8 (10.7)[a]	1.2 (1.2)[a]	5.7	1.8 (23.5)[a]
Medium-Term Economic Plan (1964–1968)	8.1 (10.6)[a]	1.1 (1.1)[a]	Approx. 2.5 (5.0)[a]	0 (14.5)[a]
Economic and Social Development Plan (1967–1971)	8.2 (10.9)[a]	1.3	Approx. 3.0 (5.7)[a]	14.5 (63.2)[a]
New Economic and Social Plan (1970–1975)	10.6 (6.1)[a]	1.9	4.4 (10.9)[a]	35.0 (1.3)[a]
Economic and Social Basic Plan (1973–1977)	9.4 (4.1)[a]	2.1 (2.1)[a]	4% level (12.0)[a]	59.0 (140.0)[a]
Economic Plan for the Second Half of the 1970s (1976–1980)	over 6.0 (5.1)[a]	1.3% level (2.1)[a]	6% level (6.4)[a]	Approx. 40.0 (−70.1)[a]
New Economic and Social Seven-Year Plan (1979–1985)	Approx. 5.7 (3.8)[b]	Approx. 1.7 (2.7)[b]	Approx. 5.0 (3.7)[b]	Balance in basic accounts
Outlook and Guideline for the 1980s (1983–1990)	Approx. 4.0	Approx. 2.0	Approx. 3.0	International harmony

[a] Actual Trend
[b] Actual Trend dependent on data until FY 1984
Notes: Real GNP growth: Average annual growth rate of GNP in real terms in the period.
Unemployment rate: Unemployment rate to be aimed at the final year of the period.
Consumer price: Average annual increase in consumer price in the period.
Current accounts: External balance in current accounts to be aimed at the final year of the period.

velopment is a function of national policy and that national policy can play a vital role in building, integrating, and stabilizing a nation.

Early Development of Post-War Economic Policy

Development of Administrative and Social Basis for Economic Development

When Japan was occupied by the Allied powers, the Japanese government desperately sought to preserve the last vestiges of national sovereignty by co-operating fully with the GHQ in implementing its directives. Measures mandated by the GHQ to demilitarize and democratize post-war Japan renovated Japan's socio-economic structure by sweeping away many pre-war institutions. Implementing GHQ directives would have been very difficult without the co-operation of the Japanese government, which was anxious to retain a role in governing the nation and rebuilding the national economy.

The government, playing an important role as an active intermediary between the GHQ and the Japanese population, steadily vitalized its administration and gradually reduced economic controls. The newly established Economic Stabilization Board (which encouraged active participation in policy-making by scholars and businessmen as well as bureaucrats from existing administrations) was released from the closed pre-war bureaucracy. This administrative vitalization produced the dynamic evolution of post-war economic policy-making, especially in the areas of economic analysis and planning.

In 1947, the Economic Stabilization Board presented to the cabinet its first economic report, released to the public as *The Current Economic Situation*. This report was compiled by Professor Shigeto Tsuru of Hitotsubashi University, in line with the administrative vitalization of involving outside systems in economic policy-making. By objectively analysing economic problems and development potentials by means of economic indicators, the annual reports addressed public concerns and familiarized average citizens with economic terminology and theory. These reports gave the Japanese people new values to replace those lost because of the war and bolstered their confidence in economic development, thus playing a major role in fostering the social basis for post-war economic development.

Though all the reports were generally of a high quality, the fiscal 1956 report was particularly memorable for its excellent description of the economic situation and its prediction of future development. It stated: "No longer are we in the post-war age in the sense that the period of simple reconstruction is over. Our future development will rely upon a positive industrial transformation, in accordance with world-wide technological innovation." It thus contained an accurate prediction of the direction industrial modernization would take — a shift from labour-intensive light industries to capital-intensive chemical and heavy industries — to raise the overall welfare.

Trial Economic Policy Programmes and Preliminary Macro-economic Planning

The Ministry of Foreign Affairs, which had the initial responsibility for co-ordination with the GHQ (including economic affairs), took the first steps in setting a basic policy orientation for economic restoration. Three study reports were compiled in 1946 setting out the essential policies needed to preserve the economy from bankruptcy. These reports were undeniably inspired by a desire to prevent the GHQ from imposing excessive restraints and reparations by explaining Japan's difficult economic situation.

Thereafter, the Economic Stabilization Board, encouraged by the implementation of the Marshall Plan in Europe, worked out several interim reports in preparation for the introduction of a medium-term economic policy with the goal of securing US foreign aid and World Bank loans. In 1949, economic policy guidelines, contained in a document entitled *Economic Rehabilitation Plan for FY 1949 to 1953,* were made public. The programme called for gradual abolishment of direct government controls and rapid industrial reconstruction, but it could not be implemented because of the deepening depression due to the Dodge Line.

In the latter half of the first post-war decade, in anticipation of transitional problems following abolishment of direct government controls, a second trial plan, The Three-Year Economic Plan, was drafted in 1951 as the Korean War began to affect the economy. Because economic planners found that the abolishment of the Economic Stabilization Board in 1952 threatened to fragment the still immature market economy (which they hoped to unify by introducing macro-economic policy management) and with direct controls ended and the market economy revived (at least for domestic transactions), they attempted to reorganize economic policy management, but without noticeable results.

These early attempts at devising medium-term macro-economic policy, which would be superseded by full economic planning in the second post-war decade, had not been officially adopted by the government, partly because Prime Minister Yoshida, an ardent supporter of economic liberalism, opposed the use of the term "plan." The medium-term policy programmes of the first post-war decade were unsuccessful mainly because externalities such as GHQ controls and heavy dependence on US foreign assistance, including procurement for the Korean War, deprived the government of sufficient power for policy management and prevented it from articulating a comprehensive, independent economic policy. Although government agencies worked out guidelines for individual sectors, such as production targets, these were not integrated into a comprehensive economic policy.

Specialized Economic Policy Management and Scholastic Meritocracy

When the Economic Stabilization Board was dissolved in 1952, the Economic Council Board was created as an independent administrative organization for comprehensive economic policy management, distinct from the sectoral responsibilities of existing agencies. Thus, economic policy management was split into two major functions, comprehensive and sectoral, with the new board responsible for comprehensive economic policy management and sectoral policy authority dispersed to existing agencies.

The Economic Council Board and the Economic Planning Agency, a successor agency formed in 1955, had authority to establish and implement economic plans as part of their responsibility for overall economic policy management. Both agencies were directed by a cabinet level minister and functioned as a permanent secretariat for the Economic Council. The council, a consultative body consisting of no more than 30 representatives from a wide range of socio-economic groups appointed by the prime minister, had the responsibility to deliberate on proposed economic plans.

A brief examination of the scholastic meritocracy system which has developed in Japanese society will allow a better sociological understanding of Japan's success in post-war reconstruction — especially in the area of economic policy management. The Meiji government, as a vital part of its modernization programme, established a nation-wide educational system and encouraged the development of a scholastic meritocracy. This national education system, in which the seven Imperial Universities (especially Tokyo University, which had the highest prestige and broadest social influence) were opened to all students on the basis of scholastic achievement, without regard to financial restrictions or family background.

Owing to its accessibility, this national educational system succeeded in placing promising young men in education, government, and leading industries and deeply imbued Japanese society with a scholastic meritocracy system. Pre-war Japanese bureaucracy formed the summit of this meritocracy system, attracting the most successful candidates from the national universities. This tradition gave the post-war government administration strong authority, despite the lost war, and thus fostered a common psychological background for administrative integrity in economic policy co-ordination. The fact that government policy-makers shared a common meritocratic background with the journalists, academicians, and businessmen involved in discussions of economic policy facilitated practical social integration. Widespread acceptance of this meritocracy helped preserve social stability based on administrative authority in post-war Japan.

The Economic Plan and Macro-economic Policy Management of the National Economy

Political Stability of the LDP and Its Policy Alternative of "Plus-Sum Game" Economic Development

In post-war Japan, the conservatives, although fragmented into several parties in the first post-war decade, have been in power continuously — with one exception: the Katayama (Socialist) Cabinet from May 1947 to March 1948. Prime Minister Shigeru Yoshida, who formed his first cabinet in May 1946 and had held office for more than six years, until December 1954, achieved a successful reconstruction of the defeated nation and solidified the power of the conservative party, despite political disturbances such as the GHQ's direct intervention in January 1947 against a general strike called by the radical labour movement.

Yoshida, who had a pre-war career as a diplomat and had been rejected as liberal and pro-Anglo-American by the militarists, devoted great effort to managing volatile externalities, including the crucial relationship with the GHQ. With his deep insight into world power politics and strong belief in a peaceful post-war Japan, persistent American requests for Japanese military contribution to the Korean War were successfully avoided. Post-war Japan's concentration on peaceful economic development was made possible by his skilful handling of the GHQ and US foreign policy.

Prime Minister Yoshida laid the foundation for the era of independent domestic development which would begin under his successors. His departure from the cabinet in December 1954 led to a historic coalition of the conservative parties in November 1955, at the beginning of the second post-war decade. The LDP, while incessantly troubled by factional struggles, has succeeded in handling internal strains and holding its coalition together, which has fostered its large political capacity to tactfully reconcile social disputes in the nation.

Despite a cabinet reshuffle in January 1960, triggered by violent student demonstrations against Japan's military commitment to the United States, the LDP has kept its hold on political power and permitted the bureaucracy to concentrate on economic policy management. The LDP, which has had to reconcile a wide range of social interests, has realistically chosen to make economic development the central national goal and prudently avoided ideological and cultural issues and, in fact, has remained in power largely because of this ability to diffuse political controversies by focusing on economic development.

From a different perspective, the LDP discovered that economic development could be used to mobilize the nation in a "plus-sum game" in which all citizens could gain without damaging others' interests while individually seeking personal profit. The LDP recognized that focusing on ideological or cultural issues might involve them in a politically dangerous "zero-sum game." As illustrated by the many nations currently suffering from poverty and political conflict, these zero-sum game issues seem to expand internal antagonisms and tend to lead to either national fragmentation or a dictatorial government.

The Japanese government deliberately focused the people's attention and efforts on the plus-sum game of economic development by presenting concrete plans for resolving people's complaints and satisfying their aspirations. Economic policy-makers successfully co-ordinated individual sectoral policies under the comprehensive policy guidelines of the economic plans. Using this approach, Japan's economy was successfully transformed from a closed market economy with government controls on allocation of economic resources to an open market economy strong enough to compete in the international market without government protection.

Public Support for the Four Goals of Economic Self-Reliance and Effective Division of Social Functions

At the beginning of the second post-war decade, having completed basic reconstruction of the economy, Japan entered a period of independent economic development, which would allow it to overcome its dangerous vulnerability to external factors. Business's sentiment reflected both optimism and anxiety about the future because of the pending decline in American procurement for Korean post-war reconstruction. Industry needed a reliable perspective for future economic development which would give it a more solid goal than profiting from externalities.

Japanese opinion began to focus on the goal of steady economic progress, as reflected in the famous statement of the fiscal 1956 economic White Paper, which declared that "no longer are we in the post-war age." In presenting the first economic plan, Prime Minister Ichiro Hatoyama challenged the Japanese people to achieve economic self-reliance. The economic plan presented an overall perspective on future development, forecasting a steady reduction in Japan's heavy dependence on volatile externalities. The plan received wide support, enabling the government to begin integrating fragmented individual sectoral policies into a consistent overall policy.

The first economic plan in its first chapter identified four central policy goals which had to be met to achieve economic self-reliance. First, the plan stated, the Japanese economy had not achieved a sustainable balance-of-payments equilibrium, as it had relied heavily on American assistance and procurement for the Korean War, which had reached US$2 billion and US$3 billion respectively during the decade. With these revenues due to drop in the near future, it was essential for the Japanese economy to achieve a balance-of-payments equilibrium in its normal foreign trade. The plan argued that the most important economic policy objective should be a major expansion of exports through industrial rationalization and enhancement of productivity, which would allow Japan to take advantage of the world-wide trend toward foreign trade liberalization. Imports, on the other hand, should be restrained to conserve foreign exchange.

The second goal was expansion of employment. Unemployment was due basically to surplus population in the productive age group (15 to 64 years old), which would increase by 12.0 per cent between fiscal 1954 and 1960, in contrast to a 5.5 per cent rise in the total population during the same period. To solve this problem, which also involved underemployment of low-wage and part-time employees, the maximum possible expansion of the Japanese economy was needed to create new jobs and raise incomes. The plan commented that, since employment could not be greatly increased in export and basic industries in view of the effort to raise their productivity, labour policy should be designed to encourage other industrial sectors, especially medium- and small-scale businesses, to absorb surplus labour.

The plan set stable economic growth as the third goal. It emphasized that, in seeking an economic expansion which would increase employment, care was needed to preserve economic stability, especially the balance-of-payments equilibrium. It held that economic growth rate targets should be established within the limits set by the balance-of-payments ceiling, which would rise parallel with international competitiveness. In this context, the plan expected international competitiveness to elevate the balance-of-payments ceiling so as to maximize economic growth.

The plan also sought to harmonize overall economic expansion and structural changes. Japanese industry, which had developed to serve the military and Asian markets in the pre-war period, needed to be reoriented toward development of the domestic and international markets, centring on the heavy and chemical industries. The plan called for structural changes to encourage adoption of new technology, industrial rationalization, and productivity growth as well as improvements in management methods, business finance, and industrial relations as preconditions for overall economic expansion.

In Japanese society, political power, which derives from the results of direct elections, is concentrated in a self-selected and spontaneous meritocracy which is distinct from the socially standardized scholastic meritocracy that produces senior bureaucrats. Although there is some danger of oversimplification, it may aid understanding to view Japanese society in terms of two coexisting meritocracies: a spontaneous self-selected meritocracy, dominant in politics and medium and small businesses which produces innovative individuals, and a scholastic meritocracy which is the basis for organized collective power.

These two groups, although prone to social tensions, are in fundamental social equilibrium and have generally shared responsibility in the post-war era. Between the legislative and administrative branches, co-operation has taken the form of a division of social functions between the generalist and the expert, with politicians acting to reconcile various interests and bureaucrats managing policy to achieve stability. In economic policy-making, the LDP has ceded wide discretion to bureaucrats, who have assumed much of the responsibility for consultations and policy co-ordination, while LDP members have retained influence primarily over the specific allocation of economic resources in order to satisfy the interests of their constituents.

Role of the Economic Council in Economic Planning

The decision-making process was critical to the success of economic plans in that the procedure used to devise plans strongly affected their workability. The first plan was written entirely by the Economic Council Board as a normal official document and was adopted by the Hatoyama Cabinet in January 1955 as an "Official Framework for Six-Year Economic Policy Management." This policy statement provoked such a strong public response that the government gained a new awareness of the public's anxiety and expectations regarding economic policy and quickly revised its policy-making procedure.

Rather than directly implementing the Official Framework, Prime Minister Hatoyama requested the Economic Council to take the primary role in devising an economic plan based upon the recently announced policy programme. The government created a strategic policy-making framework which allowed representatives of a wide range of interests to take part in economic policy formation. Economic Council deliberations provided the relevant interests, including individual government agencies, with an important opportunity for co-ordination and consultation in the process of policy-making. In other words, the Economic Council became a vital forum in which various interests were brought together, not just for negotiation or bargaining but in search for common interests in the context of the economic policy framework established by the secretariat. This sophisticated policy-making process helped Japan make economic development a plus-sum game for all sectors of society.

Formation of an economic plan begins with a request from the prime minister, which the Economic Planning Agency conveys to the Economic Council (see fig. 1). All such requests have in the past been very brief in order not to disturb the independent deliberations of the council. For actual deliberations on the economic plan, the government enlarged the council's membership and organized a number of committees on specific subjects under the supervision of the standing council.

These committees included several hundred representatives from various groups, such as financial and industrial firms, public organizations and corporations, academic and research institutions, the press, labour unions and consumer groups, government sectoral policy management councils and individual government administrations, who were appointed by the prime minister as temporary members to supplement the standing council, which consisted of no more than 30 senior representatives appointed for two-year terms. The Economic Council, organized in this way, became a forum in which consultations among various societal interests and intergovernmental policy co-ordination could occur to find a common policy objective to pursue. The discussions held in several sectoral subcommittees within the council were integrated into the deliberations on the general macro-economic policy.

Role of the Economic Planning Agency in Developing Economic Plans

In the process of developing the National Income Doubling Plan, the General Policy Committee and the Macro-Economic Projection Committee had responsibility for the overall macro-economic framework of the plan, while 17 other

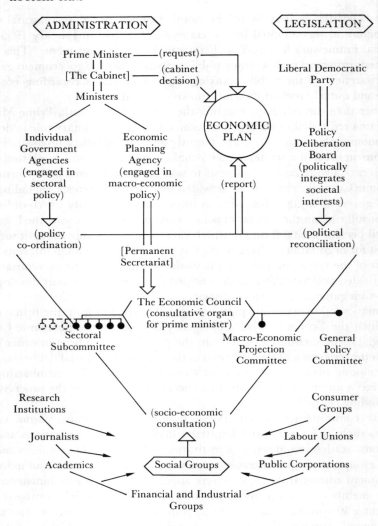

FIG. 1. Socio-economic formulation for economic planning

committees were in charge of making policy recommendations for individual public and private sectors consistent with the macro-economic programme deliberated in the former two committees. Through the entire process of formulating the plan, from the prime minister's initial request to the council through the organization of the extended council and committees and deliberations by the extended council, which took more than one year, including internal preliminary considerations by the Economic Planning Agency, the Economic Planning Agency played a leading role as a permanent secretariat.

In accordance with its legal authority as the final arbiter of the economic plan, the Economic Planning Agency has the power to appoint the members of the Economic Council, including the extended council, and to select committee members in consultation with the prime minister and leading figures on the council and other government agencies. The Minister for Economic Planning has the exclusive responsibility of supervising these arrangements as the principal director of the secretariat for the Economic Council. In particular, the choice of an appropriate chairman for the Economic Council is significant in formulating a national consensus. Although by law the chairman of the Economic Council is chosen by a vote of the members, the secretariat normally plays a vital role in identifying a widely acceptale candidate.

There are three stages in the council's deliberations. A tentative plan approved in the council discussions is drafted by the secretariat and delivered to the concerned agencies for examination since they have the final responsibility for implementing the plan in the individual sectors. Conclusions reached through this process of policy co-ordination, which the secretariat has the responsibility to arrange, are submitted to the council for incorporation in the final plan. In addition to these three stages, before the final draft is circulated in a general meeting of the Economic Council, consultations are held with the Standing Policy Deliberation Board of the LDP by the Economic Planning Agency to secure the board's approval of the plan.

The cabinet authorizes the final report submitted by the council as a national economic plan, accepting it as a consensus reached through consultation and co-ordination among a broad range of social groups. A consensus derives from the broad knowledge of experts, the sensitivities of journalists, the rational evaluations of academics, and the social dynamism of conflicting interests. The public generally views economic plans not as a product of self-interested compromise but as a well-balanced proposal calling for fair and positive contributions from every sector of society, as well as a government commitment to overall welfare.

Rational Policy Harmonization in the Economic Council and Political Reconciliation with the Ruling Party

Economic planners in post-war Japan, while applying the model of economic planning in socialist countries, developed their original methodology to address the liberal-market economy. In the policy-making process, the Economic Planning Agency, as the secretariat of the council, plays an intermediary role in consultations among various interests and in inter-agency co-ordination. The medium- and long-term macro-economic framework, which was projected by the Macro-Economic Projection Committee in the case of the third economic plan, forecasts the national account, money flows, the trade balance, and industrial input and output. These projections are used as a basic reference point in the consultation and co-ordination process through which fragmented sectoral viewpoints and interests are harmonized.

Thus, the economic planning system has introduced into the Japanese policy-making process a scientific method for societal consultation and inter-governmental co-ordination on the basis of economic projections derived from economic theory and indicators known to the public. Because of the vital role of these projections in the policy-making process, the Economic Planning Agency has continuously carried out research on economic indicators and analysis, data-oriented policy-making, econometric models, and socio-economic perspectives.

In the division of the social functions between the legislative and administrative branches, which support a social equilibrium widely accepted by Japanese society, the LDP's approval is of significance in the economic planning process as a confirmation of the party's basic posture toward economic development. Thus, the Economic Planning Agency ensures a powerful political commitment to the economic plan by the ruling party.

This system has not always worked smoothly. In the case of the second economic plan, the LDP's Policy Deliberation Board compiled an independent opinion on the economic policy programme which it announced in the middle of council deliberations. Later, the cabinet, which received the final version of the National Income Doubling Plan from the Economic Council, reacted so strongly that the Economic Planning Agency had to include a "Government Statement on the National Income Doubling Plan" at the beginning of the economic plan.

Indicative Economic Plans in a Market Economy

The first Five-Year Plan for Economic Self-Reliance gives a brief historical analysis of the economic plan and discusses its significance in a market economy. It noted that economic plans originated in the Soviet Union, where the national economy as a whole is under the direct control of the government. In World War II, many countries used economic plans to fulfill military purposes and to prevent inflation. Some of them continued to use economic plans after the end of the war for economic reconstruction.

The report argued, however, that the usefulness of economic plans is not limited to specific countries or situations and that economic plans are compatible with a market economy, in that the policy measures used to implement a plan in a liberal economy are completely different from those used in socialist or statist economies. It concluded that in a market economy, policy measures are only instruments used to develop market dynamism and are different from the government controls used to achieve plan objectives in dictatorial states.

The first plan noted that market economies develop primarily through private activities motivated by individual interest, with only limited application of direct or indirect government controls. However, the plan noted that market defects confronted the Japanese economy with major difficulties, such as economic disorder and persistent inflation during the post-war reconstruction, balance-of-payments deficits caused by excess demand, stagnating industrialization, obstinate unemployment, and business fluctuations.

It argued that these critical issues must be dealt with in accordance with medium- and long-term policy programmes, for which the economic plans were to be used to indicate collective targets for economic policy management. It concluded that achievement of these targets relies ultimately upon the public's co-operation, which could be encouraged by presenting reliable perspectives and policy programmes consistent with the overall economic policy guidelines of the economic plan.

The second economic plan, the New Long-Range Economic Plan of December 1957, discussed how the indicative plan serves to gain the people's co-operation in development. The report, emphasizing the plan's importance as a means of communicating policy to the private sector, argued that the most democratic way to implement the plan was to educate the public about the importance of ther individual roles in economic development and thus obtain their voluntary co-operation in achieving overall goals for the national economy. This plan, while admitting that different industrial sectors and social groups might have different interests and ideologies, concluded that every group could find a common interest in achieving overall economic development.

Discussing the nature of the economic plan, the National Income Doubling Plan noted that the economy consisted primarily of two sectors, the public and the private. The former consisted of collective social facilities provided by the government. For this sector, feasible and detailed projections should be provided in a plan to secure a well-balanced formation of social overhead capital in such areas as industrial infrastructure, roads, railroads, sewage, urban construction, public housing, etc. For the latter sector, which depends upon the initiative of individual persons and enterprises, a plan should provide only a reliable overall perspective for development.

The second economic plan noted that market defects hindered voluntary adjustment among private enterprises and argued that these limits necessitated indirect government intervention in the market. The plan argued that the goals it put forward, including indicative projections for basic industries, could guide individual government agencies in applying policy measures which reinforced the market mechanism. The market mechanism is not perfect, but has defects identified by recent developments in economic theory with policy implications for sectoral policy frameworks.

The National Income Doubling Plan, in its section on "Means for Implementing Policy," emphasized the transition from post-war reconstruction to economic development through active industrial transformation and proposed the institutional reforms necessary to achieve the targets of the plan. These concerns point to the vital role of the indicative economic plan in Japan, which activated individual sectoral policies to mobilize the national economy without centralized controls, dictatorship, or forcible authority.

Economic Policy Development in Major Sectors in Post-War Japan

In the first post-war decade, sectoral development policies focused on democratization and economic reconstruction. Formulation of the post-war institutional framework began while the government was still subject to external decision-making by the GHQ. Entering the period of economic self-reliance in the second post-war decade, policies were directed to the structural transformation of individual sectors in response to the comprehensive policy guideline put forward in the Income Doubling Plan.

Sectoral policies were aimed at industrial rationalization and reduction of structural discrepancies and played a leading role in the allocation of public resources to individual sectors, while macro-economic policy was used to harmonize these policies to encourage overall socio-economic development. To illustrate the development of the three major types of sectoral policy, positive and passive adjustment policies, and social capital formation policy, the following three sectoral policies are addressed: industrial policy, to illustrate positive adjustment policy; agricultural policy, for passive adjustment policy; and regional development policy, for public resources allocation policy.

Industrial Policy Development

Japan's post-war economic development cannot be understood without taking into account the rapid transformation of industrial structure. This process was characterized by rapid industrial reconstruction in the first post-war decade and intensive rationalization in the next decade. The development of post-war industrial policy, which played a vital role in this industrial transformation, was greatly influenced by the tension between strong private dynamism and a market economy insufficiently developed to accomodate it. The industrial policy-makers, struggling continuously with the shortage in foreign exchange, natural resources, and capital to improve technologies and international competitiveness, sought to rebuild production during reconstruction and later to promote industrial rationalization.

The "Highest Priority Strategy" and the Reconstruction Finance Bank

The first post-war industrial policy was devised to alleviate the severe raw material shortage of the immediate post-war period. As the initial policy of the Allied powers virtually prohibited Japan from engaging in foreign trade, raw material stockpiles were exhausted and seriously affected industrial production, which had been reduced by wartime damage. The consequent shortage of consumer goods triggered a 200 per cent inflation. To avoid a production crisis predicted for March 1947, Prime Minister Yoshida, focusing on energy supply, proclaimed in October 1946 a coal production target of 30 million tons for 1947, well above the then current production of 23 million tons.

To achieve this target, a policy framework for a "Highest Priority Strategy for Industrial Reconstruction" was developed by the Special Coal Committee chaired by a Professor Arisawa and under the authority of the Ministry of Foreign Affairs. He identified commodity shortages as the basic cause of inflation and argued that efforts to expand production should initially be in the coal and steel industries, which were essential for overall recovery of production. This strategy was designed to allocate resources to basic industries through a preferential financing system which indirectly controlled the market through credit-rationing as well as direct controls on the relevant materials. The Reconstruction Finance Bank, established in January 1947, allotted the largest share of its credit to the core industries centring on coal and steel production. Thirty-five per cent of the bank's funds went to coal mining in 1947 and thirty-eight per cent in 1948, covering more than ninety per cent of the industry's borrowing needs in these years.

The success of the priority strategy led to the adoption of an Economic Stabilization Program in December 1948 in which the Japanese government applied similar policy measures in response to a GHQ directive calling for the stabilizing of price and wage inflation by expanding domestic production to the maximum extent possible. This programme expanded the application of the priority strategy to a number of industries, such as electric power, fertilizer, textiles, and shipbuilding.

To avoid the inefficiency of a centrally controlled economy, policy measures were devised to allow buyers' discretions to assume market forces by applying a quota system. Raw materials for export products were to be allocated to factories chosen by traders who had arranged export contracts certified by the public authority.

Post-War Industrial Policy Framework and the Ministry of International Trade and Industry

The introduction of a single exchange rate of US$1 = 360 yen in April 1949 revealed the great backwardness of Japanese industry, which had been temporarily concealed by the multiple exchange rate system previously used for foreign trade. The multiple exchange rate system, supported by huge subsidies, had enlarged the price discrepancies between imported materials and exported products. A high exchange rate for the US dollar had been charged on export products: 420 yen for silk fibre and textiles, 500 yen for steel boats, 500 yen for radio sets, 510 yen for bicycles, 500 yen for dye, 600 yen for glass products and chinaware, etc. A low exchange rate for the US dollar had been applied for imported materials: 154 yen for raw rubber, 250 yen for cotton wool (exclusively for the export industry), 165 yen for wheat, and 177 yen for sugar. These multiple exchange rates had distorted overall relative prices in Japanese industry.

Once deprived of the protective multiple exchange rates, Japanese industry was unavoidably forced to cope with inefficient production, which was reflected in aging machinery and equipment, insufficient depreciation, and technological backwardness. More than 40 per cent of Japan's electric generation capacity was more than 20 years of age. Plants less than 5 years old accounted for only 4.3 per cent of the hydroelectric and 2 per cent of the coal-fired electric generating capacity. In the steel and iron industry, 40 per cent of the machinery and equipment was more than 2 years old and only 1.3 per cent was less than 10 years old. Japan's technological lag in this industry was most serious in the rolling-mill process which elsewhere had been developing rapidly. Japan had only two cold-strip mills, compared with forty in the United States. In the machine industry, 60 per cent of home-made machine tools were more than 10 years old, and all of the imported machine tools were more than 10 years old because imports were forced to stop in 1940.

The massive industrial handicaps revealed by the fixed exchange rate system forced the government to prepare a new industrial policy. The Ministry of International Trade and Industry (MITI) was created in May 1949 by unifying the Ministry of Commerce and Industry and the International Trade Agency. Its purpose was to develop an industrial policy which would enhance industrial reconstruction and be effectively linked with foreign trade policy. The policy developed by MITI was embodied in the Cabinet Decision on Industrial Rationalization of September 1949.

The policy goals of the Cabinet Decision centred on the rationalization of private industries to bring domestic prices to a level comparable with those at the international level. Significantly, MITI employed administrative guidance as a policy tool to involve the private sector in implementation of industrial policy; for example, it encouraged the formation by the Industrial Rationalization Council of industrial rationalization programmes. More specifically, companies in the basic industries and others in urgent need of rationalization were individually requested to submit their own rationalization plans to MITI, which would handle preliminary consultation with the companies concerned in conjunction with discussions by the council to establish overall goals for rationalizing production and introducing advanced techologies, after which MITI would then devise and publicize detailed programmes for specific industries.

To individually guide the enterprises' efforts to concentrate on research and development of technologies, effective introduction of advanced technologies, and rationalization of production, MITI prepared a wide range of preferential policy measures, such as favourable allocation of raw materials, relaxation of price controls, corporate tax concessions, concessionary financing, and favourable foreign currency control. The Industrial Rationalization Council was used to involve the private sector in devising policy guidelines which directed and justified applications of these preferential policy measures and the regulations on international transactions.

External transactions were institutionalized with the passage of the Foreign Exchange and Foreign Trade Control Law in 1949 and the Foreign Capital Law in 1950. These laws were intended to insure the best use of the limited foreign exchange and to control imports and capital inflows in line with the industrial rationalization programme. Within this institutional framework, MITI was given wide discretion in regulating raw-material and machinery imports and in the introduction of foreign technologies and capital investments, which it engaged to promote the development of the basic and export industries.

The Korean War and the Establishment of Preferential Industrial Policy Measures

The industrial policy framework newly established had few practical results because of the austerity policy of the Dodge Line combined with a recession in the United States in 1949. New industrial policy measures could not prevent the Japanese economy from falling into a deep recession in which imports declined and investment was suppressed as the Reconstruction Finance Bank suspended lending. The outbreak of the Korean War in June 1950, however, completely changed the situation. In the economic expansion fueled by procurement for the Korean War, the Japanese government resumed its efforts to reformulate industrial policy.

After Minister Dodge laid the foundation of economic stability, Professor Shaup of Columbia University came to Japan in September 1949 and made proposals for a fundamental reform of the Japanese tax system, in which direct taxes were emphasized as the primary source of government revenue, with personal and corporate income taxes providing national government revenue and real estate and residence taxes providing local government revenue. Indirect taxes were limited to non-essentials. While recommending that the reassessment of the fixed assets still be assessed at their pre-war values, Professor Shaup strictly opposed tax concession to promote specific policies, in accordance with the Dodge Line policy to ensure fiscal stability and fairness.

When the Korean War broke out and relieved Japanese industry from deepening stabilization depression, the government resumed the advancement of industrial policy. The Special Depreciation Promotion Act and Import Tariff Exemption Act were introduced in 1951, and the Enterprise Rationalization Promotion Law in 1952, in response to the economic upswing triggered by the Korean War.

The Special Depreciation Act, adopted in August 1951, allowed an additional 50 per cent depreciation over three years for designated industrial machinery and equipment, and ships. This regulation accelerated aquisition of advanced machinery and equipment by allowing accelerated depreciation in the early stage of capital formation. The Import Tariff Exemption Act removed import tariffs on advanced machinery and equipment not produced in Japan and judged important to technological development. The Enterprise Rationalization Promotion Law adopted in March 1952 extended tax exemptions to experimental machinery and equipment. These tax concessions, restricted to 32 designated industries, constituted a strategic tool with which to effect administrative guidance.

Japan became a member of the International Monetary Fund (IMF) and the International Bank for Reconstruction and Development (IBRD) in 1952, making it eligible for development loans. In addition to these international financial resources, the Japan Development Bank (JDB) was established in March 1951, in place of the Reconstruction Finance Bank, to supply capital exclusively for industrial investment, using postal savings funds managed by the Fund Operating Office of the Ministry of Finance. This new institutional finance system did not cause inflationary credit expansion, as had the Reconstruction Finance Bank, which was funded by budgetary deficits.

Administrative agencies responsible for industrial finance, including MITI, the Ministry of Finance, and the Ministry of Transportation, used funds available through these foreign and government institutions to provide preferential credits to support industrial development policies. Thus, the industrial policy framework strengthened by the tax concessions and institutional financing systems encouraged early formation of the fundamental industries in the first postwar decade and led to the long-lasting investment boom in the next decade.

Development of Institutional Financing and Amendment to the Monopoly Prohibition Law

The JDB played a particularly important role in industrial rationalization. Its loans were concentrated in four industries, electric power, steel and iron, shipbuilding, and coal-mining, which received 80 per cent of total JDB credits between 1952 and 1955. Hydroelectric power investment especially, which received the largest share, accounting for 53 per cent of total JDB loans in 1953, produced an electric power development boom, which stimulated, through the "investment producing investment" effect, relevant investments in cement, steel and iron, and civil engineering and construction.

Shipbuilding held the second largest share, with 26 per cent of total JDB loans. These credits accounted for 60 per cent of the shipbuilding industry's total investment funds. The JDB loans also enabled the steel and iron industry to implement the first rationalization programme between 1951 and 1953, in accordance with the cabinet decision on industrial rationalization of 1949. The Japanese government, at the same time, expanded its borrowings from international financial organizations, which totaled US$1.54 billion through 1961.

These foreign funds equaled 5 per cent of the total annual loans, on average, from the domestic commercial banks, and reached 10 per cent in 1958 and 1961. World Bank loans to Japan from 1953 to 1961 reached US$488 million, the largest figure after India. The Export-Import Bank of the United States (EXIM) lent Japanese industries US$274 million between 1956 and 1961, while foreign commercial loans amounted to US$376 million. The IBRD and EXIM loans were concentrated in the electric power and steel industries, while the foreign commercial loans went mainly to the petroleum refining and transportation industries.

The Japanese government passed a Monopoly Prohibition Law in 1947 which closely followed the United States's Sherman Anti-Trust Act. The industrial policy bureaucracy viewed this law as an obstacle to industrial rationalization, since active competition in the domestic market would cause excessive investment, over-production, and exaggerate business cycles, threatening steady rationalization conceived in the industrial policy.

An amendment to the Monopoly Prohibition Law in 1953 allowed industrial policy agencies to temporarily form two kinds of cartels, on condition of the Fair Trade Commission's concordance. Recession cartels were allowed in order to reduce serious demand and supply imbalances, and rationalization cartels were permitted if necessary for implementation of industrial rationalization programmes. Other collective industrial actions were legally exempted from the Monopoly Prohibition Law by independent laws governing development programmes for individual industries.

The Medium- and Small-Scale Enterprise Stabilization Law and the Import Transaction Law, both adopted in 1952, allowed industries to form, always temporarily, production and distribution cartels if the responsible agency found a supply-and-demand imbalance and the head of the Fair Trade Commission gave consent. Further, to assist declining industries, similar exemptions were granted under several laws, including the Temporary Fertilizer Industry Rationalization Measure of 1954, the Temporary Coal-Mining Rationalization Measure of 1955, and the Temporary Textile Industry Equipment Rationalization Measure of 1956. In growing industrial sectors, collective actions were permitted, if necessary, to introduce new technology and equipment and to receive preferential credit for rationalization.

Irreversible Shift of the Post-War Industrial Policy

As Japan strengthened its export competitiveness through active industrial investment, its impact began to be felt in the international market by the middle of the second post-war decade. Japan's first trade surplus with the United States in 1959 led to US demands for abolition of Japanese trade restrictions. As the European countries had taken rapid liberalization measures in response to similar pressure from the United States, the Japanese government began to liberalize international transactions with the cabinet decision on a "Trade and Foreign Exchange Liberalization Program" of June 1960.

The first market liberalization, which was implemented in stages between 1967 and 1976, proceeded from trade to capital movement. Abolition of the foreign exchange budget, subsequent to Japan's adherence to Article 8 of the IMF Charter in 1964, became the first change in post-war industrial policy, which had been closely linked with foreign exchange restrictions. Although this liberalization would have an irreversible effect on industrial policy in the long run, MITI was not ready to relinquish its control of international transactions and attempted to maintain its administrative power by playing on the anxiety of private industries over liberalization.

The National Income Doubling Plan, announced in the same year as the cabinet decision on market liberalization — 1960 — called for focusing industrial development on high value-added industries in growing sectors. To achieve economic rationality through an optimum international division of labour, the plan requested increased private autonomy. MITI strongly opposed this macro-economic guideline and countered with a "New Industrial Order" plan through the Industrial Structure Research Council, which replaced the Industrial Rationalization Council in 1961.

MITI argued that administrative initiative was essential in promoting collective action among private industries to counter the superior competitiveness of foreign enterprises, to which Japanese industries would be directly exposed by market liberalization. In 1963, the ministry drafted and proposed to the council a "Temporary Specific Industry Promotion Measure," which would greatly enhance the competitiveness of the automobile, specialty steel, petrochemical, and heavy machinery industries. These industries were reluctant, however, to accept further administrative guidance which would restrain their voluntary decision-making, although they favoured a policy of "autonomous adjustment" based on cartels which MITI proposed by modifying the Monopoly Prohibition Law. Lacking support from the LDP, however, MITI's proposal was not adopted.

The failure of its New Industrial Order plan left MITI in internal confusion and without a clear conception of its role in industrial policy. It took several years for the ministry to end its retrospective attachment to restrictive industrial policy and to put forward a new policy orientation. In 1971, the Industrial Structure Council, which was established in 1964 in place of the preceding Industrial Structure Research Council, presented a new policy statement, entitled "International Trade and Industrial Policies in the 1970's."

The report, which reviewed the rapid economic growth of post-war Japan, described this process poetically: "The Japanese economy has been single-mindedly climbing a steep hill-side, with its eyes focused only on the cloud above the hill top — [but now] finds itself on the hill top where it commands a wide view of the world." This expressed the feeling that Japan had just accomplished a miracle of economic development in difficult conditions but had now to reorient policy toward the quality of life and contributions to the international community.

Recent industrial policy has been urged to further promote structural adjustment, both in the internal and external aspects, facing continuous fluctuation in foreign exchange rates and global industrial transformation accelerated by deepening international interdependence. Internally, the government has inevitably strengthened its temporary adjustment policies for industries declining both in domestic and international markets, such as basic material industries and medium- and small-scale firms, fundamentally to enhance global industrial transformations with a minimum of social friction. Externally, severe trade conflicts with industrialized countries forced MITI to arrange unilateral self-restrictions on Japan's exports, without multilateral agreement on global perspectives on structural adjustment.

Parallel to these passive adjustment policies, positive industrial policy for innovative sectors has been developing in two directions. In place of forcible implementation of administrative guidance, "informative guidance" has been emphasized anew to indicate new industrial opportunities with limited use of preferential policy measures. Advanced technology development projects have been organized with government initiative to concentrate public and private resources on non-military industrial development for the future.

Agricultural Policy Development

Agricultural Structure and Land Reform in Post-War Japan

Japan's agricultural sector, unlike the non-agricultural sectors, has remained largely a traditional industry that is dominated by a strong historical and cultural commitment to rice production. Protectionist agricultural policy has in large part been responsible for the traditionalism of the sector. Historically, before industrialization, agriculture was the dominant means of production and thus deeply affected politics and culture. Local crops and family farms have survived in the face of industrialization.

Japanese agriculture has traditionally been dominated by small family farms engaged in rice production. Farmers have been limited to a very low proportion of arable land — even today the average farm is only 1.2 ha — only 18 per cent of the national territory owing to Japan's mountainous geography, which also accounts for Japan's high population density. Rice paddies, totally irrigated, accounted for 55 per cent of Japan's total area — 5.4 million ha — of farm land and pastures. In Japan, rice was the major medium of exchange and was often used for tax payments in kind. Before the Meiji Restoration, the power of feudal lords was measured by the amount of rice produced in their territories.

Even when Japan began to industrialize, agriculture made a major contribution to industrial development, by producing important export products such as silk, which compensated largely for week manufacturing exports. In pre-war Japan, the agricultural sector remained stable at roughly 5.5 million households, farming primarily as tenants. Although the share of the labour force engaged in the primary sector decreased from over 80 per cent in the early part of the Meiji Era to approximately 50 per cent on the eve of the war, the impact of early industrialization on the industrial structure was rather limited in comparison with the overwhelming industrial transformation of post-war Japan.

The land reform ordered by the GHQ immediately after the war caused a thorough structural change in Japanese agriculture. During the first half of the first post-war decade, the Japanese government drastically redistributed agricultural land, expropriating a third of the total cultivated land from absentee landlords to resell to tenant farmers. Consequently, tenant-cultivated land, which amounted to 60 per cent of total farm land in 1945, declined to 10 per cent by 1950. With the elimination of the landlords, who had had more than 60 per cent of the total farm land, independent owner-farmers became the majority in post-war Japan's rural communities. This dramatic agricultural reform, which could never have been put into action without the authority of the Occupation, strongly influenced the development of post-war agriculture.

Agricultural Development in Post-War Japan

Independent owner-farmers, including those farming some land as tenants, rose from 31 per cent of total farming households to 62 per cent at the end of land reform in 1950. The Rural Land Law, enacted in 1952 to control rural land transactions, soldified the land reform and established the basic management structure of post-war agriculture. During the food shortage of the first post-war decade, this legislation protected newly independent farmers and encouraged them to increase agricultural production. Rice yields per one hectare rose from the pre-war average of three tons (1933–1942) to three and one-half tons in 1960. With only a limited extension of cultivated land, Japanese agriculture nearly overcame the food shortages by the middle of the second post-war decade.

As food consumption rose with income, the quantity and the variety of agricultural products were greatly expanded, even though farm sizes remained small due to restrictions on rural land transactions. Compared with pre-war production (average for 1933 to 1935 = 100), agricultural production recorded striking increases in all categories in the first post-war decade, with rice reaching 138 against the pre-war figure, vegetables 201, fruits 358, eggs 1,309, beef 462, pork 1,517, and milk 1,299.

Throughout the post-war period, food consumption has changed in composition. Meat consumption rose almost five times from 5.0 kg in 1960 to 23.3 kg in 1982, on a per capita basis. Consumption of milk products tripled over the same period, while fruits and vegetables increased by 80 and 10 per cent respectively. Rice and other cereals, in contrast, declined by 30 per cent over the same 22 years. In response to changing consumption, the share of cereals in total farm output decreased, with rice declining from around half to 31 per cent while vegetables rose from 8.3 to 17.7 per cent of total production over the same period. Further, livestock products, meat and milk, doubled their shares, from 14.5 to 29.0 per cent, to equal roughly rice production in the 1980s.

The Japanese government acted early in the post-war period to encourage a switch from domestic production to imports of selective agricultural products, including wheat, soya beans, and feed grains. Recent figures indicate that Japan's self-sufficiency ratio in cereals, including self-sufficient rice production, has declined to 33 per cent due to growing imports of these selective grains, while self-sufficiency ratios remain fairly high for vegetables, fruits, dairy products, and meat.

Economic growth in post-war Japan, which more than doubled employment in both the secondary and tertiary industries in the 25 years after 1955, absorbed the primary sector's excess labour. Agricultural employment has declined by two-thirds to less than 6 million during the same period. The number of farm households, however, has only dropped from 6.1 to 4.7 million, because most farmers have not quit agriculture or left their farms, but have instead found additional employment in the non-agricultural sector. Owing to the labour-saving technology developed in post-war Japan, farmers can easily continue rice production, which has been the most protected crop by the government food control system.

As a consequence, independent full-time farm households deriving their entire income from farm production fell from 50 to 13 per cent of the total farm households, while part-time farm households with additional income from non-agricultural employment became the majority. Those gaining more than half their income from outside in particular rose to 70 per cent of total farm households. The minority of full-time farm households have taken the lead in enlarging the variety of farm products and in undertaking capital-intensive farming and import-dependent livestock production. While constituting only 13 per cent of total farm households, their production now accounts for almost 60 per cent of total gross farm output.

Narrow Alternatives of Agricultural Policy

Agricultural policy in the first post-war decade was devoted to production expansion and democratization of the rural community. Food shortages in this period were so severe that rice imports equal to a tenth of total domestic demand were necessary. The government introduced a series of measures to expand agricultural production and to ensure the stability of independent owner-farmers created by the rural land reform. The Ministry of Agriculture and Forestry developed a broad range of agricultural promotion measures, including construction of agricultural infrastructure, demand and supply adjustment programmes, a preferential financing system for agricultural production and distribution, nation-wide agricultural co-operatives, self-governing

agricultural committee systems, rural land improvement assistance, a crop insurance system, and a food control system.

Considering that the majority of Japanese belonged to farm households in the
immediate post-war era, it is understandable that these protectionist, favourable agricultural policy measures received strong social support and created a
solid foundation for economic reconstruction in those days. By 1953, food consumption had regained pre-war levels. In the middle of the second post-war
decade, post-war agricultural policy faced a critical turning point. The National
Income Doubling Plan called for a reorientation of agriculture to enhance industrial transformation and to mobilize idle resources. The economic plan
urged that agricultural policy be transformed to address structural disparities
and increasing productivity rather than continue to emphasize product expansion.

The rapid industrial transformation and global market liberalization characteristic of the vigorous economic development in the second post-war decade
enlarged the structural disparities between the agricultural and non-
agricultural sectors. Agricultural policy was thus obliged to focus on resolving
the disparities associated with the traditional structure of agriculture. A research committee on "Basic Problems in Agriculture, Forestry and Fishery"
(this committee conducted deliberations at the same time as the Economic
Council, which was developing the National Income Doubling Plan) submitted
its final report to the prime minister in 1960. This agricultural report, which
identified "selective production expansion" as the agricultural policy most consistent with the overall economic plan, formed the basis of the Basic Agricultural Act of 1961.

The Basic Agricultural Act, which formed the foundation for agricultural
policy over the following three decades, embodied three major policy goals:
"selective production expansion," focusing on the high demand elasticity
products such as milk, meat, fruit, eggs, and sugar beets; "selective import
expansion" in sectors with limited domestic production, including wheat
and soya beans; and intensive improvement of productivity of major crops,
centring on rice. These three goals were achieved through such means as encouraging farmers to introduce labour-saving technologies and to use cheap
foreign feed grains.

By applying policy measures such as price supports and favourable financial
and budgetary measures, the ministry encouraged farmers to switch to agricultural products for which domestic demand was expected to increase.
Through selective trade expansion, domestic production of wheat and soya
beans was decreasing, and dairy farmers were enlarging the import of feed
grains. These changes made a real, although limited, contribution to both the
internal and external markets. Internally, they reduced inflationary pressure on
food prices during rapid economic growth, while externally, they encouraged
the expansion of world-wide agricultural capacity.

Contradictions in the Post-War Agricultural Policy

The post-war development of the agricultural sector, especially the growth in the number of marginal production units, has been accentuated by the government's price-support policy. The discussion of structural disparities in the government economic plan provoked farmers to demand the elimination of the income disparity with the non-agricultural sectors. Farmers have used their traditionally strong ties to politicians representing rural districts to apply persistent political pressure on the government and have succeeded in gaining increases in budgetary subsidies, including rising producer prices of rice which the government has to pay.

In the last two decades, the agriculture sector has made little progress in expanding the farming scale or in reducing the income discrepancy in the face of the non-agricultural sector's rapid growth both in demand and productivity. Agricultural policy has inevitably had to accentuate a price-support policy and favour rice cultivating households because of their predominant importance in Japanese agriculture. This price-support policy, which accelerated the rise in part-time farming, delayed structural adjustment in the agricultural sector. Eventually, these policies produced a dual agricultural structure, with a minority of full-time farm households producing competitive products and part-time farm households, which formed the majority, specializing in rice cultivation to supplement family income.

Actually, the government's hefty increase in price supports for rice production resulted in an increase in part-time farmers and prevented full-time farmers from enlarging their management scale. The situation began to change gradually in the 1970s as the economy entered the stable-growth period and the agriculture sector experienced a surplus of rice production. With the budgetary restriction which kept the purchasing price almost unchanged, agricultural policy turned to a reduction of rice production.

In 1978, agricultural policy introduced a ten-year programme to convert a part of rice cultivation to other agricultural products. The plan also provided for a considerable amount of subsidies to be poured into the agricultural sector year after year. The post-war agricultural policy dependent largely on price-support measures centring on rice production — apart from the policy-maker's original intent, the policy framework and social interests reinforced each other and led eventually to intense political pressure to raise the price — is coming to an end.

Regional Development Policy

Legal Framework for Regional Development Policy

Regional development policy in post-war Japan started with the Comprehensive National Development Act enacted in 1950. This basic act, which was prepared by the Economic Stabilization Board as a fundamental legal framework for regional development policy, presented four categories of development: the national level, the individual prefecture level, the local level, which grouped several prefectures together, and the specific areas level.

The act fundamentally indicated that local authorities had the responsibility to propose regional development plans in three categories other than the national level and to submit them to the Economic Stabilization Board. The same act provided that preferential budgetary and financial supports by the national government would be given to public works and other projects in the regional plans which were approved by the board and formally designated by the prime minister through deliberations by the National Land Development Council.

In post-war Japan, local governments took the first step in working out their regional development plans of the fourth category, with selective policy targets on land and river preservation and local resource development, including construction of hydroelectric power stations. Twenty-one areas which had their specific area development plans approved by 1957 began their planned regional development by focusing on regional reconstruction, which was so urgent in the immediate post-war period. The national government, however, could not find the opportunity to adopt a nation-wide regional development plan of the first category until a nation-wide regional development issue arose in the context of a macro-economic development strategy launched by the National Income Doubling Plan of 1960.

During the absence of a comprehensive regional development plan on the national level, various pieces of legislation for regional development had been adopted independently into the Comprehensive National Land Development Act. They brought confusion to the effort to construct a framework of consistent policy management for the regional allocation of economic resources. In 1950, for example, the Hokkaido Development Act was settled independently for regional development in Hokkaido, a northern region of Japan. In addition, the Remote Islands Development Act and the Tohoku District Development Act were adopted in 1953 and 1957 respectively to draw favourable budgetary support from the national government for regional development in these less-developed areas.

Parallel to this, to cope with the excessive concentration of both population and industries in the large metropolitan areas, three Major Metropolitan Area Development acts were approved. The Capital Region Development Act, in which Tokyo and the surrounding seven prefectures were integrated, was enacted in 1956 and the Nagoya and the Osaka Metropolitan Area Development acts were brought into effect in 1963 and 1966 respectively.

Three Regional Development Strategies

When the Japanese economy entered the period of economic self-reliance in the second post-war decade, unprecedented development aimed at chemical and heavy industries occurred and a large-scale movement of population toward the three major metropolitan areas started. As a result, existing social infrastructures were quickly exhausted and the excessive concentration of population in the urban areas redirected attention to the controversial nation-wide regional development policy which had so far been neglected.

The National Income Doubling Plan made public by the Ikeda Cabinet in 1960 accelerated discussions on a comprehensive regional development plan. Because the intensive industrial development conceived in the plan called for explicit policy guidelines for the construction and regional allocation of social infrastructures, the Pacific Coastal Belt Development Strategy was proposed. This strategy indicated the Pacific coastal areas where new industrial complexes would be built with effective linkage to existing industrial basins located in the same areas.

This proposal gave rise to strong reactions from many local governments and Diet representatives from outside the Pacific coastal areas. They opposed the Pacific Coastal Belt Development Strategy and tried to win support for an industrial development plan favourable to the less-developed areas by playing on the anxiety that would be created by the critical regional discrepancies of which the economic plan had explicitly warned. As a result, the Economic Planning Agency, Regional Development Bureau (independent from the Economic Planning Bureau) started deliberations on an overall regional development plan proposed by the National Land Development Council.

In October 1962, the government adopted the Comprehensive National Development Plan, with a planning horizon of one decade. This first comprehensive regional development plan contained a Priority Area Development Strategy which aimed at large-scale industrial construction outside existing industrial basins as the fundamental policy guideline for nation-wide regional development. The strategy was embodied in the New Industrial Cities Promotion Act and the Special Areas for Industrial Consolidation Act and adopted, after many twists and turns, in the hope of reconciling the two opposing regional disparities. In July 1965, the cabinet decided to designate 15 areas as "new industrial cities," mainly outside the Pacific coastal belt area, and an additional 6 areas were designated as "special industrial areas" in the Pacific belt area.

Entering the third post-war decade, people began to stress balanced socio-economic growth to remedy the distortions which had been accelerated by the reckless industrialization pursued during the prior two decades. Prime Minister Sato, who succeeded Ikeda in November 1964, requested the National Land Development Council to start deliberating on a new regional plan. In the elaboration of a second plan, the planners came to recognize that, during the ten decades since the Meiji Restoration, national infrastructures, be they transportation networks, regional location of educational facilities, or industrial infrastructure, had no more than barely survived what had been built early in the Meiji era and which high economic growth threatened to devour.

It was decided to construct a new overhead capital network which would create a nation-wide human and physical mobility of a new dimension.

Thus, the second plan, adopted in 1969 (when the first plan, 1961–1970, was terminating) and named the New Comprehensive National Development Plan, proposed an "infrastructure network development strategy," accentuating network formations which were different from those of the first plan, which stressed a "point area development strategy."

A three-dimensional development strategy was devised to facilitate decentralization of enterprise management facilities and industrial complexes which had been concentrated in three major metropolitan areas by providing nation-wide infrastructure networks linked by highways, superexpress railways, aviation, telecommunications, and large-scale distribution bases. A Research Committee for New Large-Scale Development Projects, whose members consisted of concerned public authorities and representatives of the relevant private enterprises, was chosen to define the strategy.

Transition of Regional Development Policy Orientation

A quarter of a century after the war, Japan entered the final stage of high economic growth. The Japanese government, in accordance with the Infrastructure Network Development Strategy, proceeded to ultra-long-range projects, such as the 19 highways (stretching 7,600 km), the 2 additional superexpress railways of the Tohoku and Hokuriku regions, the New Tokyo International Airport in Narita, 2 trans-Inland Sea bridges, an undersea tunnel of more than 50 km connecting Hokkaido and the main island of Japan, and 2 large-scale industrial complexes in the northern part of Japan, Mutsu Ogawara and Tomakomai East.

Then Prime Minister Tanaka, who took office in 1972 with an optimistic spirit was determined to pursue economic dynamism to the ultimate. Construction of the infrastructure network continued, to emphasize his proposal to vitalize the Japanese archipelago — an ambition he made public in his book *Nippon Retto Kaizo-Ron*, published before his inauguration as prime minister. At the same time, Tanaka proceeded to broaden institutional reforms in order to pursue an effective national land-development policy (while simultaneously coping with vigorous real estate speculation accelerated by the so-called excess liquidity trap). As a result, the National Land Agency was instituted in 1974 as an independent administrative agency to conduct comprehensive management of land-development policies, and the National Land Use Planning Act was approved in the same year to regulate private land use.

The ultra-long-range projects, which made great progress under the Tanaka Cabinet, continued to be responsible for the construction of new national networks — at a decelerated pace, however, as the economy made the transition to stable economic growth throughout the world-wide economic upheaval of the 1970s. In the latter half of the third post-war decade (the early 1970s) the world economy faced a massive upheaval caused by the monetary and oil crises. The Japanese economy fell into a critical trap after its enthusiastic rapid economic development. The Third Comprehensive National Land Development of 1977 shifted its policy orientation from large-scale development projects to an "integrated strategy for better dwelling conditions," aiming at creating a human dwelling environment in harmony with both nature and a culture beyond materialism.

Conclusion

The economic development of post-war Japan reveals that economic development is not a quantitative expansion measured in terms of GNP but an endless process of structural transformation in industries, employment, and external economic relations. As the economy has moved from post-war poverty to its recent affluence, economic policy has evolved from one with stringent controls on excess demand (a persistent condition during the years of material destitution) into one with a means of increasing market dynamism by gradually reducing preferential and protective policy regulations which affected first the domestic and then the international economies. Economic policy development produced two major types of policy: macro-economic and sectoral. Economic planning has been used to devise macro-economic policy guidelines, which have been successfully used to integrate individual sectoral policies.

Japan's economic planners focused first on reconstruction of the industrial capacity lost in the war and then on activating market dynamism by reducing regulations on the economy. They continuously sought to encourage industrial transformation and to prevent structural disparities from eroding economic growth. Economic planning in the first two post-war decades, going through two major phases — a trial period in the first post-war decade and full implementation in the second post-war decade — succeeded in transforming a feeble, handicapped economy into a self-reliant economy with a growing domestic market. As economic self-reliance emerged in the final stage, the economic policy was reoriented toward liberalization of a market which had been isolated from international competition, thus preparing the way for a fully open market economy.

Japan's economic plans over the last two decades, however, following the methodology established in the first two post-war decades, have continued to be characterized by policies appropriate to a developing economy with large trade deficits, despite recognition of the pressing need to adapt the Japanese economy to unprecedented global changes. Essentially, Japan's economic plans have not yet been adjusted to compensate for the balance-of-payment surpluses the Japanese economy now produces or to indicate how these surpluses can be used to promote domestic and global economic equilibria.

Bibliography

Bieda, K. 1980. *The structure and operations of the Japanese economy*. New York, John Wiley & Sons.

Bornstein, M., ed. 1965. *Comparative economic systems*. Homewood, Illinois, R. D. Irwin.

Denison, E. F., and W. K. Chung. 1976. *How Japan's economy grew so fast: The sources of post-war expansion*. Washington, D. C., The Brookings Institution.

Economic Planning Agency. *Economic white paper*. Tokyo. Published annually.

Kosai, Y. 1986. *The era of high-speed growth*. Tokyo, University of Tokyo Press.

Kosai, Y., and Y. Ogino. 1984. *The contemporary Japanese economy*. New York, Macmillan.

Lockwood, W. W., ed. 1965. *The state and economic enterprise in Japan*. Princeton, Princeton University Press.

Management and Co-ordination Agency. 1985. *Organization of the Government of Japan*. Tokyo, Management and Co-ordination Agency.

Nakamura, T. 1983. *Economic growth in post-war Japan*. New Haven, Yale University Press.

———. 1986. *The post-war Japanese economy*. Tokyo, University of Tokyo Press.

Ohkawa, K., and L. Klein, eds. 1968. *Economic growth: The Japanese experience since the Meiji Era*. Homewood, Illinois, R. D. Irwin.

Patrick, H. T., and H. Rosovsky, eds. 1976. *Asia's new giant: How the Japanese economy works*. Washington, D. C., The Brookings Institution.

Shinohara, M. 1982. *Industrial growth, trade and dynamic patterns in the Japanese economy*. Tokyo, University of Tokyo Press.

Suzuki, Y. 1980. *Money and banking in contemporary Japan*. New Haven, Yale University Press.

Tsuji, K., ed. 1986. *Public administration in Japan*. Tokyo, University of Tokyo Press.

Vogel, E., ed. 1975. *Modern Japanese organization and decision-making*. Berkeley, University of California Press.

Voltho, A. 1975. *Japan: An economic survey 1953–1973*. London, Oxford University Press.

9

EXPERIENCES OF NATIONAL PLANNING IN HUNGARY

György Enyedi and György Ránki

Comprehensive Economic Planning

Origins of Planning in Hungary

Planning is so completely identified with the socialist transformation and with the establishment of the Soviet-led bloc of East European countries after World War II that one would hardly believe that some elements of planning actually appeared prior to the Second World War. Like most of the small Danubian countries, pre-war Hungary had a strong, autocratic, anti-Leftist government with a strong anti-Marxist ideology which was supported by the state, while simultaneously the idea of a free market economy was fading. The reason for this astonishing phenomenon might be found partly in the fact that the role of the state in the late-developing East European economies was traditionally more important than in Western Europe where, as early as the first half of the nineteenth century, the spontaneous forces of the economies were strong enough to lead to the process of self-sustained economic growth. Even more important, however, was the impact of the Great Depression of 1929–1933: because it almost ruined the weak Danubian states, serious questions were raised concerning the effectiveness of the free market system and the implementation of some kind of state intervention for maintaining economic equilibrium became inevitable. State interventions in the economy and planning had begun to lose the ideological stigma which connected them to socialism or communism.

The first ideas of government intervention (or planning) which emerged in Hungary were more concerned with overcoming the difficulties caused by the depression than with implementing a purposeful policy targeting economic growth. However, later, in 1938, due to strains in international relations, the Hungarian government felt it necessary to be prepared for war and a government programme in the form of a five-year plan was enacted. This programme concentrated mainly on rearmament and was actually a kind of investment programme designed to curb the economy through large government orders to rearm the Hungarian army. About 60 per cent of the investment was allocated for direct military purposes, while the remaining 40 per cent was allocated to indirect military investments — principally the development of transportation, telecommunications, and the like. This programme cannot be called a plan, however, since besides the state orders to industry and some financial steps taken to ensure monetary support for increased state orders, no direct government control or intervention was involved.

Later, government intervention was greatly extended. When World War II broke out, a government price commission was brought into being, a price freeze was put into effect, and any increase in prices required the permission of the government. Apart from government purchasing, the state also intervened in an effort to solve the more serious problems involving raw materials and energy supply. State direction appeared most obviously in the management of raw materials, where it was relatively easy to estimate reserves, needs, domestic production, and available imports and to regulate distribution on the basis of the estimates. A system of state allocations replaced the free market sale of essential raw materials. State intervention played a similar role in agriculture: distribution of existing stock through rationing, stimulation of production to meet wartime needs, regulation of the organization of production, and obligatory deliveries (at fixed prices) to the state. Through military orders, allocation of raw materials, and the control of consumption by rationing, for a number of goods the free market gave way to a system where production and distribution were directed by the state.

Intervention partly modified the money market as well. Bank credit was put under greater control; the banks were obliged to screen requests for loans closely in order to determine the borrowers' intended use. If the requests were found to be unjustifiable, they were to be rejected. Expansion of war production was directly financed by the state through large loans made to the largest companies whose work related to war production. The share of the state budget in the national income increased from 16 per cent in 1937–1938 to 33 per cent in 1938–1939, then to 40 per cent in 1941, and finally to 67 per cent in 1943.

State intervention contributed to a temporary increase in war production and in the first years of the Second World War, when Hungary was not yet directly involved, the economy was prospering and the balance between supply and demand was maintained. Later, however, there were serious shortages, inflation, wartime distortion of the economy, and capital depletion. Finally, in the last year of the war, after German troops occupied Hungary, the economy collapsed due to the increased Anglo-American bombardment, the systematic plundering by German troops, and the six months of fighting between the Germans and the Soviets on Hungarian territory in 1944 and 1945.

After the war, the country found itself in a desperate economic situation: 40 per cent of Hungary's national wealth had been destroyed, 24 per cent of the industrial capacity had been lost, a large part of the railway system and most bridges had been destroyed, and agriculture had suffered terribly. The task of reconstruction was made even more difficult by the fact that stocks of raw materials had perished, inflaion had reached unbelievable heights, and the country had to pay reparations for its participation in the war against the Soviet Union. In addition, goods were scarce and production was far below the prewar level. The newly established democratic government was obliged to maintain some form of the state intervention introduced during the war by the political system which had collapsed with Nazi Germany. Institutions such as the Office of Price and Raw Material Control actually did continue to function and new government organs were created. The state remained the major buyer of industrial goods. Now, however, the goods were being produced for reparation. Besides different control committees (connected mainly with raw material real overturn and the rationing of consumption goods in short supply), a Supreme Economic Council was established with power to control, interfere with, and even command the economy.

Due to inflation, a large part of the savings and other forms of capital disappeared. After stabilization was successfully carried out in 1946, a deflationary policy, which necessitated strong government control over credit, was introduced. A price and wage system was also established by the state. Consequently, in spite of the fact that the economy was still basically in the hands of private firms, it was closer to being a mixed economy than a market economy. At this stage, state property increased little beyond prior holdings. Legislation concerning the nationalization of the mines was in line with the economic policy followed by the Labour party in England. The ensuing nationalization of four major mining and electricity companies did extend the state sector, but it did not yet effect a change in the dominance of the private sector. The question was still unanswered as to whether this mixed economy would return to a liberal free enterprise system after reconstruction (as liberal political forces advocated) or whether systematic planning (as the Communist party advocated) would be introduced. The answer to this question was dependent on the balance of domestic and international political forces.

Nevertheless, since an acceleration in the recovering process was badly needed and since the idea of some kind of planning was alive everywhere in post-war Europe, an interim reconstruction plan for three years was accepted in 1947. In August, when the three-year plan was introduced, the private sector was still the dominant sector in the Hungarian economy. A part of the industrial sector (coal-mines, electric power stations, and the most important heavy-industry companies) had been nationalized but did not present a majority in the sector. In banking and in wholesale and retail trade, the share of state property was low. In agriculture, except for a few state farms, peasant plots were the prevailing form of land tenure (as a consequence of the 1945 Land Reform Act). Although a National Planning Office had been established, its task was to do no more than set some basic targets for the economy (in industrial and agricultural production and growth rates), to co-ordinate the most important efforts, and to influence directly or indirectly the most important investment decisions. The three-year plan represented a special combination of a mixed economy, in which a large but declining private sector was to work together with the growing state sector and in which the role of planning was combined with the broad elements of the market. Measuring the plan by its achievements, it can be called a success. Reconstruction was more or less successfully carried out. With a surprisingly high rate of industrial growth, and with state-controlled major investments, industrial production reached and surpassed the pre-war level by 1948. National income was around the pre-war level by 1949, and the income of the working class was slightly above the 1938 level. Agriculture was behind the pre-war level. It is difficult, however, to ascertain to what extent this was the consequence of the radical changes made in the land tenure system.

Establishment of a Socialist Planning System

The three-year plan was still in effect when decisive changes took place in the political structure of Hungary: transformation from a multiparty system to a one party system, from a mixed economy to a socialist economy, and from a combination of nationalized and private firms to complete nationalization. The Communist party started to fight for the extension of state property with the introduction of the three-year plan, and when Parliament accepted state control over the 10 largest banks, the financial system and the majority of industrial production went directly under state control.

The decisive turning point, however, came in 1948–1949. Due to a change in international circumstances, the Communist party, having achieved an absolute monopoly of power, turned from a strategy of gradual to one of immediate socialization. An important element in this strategy was the demand for the extension of state property. Since private ownership was regarded as harmful to economic growth and as an obstacle to economic transformation, an ambitious policy was established to liquidate private firms. In March 1948 all types of firms in private hands employing 100 persons or more were nationalized. This measure, covering 594 firms and 160,000 workers, enlarged the state sector of industry to more than 80 per cent of large-scale industry. Some key branches such as mining and metallurgy were entirely in the hands of the state: the engineering and construction industries were about 90 per cent in state hands, and the textile, paper, and food industries were around 50 per cent state owned.

Nevertheless, the nationalization process did not stop at that level. On 28

December 1949, a new decree was codified: all firms employing more than 10 workers (that is, a part of small-scale industry) were expropriated. In some cases, for example in the case of the printing industry and pharmaceuticals, every unit was nationalized. This represented not only the annihilation of the private sector in large-scale industry and banking but also a rigorous effort to eliminate private small-scale industry and private shop ownership as well. The realization of this aim, however, was carried out not by acts or decrees but by administrative pressure. One has to consider that small-scale industry played a very significant role in Hungary until the mid-twentieth century. This sector, which employed more than 40 per cent of all industrial workers, was responsible for one-quarter of the industrial output. Even in 1948 there were 180,000 artisans who employed 188,000 workers. Most of these shops, being very small, were not nationalized. Because of taxation, price controls, materials allocation, and sometimes just by bureaucratic harassment, however, the number of artisans declined to 120,000 and the number of their workers dropped to 29,000 (e.g. 19 per cent of the industrial labour force) by the end of 1950. The same trend was shown by the drop in the number of private shopkeepers in Budapest, from 20,000 to 1,300 between 1948 and 1952. The state sector completely dominated wholesale trade by 1949 and, to a great degree, the retail trade by 1952.

With the establishment of the one party system and the introduction of a new socialist constitution in August 1949, the political process of transformation had been completed: the state formally proclaimed its dictatorship of the proletariat and declared as its main aim the buildup of socialism in Hungary. In 1949, a new, five-year plan was launched. It was indicated that it would not be a plan for reconstruction nor would it be a plan for a mixed economy, where plans were merely orientation points, rather it would be a real "socialist" plan in which the whole process of economic development is included in and actually commanded by the plan. It was further asserted that in spite of different attempts and plans elsewhere, this type of plan, inclusive of all fields of economic, political, and institutional life, existed only in the Soviet Union. Therefore, the Soviet Union was to be regarded as the great example to be followed. It was all too obvious that the interpretation of the socialist plan was nothing more than the introduction of Soviet-type planning in Hungary.

What were the basic systemic features of the Soviet-type centrally-planned economy? First of all, state ownership of the means of production in every branch of the economy, but particularly in banking, industry, and trade. In agriculture, nationalized ownership of the means of production was not regarded as a pre-condition of central planning. Nevertheless, strong pressure was exerted by the state to abolish private farms and to turn them into producer's co-operative or state-owned farms. The state-owned farms were supposed to operate under the same principles as the state industrial enterprises; collective farms were strongly controlled by state regulations. Private farms were to be pushed by different types of pressure (from large taxation to high compulsory deliveries and to permanent harassment) to join the collective farms. Actually, with the exception of small household plots, the plan previewed the abolishment of all private property in agriculture.

The second most important feature of Soviet-type planning was the hierarchical economic organization, where all decision-making was concentrated at the very top. Plan targets were transmitted through administrative channels to the executors by administrative directives. This meant that decision-making was hierarchical, with the scope of decision-making possibilities automatically declining on lower levels. The major targets of economic development were made by the supreme organ of the ruling Communist party (which is actually the supreme authority in planning, and it controls all official government bodies, including the Planning Office, which was ostensibly in command of the economy).

Since it was to encompass all the economic activities of the country, a principal role was given to the national plan elaborated by the Planning Office. The plan would include the means and procedures for its fulfilment, a production plan for industry, some general regulations, and a long-range plan in addition to the current plan. Since uniformity seemed very important, targets were stated in physical units whenever possible. Although the same language might have facilitated the execution of the "orders" for the lower units and might have made it easier for local or sectoral planning agencies to disaggregate the plan targets, it was not possible to do so since, for a number of goods, physical indicators could not be applied. Therefore, some targets were stated in value terms. The plan, in the form of an order from the central authority, determined the quantity and the quality of goods to be produced as well as the means of production.

Three types of means were considered: total investments, raw materials and equipment, and manpower resources. All three were rationed: total investment by central allocation of investment funds, construction materials (and the like), raw materials, and machinery by administrative orders, and manpower resources by control of the scope of employment and wage expenditures. Resource allocation was carried out by direct command from the Planning Office. First material balances were drawn for production, allocation, and consumption; then the supply plan was formulated, indicating the allocation of raw materials, semi-manufactured products, and manufactured products among users. The balances and distribution plans were usually elaborated on an annual basis. Some, however, were for quarters as well. The number of balances was constantly increasing since this was regarded as proof of the improvement of the planning methods.

Foreign trade was regarded as a state monopoly to be executed by a number of firms, called foreign trade enterprises. These firms were in some ways intermediaries, since production enterprises had no direct contact with foreign markets. A special plan for foreign trade was usually prepared, and the implementation of this plan was strictly controlled by a strong foreign exchange control and other means.

Personal compensation was regulated by fixed wage scales — differences in reward for different skills were usually low — and was related to the fulfilment of the plan directives. Plan directives included a total wage fund at the company level. Special bonuses were given to managers upon fulfilling or surpassing the quantitative indices of the plan. Farm income, whether collective or individual, was controlled by the extremely low prices set up for compulsory deliveries and by taxation.

The price system was the weakest point in the planning. Prices were administrated and fixed by the Planning Office, and fixed prices were, in the long run, regarded as a basic element of a socialist economy (in direct contradistinction to a capitalist economy, where prices are determined by market forces). Administered prices had nothing to do with market forces but were fixed on a branchwide cost basis. Enterprises — usually in production goods industries where prices were kept extremely low — unable to produce at the given fixed price level were subsidized, and special prices were established for the consumers.

In sum, everything seemed to be forecasted, regulated, and co-ordinated with the explicit aim of minimizing the "element of chance" in economic life. Finally, trade, money, and the market were, whenever possible, forced out of the economic arena.

The application of a Soviet model of economic planning in Hungary was not entirely a free choice. The Soviet model was presented as necessary. This was partly because it was regarded as the only working planned economy having substantial success in overcoming the actual backwardness of Russia and partly because any deviation from the Soviet model was regarded as heretical.

The process of setting up the proper institutional framework for the adoption of the Soviet planning system started in the second half of 1948. When more than 80 per cent of large-scale industry became state property, the need for radical reorganization became obvious.

According to the Soviet model, the national enterprises operated as independent entities but were closely integrated with the state organization of industry. This was headed by the Ministry of Industry (reorganized in the first half of 1948), which also had operative directorial functions. Obviously it could not deal with 750 enterprises directly; consequently, in May, the network of industrial directorates was organized. The 29 directorates were partly administrative organs, but they also exercised direct control (prepared detailed plans, checked submitted plans, co-ordinated co-operative ventures, set prices, and allocated raw materials). To eliminate the somewhat contradictory nature of these functions, and to further narrow the organizational framework, enterprises with similar production processes were concentrated into horizontally organized industrial centres. This made possible the division of the administrative and direct-supervisory functions. The direct control of production, material procurement, and marketing were passed on to the industrial centres. The industrial directorates gradually became departments of the responsible ministries.

It was also recognized that the financial and credit structure should be reshaped after the state took over the 10 largest banks. These 10 banks controlled the vast majority of the financial means, deposits, and accounts. Under the new banking system, the Hungarian National Bank was given a monopoly on short-term lending in addition to its former monopoly on the issuance of bank notes. The so-called single-account system provided for all enterprise payments and receipts to go through the National Bank.

Alongside the central bank, a network of special banks was established: a bank for financing government investment (Investment Bank), a bank for dealing with foreign trade (Foreign Trade Bank), and a savings institute to deal with citizen deposits and various smaller loans. The savings institute had a large network of provincial branches. The unified direction of the transformed banking system fell to the reorganized Ministry of Finance.

Besides the supervision by the Ministry of Industry (asserted through the industrial directorates) and of the Ministry of Finance (asserted through the banking system), a very important role in industrial control was given to the National Planning Office. The newly established institution of control was well suited to the needs of a strong, comprehensively planned economy.

Upon completion of the reorganization, a five-year plan, which was not elaborated in the way that the former three-year plan had been, was implemented. Production was expedited according to detailed plans worked out for every year and every company. These plans were based on an extraordinarily great number of indicators and were considered to correspond maximally and precisely to economic laws and to the economy's best interests.

The plans prescribed precisely how much the companies were allowed for investment and spending; the amount they could use of goods, raw materials, energy, and manpower; and what they were to produce — variety, quality, quantity, and cost price being strictly defined. On the basis of these production plans, and using a system of material balance sheets, the Council of Ministers and the National Planning Office prepared the material plans. It was these plans which were used by the departments of material control in the relevant ministries and, after 1951, by branches of the Planning Office to order the yearly and quarterly distribution of materials.

The chains of directives regulating production, material supply, investment, etc., were attempts to insure that the plans would be carried out to the letter. To this end, the plans (approved by the Council of Ministers and Parliament) were broken down by years and even quarters, as well as by ministries, directorates, and enterprises. Each directive, then, became a strict, personally-addressed order. With the industrial directorates setting the quarterly production quotas and with the central agencies — the ministries included — managing the enterprises (especially in respect to their raw-material supplies), the enterprises were, for the most part, left with but a formal independence.

A special function was given to this system of command economy: it was to ignore the market forces as much as possible and to acquiesce to the control, particularly in the price system, of certain authorities as much as possible. In the beginning of the plan, the price system was still in a kind of transitory period. This period ended with the price reform of 1951, when the Soviet model was strictly applied. The basic principle of the price reform was that the cost price of the goods produced by the state sector had to be covered by the sale price of the consumer products. The means of production, however, were to be sold at cost price. The cost price, therefore, bore no fixed relation to the sale price, and a great many of the primary industrial materials were sold below cost, with substantial state subsidies. Although this was intended to be a form of encouragement for the development of raw-material-oriented heavy industry, it proved to be an aggravation.

The situation was further aggravated by the great difference between the market price and the price the producer was paid when he delivered agricultural goods to the state. The state intended to use some of the income generated in the agricultural sector from this discrepancy to increase its capital accumulation. Producers' prices in the state sector, on the other hand, were considered as more of a technical means of balancing the books. The prices of basic materials were thus kept down without regard for the growing cost price. Prices reflected real value relations less and less.

The problems resulting from this trend were compounded by foreign trade prices. The prices of export goods bore no relation to real production costs or to the domestic price level. The prices were determined, first of all, by the foreign price level and secondly by the competitiveness of these goods on the world market. The producing company, however, sold the products at the domestic producers' price to the foreign trade company, where the often significant difference between the domestic and the world market selling prices was bridged by the state's price-levelling fund. There was a marked difference between the official rate of foreign exchange and the exchange rate used in foreign trade transactions — the latter being often four to five times higher. Similarly, the government sold imported goods and materials to companies not at cost price but at the domestic producers' price. The price was usually much lower, for the same kind of product, than the import price.

During the Korean War, there was a change-over to fixed prices in CMEA (Council of Mutual Economic Assistance) foreign trade in order to eliminate the unfavourable effects of the price fluctuation on the world market caused by the war boom. Subsequently, the rigid price system of the CMEA market became totally independent of the world market price levels and price ratios. This simplified economic planning, since it removed the spontaneous effects of price fluctuations. As a result, however, the price system did nothing to stimulate economic activity and efficiency because the organic relationship between input and output had been totally destroyed.

The price mechanism thus had real price functions in only one very limited sphere of the domestic market — consumer goods. Even here, however, the pricing system affected only demand, not supply. The confinement of market effects to such a narrow area made the companies practically independent of responsibility; marketability, cost, quality, or the technological standard of their goods played no part in the companies' standing.

The companies' interest in fulfilling central directives was reinforced by the system of bonuses and wages. Since it was impossible for a company to follow the comprehensive system perfectly, they concentrated their resources on fulfilling those plan indicators which were the most important — the most rewarding — to them. The framers of economic policy, however, tried to insure that this coincided with the most dynamic production growth possible. Of the 200 central bonus regulations issued between 1950 and 1955, the fundamental one issued on 1 November 1952 motivated companies to achieve targets — in both quantity and quality — by making the fulfilment, and even overfulfilment, of the production plan the primary bonus criterion. The system of central planning worked out in the late 1940s and early 1950s was adequate for a maximal rate of development (one strongly concentrated on primary production) because it was essentially the strategy of a war economy.

It soon became clear that the system of central planning — by separating the companies' activities from the effects of price and the market and by materially motivating them to achieve quantitative growth — was encouraging the development of a special kind of hierarchy in which all objectives became subordinate to fulfilling and overfulfilling the plan. Prescriptions for the increase of efficiency, for improvement of quality, for material savings, reducting of costs, etc., became less necessary. Central planning thus led to the partial and somewhat contradictory realization of the economy's objectives. It might be noted that in a number of fundamental respects, planning led to consequences quite contrary to the original intentions.

One might argue that the strong centralization and command system was not simply a copy of the Soviet model but was rather the endogenous demand for reorganization of the economy. First, since one of the basic weaknesses of the capitalist model (based mainly on the experience of the depression of 1929–1933) was the lack of a macro-economic approach, the anarchy of individual and conflicting interests, it was obvious that a macro-economic approach was needed and that it could not be applied only from above. Although production reached the pre-war level, it was open to question whether the demand for production growth could be met by the relative short supply without a strict command system. Arguments were brought up for central control in clear reference to the fact that most of the former managers (proprietors) were dismissed as a result of nationalization and that former skilled workers, technicians, or intellectuals, with at best limited managerial experience, took over the positions. The state hastened to augment their education. Further, in a kind of cultural revolution, the state started to train working-class people for higher jobs. Nevertheless, for the time being, the major policy was to carry out orders well, and bureaucrats were needed more than innovators. Last but by no means least, the economic policy adopted in the 1950s seemed in fact to demand strong centralization. Rapid industrialization and the unprecedented growth rate could not have been achieved without a strong command system and the concentration of forces to carry out the most important tasks.

Planning was not only the system of the economy but the economic policy as well. The essence of Soviet economic policy lay in a strategy of forced industrialization to overcome the underdeveloped status of the country. For this reason, a relatively high share of the GNP was allocated to investment, and the majority of this investment went to the traditional heavy industry sectors such as mining and metallurgy. Other branches of industry, such as agriculture and the infrastructure, for example, were neglected. To achieve these high growth rates, a vast amount of underemployed labour was transferred from agriculture to industry. We may characterize this type of industrialization as import-substitutional industrialization. Import-substitutional industrialization was present in the East European economies long before the socialist transformation, but planning and government orders instead of the market made it more effective.

The industralization process had one more benefit: the enormous demand for labour, which changed the entire social composition of the population, assured a high employment rate. Income distribution followed egalitarian concepts. However, this may have been more of an obstacle than an accomplishment of the planned economy, since it encouraged a lack of individual incentives for higher productivity.

Functioning of "Classical" Centralized Planning (1947–1957)

The first five-year plan focused on the forced industrialization of Hungary during one planning period. It aimed primarily to accelerate economic growth by increasing the amount of investment and capital accumulation. Before its official acceptance, the plan was modified three times. In each instance the amount designated for investment increased considerably.

During the plan period, one more drastic revision occurred when the growth target of the national income was increased from 63 to 130 per cent and that of industrial output from 86 to 210 per cent. That is, instead of a 13 per cent annual industrial growth rate, the new version envisioned a yearly industrial growth of 26 per cent.

More than half of the total investment was to go to industry, and 90 per cent of industrial investment was to be channelled into heavy industry. Two-thirds of the total heavy industry investment went for the development of mining and metallurgy. The index of metallurgical investment reflects the extraordinary dynamism of the investment policy in these branches: with 1950 equal to 100, the investment index in 1951 was already 264, in 1952 it was 463, and in 1953 it was 498.

In addition to the special preference given to the production of strategic materials, great efforts geared to achieve economic self-sufficiency were made. Instead of building up a multinational economic collaboration with neighbouring countries, industrialization was based on the importation of Soviet raw materials and on the building-up of a comprehensive processing industry able to produce practically everything. This trend was partly forced upon Hungary by the fact that the cold war had all but abolished the traditional economic ties with Central and Western European countries.

Clearly, the economic strategy had a two-pronged emphasis: (1) an increase in the production of basic materials and (2) the achievement of economic self-sufficiency.

This type of economic policy, however, further reinforced the inherent deficiencies of Soviet type planning, so well characterized by Maurice Dobb:

Problems of economic planning seem to acquire a resemblance to the problems of military strategy, where in practice the choice lies between a relatively small number of plans, which have in the main been treated and chosen between as organic wholes, and which for a variety of reasons do not easily permit intermediate combinations. The situation will demand a concentration of forces around a few main objectives and not a dispersion of resources over a very wide range.[1]

The centralized disposal of economic resources combined with public ownership of the major factories and central planning overcame the vicious circle of poverty. This breakthrough was possible on the supply side by collecting all surplus and investing it for selected purposes and by reducing the investment going into consumption or less-preferred productive sectors; the breakthrough on the demand side came through the orders of the state. However, while some sectors were selected for growth, others were neglected because they allegedly did not contribute directly to further growth. The differences in growth rates caused shortages and strains, and overcoming these bottlenecks became the new target. This required the alteration of some principal goals in order to achieve greater dispersion. However, the strict system of hierarchical planning and the given economic policy made alterations increasingly difficult.

Among the many bottlenecks, contradictions, and disadvantages produced by the centrally planned economy and the high-investment, high-growth economic policy, one may cite the following:
— Decline of capital-output ratio
— Huge stock of unsaleable goods due to global fulfilment of the plan (1952–1954 stock growth was 73 per cent, production 13 per cent)

— Low productivity and technological level
— Poor quality, little variety
— Enormous bureaucracy for control
— Waste of materials, increased foreign trade dependency of a resource-poor
    economy (energy, raw materials, machinery, spare parts)
— The existence of underemployment or disguised unemployment
— High investment rates, low living standard
— Shortages and a low level of international division of labour

Let us elaborate on a few of these issues. One of the most common practices was the "global fulfilment" of plan targets. For factories where targets were given in value terms, it became a custom to use great quantities of expensive materials to increase production value. Thus, while in 1949 100 forints of materials consumed yielded 100 forints of value added, in 1954 it produced only 71.

Some companies often "fulfilled" the plan by producing huge stocks of unsaleable goods. Paradoxically, "overfulfilment" of the overall production plan led to an anarchy of production because companies produced, not the goods specified, but needless stocks of easily manufactured, material-intensive goods. They overfulfilled the plans for heavy casts, but neglected the manufacture of light ones. Thus the companies accumulated great stocks of unsaleable goods — goods entailing a great deal of material and labour.

Between the last quarter of 1952 and the last quarter of 1954, the stocks of finished goods grew by 72 per cent, while industrial production growth trailed behind at 12.7 per cent.

The introduction of planning based on the nationalization of the large factories might have removed a number of obstacles since — theoretically — company secrets ought to have been replaced by the utilization of effective and productive methods. However, when the existing monopolies and oligopolies were abolished, new monopolies were created. Monopolizing the domestic market and enjoying protection from risks, the companies lost interest in technological modernization. New stimulus was given to meet the requirements of technological development. Sometimes, however, the contrary occurred: the race to increase production and fulfil the plan discouraged technological development; it was much easier to stick to traditional goods to achieve maximal results in quantity.

This led to a decline in the quantity and variety of goods in the market. Large-scale production of consumer goods was easier, and therefore only 16 kinds of men's shoes were, for example, produced as opposed to the 90 kinds which had been produced before. The prevailing idea was that planning would provoke national unrest if it conflicted with individual (company) interest. However, since this proved not to be the case, the planners, in order to make sure that their instructions would be carried out, increased administrative regulations. For example, early on, ten-day production reports were collected and numerous regulations were issued. In the first half of 1951 every mine received

1,025 ministerial regulations and orders. All this resulted in an increase of bureaucracy and contributed to the shift in the blue-collar-to-white-collar worker rate. Since administrative regulations were often ineffective, legal measures were increasingly taken to ensure the necessary plan discipline. Nevertheless, the economy did not work as had been expected; maximum waste of materials and labour was generated in the fulfilment or overfulfilment of plan targets.

The overcentralized system of planning was fraught with grave contradictions. In the short run, it may well have been inaccurate to attribute to the primary central goal what was, in fact, achieved by the strained rate of economic development which the system of planning had indeed promoted for a certain length of time. In the long run, however, this system was inadequate to serve the central goals of development, as the contradictions that arose shot holes in the system — holes through which increasing amounts of the GNP disappeared in the process of reproduction. The gravest of these "holes" — one that can be traced statistically — was the growth of unsaleable stocks and of incompleted investments. There can be no doubt that between 1949 and 1953 a significant part of Hungary's national income flowed away through these channels. With the national income computed at constant prices, we find that uncompleted investments and accumulated stocks absorbed about one-fifth of the growth of national income. Although this can be taken only as a rough estimate — intensive investment activity being necessarily associated with increasing stocks of unfinished investments — it definitely points to the consequences in the 1950s of the economic policy and system of central planning — consequences which were to become obstacles to further progress.

In agriculture, since socialist ownership was still far from being prevalent, the government pushed hard to set up collectivization by pressuring individual peasant farmers to join the co-operative farms. By the end of 1949, only 1,300 co-operatives, with a relatively insignificant number of members, were established. However, these co-operatives had been founded on a voluntary basis. After 1950, the government used constant harassment combined with ruthlessness to oblige the peasants to join the co-operatives. The above efforts were joined by high taxation, low prices, elimination of private markets, and the substitution of a compulsory delivery system. Agricultural production declined and its level remained, even during the early 1950s, below the pre-war level. Because of the harassment, a large number of peasants became disenchanted, abandoned large quantities of arable land, and left the villages.

The number of co-operatives increased — by the middle of 1953 they included more than 300,000 peasant families and about a quarter of all arable land — but they were not successful. Because economic policy dictated that all resources be channelled into industry, the co-operatives were deficient in machines and fertilizers. In addition, they were unable to lure other peasants to join them because production and income were at a very low level. The economic policy deliberately exploited agriculture in favour of heavy industry.

Political changes brought about by the death of Stalin in 1953 served to ease the pressure and tension prevailing in the country as a result of the decline in the living standard, shortages, and decay in the agricultural sector. By a party decision, the impossible targets of industrialization were made public. Further, because the party criticized the existing economic policy, the former party leader Mátyás Rákosi was replaced by Imre Nagy as prime minister. In 1953, an increasing amount of comprehensive criticism was accepted with the aim to ease tension and to modify the course taken.

The first programme strongly criticized was forced one-sided industrialization. More moderate growth coupled with considerable structural changes was advocated. The importance of agriculture, food processing, and consumer goods industries was stressed. With the moderation of investment, proportions between accumulation and consumption shifted and an actual rise in the standard of living seemed feasible. Forced collectivization was abandoned and withdrawal from the collective farm system was allowed. As a consequence, the membership and area of collective farms dropped by 40 per cent.

The road to reform, however, was not an easy one. Ideological premises and myth, as well as vested interests, were still very strong. Rákosi remained the head of the party and attempted to minimize the error in the course taken by blocking every effort to carry out radical corrections. Actual proposals for reforms were far from radical; all criticism concentrated on economic policy. The system of central planning was not called into question and therefore remained unchanged. Even when criticism was directed at economic policy, it was conceded that forced industrialization could be useful but that, due to the poor resource endowment in Hungary, its attempted application was an error. Serious ideological and political battles concerning policy ended, after a year and a half, with the defeat and removal of Imre Nagy.

In 1954 Rákosi drastically decreased the modification efforts and started to use ideological arguments as grounds for carrying out former economic policy (with slight cosmetic changes). If only less than radical changes were allowed in the economic policy, changes in planning, which had not been criticized, were of even less significance. Measures such as the proposed reduction of administrative staff proved to be temporary. In the end, administrative measures and other phenomena which were inherent in the economic mechanism remained basically unchanged.

Nevertheless, some far-reaching criticism began to appear in the economic literature. Numerous proposals were made to reduce overcentralization, to pay greater attention to costs, prices, and profitability, and to establish a balance between supply and demand. The idea that nothing short of economic policy correction would be sufficient to solve Hungary's problems was first published in the summer of 1956. "A consistent and radical reform is needed" was the message.

This reform was supposed to combine the planned economy with a market economy. However, even the reformers in the government thought that the given planning system was adequate and that certain modifications (e.g. limiting directives, giving more independence to firms, and introducing slight reform in the price system) would be sufficient.

The difficulties in the economy and the slow improvement due to the delay in the implementation of reform contributed considerably to the political crisis developing in the country which culminated in the tragic events of October 1956.

Transition from Central Planning to Substantial Reforms

The new Kádár government, imposed by the Soviet Union after crushing the 1956 revolt, tried to ease its unpopularity by giving serious consideration to far-reaching economic reforms. A committee of experts was appointed to elaborate on the principle of the new economic and planning policy. They produced a radical proposal for a comprehensive reform which aimed at replacing compulsory plan directives with a controlled market mechanism which would introduce real prices and profit motivation. Alongside these radical proposals, the blueprint retained centralized investments, financed entirely by the state budget.

Concurrently, however, conservative political groups (supported from outside) initiated a strong ideological offensive, branding any modification of the planning system as non-socialist. As a result, the road to reform was blocked and the plan rejected.

Although no radical changes took place, some corrections in economic policy were accepted (mainly along the lines advocated by the deposed Imre Nagy government). The most important and the most far-reaching correction was in agricultural policy. First of all, to regain the political support of the peasantry, the government cancelled the collectivization policy. When two-thirds of the members of the collective farms left, the government made a strong pledge not to use political harassment to coerce them. At the same time, a decision was made to abolish the compulsory agricultural delivery system and the centrally determined compulsory sowing plans. With this, the basic pillars of the command economy in agriculture were destroyed. Nothing remained between the peasantry and state but the market connection.

The state organs delivered the agricultural products and paid market prices when they wanted to make a purchase. (When delivery was compulsory, it was possible to pay artificially low prices because the peasants had no choice but to deliver the goods.) Instead of compulsory sowing plans, the state used economic means, primarily price incentives and tax differentiation, to encourage production and to influence structural changes. Earlier planning directives were replaced by contracts signed by both farmers and state trade company representatives.

In one sector of the Hungarian economy, then, a controlled, planned market economy was introduced. This was a pioneering step towards a new economic model.

(It may be interesting to note that we were witnessing a similar phenomenon in the People's Republic of China, where economic reform — for example, "the responsibility system" — was introduced first in the agricultural sector.)

The abandonment of collectivization did not fare so well. In 1957 a new agrarian policy was shaped to achieve dynamic growth in production that was to be accompanied by a gradual but deliberate merger with the collective farms. However, the collective farms did not necessarily have to be built upon the Soviet model. In addition, different forms of co-operatives were allowed. The co-operatives were to obtain considerable support from the state to enable them to reach full mechanization and higher yields and income. The price structure changed and low agricultural prices no longer served as a price disparity for supporting quick industrialization by absorbing surplus from agriculture.

This strategy was soon abandoned, however, and a new drive for collectivization commenced in the beginning of 1959. Its method was remarkably different from the previous drive. No police force or direct economic coercion was used, no punishment was administered against those who did not join, and even well-to-do peasants were allowed to join the co-operative. The whole drive for collectivization, instead of requiring decades, was completed in two years. In February 1961, 95 per cent of the arable land belonged to co-operatives or state farms.

This radical change in strategy was closely connected with a comprehensive policy change in the East European socialist countries towards the establishment of a more ambitious industrialization programme and the completion of collectivization. Some of these countries, following the Chinese example, declared the programme a "great leap forward," and a drive to catch up the most developed capitalist countries in 15–20 years was advertised.

Even though the revised agricultural policy returned to the traditional collectivization pattern, the emerging collective farms represented a new model, comparable to the kolkhoz-type in many respects. The government, having learned the lessons of the early 1950s, did not want to paralyze private farming by forcing the peasants to join co-operatives. On the contrary, a tremendous effort was made to establish the material basis for co-operatives and to allow flexibility. However, unlike the kolkhoz-type collective farms, a new income system was introduced, several forms of crop-sharing were used inside the co-operatives, and about 40 per cent of the animal stock remained in private hands on the private plots (one hectare) which were allotted to each member of the collective farms. The peasants were given the right to elect the director of the co-operatives, and, as a result, they were basically chosen from among experienced farmers, even from the most well-to-do elements — kulaks — who were formerly purged. Indeed, they became key personalities in the new co-operatives. The foundation for a modern agricultural enterprise was also helped

by allowing additional industrial activities (i.e. establishment of food processing, building, and machine-repair shops) inside the co-operatives.

All these served the unchanged aim of the so-called dual target, that is, to
achieve dynamic agricultural growth and collectivization simultaneously. As a
result, for the first time in the history of the collectivization of agriculture, the
number of livestock did not decline. Between 1959 and 1961 gross agricultural
production increased by nearly 10 per cent (although net production declined
by about 10 per cent).

The rejection of the plan for comprehensive reform in 1957 did not mean that
the idea of enacting smaller modifications was given up as well. The prevailing
concept of the Communist party was that, if after abolishing compulsory delivery economic policy were radically modified, there would be, in addition to
minor alterations, a necessity for comprehensive changes in the planning
system.

Some reform measures were implemented even during these years, but they
were rather contradictory and remained basically inefficient. Among those reforms, the price reform aiming to base prices on real values was the most promising. However, since prices remained fixed and factory and consumer prices
remained unrelated to changing market conditions and expenses, the system
became artificial again and had only short-term consequences.

Criticism was still focused on economic policy, with no recognition of the
problem of the economic mechanism as such. Criticism called attention to the
fact that in shaping economic policy Hungarian national circumstances (poor
resource endowment) were completely neglected; rapid industrialization, overcentralization, and all other economic problems were merely regarded as consequences of bad planning.

Some of the economic policy targets were changed after 1953, but the system
of central planning basically remained the same. The system of planning concealed real value and price relations behind an artificial price system which
made the realistic evaluation of the economy impossible and encouraged quantitative production growth independently of costs.

After 1956, the idea of combining a planned economy with a market economy
was raised, but the government, under the given political circumstances, decided on half-measures instead of radical reform.

From 1957 on, many important steps were taken to avoid former mistakes.
First of all, the system of compulsory agricultural delivery was replaced by a
"buying-up" system; while in industry the new profit-sharing system improved
on the system of incentives. The system of controls was modified through the
significant reduction of directives and plan indicators, the introduction of qualitative indicators, the establishment of a community development fund, and
through the introduction of a bonus system.

Much was expected from the changes in the economic policy which had been
the focus of the government programme. Substantial wage increases were intro-

duced, and, by the implementation of a policy of gradual, moderate improvement, real income grew by more than 50 per cent between 1958 and 1968. Obviously this policy could not have been carried out if the former, overly ambitious accumulation and investment plan had not been dropped. The policy of forced industrialization lost impetus, and the share of accumulation in the GNP decreased from 35 per cent to around 20 per cent. It was realized that industry must be restructured according to domestic circumstances and autarchic industrialization had to be discontinued. Instead of the high-energy and raw-material consuming branches, the electro-technical, chemical, and consumption-goods industries were stressed. High priority was given to modern technological advancements and qualitative competitiveness. Not only was the share of industry in the investment programme decreased and more support given to agriculture and infrastructural investment but the very structure of industrial investment was changed considerably.

Even with all these good intentions, some contradictions were difficult to overcome. All industrialization required an increase of energy and raw-material consumption. Since no proper division of labour had been established among the socialist countries, the planners were obliged, although with greater moderation, to continue the traditional support of iron and steel. Even though greater moderation was exercised, almost half of all investments were absorbed. The drive for modernization of the industrial structure, with a significant chemical industry programme based on Soviet oil and natural-gas deliveries, proved to be very expensive; it created new imbalances between industries and processing branches. In sum, despite a change in aims and actual effects, no radical changes took place in the industrial structure, and the modernization of the processing industry was further delayed. It became increasingly clear that the government intention to successfully carry out a different economic policy failed to reconcile the diametrically opposed interests of the firms, due to the lack of market incentives and real value categories.

Nevertheless, the early 1960s cannot be regarded as a failure because (besides the improvement of the living stardard) even these rather partial and inconsistent alterations represented a modification of the previously adopted forced-industrialization strategy and planning concepts of Stalin. Even if the essence of the model remained untouched in several fields, the agricultural reform set a precedent: the possibility of combining planning and the market. Even the minor, partial reforms were more important than their immediate impact; they proved that the possibility of change existed, and they represented a more pragmatic attitude toward an acceptance of reality. Now that the door was open to practical corrections and revisions, further reforms followed. An analytical, critical approach was initiated (although the apologetic approach still existed and periodically confronted the new efforts of change).

The mid-1960s, in a sense, became a turning point. There were no dramatic events or tragic shocks as in the previous decade. Circumstances, however, changed crucially. The unlimited labour sources, which had created an easy way to extend industrialization, were soon to be exhausted. The level of per capita GNP approached the pre-war Western European level, and the country was on the verge of the historical transformation from an agrarian to an industrial structure; it would be impossible to turn back.

Particular tension appeared in the field of foreign trade. Due to the failure to restructure and modernize, Hungarian exports were unable to match increasing import needs, and a large trade deficit began to appear. Phenomena thought to be of the past reappeared. Factories were again producing unsaleable, low-quality products, and stocks accumulated at a high rate, absorbing a part of the national income. Another large burden was placed on the economy by the unfinished investment programme resulting from the lack of material incentives and from the lack of a sense of responsibility regarding the investments since they were provided to the firms by the state free of charge.

In the middle of the 1960s, it became clear that a transition in economic policy from import substitution to export orientation could be achieved only if a real improvement could be realized in the directing system. In the middle of the 1960s, the need for reform was in the air in all the socialist countries. Even in the Soviet Union some debate arose in this direction. A new major reform was instituted in Yugoslavia, reform preparations were begun in Czechoslovakia, and Polish economists also came up with proposals for far-reaching reforms. At the end of 1964, the decision to prepare a comprehensive reform plan was accepted by the leading authorities in Hungary. By the end of the next year, the Central Committee of the Hungarian Socialist Workers party accepted in concept the reform which was actually implemented in January 1968.

The "New Economic Mechanism"

The economic reform, or the "New Economic Mechanism" as it was called, did not abandon central planning but reduced its sphere of influence and changed its methods. Compulsory plan directives were replaced by market relations and market prices. The central plan was largely limited to decisions on the government macro-economic level. On the level of firms in the micro-economy, instead of compulsory orders indirect economic regulations were introduced to influence economic activity. Sectoral planning was totally abandoned.

Medium-term and annual macro-economic plans continued to be prepared by planning authorities; plan targets became primarily indicative binding on ministries but were no longer used as the basis for commodity allocation or incentives. The annual plans still prescribed some economic regulators, for example, credit policy, price system, and state investment. In central planning, however, the emphasis was to shift towards the use of the five-year plans as guides for enterprise and for long-term state investment policy. Resource allocations were altered by inter-enterprise contacts.

Planning, through public authorities, maintained decision-making power over infrastructural and social investments, and over industrial investment that increased capacity by over 25 per cent, necessitated substantial imports, or involved the establishment of new factories. Nevertheless, a substantial part of the remaining administrative authority over enterprises was taken from the Planning Office and branch ministries and redistributed among the banks, the Materials and Price Office, and the functional ministries (finance, labour, foreign trade). The branch ministries were to continue to exercise "ownership" rights (primarily through managerial appointments) as well as to prepare sectoral development plans. But the intervention of the branch ministries in enterprise decision-making was to cease.

Since it had been formulated that the essential task of a national economic plan was to provide efficacious impetus to economic development, and since wide paths for unfolding initiatives had been found more productive in accomplishing this end, the decision that the role and the function of the plan had to be changed was accepted. Whereas the old plan had been regarded as a command, the new plan was viewed as and was starting to function as a basis of control and perspective.

Less minutely detailed than the prior plans, it concentrated on major objectives such as the rate of growth and the main structural proportions of the national economy.

Automatically, the former basis (one-year plan) had lost its importance, and the function of long-range planning increased, like the five-year plan, as a decisive tool of control and, like the 15–20 year plans, for setting objectives.

The system of planned control included "planning on the preparatory process representing a preliminary to the complex economic decisions and an instrument serving to specify the ways and means of their realization; secondly, the regulations based on the national plan, which determined their economic contexts, and consisted of direct and indirect measuring influencing economy; thirdly, the system of economic organization" (István Hetényi, then deputy president of the National Planning Office). According to this basic interpretation, important differences were to be made between purpose and controls of the long-term plan, the five-year plan, and the annual plan.

The long-term plan was supposed to deal with the following:
— General growth rate and the structural changes of the economy
— Concepts concerning international economic relations
— Growth rate of basic branches of the economy
— Regional development
— Proportion between investment and consumption

The five-year plan was supposed to be elaborated by looking at the same issues in a more concrete form, by describing and quantitatively determining the main development targets stated above, and by designing the ways and means to realize the objectives. The annual plan was the yearly implementation of the objectives of the long-term or the five-year plan, adjusted to meet new circumstances. Measures of particular importance were those concerning the balance of revenue and expenditure in the state budget, the adaptation of the credit policy, and wages and price policy. The leading role of the National Planning Office was maintained, although its influence was greatly diminished. Its responsibility was comprised of the conceptualization of economic policy, the establishment of proportions, and the co-ordination of the major means of its implementation. (Needless to say, the methods applied to the analysis of the economy no longer resembled the methods used in the 1950s.) The activities and the influence of the various branch ministries were not abolished, but their role in planning was designed more or less by stressing the following functions:

1. Elaborate upon conceptions of technological and economic development for certain spheres of economic activity
2. Work out concrete proposals on every aspect of the development (technological economic parameters) inputs needed (correlation with other branches), effect on economic growth in international balance of payments and balance of trade
3. Design large individual investment proposals
4. Finally, the functional ministries and the banks were supposed to review and co-ordinate the cross-sectoral economic activities of the economies by proposing the necessary economic regulations and adjusting the proper control system

As can been seen, in spite of the decreasing role of central planning, and in spite of the attempt to include much wider elements of the market economy in the processes of economic development, the leading role of the plan was preserved in the economy of Hungary even after the reform of 1968.

The implementation of the plan was aided by a system of regulations which contained a large number of elements, such as a new price system, a new form of taxation and subsidies, a modified wage policy, and even some specifications for investment policy on the company level. Certainly the new price system was the most important of these regulations. Artificial prices, characteristic as they were in traditional planning, were replaced by a new system that more accurately reflected costs and market fluctuations.

Prices in the new system became transmitters between producers and consumers and, in effect, reoriented firms toward creating incentives and interests. There were, however, controlled and planned markets and prices. The reform did not aim at linking domestic prices directly with world market prices. The debates which preceded the implementation of the reform warned of the danger of inflation and of the devastating effects of the transition from a hermetically sealed market to a more open economy. The government wanted to avoid these side-effects. Built-in safeguards, where price spheres were distinguished, assured a more gradual transition.

Price spheres were as follows: (1) centrally fixed prices (for fuel, raw materials, basic agricultural and food products); (2) prices which could change within centrally regulated limits (certain materials and some mass consumption goods); and (3) free prices (machines, semi-finished products, consumer goods). In the beginning, 70 per cent of factory prices were either fixed or maximized prices, but within five years this sphere diminished to 35 per cent, while free prices increased to 65 per cent. Some 50 per cent of consumer prices at the time of the reform were fixed or a ceiling was set; this share did not decrease much: in five years, the sphere of free consumer prices increased to only 53 per cent. Factory and consumer prices were linked to each other and thus changed together after the reform. Nevertheless, state control of consumer prices remained strong in order to counter-balance inflation.

Subsidies continued to play an important role in staple products of mass consumption (i.e. basic foods, services, etc.). To avoid negative social reaction, a comprehensive reform of consumer prices was delayed and a policy of "permanent but gradual" price modifications was accepted. Prices began to rise in the first few years at an annual rate of two to three per cent and then increased to three to four per cent.

Controlled market prices represented a certain compromise between the reform's aims and the socio-political realities. Indeed, they helped to avoid most of the undesirable side-effects, but at the same time limited the effects of the value and market orientation as well.

The system of more flexible prices and less governmental control assumed that management would receive a greater range for expressing independent actions and decisions. Since a part of its profit remained within the firm, a special incentive was given to production. However, management did not entirely have a free hand. It had first to create a special fund from the remaining profit for welfare expenses, for reserve, and for investment; and only the smallest part of the profit was left free for profit-sharing purposes. Although managers had received more freedom in implementing a wage policy than before, they were limited here also by another major compromise that was built into the reform, namely central wage regulations which fixed the average wage level of the firms, and rules were similarly strict concerning the annual increases in a firm's average wage or total wage bill.

This strong state intervention was retained because of fear that firms would dismiss a large number of workers to increase productivity, which would undermine the full employment policy and embarrass the government. Actually, no lay-offs were effected after the introduction of the New Economic Mechanism. Nevertheless, the maintenance of strong government control was rather counterproductive because it preserved low efficiency and underemployment and failed to stimulate higher productivity. Concessions, which made possible higher differentiations among wage categories — instead of a 1:3 ratio, the differences between the top and the bottom categories increased to 1:9 —

did not counterbalance the impact of regulations. The contradictions of the wage regulation were further aggravated by the fact that the government (for social policy reasons) further increased allotments in excess of wages, for example subsidies on foodstuff prices, free health and educational services, allowances for families with many children. The average percentage value of these allotments to wage increased from 18 per cent in 1960 to 27 per cent in 1975. Obviously, these allotments had nothing to do with skill, efficiency, or productivity.

Further, basic elements of the reform modified the investment system. The different sources of state income concentrated 35 per cent of the national income into the state budget. That was the source of state investment which, however, represented only 47 per cent of total investment. Another 10 per cent was financed through loans from the National Bank. These investments were channelled into infrastructure and used to finance energy projects as well as to reach new major central investment targets. More than 40 per cent of investments, however, were covered by the investment funds of the firms. It was a giant step forward when compared to the unrealized reform proposals of 1957, which had aimed at keeping central (for the firms, free of charge) investments financed from the state budget as a basis of planning. The reality, nevertheless, reflected a much less radical change, since a great part of the business investments were linked to the central plan, which served as an additional financial source. Changes were made either by informal ministerial intervention ("suggesting" that the firms join a central investment project) or by the granting of state loans if the firm joined a central investment programme. According to certain calculations, no more than one-sixth of the firms' investments were actually independent.

It ought to be clear from this very sketchy presentation of the New Economic Mechanism (where we tried to elaborate more on the features of planning than on other issues) that, in spite of substantial changes in the system, a number of contradictions still prevailed, and a balance between planned and market elements and between long-term economic growth and short-term social impacts was still far from being realized.

Experts like Paul Marer stress that one of the basic deficiencies in the new system was the lack of reform on the institutional side of the mechanism. A highly concentrated industrial organization, a banking system built upon the absolute monopoly of the central bank, and foreign trade enterprises bearing little in common with flexible market orientation remained quite common.

Marer also tried to summarize the specific problems which were not solved in this special combination of planning and market orientation. According to him, the reform (for all its good intention) did not sufficiently encourage competition. In fact, due to the high concentration of the industry in a relatively small market, competition was confined even more than usual in a centrally planned economy. The shortcomings of the price system also moved things in that direction.

Since a wage system impeded worker mobility, not only was no real market labour created but the underemployment as well as the swelling work force in the factories contributed to a permanent labour shortage. Incentives for profitable investment were not yet present. However, investment incentive from the central budget was increasing. This seemed to be particularly the case for the huge enterprises, where management continued to rely on higher authorities for their decisions rather than working independently for greater profits. Maintaining good terms with the supervising authorities remained the primary objective of the managers, who were still appointed by the ministries.

Despite all the shortcomings of the New Economic Mechanism, the abolition of the command economy and the special combination of planning with the market brought a new upswing to the Hungarian economy. The five years of economic development following the introduction of the reform are numbered among the best in Hungarian economic history. With an average annual growth of net national product of over 6 per cent, a relatively lower level of employment growth (around 1 per cent), and the improving growth of labour productivity (around 2–3 per cent), the Hungarian GNP per capita growth was more than 3 per cent in this period. During these 5 years, net national product per capita increased by 40 per cent. The former declaration of economic growth was reversed, and the improvement in the efficiency of investment made a high growth of consumption possible (a yearly average of 5–7 per cent).

Previously labour input — complemented with a high ratio of capital investment — was the major element in growth; now total factory productivity had more than doubled by reducing inventory ratios and improving technology. Growth rates were averaging 7 per cent in the manufacturing industries during these years, and achievement was even better in agriculture. The introduction of more flexible planning, the reinforcement of the independence of the agricultural co-operatives, the incentives given to raise production, and the successful combination of large-scale farms (co-operatives and state farms) with a large number of household plots made agriculture successful in every respect. The growth rate of gross output nearly doubled, approaching 3 per cent, and, due to low population growth, food production per head grew nearly at the same rate. Wheat and maize yields more than trebled in 10 years, and a shift occurred vis à vis production and export of goods of higher value.

Stop and Go: Responses to the World Economic Crisis

First Response: Recentralization

The continued development and further radicalization of the reform began to crumble in 1972 and 1973. The attack came from two directions. The worldwide economic shock triggered by the oil crisis and its immediate consequences hit Hungary particularly hard. Because of its poor natural endowment, Hungary was heavily dependent on the import of oil and other raw materials. Rising import prices (more than 70 per cent during the next five years) caused a serious deterioration in terms of trade (20 per cent between 1973 and 1978). According to some estimates, the loss incurred by the deterioration of terms of trade ranged around 5 per cent of the average annual national income. The trade deficit began to rise and quickly reached a peak in 1978 of almost US$1 billion. Hungary began to borrow heavily and the national debt rose to US$5 billion. Obviously, the new situation in the world market demanded changes in Hungarian economic policy. Nevertheless, the changes which took place did not help to overcome the difficulties. Quite the contrary, Hungary was quickly manoeuvring itself into an increasingly difficult economic situation.

The oil crisis broke out during a counterattack mainly by domestic political pressure groups opposed to the reform. A special political coalition was formed among ideologists who regarded the reform ideas as a challenge to the ideological principles of socialism established in the Soviet Union. Also included were bureaucrats who were afraid of losing control over society by allowing too much spontaneous economic activity; planners who felt the growing independence and market orientation of firms would undermine their authority; top managers of some of the major firms who felt their job under competitiveness would become more difficult; and some trade union leaders who were under the impression that social groups other than blue-collar workers would benefit more from the reform and that the reform was causing inequality and social tension in society. Ideological and social arguments well supported by economic arguments pointed to one possible solution: a return to stronger state intervention and recentralization.

The counterattack efforts realized their first achievement when the 50 largest enterprises were placed under special direction and, by this act, were exempted from a large number of the rules introduced by the recent reform. The same drive toward recentralization dictated the decision to, in the interest of greater efficiency, compel small- and medium-sized firms to merge with larger enterprises. Through this, the monopolistic or oligopolistic position of the large enterprises was strengthened. By a series of new regulations — allegedly fighting against unjustified profits or income inequality — restrictions were imposed on the entrepreneurial activity of the medium-sized or smaller firms. In agriculture — allegedly to combat speculation — the co-operative's activity was restricted again, and those selling goods from private plots underwent special harassment. Taxation did not stimulate economic activity, and no inducement was given to innovations — quite the opposite, the aim was to discourage everybody from looking for extra income.

Due to the excessive increase in prices on the world market, Hungary's domestic prices should have changed in the spirit of the reform. However, the government, fearing inflation and regarding the price increase as a temporary, cyclical phenomenon, wanted to protect the domestic market from the impact of a price increase. It decided rather to counterbalance the import of price increases by government subsidies on a more or less industry-by-industry or firm-by-firm basis. As a result, domestic prices were again completely isolated from world market prices as the whole price system of the reform practically collapsed. Firms actually did not feel the increase in raw material prices since the state — which bought the raw materials at higher prices — was still providing them the same quantity at almost the same prices. None of the factories had any real reason to exercise caution when using raw materials, gasoline, etc. Even the discrepancy between consumer and producer prices survived and threatened to regain the level of the 1950s and 1960s.

The government tried to fight inflation on the domestic level by recentralization, undermining any serious efforts to adjust domestic prices to world prices. The foreign trade sector was zealously involved in an attempt to overcome the serious balance-of-trade deficit. On the one hand, a large number of stringent import restrictions were reintroduced, while on the other hand rapid economic growth was supported for an offensive export policy. Again, large sums were invested in various projects, anticipating that their production would increase exports significantly. Large amounts of money for investment were borrowed to cover the balance-of-trade deficit (mainly from Western countries). A vicious circle was created: to ease the pressure from outside, Hungary again tried to be more autarchic, and striving for greater autarchy increased outside pressure. Indeed, 1973–1978 were the years when the reform was stalled, if not entirely abandoned.

Free labour migration and investment, limited through the increasing influences returned to the ministries, were put under stricter control by higher authorities, including the National Planning Office. Export incentives were reduced, credit was restricted, and freedom of the firm in making investment decisions was limited to the priorities set up by the National Planning Office. Through the allocation of budget support, the role of supervisory organs (their decisive influence at the upper — Planning Office — and middle — ministries — levels increased again) was felt not only in controlling the economy but also in directing it.

This setback lasted nearly five years before it was finally acknowledged that this policy could not be continued. By trying to isolate the economy from the adverse impact of world market developments, the prevailing mechanism was actually making things worse through strengthening the inefficiency and inflexibility of the firms and by carrying out an import-substitution policy.

New Wave of the Reform

The first sign of the government's return to the reform was a new declaration on long-term economic strategy at the end of 1978. It was acknowledged for the first time in Hungarian economic policy that there should be a shift from import-substituting industrialization towards an export-oriented industrialization, necessitating a restructuring of the export and production base. Most of the previously (in 1956 or in 1965) declared, but only partially realized or failed, targets of high productivity, selective industrial development, technological up-to-dateness, and competitiveness, etc., were emphasized again.

Without a doubt, the new wave started under very difficult economic conditions; one third of total capital accumulation came from unsold stocks and unfinished investments, and net foreign debt reached US$4.6 billion in 1978. One of the first measures was a new price reform. To eliminate subsidies, a major consumer price increase was carried out. As a consequence, the inflation rate increased to 10 per cent in 1979 and 1980 and then declined to 5–7 per cent. The rearrangement of factory prices went further. It not only remodelled the price system according to real input and value but, for the first time, it linked price formation with world market prices. As opposed to 1968, factory prices from 1980 were calculated on the basis of export profit in the case of the firms which exported at least 5 per cent of their production. It covered not less than 70 per cent of Hungarian industrial production. Subsidies, nevertheless, still survived and basically characterized the prices of services, transportation, and rents.

The reform radically broke with the compromise of 1968 and started to change the untouched institutional system as well. Three major steps warrant special attention. Reflecting the philosophy of strengthening the independence of the business sector, the classical central directing institution of industrial branch ministries was, in 1980, reorganized into one ministry of industry which, unable to direct or interfere in a firm's affairs, functioned as a policy-making body.

Since most of Hungary's large enterprises were a conglomeration of formerly independent factories put together to facilitate central planning, they did not yet have the advantages of large-scale production. Production was mainly connected with small factories without economies of scale but with a monopolist's position in the market. After 1979, half of the existing large trusts dissolved or were broken up into independent enterprises. This process offered strong encouragement to the small and medium-size enterprises. In addition to the 300 new enterprises which came into being by reorganization, special support was provided to establish small factories for the dual purpose of increasing competition and satisfying the consumption needs of the population. Earlier regulations concerning the activity of small enterprises were reinstated, and an unprecedented level of freedom of action was given them. Small-business activity was not limited to the state or to the co-operatives; private ownership of small enterprises was allowed. Particular preference was given to private enterprises in the service sector; nevertheless, even direct industrial activity was no longer regarded as taboo. The majority of state-owned restaurants and small shops were given over to private individuals on a rental basis.

They had to pay the state a fixed sum over a certain period, but otherwise they were absolutely independent. Several forms of incentives were granted to initiate additional labour input. Workers and engineers could form special small enterprises within the state firm and make contracts with it. They could use the firm's machinery and equipment and work after hours for the firm in accordance with the terms of a regular contract. Some huge firms made dozens of such contracts with small enterprises, formed within their own framework.

A sort of "after hours" private industry was allowed. Workers or intellectuals could obtain permission to use their cars as private taxi cabs. Skilled workers could get licenses and officially act, after hours, as plumbers, carpenters, mechanics, etc.

Now, methods for appointing managers in state industry and state farms might also have far-reaching social consequences. From 1985, new managers in state enterprises will be elected by the workers' council, for a five-year period. The elections will be advertised, and there will be no restrictions preventing one from accepting applications for candidacy. The election was an important step towards the self-management of state enterprises based on workers' participation. A small number of state firms, which have a public service character (e.g. electric power plants), will continue the former system (appointment of managers by the ministries), but they also will have a workers council as an advisory board.

Besides other equally important institutional changes, such as the limitation of bureaucracy and enlarged foreign trading rights for the industrial enterprises, we would like to mention the changes in financial intermediaries and instruments resulting from the repeal of overcentralization in this field, that is, the change in the fucntion from a supervisory role, where intermediaries act as a watch-dog in the implementation of the macro-economic plan, to the traditional role where lending is more connected to the rate of return and interest rates have a greater effect in the distribution of credit. With this change, competition and market orientation were promoted and the financial institutions became less an agent of the state and more a business partner in the economic community. Foreign banks were allowed to operate in Hungary, and some steps were taken to create an institutional framework for domestic financial intermediaries.

The results of these new steps in the implementation of the reform are far from being fully realized; in a large number of fields new measures are expected. It is too early to try to assess the achievements, particularly since, although it is not the beginning, it is even less the end of the process. However, the direction of the process is clearly toward establishing an economy which will be based principally on socialist features, that is, on common property, where planning will play a significant role in everything from the establishment of targets and perspectives to the partial regulation of production decisions and income distribution. But private property is allowed and even supported, up to a given level. Planning gives significant latitude to market forces. Greater reliance of economic decision-making on competition and market forces brings about several merits: (1) restrictions on bureaucratization of the economy, (2) greater implementation of modern technology and hence an increase in efficiency, (3) restraint on monopolistic positions, (4) a sustained growth rate, and (5) realization of a more realistic and desirable rate of capital accumulation.

Obviously the aim of the reform was not only to restrict planning but, just as importantly, to improve the planning methods. This improvement also went in the direction of decentralization; enterprise plans are not supervised by the central authorities who set up the plans but by independent agencies. These agencies — research institutes — may have the right to suggest a modification or adjustment of the central plan based upon the aggregation of the enterprise plans.

The reform will not diminish the importance of planning, but its content and mechanism are changing. Central government planning focuses on the conditions and the regulatory system of the economy, instead of the production itself. Long-term plans are of greater importance than they were earlier. Medium-term (five-year) plans design the framework of economic manoeuvring, and they act as guidelines for economic policy rather than directives for economic management.

The Hungarian reform is unique among the socialist countries, although others have also recognized the need for change. Since the country is moving toward a mixed centrally-planned-market-oriented-socialist economy, their experience may be meaningful for re-evaluating the traditional — and dogmatic — "planning *versus* market" and "socialist economy *versus* mixed economy" ideas.

Before concluding the planning experiences, let us summarize the characteristics of regional planning. Planning on a regional level follows the main paths of macro-economic planning, but clearly it has independent features, too. "Regionalism" stems largely from political traditions, territorial differentiation, the multinational or homogeneous population structure, etc., of a given state, although the basic characteristics depend on the centralized or decentralized structure of the existing political power.

Planning on the Regional Level

A History of Planning on the Regional Level

Comprehensive economic planning was first introduced in the Soviet Union in the 1920s. Representing an enormously differentiated and multinational state, the Soviet government has attempted to achieve the primacy of social solidarity over regional loyalties. Regional planning was integrated within a strongly centralized planning system. Regional development targets — for example, industrial and mining development in Siberia — were formulated according to sectoral interests or strategic viewpoints rather than to local (regional) interests or desires. Nevertheless, regional differences have diminished greatly since the beginning of the Soviet industrialization programmes.

Historically, socio-economic planning started on the regional level in western economies. As a consequence of the 1929–1932 economic crisis, planned government intervention was executed in regions seriously hit by the crisis (e.g. the Black Country in England and the Appalachian region in the United States). There were some sporadic government efforts for influencing regional development (e.g. by the optimal location of agriculture) in pre-war Hungary, too.

Regional plans have similar goals in both market and centrally-planned economies. Generally speaking, regional policies seek the *levelling of regional disparities*. Disparities differ from country to country and depend on the size, economic maturity, historical traditions, etc., of the given states. The following are some special features of regional planning in socialist countries:

1. Regional plans cover all aspects of socio-economic life, from production to public services. For a long time, production goals were unilaterally stressed because it was assumed that industrial growth would lead automatically to the improvement of living conditions.
2. Regional plans cover *all* regions of the country and give a framework for regional distribution of national (comprehensive) planning targets and development funds. (There are special planning regions, for example, tourist regions, too.)
3. Regional development — in most socialist countries — is centrally designated. Central decisions are channelled to the local level through different government agencies and through public administration; local initiations thus have a rather limited impact on the plans. The role of local authorities is to convey government will *to the local* level rather than to express local interests.

The different stages of post-war economic development were characterized by distinct regional and urban policies.[2] Following is an examination of these stages.

First, immediately after the war — as discussed earlier — the non-agricultural sector of the economy passed almost completely into state ownership. Parallel with this action was the introduction of comprehensive planning. The first post-war economic plan (1946–1948) aimed at the reconstruction of the heavily damaged economy. The First Five Year Plan (1949–1954) had an ambitious programme of rapid industrialization. Hungarian leadership totally adopted the Soviet economic model, including the high priority given to heavy industry and the strongly centralized economic management system. Central planning authorities prescribed detailed directives to the enterprises and the non-productive sectors alike.

This strongly centralized planning system allowed no room for regional planning. The economy was directed by sectoral plans. The First Five Year Plan had some regional targets (e.g. industrial location on the rural Great Plain), but there was neither an organization nor a decision-making system for regional development. In 1950, the council (soviet) system replaced earlier local authorities. Local and regional authorities had the mere task of conveying the central government's will on the local level. Self-government — which was traditionally poorly developed in Hungary — was practically abolished.

The new system inherited important territorial inequalities from pre-war Hungary. Manufacturing was excessively concentrated in Budapest, the capital city. The city alone employed 60 per cent of the total industrial work-force in 1930. The mining and heavy industry regions were cut out by the new borders established after the collapse of Austria-Hungary in 1920. Besides Budapest, Györ was the only developed manufacturing centre. A number of small-company or mining towns in the Hungarian highlands bore the marks of industrialization. Hungary's greatest land mass, however, lay in a poorly developed rural zone, where traditional agriculture offered neither capital accumulation nor a market for industry.

Uneven industrial development was reflected in the urban network, too. In additon to Budapest, with a population of 1.8 million in 1941, only two provincial cities had more than 100,000 inhabitants. Both cities — Debrecen and Szeged — were former rural market towns, with very poor industrial functions. There was no urban network in the modern sense of the word. Most cities had a pre-industrial social structure as far as market functions and limited attraction zones were concerned.

Extensive industrial growth had important regional effects. Budapest's dominance in industrial employment had somewhat diminished and new industrial regions grew in the Hungarian highlands near the coalfields and ore (mostly bauxite) deposits. As a whole, the first wave of post-war industrialization sharpened regional differences between industrialized and rural regions. Since heavy industry was concentrated in a few locations, most of the rural areas remained untouched by industrialization. Massive migrations from the overpopulated rural areas brought new manpower to Budapest and the freshly industrialized north-east-south-west "energy axis" of the country. Great Plain cities which had lost their earlier market functions had a migration similar to that of the villages. This was a normal phenomenon; industrial take-off has always had a polarized regional structure. The rural-urban dichotomy sharpened even within the new industrial regions because dynamism was concentrated in the newly industrialized — or, in a few cases, newly established — urban centres. Thus, there was no possibility of formulating the usual regional planning target (welfare in character) or regional levelling.

Second, the transitory decade between 1957 and 1968 was marked by the introduction of a regional policy.

In 1959, at the Seventh Congress of the Hungarian Workers' Party, the first comprehensive regional policy was formulated. The timing was connected to the final wave of collectivization, when great masses again left agriculture. The government intended to keep these people near their domicile and employ them, if possible, within a commuting distance in order to avoid further growth in the hypertrophic capital.

Industrial decentralization was the key element to this regional policy. For this purpose, the following measures were taken:

1. Five regional centres (Miskolc, Debrecen, Szeged, Pécs, and Győr) were designated as "counter-poles." They received priority from the point of view of industrial location and urban development to counterbalance the overwhelming economic role of Budapest. Thus, Boudeville's well-known growth pole theory was applied. The development took place frequently at the growth centres, without having much impact on their outer regions; greater regional imbalances resulted. Growth was stimulated primarily by direct government investments into the local industry, since infrastructure usually remained neglected.
2. There was a general stimulus for industrial enterprises in Budapest to establish new plants in provincial cities.
3. The establishment of new industrial plants in Budapest (later in the whole metropolitan area of the city) was prohibited.
4. A number of industrial plants (with 20,000 employees) were designated for mandatory relocation from Budapest to the provinces, mostly for physical planning reasons.

This strategy proved to be basically successful. The main results were as follows:

1. Population growth in Budapest slowed remarkably. The number of industrial workers and employees reached its maximum (700,000) in 1964. Since then, industrial workers have diminished in number to 420,000. Industrial relocation from Budapest played a minor role in this decline. Industrial decentralization placed a great part of the young people entering the labour market in the countryside, leaving the continual "hunger" for manpower in Budapest unsatisfied.
2. Modern industry was located in a number of provincial cities, making industry the main force behind urban development. The industrial decentralization contributed to the formation of a modern urban system, helped to level the employment rate among different regions, and diminished interregional migration.
3. Industry also moved into the agricultural regions. An important part of the agricultural manpower surplus was absorbed by industry. The rapid tech-

nical modernization of agriculture, in addition to the abolishment of rigid centralization in planning and management, led to a substantial growth in the income of co-operative farmers. The average industrial and agricultural income became equalized by 1968. Consequently, the regional income disparities have diminished greatly.

Third, the introduction of the New Economic Mechanism in 1968 — discussed earlier — had an important indirect effect on regional development. For example, when industrial enterprises became the primary decision-making units for their own new investments, decentralized decision-making permeated throughout the enterprises.

As a consequence of the New Economic Mechanism, a new regional and urban policy was worked out. This policy was more moderate than the reform itself — while at the same time, recentralization efforts were losing momentum.

In 1971, the government adopted three fundamental resolutions which reformulated the aims and methods of regional planning. The first defined two basic aims for regional policy and planning.

1. "It should ensure the efficient utilization of the resources of different regions and the modernization and rationalization of the settlement network"
2. "By equalizing regional differences in employment, economic activity, and infrastructure, the regional policy and planning should reduce differences in the standard of living and cultural enrichment"

In the new regional policy, in addition to economic levelling, the reduction of differences in living conditions also became an important target. Earlier, it was supposed that economic development would automatically lead to an improvement in living conditions. That proved not to be the case. For example, the development of rural infrastructure and rural services lagged behind the growth of agricultural output and rural income.

The second government resolution was embodied in the National Settlement Network Development Concept. According to this concept, different hierarchical levels and their centres were identified (130 towns and large rural communes). Each hierarchical level was determined by population size, the size of the attraction zone, the infrastructural level, the variety of public services available, etc. Then county councils in turn determined local centres (about 800 in the country) to assure basic services in each region and to channel the central development funds towards the planned urban network.

The third resolution prescribed the system of regional planning. It expanded the decision-making power of local and county authorities (councils).

In the early 1970s, economic growth continued. Searching for manpower, industry continued to move to the rural area. Half of the new industrial manufacturing plants were located in rural communes between 1968 and 1973.

Industrialization in the rural areas later slowed, but due to the decline in industrial employment in metropolitan areas, the share of rural industry in terms of employment continued to grow. Over one-fifth of the total industrial workforce was employed in the manufacturing industry of rural communes — almost the same number as in Budapest! — by the late 1970s. This extensive territorial industrial dispersion was facilitated by the unusually large concentration of population in Hungarian villages (the national average of 1,800 inhabitants bypassed that of 3,000 inhabitants on the Great Plain). Migration from rural to urban areas diminished.

The government was able to assure full employment even during the industrial stagnation of the second half of the 1970s, but it reduced subsidies for backward regions and generally in the non-productive areas (i.e. infrastructure and public services).

Contradictory moves were promulgated during the 1970s in view of regional development. The economic levelling continued: the difference between the most and the least industrialized countries was fourfold in 1970 and only twofold in 1980 (in the number of industrial employees per 1,000 inhabitants). Due to the successful performance of agriculture, rural areas also advanced economically.

Regional tensions shifted from the macro-regional to the micro-regional level. The urban-rural dichotomy still existed, due partly to the urban-centred regional policy and partly to the general neglect of the development of infrastructure. Settlement development remained centralized, although the government shared its redistributive role with county councils. Local financial resources remained insignificant and the central (i.e. government and county council) development funds were located almost totally in the cities. In 1979, only 10 per cent of the central settlement development fund was devoted to rural communities, where 47 per cent of the country's population lived (1969: 23 per cent, which ratio was reached again by 1984).

The implementation of the National Settlement Network Development Concept was clearly successful in developing the urban network. The population of Budapest started to decline; the medium- and small-city network expanded. The development of the modern urban network was basically finished.

In addition, recentralization attempts had influence on regional development. For example, territorial decentralization of industry was accompanied by organizational centralization. Small local enterprises were absorbed by large enterprises. Forty per cent of the industrial plants had their headquarters in Budapest. This ratio is over 70 per cent in the case of large (over 3,000 employees) manufacturing enterprises.

A movement toward stronger centralization characterized the 1970s in rural public services (i.e. public administration, public health, public education, retail trade). Key words for this centralization were "modern" and "efficient." This time not the Soviet but the "developed Western" pattern had to be followed. Given the level of the Hungarian communications system, these service models proved disadvantageous for the rural population.

Local authorities in each settlement had but symbolic power, despite the declared principles of self-government and the definition of a new task of local councils to express local interests. Local resources became strongly centralized, and their redistribution among counties and settlements again became strictly controlled by central (government) agencies.

New Waves of Reform and the New Regional Policy

The 1980s have been characterized by important changes both in economic and regional policies. In economic policy, the basic aim has been to make our economy more competitive in the world market. This aim has necessitated substantial modernizing and restructuring of production, chiefly in industry. The short-run aim has been to keep the country accessible to the international financial market, which has required a very strict control over government expenditures. At the same time, regional policy has had to undergo major changes. It has become clear that the problems of uneven regional development in the 1980s cannot be managed by the techniques of intervention employed during the 1960s and 1970s.

A consideration of some of the fundamental questions for the 1980s — or for a longer period — follows.

First, what kind of growth-stimulation policy is possible for regional development? There is a growing number of studies dealing with the role of technology change or the propagation of innovations in regional policy. Nevertheless, because of the lack of empirical studies, we are still uncertain whether the technological impact will have a new regional concentration effect. Heavy concentration of R&D capacities in the big cities — primarily in Budapest — and the outmoded technology which is used in certain provincial plants suggest a need for a new territorial concentration. Greater flexibility within the small firms, which are prevalent in the countryside, and the possible development of microelectronics may help to preserve the relatively deconcentrated character of production. Another question, which has never been analysed from the point of view of regional development, concerns the future importance and location of the "second economy." A part of this economy is "black" (half-legal or illegal) and is attractive to people in the large cities where control is more difficult. Auxiliary farming, another part of the "second economy," may substantially augment family income in rural areas where statistical (official) revenues are low.

Two guidelines were adopted for government interventions. The first stated that the government should intervene to assure full employment. Government interventions were particularly needed in the traditional area of heavy industry rather than in the rural zones. The second guideline recognized the need to continue regional levelling. The two basic services of education and public health were considered to be of great importance in this matter.

Another question that arises is: How should the National Settlement Network Development Concept be remodeled? A new redistribution system of government funds, greater independence of local authorities related to financial and other matters, increased citizen participation, and enhanced regionalism in settlement development are planned.

Between 1981 and 1983, three groups of experts worked out guidelines for a new settlement and regional development policy, dealing with trends in urban transformation, with the new system of financing to be controlled by local councils, and with the decentralization of public administrative power. The government accepted the suggested new settlement and regional policy in 1984. It was passed by the Parliament as a law in the spring of 1985. The law contains substantial changes in the decision-making system of regional development. The most important new elements are taken up in the following.

New regional policy does not intend to infringe directly into the economic sphere. It can be assumed that structural changes will reflect the economic activity. A clear strategy for structural changes does not yet exist, just as one did not exist for quantitative changes (i.e. for economic growth).

Structural changes in the industry of a given region or city will certainly affect the need for local resources and manpower; it will also affect intra- and inter-regional relations, commodity flows, etc. The magnitude and the direction of these changes are still uncertain.

The Hungarian government intends to maintain full employment in the future. It is a realistic aim since the size of the working-age population is diminishing and the tertiary sector can absorb a certain amount of surplus manpower from industry. Structural changes will certainly disturb the local (regional) labour market, although the outcome of the disturbance is uncertain. The government recently introduced a programme of retraining to prepare for the possible manpower surplus, but the regional relocation will not be easy. After 40 years of continuous "manpower shortages" (i.e. underutilization of the employed manpower), these problems will prove difficult to manage.

Former regional policies in Hungary formulated economic targets and justified intervention into the economy. New regional policy has to prepare alternative responses for economic changes which are in many respects still uncertain. Fundamental changes in financing settlement development are planned. New measures were introduced as of January 1986. First of all, while the importance of the centralized redistribution system will be reduced, local financial resources (local taxes) will gain in importance. Second, the distribution of resources from the central budget will be effected according to clear norms and rules instead of the frequent "informal bargaining" between local and central authorities which has been typical until now. Local authorities will have complete control over the utilization of their financial resources (presently, the share of new investments and the proportion of expenditures for housing, public health, and public education are fixed).

Local councils are expected to express and to follow local interests. This is an important change in a socialist country; earlier, the expression of valid local interests was denied. Attempts were made to induce citizens' participation in local decision-making. According to calculations, in the new resources allocation system, the share for rural communes in the central development fund will rise to 30 per cent.

The importance of regional and urban planning has been stressed by the general political atmosphere in the country. "Decentralization" has become a key word for further political and economic development.

Decentralization came first from the economic reform — as mentioned earlier — which began more than 20 years ago. This reform incorporates various programmes of decentralization of economic power from government agencies to the enterprise or plant level. In a certain way, the re-establishment of the private economy and the great importance of its special form, the so-called second economy, also imply an organizational decentralization in the economy. The economic decentralization aroused a greater interest among economic management units in settlement development and created a closer relationship between managers and local authorities.

Earlier, the central government was in charge of a wide range of welfare programmes — from cheap government housing to subsidizing every type of cultural event — which became impossible for the government to execute under the strain of the long years of economic restrictions. Consequently, the government is withdrawing from some of its earlier commitments (e.g. in 1987 the share of government housing dropped to less than 10 per cent of the total new housing units built in a year), leaving some tasks for individuals and the local communities. This process gave more duties and responsibilities but, logically, also more rights to the local communities.

The above-mentioned decentralization means the transfer of power to the regions and to the local communities. The smoothness of the transfer of power depends on the answers to the following questions: Will it lead to the formation of real local governments? How well are the local communities and local authorities prepared for their new responsibilities? To what degree will it be possible to develop horizontal connections among different institutions, agencies, and firms functioning within the same settlement? How can the government continue its policy of regional levelling since presumably greater local independence will strengthen regional differences? Through which organizations can local societies and different interest groups express their interests? This long list of questions, as yet unanswered, suggests the depth of the changes that will be necessary for the successful implementation of the new regional and settlement policy.

Conclusions: The Impact of Planning on Hungarian Development

In concluding the history of economic and regional planning in Hungary, we shall try to answer the following questions:

1. What advantages accrued to Hungary by planning?
2. What were the major problems confronted in the planning process at different points in time and what were their causes?

Achievements of Planning

Central planning (i.e. government intervention in the operation of the economy) existed in pre-war capitalist Hungary. Because of the lateness of the industrial revolution, the free market system was never fully developed and modernization in the peripherally developed states needed stimuli and interventions from the government, since "from bottom to top" there were neither enough local resources nor enough societal stimuli.

Post-war nationalization of the economy made central planning inevitable; the state as an owner had to control and direct its economy.

Central planning had certain advantages over a market economy in the period of industrial take-off. It made possible massive allocation of national resources to many sectors, including the energy industry and heavy industry, where profitability was low or nonexistent, enabling Hungary to industrialize rapidly. War-stricken and poorly developed, Hungary needed rapid growth at that time. Rapid industrialization influenced the social restructuralization of Hungary. Planning has been the fundamental instrument for bringing about the necessary structural changes in the economy which later led to a substantial improvement in efficiency and productivity. A market economy — even with some government subsidies — could not have supported such massive investments.

A brief overview of the most important economic accomplishments since the introduction of planning must begin by acknowledging the results of industrialization, since industrialization was the focal point of the socialist transformation. Although the high growth rate experienced during the forced industrialization of the 1950s slowed, it nevertheless maintained a 6–7 per cent yearly growth until the end of the 1970s. The level of production increased eight times between 1950 and 1980; per capita industrial production ranked Hungary in the middle among the 30 most industrialized nations of the world.

Hungary was an agricultural-industrial country after the Second World War. At the end of the 1940s, more than half of the population worked in the agricultural sector and around a quarter were involved in industrial production. By 1975, the proportions were almost reversed: around 40 per cent of the population worked in industry as opposed to less than 20 per cent in agriculture. Hungary had become an industrialized country.

TABLE 1. Output of energy and raw material production

Year	Electric power (million kWh)	Coal	Iron	Steel
		(1,000 tons)		
1938	1,979	9,360	355	647
1950	3,001	13,268	457	1,048
1960	7,617	26,524	1,249	1,887
1970	14,542	27,830	1,822	3,108
1980	23,874	25,701	2,214	3,764

Source: *Magyar Statisztikai Évkönyv* (Statistical yearbook of Hungary), 1981, pp. 7–8.

Economic policy was to make industry the largest sector of the economy. Basic structural changes took place within industry as well. We mentioned — and even criticized — the fact that heavy industry had initially received an overwhelming share of the investments. Due to this, the share of heavy industry in production value increased considerably. On the other hand, the relative share of the food and textile industries declined. Energy and raw material production also increased rapidly, as table 1 reveals.

The engineering and chemical industries were at the top of development. Four or five times more equipment and machinery, and twenty to thirty times more electrical equipment, were produced than had been before the war. A durable consumer goods industry was created. Chemical industries, with a strong export-oriented pharmaceutical industry, grew particularly fast during the late 1960s and early 1970s when development programmes were concentrated in these branches. Table 2 illustrates the substantial changes in structure which have occurred in Hungarian industry during the last few decades.

Due to the low efficiency of capital investment, or because of overinvestment, proper care was not given to maintenance, and the proportions between investment in buildings and machines were unbalanced. In the period of reform, productivity rose very quickly; during centralization, its growth was slow and occasionally even the reverse was the case.

The growth of agriculture was particularly slow in comparison with industry. Nevertheless, two periods can be clearly identified in the history of Hungarian agriculture. During the 1950s, in the time of forced collectivization when agriculture was entirely neglected in the investment process, agricultural production actually declined for a number of years (1952 was 14 per cent less than in 1950). Even after 1956, production growth was slow: in the early 1960s it was about 20–25 per cent above the 1950 level but still below the pre-war level.

Following the success of collectivization, the trend altered in the 1960s. From 1965 to 1980, the production index increased from 127 to 207. The growth rate was 3 per cent in the early 1960s and increased to 5.5 per cent in the early

TABLE 2. Structure of industry according to branch (%)

	Work force			Gross value of production		
	1938	1965	1980	1938	1965	1980
Mining	12.5	13.1	7.1	5.6	7.3	6.2
Metallurgy	—	7.2	6.0	—	12.7	10.2
Iron and metal	15.4	—	—	13.3	—	—
Engineering	12.2	30.2	32.0	9.2	24.7	23.0
Electrotechnical	2.1	2.8	2.2	4.2	5.1	4.3
Building material	9.3	6.0	4.9	3.4	3.6	3.3
Chemical	4.9	5.9	6.9	9.1	9.6	19.3
Heavy industry total	56.4	65.2	59.1	44.8	63.0	66.3
Textiles	19.3	11.5	7.4	14.4	7.6	4.6
Clothing	3.1	3.0	4.8	2.4	2.4	1.8
Leather	3.1	3.2	3.7	3.7	2.1	2.3
Wood	3.8	3.4	3.0	2.4	2.3	2.2
Paper	1.7	0.9	0.9	1.9	0.9	1.3
Printing	2.3	1.3	1.2	1.6	0.8	0.9
Other light industry	—	1.9	4.3	—	0.8	0.9
Light industry total	33.3	25.2	25.3	26.4	16.9	14.0
Food processing	10.3	9.6	12.2	28.8	20.1	18.3
Others	—	—	3.4	—	—	1.4
Total	100.0	100.0	100.0	100.0	100.0	100.0

Sources: *Magyar Statisztikai Évkönyv* (Statistical yearbook of Hungary) 1980, 1981, p. 184 and pp. 40–50; T. I. Berend, *A szocialista gazdaság fejlödése Magyarországon, 1945–1975* (The development of the socialist economy in Hungary, 1945–1975), Budapest, Kossuth, 1979, p. 182.
Note: Iron and metal industry was grouped partly into metallurgy, partly into engineering in post-war statistics

TABLE 3. Average production and yields

	1931–1940		1951–1960		1961–1970		1971–1980	
	1,000 tons	t/acre	1,000 tons	t/acre	1,000 tons	t/acre	1,000 tons	t/acre
Wheat	2,196	0.79	1,899	0.85	2,583	1.25	4,741	2.13
Maize	2,185	1.08	2,783	1.26	3,654	1.68	6,128	2.60
Sugar beet	965	11.71	2,265	11.47	3,532	16.14	3,538	20.57

Source: T. I. Berend, *A szocialista gazdaság fejlödése Magyarországon, 1945–1975* (The development of the socialist economy in Hungary, 1945–1975), Budapest, Kossuth, 1979, p. 205.

1970s. In the 1970s, Hungary's agricultural growth rate was second only to that of Holland in the world. Since a million peasants quit the agricultural sector during these years, decreasing the agricultural population by 55 per cent, the growth could not be attributed to an increase in the agricultural work-force. Quite the opposite, growth in agricultural output occurred because production per capita has more than quadrupled during the last 30 years. The main factors responsible for this phenomenal growth rate were the rapid advance of mechanization, the intensification of production, and the large increase in yields.

Animal power almost disappeared from agriculture, while the number of tractors increased from 13,000 to 123,000. Basic work, such as ploughing and harvesting, became entirely mechanized. Intensification of production and the large increase in yields were partly the result of an increase in the amount of fertilizer used. Instead of 3 kg of fertilizer per acre (1931–1940 level), 30 kg per acre were employed in 1960, 100 in 1970, and 250 in 1980.

Because of Hungary's limited natural resources, the growth of production usually entailed an even greater increase in foreign trade. For every percentage of increase in the national income there was a 1.29 per cent rise in foreign trade in the early 1950s and a 1.89 per cent to 2.00 per cent increase in the 1960s and 1970s. In the 1950s, imports and exports amounted to 25 per cent of the national income. By the late 1970s, they amounted to 55 per cent.

The structure and direction of foreign trade also changed. In imports, relative weight of industrial goods declined while that of fuel, raw materials, and semi-finished goods increased considerably. With regard to exports, before the war, foodstuffs and agricultural products made up about 60 per cent of all exports, and the share of industrial products was about 13 per cent. Today, more than 50 per cent of all exports consist of machinery and other industrial consumer goods. In the 1940s, after the socialist transformation and the establishment of the CMEA, the role of the Soviet Union increased quickly in the foreign trade of Hungary; later on, when technological development was given a higher priority, the role of the Soviet Union declined, while that of the developed industrial countries started to increase. In the early 1980s, the CMEA accounted for around 50 per cent of Hungarian foreign trade, with developing countries making up about 55–60 per cent and Western countries around 40 to 45 per cent of the remainder.

In terms of trade structure, two entirely different pictures emerged. In the Eastern market, Hungary was mainly an exporter of industrial goods and an importer of raw materials and oil. On the other hand, in the Western market, Hungary was a dominant exporter of foodstuffs and agricultural products and an importer of investment goods and technology.

On the whole, national income has almost quintupled during the 30 years since planning became the basic element of the Hungarian economy. In the first decade, growth was 77 per cent, in the second decade, 63 per cent, and in the third, 60 per cent. The per capita national income rose four and a half times, at an average annual rate of 5.8 per cent. The Hungarian per capita income was 75 per cent of the average per capita income among European countries in 1950, and by 1980, it had reached the European average per capita income. The underdeveloped state of Hungary was considerably rectified during these 30 years.

Concerning prices, one can observe several phenomena. There was no direct relationship between wholesale prices on the one hand and consumer prices on the other; more interestingly, the two sets of prices seemed to be entirely different in structure. There seemed to exist several reasons for this lack of a relationship between the two sets of prices. First, the quantity of consumer goods and services had to be planned within the perceived wage bill. Second, prices did not reflect relative scarcities because of the turnover in workers, taxes, and price subsidies. Third, the prices of commodities traded with other socialist states were tagged to the world market prices of the immediate past which, by definition, were subject to periodic revisions. Fourth, the prices of commodities traded with Western economies were not aligned with the subsidized domestic prices through the undervalued Hungarian currency *vis-à-vis* the currencies of the Western economies. (It may be of interest to note that the exchange rates between Hungarian currency and the Western currencies did not effectively reflect the relative purchasing power of Hungarian currency; the official exchange rates merely served the accounting function, because the specified amount of exports and imports was mandated by the plan.)

Money and credit had a secondary or passive role. Since allocation of resources and goods was made primarily in physical terms, credit was used to provide enterprises with the financial resources necessary to carry out the planned investments which would enable them to fulfill the targets of the plan. No direct relationship was established between the financial means provided by the state, the profitability of production, and the performance of the enterprise. No reciprocal credit among economic organizations was allowed and the state bank was actually granted a credit monopoly. The state budget, centralizing and redistributing income for public consumption, was the other source of credit.

The enterprise was the basic unit used to carry out the plan. In a legal sense, the enterprise was autonomous; it had its own working capital and was permitted to conclude civil law contracts. However, the enterprise paid strict respect to planned production and exercised strict financial discipline. The means at the disposal of the enterprise were stated annually in the plan, and the principal duty of the company manager was to execute the plan's instructions and accomplish production goals. Hence, in contrast to the legal sense of autonomy of the enterprise, in actuality, all directives were unconditionally binding.

Nevertheless, after economic growth had accelerated and a higher standard of living was achieved, the marginal efficiency of central planning declined considerably, and it became evident that a common understanding regarding the organic linkage of central planning with the market was badly needed. Hence came the efforts for economic reform, as discussed earlier in this paper.

At this point, a listing of important successes in regional and urban development seems to be in order. The economic development in the 1960s and 1970s resulted in a substantial regional levelling with respect to industrialization, urbanization, and living conditions. This levelling greatly diminished inter-regional migration. A few decades before, the oversized capital city of Budapest (in sharp contrast to the underdeveloped rural areas and the pre-industrial rural market towns which had dominated the country's territory) had been, practically speaking, the only modern city in Hungary. As a consequence of settlement network planning, a modern urban network was shaped with the aid of a greater proportion of the nation's capital, and the rural-urban dichotomy was significantly eased.

Thirty-five years of central planning, with its successes and failures, has resulted in many experiences which will be briefly summarized in the following pages.

Experiences of Planning

The nature and role of central planning are a crucial issue. The issues regarding the government's ability to concentrate the nation's resources for given developmental targets deserve consideration also. Hungary's experience may serve as a case in point. The tutelage of the state made the micro-economic sphere indifferent to enterprise management and cost-benefit calculations, etc. Because the central planning authorities expected obedience from enterprise employees, the latter rightly supposed it to be the government's duty to solve all their problems. The 1968 economic reform, which declared the independence of the enterprises, found planners and enterprise managers unprepared. The first reaction was the recognition that to achieve enterprise independence, not only a change in the attitude of the managers but also a possible change in their location would be required. However, the inelasticity inherent in the planning system itself and in the system of state ownership rather limited the possibilities for management manoeuvring. The definition and the role of central planning had to be changed. As a result of this renovation, the task of central planning — as opposed to direct economic intervention — would now involve (1) forecasting the external conditions for the economy; (2) planning the societal processes related to the economy (education and training, mobility, health services, demographical movements, urban development), and (3) forecasting the qualitative characteristics of economic activity.

The forms assumed when exercising state ownership in the economy have been another topic of much discussion. When state ownership plays a significant role in an economy, questions concerning the efficiency and competitiveness of state enterprises inevitably arise. These questions and their answers have been important to Western European economies where state ownership is exercised, and they have a vital importance in socialist countries as well.

The low efficiency level in state industrial enterprises in Western economies points to two important factors: (1) traditional sectors (energy, steel, etc.) dominate state industry and (2) in many cases (e.g. the mining industry in Britain) nationalization was the result of an attempt to save an important but less-profitable industry from economic disintegration.

Another widespread problem in both the East and West concerns the method of state control used with state industry when the industry is considered to be a part of the bureaucratic machinery of the state which is managed through public administration. The value system employed by those in public administration differs greatly from that of those involved in economic life. Public administration assures precise execution of laws or decrees; it does not tolerate improvisation or the use of original ideas by leading officers. Public administration serves to stabilize a given political power; its efficiency is judged in political rather than economic terms. A model government officer who is selected at least partly because of political considerations probably will not be the best business manager.

In order to improve the flexibility and competitiveness of firms, the state needs to (1) eliminate its role of providing public administrators to manage firms and (2) redefine its role in the area of sectoral control.

Self-management seems to be a possible solution to the first problem. As noted earlier, important measures were taken recently towards self-management in state enterprises (the establishment of workers' councils, the election of managers by employees). It is too early to predict how the self-management system will develop and how the state will exercise its right and power of ownership in the new situation. However, one may observe that state ownership may create a monopolistic situation in the market which in turn may have an inflationary effect.

Sectoral control by the state should not be defined in terms of its control of enterprises; rather it should be defined in terms of its promotion of technical progress, market control, and the promotion of those inter-industry relations which serve priority objectives.

The history of economic reform offers some useful insights, too.

First is the fact that the economic reform was introduced in one day — 1 January 1968 — and the totally new system, which encompassed the whole economy, proved to be successful. It was thought, and we feel it to be correct, that to change a few details of the old system or, alternatively, to introduce the new system to a few enterprises at a time would be disastrous.

Certainly, the introduction of a basically new management system meant taking great risks. One cannot calculate all the possible effects of the changes. For example, politicians' interest in a stable political situation forced economic pragmatism into compromises designed to minimize risks. Compromises were necessitated by external factors, too (e.g. the unchanged nature of CMEA co-operation). These inevitable compromises resulted in a number of half-solutions which diminished the efficiency of the reform and created an unhealthy atmosphere for further development.

One of the results of these half-solutions was that institutional changes were slower than functional changes. Sectoral ministries lost their right to give planning directives for enterprises, but as their structure remained untouched, they tried to regain control over the micro-economic sphere under new forms. Directives were replaced by "expectations" and "guidelines" — and most of the managers (nominated for their posts by the ministries) got the message. We moved away from half-solutions when sectoral industrial ministries merged to create a Ministry of Industry. Its internal structure (there are no sectoral departments) made direct interventions in production impossible.

Another half-solution — namely, a market that is simulated — is still in existence, and an active use of the market mechanism is difficult. Because of the hard currency shortage in Hungary — and because of the lack of convertible currency even within the CMEA market — foreign trade is strictly controlled by the state. Thus, imports are not on a competitive footing with home industry. Since the size of the country is limited, it is difficult to avoid monopolistic situations in certain industries. In the early 1980s, a number of state trusts were dissolved for stimulating competition.

The price and wage system contains many half-solutions, too. In the "classical" central planning period, prices of consumer goods and basic services were heavily subsidized; there were a number of free public services; and the wage level was calculated to make possible a modest standard of living. In 1968, there was no possibility for a sudden change. A new price system, which reflects the market situation and world market prices, necessitated drastic cuts in price subsidizing, that is, a substantial rise in prices of basic goods and services. This new price policy pre-supposed a radical transformation of the wage and income policy.

There were several measures taken to bring about a solution, as mentioed above, but they were decided upon while under the pressure of the economic crisis. The changes in single elements of the price-wage policy were uneven; in the early 1980s, real income dropped; accessibility to the second economy (i.e. extra work and income outside the main occupation) became a very important element of the family income, etc. Let us take an example: In the 1950s, one assumed that housing would be assured by low-rent government housing. Later, government housing focused on subsidizing co-operative construction. Now, four-fifths of all new housing units are built privately (mostly by private contractors, with much of the work done by family members), and government subsidizing is limited to low interest credits. Wage increases lagged behind the enormous changes that occurred in the housing and real estate market, so the wage-price relationship became disproportionate.

Many of the contradictions result from the fact that most of the industrial firms sell on three markets (e.g. home, Western, and CMEA markets), where prices, the mechanism of marketing, and taxes or subsidies differ sharply.

In 1987, after the present chapter had been written, a new era of reform began in Hungary. In the economic sphere, the expansion of the private sector and changes in finance (e.g. the introduction of value-added and personal income taxes, and the establishment of a multilevel banking system) were the most significant. The fact that the reform extended to political institutions, remodeling of party functioning, restructuring of the central and local governments, and the re-emerging of civil society was of great importance.

We can conclude that the Hungarian experiments in the organic combination of planning with a market in a kind of mixed economy merits attention. Whether these experiments will be successful is still an open question; and the proper answer can be given only after a few years of experience. Nevertheless, we have to bear in mind that economic development is never simply a chain of economic acts and that it can be understood only as an institutional form of interaction between man and nature in the context of society as a whole.

Notes

1. *Soviet Economic Development*, p. 6
2. "Regional and urban" policy and planning mean: (a) planning of socio-economic development of regions; (b) planning of territorial distribution of certain activities (e.g. industrial location); and (c) planning of transformation of the settlement network. We do not incorporate physical planning into regional planning.

Bibliography

Barta, Gy (Ms). 1982. "The development of industry and the industrialization of villages." In Gy. Enyedi and I. Volgyes, eds., *The effect of modern agriculture on rural development*, pp. 241–259. New York, Pergamon.

Bauer, T. 1981. *Tervgazdaság, beruházás, ciklusok* (Planned economy, investments, cycles). Budapest, Közgazdasági és Jogi.

Berend, T. I. 1983. *Gazdasági útkeresés 1956–1965. A szocialista gazdaság magyarországi modelljének történetéhez* (Economic reorientation 1956–1965. Toward a history of the socialist economic model in Hungary). Budapest, Magvető.

Berend, T. I., and Gy. Ránki. 1974. *Hungary: A century of economic development*. New York, Barnes and Noble Books.

Borai, Á. 1978. "Industry in Hungarian towns." In Gy. Enyedi, ed., *Urban development in the USA and Hungary*. Budapest, Akadémiai.

Enyedi, Gy. 1979. "Economic policy and regional development in Hungary." *Acta Oeconomica*, vol. 22, nos. 1–2, pp. 113–126.

————. 1987. "Regional development policy in Hungary." *International Social Science Journal*, 39(2): 253–263.

Friss, I. et al. 1976. *Gazdaságpolitikánk tapasztalatai és tanulságai 1957–1960* (Experiences and lessons of our economic policy). Budapest, Akadémiai.

Gábor, R., and P. Galasi. 1981. *A "második gazdaság"* (The "second economy"). Budapest, Közgazdasági és Jogi.

Gadó, O. 1972. *Reform of the economic mechanism in Hungary: Development 1968–1971*. Budapest, Akadémiai.

Hare, P. A., H. K. Radice, and N. Swain, eds. 1981. *Hungary: A decade of economic reform*. London, Allen and Unwin.

Hudson, R., and F. R. Lewis. 1984. *Regional planning in Europe*. London, Pion.

Kornai, J. 1980. *Economics of shortage*. 2 vols. Oxford, North-Holland.

————. 1959. *Over centralization in economic administration: A critical analysis based on experience in Hungarian light industry*. London, Allen and Unwin.

Kuklinski, A., ed. 1975. *Regional development and planning*. Leyden, Sijthoff.

Lackó, L. 1984. "Assessment of regional policies and programs in Eastern Europe." In G. Demko, ed., *Regional development problems and policies in Eastern and Western Europe*, pp. 134–157. London, Croom Helm.

Lappo, G. 1976. *Geographical aspects of urbanization studies*. Soviet Geographical Studies. Moscow, USSR Academy of Sciences, National Committee of Soviet Geography.

Nekrasow, N. N. 1978. *Területi gazdaságtan* (Regional economics). Budapest, Közgazdasági és Jogi.

Nyers, R. 1968. *Gazdaságpolitikánk és a gazdasági mechanizmus reformja* (Our economic policy and the reform of the economic mechanism). Budapest, Kossuth.

Portes, R. 1969. *Economic decentralization and industrial enterprise in Hungary, 1957–1968*. Oxford, Oxford University Press.

Ránki, Gy. 1963. *Magyarország gazdasága az elsö 3 éves tery idöszakában* (Hungarian economy in the period of the first 3-year plan). Budapest, Közgazdasági és Jogi.

Robinson, W. F. 1973. *The pattern of reform in Hungary: A political, economic and cultural analysis*. New York, Praeger.

Tatai, Z. 1984. *Iparunk területi szerkezetének átalakulása* (Transformation of the regional structure of our industry). Budapest, Kossuth.

Tímár, M. 1968. *Gazdasági fejlödés és irányítási módszerek magyarországon* (Economic development and our methods of monitoring the economy in Hungary). Budapest, Közgazdasági és Jogi.

CONTRIBUTORS

E. O. Adeniyi, Director, Manpower Development Department, Nigerian Institute of Social and Economic Research, Ibadan, Nigeria

A. I. Ayodele, Nigerian Institute of Social and Economic Research, Ibadan, Nigeria

V. P. Diejomaoh, Chief, Jobs and Skills Programme for Africa, International Labour Office, Addis Ababa, Ethiopia

György Enyedi, General Director, Center for Regional Studies, Hungarian Academy of Sciences, Budapest, Hungary

Godfrey Gunatilleke, Director, Marga Institute, Colombo, Sri Lanka

Lai Yew Wah, Lecturer, Department of Economics, School of Social Sciences, Universiti Sains Malaysia, Penang, Malaysia

L. P. Mureithi, Associate Professor of Economics, Economics Department, University of Nairobi, Nairobi, Kenya

György Ránki, Deputy Director of the Institute of the Hungarian Academy of Sciences, Budapest, Hungary, and Hungarian Chair Professor for Indiana University, Bloomington, Indiana, U.S.A.

Kouichi Tani, Senior Planning Officer (Industry), Planning Bureau, Economic Planning Agency, Tokyo, Japan

Tan Siew Ee, Lecturer, Department of Economics, School of Social Sciences, Universiti Sains Malaysia, Penang, Malaysia

Miguel Urrutia, Manager, Economic and Social Development Department, Inter-American Development Bank, Washington, D.C., U.S.A.

Setsuko Yukawa, Professor of Economics, Kyoto Sangyo University, Kyoto, Japan